HISTORY OF THE
BALTIMORE AND OHIO RAILROAD

HISTORY OF

THE BALTIMORE

AND

OHIO RAILROAD

John F. Stover

Purdue University Press
West Lafayette, Indiana

Book and jacket design by James McCammack

Published in 1987
Printed in the United States of America

Library of Congress Cataloging-in-Publication Data

Stover, John F.
    History of the Baltimore and Ohio Railroad.

    Bibliography: p.
    Includes index.
    1. Baltimore and Ohio Railroad Company—History.
I. Title.
HE2791.B3S76 1986   385'.065'74   86-9353
ISBN 0-911198-81-4

To Carissa, Sean, Shelly, and Rhys

Contents

. . . .

Illustrations

· · · · · · · · · · · · · · · · ·

Pictures and Maps

Tables

Preface

• • • • • • • • • • • • • • •

When Charles Carroll and Philip Thomas laid the first stone on the Baltimore and Ohio Railroad on Independence Day, 1828, they were starting a railway which was unique in several ways. The B&O was the first railroad to challenge major canals for the western trade. The new line was also the first regional railroad with a projected route over the mountains to the Ohio River. Finally, the engineering problems facing the projected railway were so varied that a railway editor called it the "Railroad University" of the nation.

A quarter of a century after the Independence Day ceremonies, the B&O was completed to Wheeling on the Ohio, and a few years later was providing service to St. Louis and Chicago. When the railroad celebrated its centennial with the Fair of the Iron Horse, it could look back on a century of service including periods of depression and prosperity, a receivership, and aid to the nation in two major wars. During those decades the Baltimore and Ohio had helped transform an agrarian and undeveloped society into the industrial urban economy of the twentieth century. In 1962 the B&O agreed to merge with the younger and more prosperous Chesapeake and Ohio Railroad and has been a part of the Chessie/CSX system ever since.

Many different people have helped make this book possible. My two longtime friends, Richard C. Overton and Thomas B. Brewer, both gave excellent advice in the early planning of the volume. Assistance was also given by three Purdue colleagues, Profs. Donald J. Berthrong, John J. Contreni, and Laszlo L. Kovacs.

Marion E. Smith, manager of the B&O Railroad Museum in Baltimore, and her staff showed me every possible courtesy during several visits to the B&O archives in the museum. Milton B. Dolinger, Franklyn J. Carr, and Lester C. Roig, all of the Chessie headquarters staff in Cleveland, were helpful during the early planning and research of the volume. The respective staffs of the Eleutherian Mills Historical Library in Wilmington, Delaware; the Maryland Historical Society in Baltimore; and the Manuscripts Division of the Library of Congress all gave extensive assistance during several research trips. I also received aid from the staffs of the

Goss Library and the Krannert Library at Purdue University. Carol N. Stix of the Association of American Railroads; John H. White, Jr., senior historian with the National Museum of American History, Smithsonian Institution; Marion E. Smith, B&O Railroad Museum; and P. E. VanCleve of the Chessie Systems, were also generous with their time in helping me collect photographs and maps for the history.

Prof. William J. Whalen, Verna E. Emery, and James M. McCammack, all of the Purdue University Press, have given helpful advice in the editing and production of the volume. Finally, I wish to acknowledge the services of three very competent secretaries: Joyce Good, Grace Dienhart, and Judy McHenry.

West Lafayette, Indiana   John F. Stover
July 4, 1986

HISTORY OF THE
BALTIMORE AND OHIO RAILROAD

Chapter I

. . . .

A Tale of
Three Cities

EARLY IN 1815, THE NEWS OF ANDREW JACKSON'S GREAT
victory at New Orleans was quickly followed by word that the
signing of the Treaty of Ghent had ended the War of 1812. The
sequence of these two events gave the American public an impression of victory, even though the war had really ended in a stale-
mate. In the years after the war, a great wave of nationalism swept
the country, and most Americans believed that their nation had
achieved a new and distinctive maturity. During this decade, the
nation's population increased by a third, the growth of manufacturing gave the country a new economic independence from Europe,
and an expanding frontier created a new West.

  With peace, the nation quickly turned to internal improvements. Citizens and political leaders alike were excited about new
modes of transportation. In the first years of the century, both
Thomas Jefferson and Albert Gallatin, his secretary of the treasury,
had sponsored extensive plans for major public improvements. In
the years after the war, Henry Clay, in his American System of
economic growth, stressed the need for improved roads and projected canals. In 1817 John C. Calhoun, at the time a nationalist
leader and a sponsor of internal improvements, said: "We are
greatly and rapidly—I was about to say fearfully—growing. This is
our pride and our danger; our weakness and our strength. . . . Let
us, then, bind the Republic together with a perfect system of roads
and canals."[1]

A "perfect system of roads and canals" certainly did not exist in 1817, but progress was being made to improve the nation's transportation. On February 6, 1815, less than a month after the Battle of New Orleans, Col. John Stevens of Hoboken had obtained from the New Jersey legislature the first railroad charter in the nation—a grant to construct a railway between the Delaware and Raritan rivers. In 1817 the longest canal in the nation was only twenty-eight miles in length, and the total canal mileage in America was no more than 100 miles. But early in April of that year, the New York legislature authorized the construction of the Erie Canal, a 364-mile project. The next year saw the completion of the National, or Cumberland, Road to Wheeling, Virginia,[2] an event which made the westward migration to the new states of Indiana and Illinois much easier. Hundreds of other new roads and turnpikes were chartered in northeastern states during the decade.

In 1818 the typical western emigrant probably floated down the Ohio River from Wheeling on a flatboat, but in that year at least a dozen small steamboats were already plying western rivers. The number of steamboats on western waters would increase at least tenfold in the next decade. Early in 1825, Colonel Stevens confounded his critics, who were scoffing about his chartered but unbuilt railway, by operating the first locomotive to run on rails in the nation. The colonel's hardy houseguests could ride in his sixteen-foot "steam waggon" around a short circular track on the ground of his Hoboken estate at speeds of up to twelve miles an hour. The public was excited about the new modes of transport in those early years of peace. Taverns, public markets, and exchanges across America heard the heated arguments of merchants, politicians, and farmers as they advanced the rival claims of turnpikes and canals, of steamboats and railroads.

These postwar years also saw the rise of the New West. During the three and a half decades between the Declaration of Independence and the War of 1812, only five new states had been added to the original thirteen. In the first half-dozen years following the War of 1812, six additional states—five of them in the west—were admitted to the Union: Indiana (1816), Mississippi (1817), Illinois (1818), Alabama (1819), Maine (1820), and Missouri (1821). The appearance of the New West, according to Frederick Jackson Turner, "was the most significant fact in American history in the years following the War of 1812."[3] Certainly the western states located beyond the Appalachian Mountains were yearly attracting many new settlers in the early decades of the nineteenth century. During the teens, thousands of Americans moved westward over the National or Wilderness roads or down the Ohio River by flatboat. In the twenties, the migration was aided by the Erie Canal and by dozens of new sidewheelers or stern-wheelers on western rivers.

TABLE 1. Population Growth of the Western States

	Admitted	1810	1820	1830
Kentucky	1792	406,511	564,317	687,917
Tennessee	1796	261,727	422,823	681,904
Ohio	1803	230,760	581,434	937,903
Louisiana	1812	76,556	153,407	215,739
Indiana	1816	24,520	147,178	343,031
Mississippi	1817	40,352*	75,448	136,621
Illinois	1818	12,282	55,211	157,445
Alabama	1819		127,901	309,527
Missouri	1821	19,783	66,586	140,445
Total of the Western States		1,072,491	2,194,305	3,610,532
Total U.S. Population		7,239,881	9,638,453	12,866,020
Western Population as a Percentage of Total U.S.		14.8%	22.7%	28.0%

The population of the Mississippi Territory (Mississippi and Alabama) was 40,352 in 1810.

In the twenty years between 1810 and 1830, the growth of western population far outstripped the nation's growth. The national total increased 77 percent in that score of years, while the population of the nine western states far more than tripled. By 1830 the three oldest states of the West—Kentucky, Tennessee, and Ohio—together had a population of more than 2,300,000, well above the total for the six New England states. During the same twenty years, the two most populous coastal states—New York and Pennsylvania—had respective population increases of 100 percent and 67 percent. In the same years, the population of Ohio climbed fourfold, while that of Indiana and Illinois grew a dozenfold or more.

This great increase in population in the newly settled western states plus significant improvements in transportation caused a striking growth of domestic commerce in the first decades following the War of 1812. The revolution in transportation appeared in the first third of the nineteenth century with the appearance and rapid development of turnpikes, steamboats, canals, and railroads. These new facilities of transport quickly extended the volume of domestic commerce as each new mode of transport lessened the difficulties and cost of internal trade.

This growing trade with the New West in the early nineteenth century was of major concern to the merchants and mercantile houses of the major seaport cities along the Atlantic seacoast. In 1810 the five major eastern seaports from north to south were Boston (population 33,000), New York City (96,000), Philadelphia (92,000), Baltimore (36,000), and Charleston (25,000). Of the five cities, Boston and Charleston were by far the least important in the growing domestic trade with the West. Charleston had a slowly expanding population and economy in the first decades of the nineteenth century and had no readily available and viable trade routes to western markets. Boston, which had been the leading mercantile city in the midcolonial period, had been surpassed by her southern rivals by the end of the American Revolution. In the competition for the western trade in the new century, Boston suffered from the geographical handicap of definitely being more remote from western markets than the seaports of the mid-Atlantic states.

Clearly the principal seaport cities in the states of New York, Pennsylvania, and Maryland were destined to play the major role in the expanding domestic trade with the West. In the decades between the War of 1812 and midcentury, the leading merchants of New York City, Philadelphia, and Baltimore increasingly turned their attention from wharves and seaborne commerce to the internal western trade moving by canal and railroad. Between 1810 and 1850, the aggregate populations of these three cities increased nearly fivefold while that of the entire nation little more than tripled. New York City with an 1850 population of 515,000 was, by far, the largest American city. Philadelphia was easily in second place with 340,000. Third place Baltimore with 169,000 had a population nearly as great as that of Boston and Charleston combined.

• • • • • • • • • • •

The commercial growth of New York City in the first half of the nineteenth century was indeed phenomenal. In the decade after 1800, its population had passed that of Philadelphia, a city which earlier had replaced Boston as the most populous city in America. The growing population, trade, and wealth of New York City was the result of several factors. New York City possessed one of the best natural harbors in the nation. After the War of 1812, the British chose New York as the major American seaport in which to "dump" their varied manufactured products. Rather quickly Britain's imported goods were disposed of profitably through auction sales managed by New York merchants. Philip Hone, later to be remembered for his diary of life in the city, grew rich in the auction business and soon retired with a fortune. New York State in 1817 passed legislation which reduced taxes on sales at auction and greatly increased the growth of the city as an import center. Very quickly more and more inland merchants began to do their major buying in New York City.

Another factor in New York's prosperity was the establishment of a regular packet service across the Atlantic. This service was inaugurated during the first week of January 1818, when the ship *James Monroe* (424 tons burden) left New York for Liverpool and the *Courier* (381 tons burden) cleared from Liverpool for New York. Both vessels were square-riggers and fitted out with improved passenger accommodations in addition to cargo space. These two vessels along with two other sister ships formed the Black Ball Line which promised the public regular passenger packet service with a ship sailing each month from each port on a specified day and hour. Prior to the new service, both shippers and Atlantic passengers had been forced to use a transatlantic service plagued with vague and indefinite dates of departure. The Black Ball Line was organized by Jeremiah Thompson and four other New York textile importers. Thompson had been an English merchant-shipowner who moved to New York in 1801. The new packet service of the Black Ball Line proved so popular that many rival packet lines were soon also serving the expanding commerce of New York. In the same years, rival packet lines were organized in Boston, Philadelphia, and Baltimore, but most were short-lived, and none offered any serious competition to the New York packets.

In the early postwar years, the merchants of New York City also expanded their coastwise trade both to the north and the south. Much of the New York commerce with the coastal area from Maine to the Gulf was provided by sloops and schooners, weighing from 25 to 175 tons. Much of this coastwise trade brought growing quantities of southern cotton to New York for export.

The several factors of an excellent harbor, an effective auction sales system, the introduction of a regular transatlantic packet service, and a growing coastwise trade all combined to make the commerce of New York grow faster than her rival seaports. In 1822 the British consul stationed at New York City reported to London that while the commerce of New York was growing, that of Boston, Philadelphia and Baltimore was declining. The following year, the members of the New England Society recognized the supremacy of New York with the toast: "The City of New York—the emporium of America; commerce her glory, rivalship hopeless."[4]

Certainly in the decade after the Treaty of Ghent, New York City enjoyed a dramatic increase in foreign trade, both imports and exports. In 1815 the value of exports shipped out of New York City was $10 million, a small fifth of the national total. By 1825 annual New York exports had increased to $35 million, a large third of the national total of $99 million. In that same year, Philadelphia's exports were valued at $11 million while those of Baltimore were $4 million. The same dominance by New York was true for imports. In 1825 New York imports were valued at $49 million, or more than half the national total of $96 million. The imported goods arriving in Philadelphia that year were valued at $15 million, while those of Baltimore amounted to only $4 million. New York City held the same advantage over her rivals in immigration. In 1825, 12,000 immigrants arrived in the United States with 7,000 stepping on shore at New York. Some observers living in the rival seaports were ready to admit the success of New York. In Baltimore, Hezekiah Niles, father of twenty children and longtime editor of *Niles' Weekly Register*, wrote: "The New Yorkers *deserve* success for their enterprise. There is a good spirit among the citizens to advance the business of New York. Let it be imitated—not envied."[5]

By 1825 New Yorkers had clearly achieved dominance in the area of foreign trade. In that same year, they added a certain frosting to their cake with the completion of the Erie Canal. Because of the canal, the merchants of New York City were soon to have the same position of leadership in the western trade that they had earlier achieved in foreign commerce.

The idea of connecting the waters of the upper Hudson River with Lake Erie dated back to the early 1770s when Gov. William Tryon of New York had recommended such a project. Later, in 1777, Gouverneur Morris endorsed the idea of a waterway westward to Lake Erie. After the Revolution, in the early 1790s, a short-lived company headed by Gen. Philip John Schuyler attempted to build short canals along the lower Mohawk River. But the major advocate of the proposed Erie Canal was DeWitt Clinton, three-time mayor of New York City and later governor of the state. Clinton did not receive much support for his project in the early years. He recalled that in 1808 President Thomas Jefferson turned down his request for federal aid with the comment: ". . . you talk of making a canal 350 miles through the wilderness—it is little short of madness to think of it this day."[6] Despite such opposition, Clinton persisted, and in the spring of 1817, the New York legislature approved a state financed project for the building of a 364-mile canal from Albany to Buffalo on Lake Erie.

The digging of the Erie started on July 4, 1817, at the little wilderness village of Rome, New York, a location where work could proceed through level terrain in both directions at once. Much of the construction was bid out to small contractors, often well-to-do local farmers, who agreed to dig a short length of the canal for a fixed price. Their workers were native New Yorkers or recent Irish immigrants, who were paid fifty to eighty cents a day plus rations of food and whiskey. Their tools at first were spades, picks, axes, and wheelbarrows, but those were soon supplemented with horse-drawn scrapers, carts, and huge circular "stump pullers." Fortunately there were no major hills or mountains to cross, but there was a total drop of 565 feet between the level of Lake Erie and the Hudson River at Albany. Eighty-three locks, with lifts varying from six to twelve feet, were built to take care of the several ascents and descents as the waterway crossed the state.

Construction of the canal during the eight years was slow but steady. In the fall of 1819, the canal commissioners navigated the canal from Utica to Rome. About 220 miles of the new waterway were in use by 1822. Soon the merchants of Buffalo were claiming that the partially completed Erie Canal had already cut freight charges from New York to the low figure of $37.50 per ton. New traffic crowded in as each new section of the canal was opened, and the tolls collected helped hasten the completion of the project. In the spring of 1825, Lafayette, as he finished his grand tour of America, traveled much of the distance between Buffalo and Albany on the nearly finished waterway.

The celebrations of the canal's completion started on October 26, 1825, when five canal boats departed from Buffalo to Albany and New York City. On board the *Seneca Chief*, the lead boat of the little flotilla, were Governor Clinton, assorted dignitaries in beaver hats, and two brightly painted kegs filled with water from Lake Erie. The growing string of canal boats reached Albany on November 2, and New York City two days later. Surrounded by hundreds of boats, the *Seneca Chief* finally reached lower New York harbor where DeWitt Clinton emptied a keg of Lake Erie water into the ocean. After the expenditure of $8 million and eight years of hard labor, the Erie Canal was open. Former President Thomas Jefferson had already admitted the error of his earlier statement concerning the wisdom of building the canal.

The financial success of the Erie Canal was immediate. At Schenectady the yearly canalboat traffic increased from 6,000 boats in 1824 to 15,000 in 1826, and 23,000 by 1834. In 1826, the first full year of complete operation, the canal tolls collected were nearly $700,000, and before long were well over $1 million. Within little over a decade, the toll revenue had paid for the canal. By the mid-1820s, New York was well out in front of her rival seaports to the south, Philadelphia and Baltimore, in her quest to dominate the trade with the western states.

There were three aspects to the triumph of the Erie Canal. The Erie was the *first* completed project as the rival seaports sought supremacy in the western trade. The completion of the Erie in 1825 predated the completion of the Main Line Canal of Pennsylvania and Philadelphia by nearly a decade, and it was many more years ahead of the canal and railroad that Maryland and Baltimore would soon be building. Secondly, New York was favored by having the *best* route to the West. The "water level" route of the Erie crossed hills and elevations far lower than those of Pennsylvania and Maryland. The highest point on the Erie was less than one-third the height of the mountains crossed by the Pennsylvania project, and the cost per mile of the Erie was only one-third the per mile cost of the Chesapeake and Ohio Canal. Finally, within just a few months, the Erie was proving to be a *profitable* venture. The Pennsylvania Canal never proved to be profitable, and the railroad built by Baltimore would take years to return a substantial profit.

• • • • • • • • • • •

In the mid-1820s, the state of Pennsylvania certainly possessed no internal improvements to aid the merchants of Philadelphia comparable to the bonanza of western trade which the Erie Canal would soon give to New York City. By 1825 Pennsylvania was second among the states in turnpike mileage, exceeded only by New York. The Keystone State had built the first successful American toll road when the sixty-two-mile Philadelphia and Lancaster Turnpike was built between 1792 and 1794. The hard surfaced twenty-four-foot-wide road had cost $465,000 to build or $7,500 per mile. Travelers enjoyed the smooth ride, and the young Englishman Francis Baily spoke of the new turnpike as a "masterpiece of its kind."[7] Business was brisk at the nine tollgates along the sixty-two-mile route, and by the turn of the century, annual toll revenue was up to $200,000 or more, a figure which paid operating expenses, road repairs, and yearly dividends of about 2 percent. Such a rate of return was indeed modest, but the heavy traffic on the road soon inspired many other promoters to project and build additional turnpikes in Pennsylvania, in other mid-Atlantic states, and in New England.

Early in the nineteenth century, Pennsylvania chartered many new turnpikes. By 1821 about 150 turnpikes had been projected in the state with a planned total route of 2,500 miles, of which 1,800 miles had been finished. More than two-thirds (1,250 miles) of the completed mileage was built with stone. Of the $6,400,000 invested in 150 companies, more than one-third— $2,240,000—had been provided by the state. Pennsylvania was by far the most generous of the states in providing public funds for turnpike construction. By 1828 the completed turnpike mileage in the state was 2,380 miles. On many of the roads the traffic was heavy, but, even so, few made a profit for their owners. Samuel Hazard, Philadelphia merchant-editor, wrote in 1828 concerning the turnpikes of Pennsylvania: "None have yielded sufficient to remunerate the proprietors. Most of them have yielded little more than expenditures for repairs."[8] The system of turnpikes in Pennsylvania included several routes across the mountains to Pittsburgh and the Ohio River, but none could successfully compete in freight charges with the Erie. On a mountain road four to six draft horses could pull perhaps four tons by wagon—on a canal a single horse could pull a canal boat with a capacity several times that of a Conestoga wagon.

The merchants of Philadelphia, as they viewed the completion and early success of the Erie Canal, desperately desired a new route to the West that was more competitive than the Conestoga wagon freight service to Pittsburgh. But the men of Philadelphia had many obstacles to overcome: the Allegheny Mountains were high, the teamsters and turnpike innkeepers opposed the canal, and critics of canals suggested that a railroad line would be better. The businessmen of Philadelphia would not be discouraged. They employed William Strickland, a local architect and engineer, and sent him abroad to study the latest railroads and canals in Europe. Despite the opposition of legislators from the northern part of the state, they convinced the state government to sponsor and finance the construction of the Pennsylvania canal system, a strange combination of horse-drawn railway, canals, and inclined planes. The completed system was to extend 394 miles from Philadelphia to Pittsburgh.

The first spadeful of earth was turned on the middle section of the Main Line Canal, running from the Susquehanna to Hollidaysburg, on July 4, 1826. (It soon became the custom to start all new American canals on Independence Day.) Some of the canal workers came from the completed Erie, including two top engineers, Nathan Roberts and James Geddes. Canal-digging techniques had improved since the start of the Erie, and the construction up the banks of the Juniata River moved ahead steadily even though the river banks were steep. When in 1832 the canal had been completed up to Hollidaysburg, 111 locks had been built in the 173-mile canal. While the Juniata division was being dug, Canvass White, another civil engineer who had helped with the Erie, was directing construction of the Portage Railroad over the crest of the Alleghenies between Hollidaysburg and Johnstown. The thirty-five-mile railroad crossed the nearly 2,300-foot summit of the mountains with a series of ascending and descending inclined planes. Horses pulled the cars on level surfaces while a motorized cable was used on the slopes. At the summit, a hotel accommodated passengers who wished to spend the night before starting the downward trip. The Portage Railroad was completed in 1828. Two years later, in 1830, the western section of the Main Line Canal, from Johnstown to Pittsburgh, was opened.

East of the Susquehanna, an indirect route to Philadelphia was available via the Union and Schuylkill canals, but the business interests of that city desired a faster, more direct service. Accordingly, the seventy-five-mile state railroad was constructed to Columbia on the Susquehanna and completed by 1834. The entire 394-mile Main Line running west to Pittsburgh, built at a cost of $10,000,000, was thus fully open for business in 1834. The merchants of Philadelphia were proud of their new connection with the West. Mathew Carey, Philadelphia editor, economist, and longtime sponsor of internal improvements, claimed in 1831 that no other nation had ever built so ambitious an internal improvement in so brief a period.

However, the Pennsylvania system never approached the success of New York's Erie Canal. The hills and mountains of Pennsylvania were steep, the 174 locks on the Main Line were more than double the number required on the Erie, and the transfers from railroad to canal to inclined plane were difficult and time-consuming. Even the novel idea of using sectional canalboats which would be lifted on and off rail cars remained a slow and expensive process. The new route never paid its way and soon was running the state into debt. The Main Line, which would later bring prosperity to the seaport and the state, would be a railroad and not a faulted canal.

•   •   •   •   •   •   •   •   •   •

Baltimore also realized it needed to adopt a new course of action if it were to successfully challenge the newly built Erie Canal. By 1825 the city had enjoyed seventy-five years of rapid growth both in population and in trade. Twenty-five years before the Declaration of Independence, Baltimore had been a tiny settlement of 200 people and perhaps 24 houses. Just prior to the Revolution, it had a population of over 5,000. After the Revolution, it began to gather in the rich tobacco and grain trade of the upper

Chesapeake and grew to more than 13,500 in population in 1790, the year of the first United States census. Her population nearly doubled during the 1790s, and by the turn of the century, she ranked third among all the cities in the nation. During the first two decades of the nineteenth century, Baltimore easily surpassed her trading rivals in the Chesapeake region and claimed a population of 62,700 by 1820.

In these years, the merchants and ship captains of Baltimore successfully expanded their coastal and foreign markets with their graceful and speedy Baltimore clippers. These long, low, flush-decked schooners not only engaged actively in legitimate trade, but also enlarged their reputation for speed with reported activities as pirate craft, illegal slavers, and privateers during the War of 1812. Since the late eighteenth century, Baltimore had expanded trade with the West Indies, sending Maryland and Virginia flour, food products, and iron to the South in exchange for sugar, cocoa, and rice. Later Baltimore had a growing trade with Brazil which exchanged coffee for the quality flour from Howard Street. The Maryland seaport was for some years a major importer of guano from Chile which was desired as a fertilizer by many American farmers.

Baltimore in the early nineteenth century.
(Courtesy, Baltimore and Ohio Railroad)

The domestic trade of Baltimore with southern Pennsylvania and western Maryland and beyond grew in the same years that her foreign trade had expanded. Like Philadelphia, Baltimore depended on the new turnpikes for much of her western markets. Between 1798 and 1816, seven turnpikes were projected to points toward the north and the west. One of the more important of the seven was the sixty-two-mile Baltimore and Frederick Town Turnpike, which was chartered in 1805. This toll road was the first leg in an improved highway running westward to Cumberland on the upper Potomac. While there were several delays in construction, the turnpike from Baltimore to Cumberland was completed within a few years.

The National, or Cumberland, Road was clearly the most important turnpike in the developing western trade of Baltimore. Baltimore was the only eastern seaport to benefit in a major way from the building of the National Road. When President Thomas Jefferson signed the National Road Bill on March 29, 1806, he was approving legislation which would result in the longest, best-known, and most expensive turnpike in the United States. The act provided for a cleared right-of-way four rods wide, with a central carriageway composed of stone and gravel. Contracts for construction were not let until 1811, and the War of 1812 further delayed the project. As each section west of Cumberland was finished, it was opened to the public. Finally, in 1818, the entire 130-mile turnpike was completed to the steamboat landing in Wheeling, Virginia.

No tolls were charged on the road in the early years of its operation even though its construction had cost nearly $13,000 per mile or more than $1.5 million, all of it paid by the federal government. Travel on the new road was soon brisk, with mail coaches, stagecoaches, Conestoga wagons, and westward moving settlers all crowding the new route. The Philadelphia merchant-traveler John Melish called the road "the finest road in the world."[9] *Niles' Weekly Register* was soon reporting that congressmen could easily travel to and from their western homes at the rate of a hundred miles a day. In the middle 1820s, Congress provided for the westward extension of the National Road, now often called the "Old Pike," and by 1833 the road had been extended westward to Columbus, Ohio. Jonathan Knight, a self-taught engineer-surveyor from Pennsylvania who had helped survey the first section of the road, was appointed to plan the extension west of Wheeling.

The heavy traffic on the road quickly changed Wheeling from a struggling settlement on the eastern bank of the upper Ohio to a bustling market town soon to have paved streets and brick buildings. Before long the merchants of Pittsburgh were complaining about the trade lost to their rival down the Ohio. Baltimore was the source of most of the westward moving traffic, and the destination of much which was headed east. Four- and six-horse teams pulled heavily loaded Conestoga wagons on a regular schedule, sometimes traveling night and day between Baltimore and Wheeling. The businessmen and bankers of Baltimore, meeting in their new Exchange, noted with approval local editorial claims that Baltimore was two hundred miles closer to the navigable western waters than New York City, and had a comparable advantage of one hundred miles over Philadelphia. Also roughly half of the Baltimore route west was over the tollfree "Old Pike," an economy not available on the Pennsylvania roads. Finally, while severe winter weather slowed and even occasionally halted the turnpike traffic, all road traffic had a much longer season than canals, which were closed four to five months each winter. But the much cheaper basic freight rates offered by canals, like the Erie, far outweighed the advantages offered by the best wagon freight service. By the middle 1820s, the merchants of Baltimore were well aware that their National Road was no match for the Erie Canal.

Even so, Baltimore in the decade of the twenties was a growing and thriving city filled with prosperous merchants. The citizens of the city were proud of their recent accomplishments. The pretty and well-protected harbor was crowded with tall copper-hulled ships from Liverpool and Amsterdam, from LeHavre and Bordeaux. Swift schooners unloaded their cargoes on wharves crowded with goods from Halifax, Boston, Havana, and southern coastal ports. Steamboats gave daily service to Annapolis, Norfolk, and Washington. Baltimore was an important stagecoach terminal. Changing horses every dozen miles or so, stage lines were carrying passengers and the United States mail west to Wheeling in three and a half days. The Baltimore skyline was growing and changing. Patrons of the arts could attend a theater lighted by a new illuminating gas. Benjamin Henry Latrobe had designed for Baltimore the first Roman Catholic cathedral in the United States, completed and dedicated in 1821. During the decade, work continued on the 178-foot Washington Monument, an obelisk which predated the larger memorial in the District of Columbia.

But the merchants and bankers of Baltimore—men like Philip E. Thomas, George Brown, and William Patterson—knew that some drastic new action would be necesssary if Baltimore was to meet the challenge of New York's Erie Canal. Philip E. Thomas, a pleasant and articulate Quaker, was a hardware merchant before becoming president of the Merchants' Bank in Baltimore. In 1825 the Chesapeake and Ohio Canal Company was revived, and Thomas was appointed a commissioner representing Maryland in the new canal organization. By the fall of 1826, however, Thomas had resigned this position. He was convinced that the proposed canal, since its intended route along the Potomac would be many miles distant from Baltimore, could never materially aid the commercial position of his city. George Brown was the banking partner and son of Alexander Brown who had migrated from Ireland to Baltimore in 1800. Alexander Brown had quickly expanded his original small business of importing Irish linen and eight-day clocks first into a broad gauge import-export firm, and later into banking. By the 1820s, his banking firm of Alexander Brown and Sons was one of the strongest financial institutions in Baltimore. William Patterson was a small spare man who had migrated as a youth from Ireland to America before the Revolution. During the war, he had made a fortune importing supplies and munitions for the patriot army. In 1778 he moved to Baltimore where he continued to prosper as a shipowner and merchant. Patterson's daughter Betsy had married Prince Jerome Bonaparte, younger brother of Emperor Napoleon I.

In 1826 William Patterson, Philip Thomas, Alexander Brown, and his son George Brown were all hearing more and more about a new mode of transport, the railroad. The year 1825 had seen not only the opening of the Erie Canal in America, but also the completion of the Stockton and Darlington Railway in England. Alexander Brown's oldest son, William, had been in England since 1809, where he headed the English branch of the family bank. By 1826 William was writing enthusiastic letters to his father and brother George concerning the early success of the Stockton and Darlington. In the same year, Evan Thomas, brother of Philip Thomas, was in England making a personal inspection of the newly opened English railroad. Col. John Eager Howard, former governor of Maryland and former United States senator, in the fall of 1826, gave a dinner party for some of his friends. Evan Thomas was present and gave a vivid review of the Stockton and Darlington Railway, which much impressed the Colonel's guests. Clearly the merchants and bankers of Baltimore were soon to seriously consider the building of a railroad to the west.

Chapter II

. . . .

Baltimore Obtains a Railroad Charter

IN THE EARLY WINTER OF 1826–27, THE BUSINESSMEN AND merchants of Baltimore continued their discussion of canals and railroads. During the month of February 1827, several meetings were held in the home of George Brown where the business leaders of the city endeavored to decide the best way for Baltimore to keep and increase her share of the western trade.

About two dozen of the leading citizens of the city met at the Brown residence on February 12, 1827, to examine documents concerning the relative advantages of canals and railroads. William Patterson was appointed chairman of the session, and David Winchester, who had extensive real estate and insurance interests in Baltimore, was selected secretary. It soon became evident that there was little enthusiasm for canals. Philip Thomas had definitely given up on the Chesapeake and Ohio Canal when he resigned his position as Maryland commissioner the previous July. The latest cost estimates on the 340-mile proposed canal to the Ohio were above $22 million, far above the estimated costs of a railroad. The projected route of the canal along the Potomac would require a forty-mile branch canal over fairly high hills to reach Baltimore, and many experts wondered if sufficient water was available to fill the branch canal once it was built. Finally it was felt that the three District cities of Washington, Alexandria, and Georgetown, located at the eastern terminal of the canal, would benefit far more from the projected waterway than Baltimore.

When the group at the George Brown house turned their attention to the subject of railroads, they eagerly listened to the impulsive enthusiasm of Evan Thomas. But they were probably more convinced by the calm, well-balanced observations made by Evan's brother, Philip E. Thomas. Later in the evening of the twelfth, a seven-man committee, with Philip Thomas as chairman, was appointed to make a subsequent report on the practicability of a railroad to be built from Baltimore to the Ohio River. The other six men on the committee were: Benjamin C. Howard, son of John Eager Howard; George Brown; Talbot Jones; Joseph W. Patterson, son of William Patterson; Evan Thomas; and John V. L. McMahon. Of the seven men, all except Evan Thomas and McMahon would subsequently become directors of the B&O.

A week later, on February 19, 1827, the seven-man committee reported back to the larger group, again in session at the residence of George Brown. The chairman, Philip Thomas, noted that Baltimore had a geographic advantage over both New York City and Philadelphia, being 200 miles closer to the Ohio River than the former city, and 100 miles closer than the latter. Thomas pointed out that turnpikes and canals had both faced strong opposition when first introduced and attempted, but that both had proven very successful modes of transport. The committee felt confident that while railroads were still in their infancy, they would, in time, prove to have great advantages over both turnpikes and canals. They believed that the railroad experience of England, while limited, already was proving railroads would soon generally replace canals. The committee had great confidence in the continental westward expansion of American population and believed that in future decades the western trade would greatly increase. Therefore, the seven-man committee on February 19 recommended the immediate construction of a double track railroad across the Allegheny Mountains to the Ohio River.

The two dozen men assembled in the Brown residence that evening promptly endorsed and approved the recommendations of the Thomas committee. They approved a resolution that an immediate application be made to the Maryland legislature for an act to incorporate a joint-stock company to be called the Baltimore and Ohio Railway Company. They decided to seek a charter which would permit a capital stock of $5 million. A twenty-five-man committee, basically consisting of the men present there, was appointed to prepare the formal charter application to the Maryland legislature. Finally they appointed a smaller committee to visit and examine the two short railways then in operation in the United

States, the Mauch Chunk line in Pennsylvania and the Quincy railroad in Massachusetts.

The seven-man committee headed by Philip Thomas decided to publish their full report of February 19 in a small pamphlet with the imposing title, *Proceedings of Sundry Citizens of Baltimore, Convened for the Purpose of Devising the Most Efficient Means of Improving the Intercourse Between That City and the Western States.* About 1,500 copies of the small booklet were printed in Baltimore, probably in March 1827, with the cost of publication provided through a ten-dollar contribution paid by each of the two dozen "sundry citizens" who were meeting at the Brown residence. In the early weeks of the spring of 1827, many citizens of Baltimore had an opportunity to read the *Proceedings of Sundry Citizens of Baltimore.*

The man who had drafted the charter for the proposed railroad was John Van Lear McMahon, a member of the Thomas committee and one of the youngest men in the Brown-Thomas group. Born in 1800 in Cumberland, Maryland, McMahon had graduated from the College of New Jersey, now Princeton University, in 1817, and had been admitted to the bar in 1819. In 1827 he was serving his second term in the Maryland House of Delegates, representing a Baltimore district. The young lawyer in many ways modeled the railroad charter upon the earlier charters of turnpike companies. The twenty-three sections of the charter gave the new railroad many rights including the use of steam locomotives and exemptions from certain state taxes. When McMahon was reading the draft of the charter to members of the Brown-Thomas group, he was reportedly interrupted by the venerable white-haired, merchant-banker Robert Oliver, who said "Stop, man, you're asking for more than the Lord's Prayer."[1] McMahon responded that all the rights and privileges were necessary and the more they requested the more they would receive. In later years, many other railroad charters would be modeled upon the charter drafted by McMahon.

The charter for the Baltimore and Ohio Railroad was presented to the Maryland legislature late in February by McMahon, and the act of incorporation was passed with very little opposition on February 28, 1827. The act provided for capital stock of only $3 million, but the thirteenth section permitted the president and board of directors to later increase the capital stock by the addition of as many new shares as they might deem necessary. Of the 30,000 shares of stock at $100 each, 10,000 shares were to be reserved for subscription by the state of Maryland, 5,000 shares for subscription to the city of Baltimore; with the remaining 15,000 shares open to individuals or corporations. The Maryland act of incorporation was confirmed by the state of Virginia a week later on March 8, 1827, and the charter was also confirmed by the state of Pennsylvania on February 22, 1828.

The general citizenry of Baltimore welcomed the news of the actions taken by the merchants and bankers of the city and subsequent railroad charter granted by the Maryland legislature. Their enthusiasm for the railroad project was soon reflected in the pages of *Niles' Register* during March and April 1827. In its issue of March 17, 1827, that paper reported: ". . . it is with no ordinary feelings we announce the fact—that a plan for making *a railroad from the city of Baltimore to some point on the Ohio river*, has been considered and adopted by certain of our most intelligent, public spirited and wealthy citizens, and a bill to incorporate a company for this purpose, with a capital of $3,000,000, has passed the legislature of Maryland."[2]

Niles' Register was also quick to point out all the advantages the proposed railroad to the Ohio offered over the rival Chesapeake and Ohio Canal. The lowest estimated cost of the C&O Canal to the Ohio River was given as $12 million while the highest estimate for the railroad was only $5 million. The estimated distance for the two projected works to the Ohio was 390 miles for the canal and only 250 miles for the railroad. The paper estimated a ton of freight moving from Pittsburgh to Baltimore by canal would pay freight charges of $5.85. The same shipment moving over the projected railroad would pay only $2.50, or about one cent per ton-mile. The estimated time required for the shipment was 214 hours by canal and only 62 hours by rail. It is quite certain that most of these estimates in the pages of *Niles' Register* came from the small pamphlet *Proceedings of Sundry Citizens of Baltimore*, prepared by the Thomas committee.

The passage of time would prove the above comparisons to be rather overdone and extravagant. The C&O Canal finally reached Cumberland in 1850, with $11 million spent on the 184 miles of completed waterway. When the B&O Railroad reached Wheeling in late December 1852, more than $15 million had been spent on the 375-mile railroad to the Ohio. Railroad freight charges at midcentury for movement over the mountains to the Ohio River were at least two or three times the penny per ton-mile estimated in 1827.

Later in the spring of 1827, a report of the activities of the committees which visited and examined the Mauch Chunk line

Philip E. Thomas, first president of the railroad, 1827–36.
(Courtesy, Baltimore and Ohio Railroad)

in Pennsylvania and the Quincy railroad in Massachusetts appeared in the pages of *Niles' Register.* The three-man committee consisted of Philip E. Thomas, Alexander Brown, and Thomas Ellicott. Thomas Ellicott, like Brown and Thomas, was the president of a Baltimore bank, the Union Bank of Maryland. The three men first visited the Mauch Chunk Railroad, a nine-mile line used to transport coal down a mountainside from a coal mine to boats on the Lehigh River below. The railroad, completed earlier in the year, was operated by gravity and horse or mule power. The three bankers were taken up the entire road in an empty wagon, pulled by one horse, at the rate of four miles an hour, and descended by gravity in forty-five minutes, reaching at times a speed of twenty miles per hour.

After leaving Mauch Chunk, Pennsylvania, the Baltimore committee proceeded to Boston to examine the three-mile Granite Railway, opened in Quincy, Massachusetts, by Gridley Bryant in October 1826. Bryant, a Yankee engineer-inventor, used horses on the broad gauge railway to move granite blocks from a quarry down to a Boston Harbor dock. The granite was being used in the construction of the Bunker Hill Monument. According to the *Niles' Register*, the three-man committee, after visiting the two short railroads, were "entirely satisfied that there will be no difficulty in constructing the proposed rail way from the city of Baltimore to the Ohio River, nor have they the smallest doubt, but that there is ample skill in our country for the execution of this part of the work."[3]

The subscription books for the capital stock of the Baltimore and Ohio were opened three weeks after the charter was granted by the state of Maryland. The subscription books were opened for twelve days, from March 20, 1827, through March 31, 1827, at three different locations. Subscriptions were available in Baltimore at the Mechanics' Bank, of which Philip E. Thomas was president, at the Farmers' Branch Bank in Frederick, and at the Hagerstown Bank in Hagerstown. The shares had a par value of $100, but only one dollar had to be paid down at the time of subscription. Interest in the railroad stock was high, and for a while it seemed that everyone in the city wanted stock. When the books were closed on Saturday, March 31, it was discovered that 36,788 shares had been subscribed just in Baltimore. Far lesser amounts had been taken in the two smaller towns to the west, but clearly the total subscriptions were far above the 15,000 shares available to individuals. Naturally the available shares had to be properly apportioned among the subscribers as provided in the charter. During March, the city of Baltimore had subscribed to the 5,000 shares available to the city by the terms of the charter.

The first board of directors of the Baltimore and Ohio Railroad was elected on April 23, 1827. The twelve men named as stockholder directors that day were: Charles Carroll of Carrollton, William Patterson, Robert Oliver, Alexander Brown, Isaac McKim, William Lorman, George Hoffman, Philip E. Thomas, Thomas Ellicott, John B. Morris, Talbot Jones, and William Steuart. All twelve men were included among the two dozen business leaders who had met in George Brown's home back in February. The next day, April 24, 1827, the company was formally organized and incorporated with Philip E. Thomas elected president and George Brown, treasurer. Earlier, on April 2, 1827, Solomon Etting and Patrick Macauley had been appointed by the city council as city directors representing Baltimore.

One of the first concerns of the projected railroad was to gain some knowledge of a probable route to the west and to make a preliminary survey of the route from Baltimore west toward the Potomac and the mountains beyond. For this, engineers were needed, and the only school of engineering in the nation was the Military Academy at West Point. The General Survey Act, which was passed by the United States Congress in 1824, permitted the president to authorize surveys of canals and roads. By 1825 the United States Congress was showing a growing interest in railroads, and by 1827 the president was willing to permit army engineers to make railroad surveys under the act of 1824. In April 1827, political friends of the Baltimore and Ohio petitioned the secretary of war, James Barbour, for federal aid in the early survey work for the projected railway to the west. Quite quickly the War Department selected three engineering parties, headed by Dr. William

Howard, Lt. Col. Stephen H. Long, and Capt. William G. Mc-
Neill, to help the Baltimore and Ohio survey. In mid-June 1827,
Secretary of War Barbour notified President Thomas of the B&O
that the costs of the survey would be charged to the government,
since the undertaking was considered to be of national importance.

Niles' Register noted that Dr. Howard, Lieutenant Colonel
Long, and Captain McNeill had arrived in Baltimore early in July
1827. The paper further reported: ". . . the three U.S. engineers
. . . yesterday attended a meeting of the board of directors . . . we
feel perfectly satisfied the work will be pursued with a zeal and
application worthy of its magnitude and importance. The prompt-
ness with which the aid of these scientific gentlemen has been
furnished, is an evidence of the favorable light in which this great
national object is regarded by the general government."[4] Dr. William Howard, United States civil engineer, started to work on the
B&O survey, but later was transferred to South Carolina where he
surveyed the route of the proposed railway from Charleston to
Hamburg. The forty-two-year-old Lt. Col. Stephen H. Long, a
Dartmouth graduate in 1809, had entered the United States Army
as a second lieutenant of engineers in 1814. He had taught mathematics at West Point for two years and had commanded a lengthy
expedition to the Rocky Mountains where he discovered the peak
which bears his name. After working on the Baltimore and Ohio
survey for several months, Colonel Long was made a member of
the board of engineers on January 1, 1828. The twenty-six-year-old
Captain McNeill was a West Point graduate of 1817. The three
survey parties were aided by several United States lieutenants on
topographical duty, plus two United States assistant civil
engineers.

In June 1827, President Philip E. Thomas also asked Secretary of War Barbour if Jonathan Knight, then employed by the War
Department in surveying the National Road in Ohio, could be
spared by the government to help with the survey of the Baltimore
and Ohio. The secretary of war agreed to the request since he felt
that railroads could serve to help the security of the nation as well
as advance the commerce of the country. Jonathan Knight, a
Quaker, as was Philip Thomas, was known as a prominent and able
engineer, even though he had a tendency to engage in bitter disputes with his associates. When Knight joined the Baltimore and
Ohio, he brought with him Casper W. Wever, who, as superintendent of construction, had built many miles of the National Road in
Ohio. Wever was soon given the same title and position on the
railroad, with a salary of $2,000 per year. On January 1, 1828,
Jonathan Knight was appointed a member of the board of engi-

neers, joining Colonel Long and President Thomas in that position. Colonel Long and Jonathan Knight were paid $3,000 annually. By 1828 the railroad itself was beginning to pay much of the cost of the survey work. The support provided by the federal government consisted only of the basic salaries of the army officers heading the surveys. The railroad company paid the wages of the civilian chain bearers and axe men, plus the cost of wagons, tents, and other required supplies needed in the field.

President Thomas and his board of directors, during the early survey work, leaned heavily upon the advice of Colonel Long and Jonathan Knight. Long and Knight decided that their first problem would be to survey a preliminary route from Baltimore to the Potomac River valley, which they intended to reach at a point some fifty to sixty miles west of Baltimore. Once having reached

Surveying for the railroad in the upper valley of the Potomac. From a painting by H. D. Stitt. *(Courtesy, Baltimore and Ohio Railroad)*

the Potomac, they hoped to basically follow the valley westward to the base of the Alleghenies near Cumberland. As they viewed this terrain between Baltimore and Cumberland, the two men made basic decisions concerning grades and curves. They were worried about the ability of steam to haul tonnage over grades that were too steep and thus agreed that grades should be limited to no more than 0.6 percent. Any grades steeper than 0.6 percent would have to be overcome with inclined planes of some sort. They intended to permit fairly sharp curves of fourteen to eighteen degrees as they followed the winding streams of Maryland and Virginia. They proved to have been far too pessimistic about the ability of steam locomotives to climb grades. A better route would have been one with steeper grades and wider curves. However, the route taken to the Potomac proved to be one of rather sharp curves and generally low grades.

Clearly the best route from Baltimore west to the Potomac would follow the Patapsco River valley from Baltimore up to its source forty miles west of Baltimore, and then follow the basin of the Monocacy River southwest to the Potomac at a point a few miles downstream from Harpers Ferry. The top of the watershed between the Patapsco and Bush Creek, which emptied into the Monocacy, was known as Parr Spring Ridge and had an elevation of about 600 feet. This ridge would obviously have to be crossed by inclined planes.

Since the Patapsco emptied into the Chesapeake several miles south of Baltimore, the easy way for the rail route to reach the river was to follow the harbor shore south to the river's mouth near Brooklyn. The city fathers, who were being asked to have the city of Baltimore subscribe to capital stock, feared that such a route would result in an expanded commercial development well south of the city and to the detriment of Baltimore. The city, therefore, insisted that before it would honor its $500,000 stock subscription, the railroad must agree to enter the city at an elevation of sixty-six feet above sea level. This "sixty-six foot agreement" made impossible the harbor level approach to the river and forced the railroad to gain the valley of the Patapsco several miles upstream at Relay Station, not far from where the Washington Turnpike crossed the river. It was decided to enter the city at a point a little southwest of Pratt Street, a location which was about one dozen blocks west of the harbor and the center of Baltimore. This first construction was at the required elevation of sixty-six feet above sea level.

The route up the Patapsco River was not easy. Almost more of a creek than a river, the waterway consisted of sharp curves, rocky spurs, and narrow gorges. At least the upward grade was well within the grade limits of 0.6 percent set by Long and Knight. But the wriggling route was far from direct—the sixty-two-mile completed route to Frederick would be a dozen miles longer than that flown by a crow. But President Thomas and his directors were satisfied with the progress. On October 1, 1827, Thomas wrote in the *First Annual Report* of the railroad: "These officers [of the topographical corps] have examined various routes from the city of Baltimore to the valley of the Potomac, and along that ravine as far as Cumberland. They are now engaged in a general reconnaissance of the country between the Potomac and the Ohio rivers."[5]

Many questions were, of course, yet unanswered. Would the railroad reach the Ohio at Wheeling—or Pittsburgh—or somewhere else? Would the gauge of the track be 4 feet 6 inches, or 4 feet 8-1/2 inches? Should the car wheels have flanges on the outside or the inside of the rail? Should the wheels be fastened to the axles or run free? But during the long winter months of 1827–28, more and more progress was being made. In early November 1827, Colonel Long reported to the top officials of the railroad that preliminary examinations had been completed of four different possible routes from the upper Potomac valley over the Allegheny Mountains to river valleys which could be followed on to the Ohio River.

Also in early November, President Thomas invited the public to make bids, no later than January 15, 1828, upon stone, timber, and iron bars of various dimensions, all of which were to be delivered to the railroad in Baltimore on or before July 1, 1828. The finances of the Baltimore and Ohio were strengthened early in March 1828, when the Maryland legislature passed an act which provided that the state of Maryland should subscribe to 5,000 shares, or $500,000 of the stock of the Baltimore and Ohio railroad. The favorable vote for the subscription was forty-five to twenty-three in the House of Delegates and eight to three in the Senate. The state legislation favoring the new railroad was greatly aided by the support and influence of John McMahon, the state legislator who earlier had written and sponsored the railroad's charter.

Also by March 1828, the capital stock of the company had been doubled from $1.5 million to $3 million. The new issue of stock was quickly subscribed. The officials of the Baltimore bank, Alexander Brown and Sons, wrote to Thomas Kennedy of Hagerstown in late February 1828: "The Railroad stock is subscribing for with great avidity. It is expected much more will be subscribed than is wanted. . . . It seems to be growing in the confidence of the community."[6] Thus in his *Second Annual Report*, President Thomas was able to report: "There has also been a further augmentation of the stock of the Company . . . making the amount of the entire capital at this time, four million dollars."[7]

During the early months of 1828, Philip Thomas and his fellow directors were less successful in obtaining direct financial aid from the federal government. Thomas and his associates in early January sent a memorial to Congress requesting a stock subscription by the United States government. The United States Senate committee receiving the memorial reported a bill calling for a capital stock subscription of $1 million. A favorable report was also obtained from a committee in the House of Representatives, but the report was made so late in the session than no final action was possible. A subsequent report to Congress in 1829 also failed to result in a stock subscription. Some opinion at the time held that opposition to the request by friends of the rival Chesapeake and Ohio Canal was responsible for the failure to obtain financial support from the federal government.

By the late spring of 1828, the management of the Baltimore and Ohio decided that enough progress had been made for them to have a formal and official commencement of their railroad. A committee of arrangements consisting of the four directors, George Hoffman, Alexander Brown, John B. Morris, and Patrick Macauley, released the following public notice: "The directors of the Baltimore and Ohio Rail Road Company have resolved, that the road shall be commenced on the *fourth of July* next."[8] All the major canals built, or building, in the nation had been started on Independence Day—the Erie on July 4, 1817, the Ohio and Erie on July 4, 1825, and the Pennsylvania Grand Canal on July 4, 1826. The officials of the Baltimore and Ohio did not propose that their great endeavor be in any way inferior to the major internal improvements of New York, Ohio, or Pennsylvania.

The directors were also agreed that their railroad should have a cornerstone and that it should be laid by representatives of the Masonic Lodge of Baltimore. These men, plus representatives of the learned professions and the different trades of the city, were all invited to meet in the Baltimore City Council chambers on Monday evening, June 9, 1828, to help plan the great Independence Day event. It was also agreed that Charles Carroll of Carrollton, stockholder, director, and sole surviving signer of the Declaration of Independence fifty-two years before, should turn the first bit of earth for the new railway. The event was to take place at Mount Clare, the estate of a relative, James Carroll, located on the western edge of Baltimore.

By the standards of the Chesapeake, it was a reasonably cool and crisp July morning. There was an unprecedented bustle through the city that Friday morning for it was to be a very special Independence Day for Baltimore. The pavements, walks, and convenient windows and balconies were all crowded at an early hour with hundreds of country and city folk seeking vantage points for the monster parade scheduled to start at eight o'clock. The inns and taverns were all jammed, especially the Golden Horse, the White Swan, and the May Pole, located out on Paca and Franklin Streets on the way to the Frederick Pike and the National Road. In the center of the city, hotels and inns like the Bull's Head, the Fountain Inn with its famous swinging sign, and the newer Indian Queen were equally crowded. Stage coaches, farm wagons, and carts had brought hundreds of visitors into the city during the past week.

The laying of the first stone, July 4, 1828. From a painting by Stanley M. Arthurs. (*Courtesy, Baltimore and Ohio Railroad*)

In the past few days, other hundreds of city dwellers and artisans and their apprentices had put in long hours of extra labor fashioning and completing dozens of floats which would represent the guilds and trades of the city: the tailors, blacksmiths, bakers, victuallers, bleachers, Windsor chair makers, rope makers, and ship captains, mates, and seamen. All had been busy in preparing for the Baltimore and Ohio Railroad parade. The parade of floats, bands, military units, railroad officials, and assorted dignitaries and political figures finally reached the James Carroll estate by mid-morning. There was general agreement that the high point of the monster two-mile parade had been the good ship *Union*—a twenty-seven-foot miniature brig with full rigging, sails and flags in place, and manned by a crew of distinguished city shipmasters.

After a prayer and appropriate introductory speeches, Charles Carroll pushed his spade deep into the ground to turn the first earth. As he laid aside the heavy spade the venerable gentleman said to one of his friends: "I consider this among the most important acts of my life, second only to my signing the Declaration of Independence, if even it be second to that."[9] The grand master and other officials of the Masonic Order lowered and placed the square granite block in its intended resting place. The *Baltimore American* reported that the ninety-year-old Carroll refreshed himself after his labors with only a glass of water. Since whiskey was but three cents a glass in some of the local taverns, many of the celebrants that Independence Day were not so temperate.

One of the nation's political figures not present at the Baltimore and Ohio ceremony was the president of the United States. That very same Fourth of July, President John Quincy Adams was forty miles away down at Georgetown, using a ribbon-bedecked spade to start the rival Chesapeake and Ohio Canal. Adams had a little trouble as he later wrote in his diary:

> It happened that at the first stroke of a spade it met immediately under the surface a large stump of a tree; after repeating the stroke three or four times without making an impression, I threw off my coat, and resuming the spade raised a shovelful of earth, at which a general shout burst forth from the multitude. . . . It struck the eye and fancy of the spectators more than all the flowers and rhetoric in my speech."[10]

Future years would find that the project started that Independence Day by the aging Charles Carroll would be far more successful than the one sponsored by an American president.

Chapter III

. . . .

First Rails

THE ENTHUSIASM AND OPTIMISM CONCERNING THE NEW railroad could not be expected to long continue at the same high pitch shown in the first days of July 1828. Soon there were rumors of dissension and discord among the directors and engineers of the railroad. Certainly the directors were facing perplexing problems and were bothered by a variety of oppositions. The rival Chesapeake and Ohio Canal advocates were quick to find fault with the new railroad. Federal influence seemed to support the C&O, since the head of the waterway project held a high post in the House of Representatives down in Washington. Closer to home, the malcontent Richard Caton was threatening to build his own railroad west to the Ohio.

The friends of horsepower and the advocates of steam locomotion continued their noisy debates. When the stockholders and citizens of Frederick City discovered that the preliminary route laid westward to the Potomac missed their fair city by two or three miles, they loudly protested to President Thomas and his board of directors. There were vigorous arguments concerning the route the railway would follow into town from the location sixty-six feet above sea level on the western edge of the city. Many believed the track should go down the center of Pratt Street to the docks of the inner harbor. This naturally brought angry dissent from Pratt Street householders who hated to see their lamp posts, trees, and hitching posts disturbed by the railroad. Some listeners wondered how a railroad that was having so much difficulty with the gutters of Baltimore could possibly consider surmounting the high summits of the Alleghenies.

Many believed the mountain slopes could only be con-
quered with inclined planes. Forty years later, in 1868, John H. B.
Latrobe, son of an architect father, and himself a lawyer, inventor,
and B&O counsel for half a century, recalled an engineer's early
dream of crossing the mountains: ". . . A double track of road was
to be constructed up and down them, as straight as an arrow. . . .
That a mountain road must necessarily be a serpentine one . . .
never seemed to have entered the head of the distinguished gentleman."[1] Most of the road was to be built level or, at least, not
more than a 0.6 percent grade. On one occasion, Alexander
Brown, the shrewd merchant-banker and a company director, successfully insisted that a deep cut being dug in the autumn of 1828
should not be absolutely level, but rather should build at a slight
incline to aid drainage. The general dissension and early errors in
planning often made it difficult to raise the money necessary for the
early construction. Many stockholders complained bitterly as they
were asked for additional payments in hard cash.

In spite of the opposition and varied problems, construction
of the railroad started shortly after the laying of the cornerstone.
On July 7, 1828, the definitive location and staking of the line out of
Baltimore was started by a party under the direction of Capt. William McNeill. A week later, on July 14, Lieutenant Colonel Long
and Jonathan Knight published advertisements asking for proposals and bids on the first twelve miles, from the outskirts of Baltimore to Ellicotts Mills. The bids for grading and masonry work
were to be presented during the first eleven days of August, with
the bids to be opened at Barnum's Hotel on August 11, 1828. The
bidders were required to provide certificates of character and testi-
monials of their professional skill.

Ellicotts Mills, the terminal of the first projected trackage,
had been settled by three brothers, Joseph, Andrew, and John
Ellicott, who moved from Bucks County, Pennsylvania, to Maryland in 1772. The three brothers, all good Quakers, purchased land
and mill-sites on the Patapsco River, about ten miles west of Baltimore, under the firm name of Ellicott and Company. They built
mills for the grinding of grain, much of which, at first, was grown
on their own land. As they prospered, they built roads for their
wagons to Baltimore at their own expense. When a fire in 1804
destroyed many of their buildings, they were quickly rebuilt. Ellicotts Mills later became Ellicott City.

As the bids for construction were accepted and graded, the
twelve-mile line west to Ellicotts Mills was subdivided into
twenty-six separate contracts. Philip Thomas in his *Second Annual*

Report, October 1, 1828, estimated that the completed twelve-mile road to Ellicotts Mills would cost about $17,000 per mile to complete. In November 1828, President Thomas sent Jonathan Knight, Captain McNeill, and Lt. George W. Whistler to England to study the methods of railroad construction in that country. Earlier, on October 1, 1828, Captain McNeill had been made a fourth member of the board of engineers. Lieutenant Whistler, a West Point graduate in 1819 and husband of the good lady later portrayed in *Whistler's Mother*, had recently been assigned by the War Department to assist in the Baltimore and Ohio surveys. The trio of engineers spent several months in England studying the two major English lines, the Stockton and Darlington and the newer Liverpool and Manchester, then being constructed. They found little terrain in England similar to the tortuous river valleys or high mountains of Maryland and Virginia. But upon their return, they strongly urged that the Baltimore and Ohio should be built in the standard English gauge of 4 feet, 8-1/2 inches.

During the winter months of 1828–29, Lieutenant Colonel Long was theoretically in charge of construction and engineering matters. However, superintendent of construction, Casper Wever, an aggressive manager of contractors but not a member of the board of engineers, began to increasingly take charge. President Thomas evidently trusted Wever more than Long and often bypassed Long as he gave direct instructions to Wever. Wever and Long differed on the design of bridges and other substructures. Long, along with most army engineers, preferred wooden bridges and trestles to those of stone. Wever, on the other hand, much preferred the more permanent, and expensive, stone bridges and heavy earth fills. Thomas and his directors clearly favored Wever and his stone bridges. Two such bridges were built in the first few miles of line. The Carrollton Viaduct, built with 12,000 perches of stone and an arch eighty feet across, carried the line over Gwyuns Falls just west of the site of where the first stone was laid for the roadbed, and was finished in November 1829. The Patterson Viaduct, another of Wever's bridges, carried the railroad over the Patapsco halfway between Relay House and Ellicotts Mills. Lieutenant Colonel Long did design and build a wooden bridge to carry the Washington Turnpike over the tracks of the railroad.

The first track went down early in October 1829, with Lt. George W. Whistler in charge. Several methods of constructing the first track were followed in the early miles of track laying. Some track consisted of wrought iron strap rail laid directly upon longitudinal stone sills, while other track had the strap rail attached to wooden stringers fastened to stone blocks. A third method had the rail on wooden stringers which were laid on wooden sleepers or ties located about four feet apart. The *Fourth Annual Report* in 1830 reported that the first two methods using stone sills or stone blocks cost from $5,000 to $6,500 per mile of track (track materials and labor of laying) while the track with wood stringers and sleepers cost only $4,000 per mile. Before long, all the track was being laid with wood rather than stone. The strap rail, used in all three methods, consisted of wrought iron 5/8 inches thick, 2-1/2 inches in width, and 15 feet in length. Such rail weighed no more than fifteen pounds per yard, and was imported from England at a cost of from $55 to $60 per ton. Such rail produced in the United States cost up to $90 per ton. All the track, whether laid on wood or stone, was provided with a sufficient earth cover between the rails for a horse path.

By the end of 1829, nearly eighteen months after the 1828 Independence Day celebration, about three miles of track had been laid in three separate places—one and a half miles west and south of Baltimore running from Pratt Street out to the Carrollton Viaduct, and two shorter sections near the Patterson Viaduct and at Ellicotts Mills. The work at Ellicotts Mills had only been well begun when N. H. Ellicott wrote Philip Thomas on November 3, 1828: "As the rail Road opposite to our mill is in a state of considerable forwardness . . . a suitable turn out place . . . will be attended with much less difficulty now than when the road is completed."[2] In due course, Casper Wever provided Ellicott with his switch and siding. On December 28, 1829, Alexander Brown wrote to his banker son William, in Liverpool, England: ". . . A vast amount of money has been expanded more than ought to have been by the ignorance of our Engineers. We think it likely the board will find it convenient to part with all of them shortly except Knight. . . . One track of our road about 1-1/2 miles is completely finished, which seems to answer our most sanguine expectations. . . . Many mistakes have been made which we hope will be guarded against in future."[3]

Alexander Brown and the other directors celebrated New Year's Day, 1830, a mild and beautiful day for midwinter, by riding the new railroad from Pratt Street out to the Carrollton Viaduct and back in a horse-drawn car. The postmaster general, William T. Barry, up from Washington by the turnpike coach, was a guest on the trip, which reached the new granite bridge in six minutes—at the rapid rate of fifteen miles an hour. A week later, on January 7, 1830, the mile and a half ride was opened to the public. One-way tickets were nine cents or three for twenty-five cents. The Baltimore and Ohio was producing its first revenue. On January 16 many members of Congress came up to Baltimore for a special ride on the new railroad. Public demand was good in the winter weeks and frequently one horse pulled four cars with a combined capacity of 120 passengers.

Alexander Brown was a good prophet concerning changes in the engineering department. On January 4, 1830, the four-man engineering board was dissolved, and on February 11, 1830, Jonathan Knight was appointed chief engineer, with salary effective January 1, 1830. The work of the army engineers on the Baltimore and Ohio ended during the first few months of the new year. Lieutenant Colonel Long left for other duties in March, while Captain McNeill and the other army officers left for new assignments later that spring. Jonathan Knight had the sole responsibility for engineering, design, and construction. He would hold the position of chief engineer until March 31, 1842.

The early construction and track laying had been slow and not without some accidents and problems. There were problems with labor as well as with the engineering staff. In mid-February 1829, four workmen, all natives of Ireland, had been killed when a deep cut they were digging through a hill collapsed and buried them. During the summer of 1829, labor problems had arisen growing out of the excessive use of liquor. Whiskey was freely sold at most of the workmen's camps, and the over consumption of liquor led to frequent brawls. In mid-August 1829, a labor disturbance, described as "riots" by *Niles' Register*, followed the discharge of several workers by Thomas Elliott, a contractor on the tenth section of the road. The discharged workers threatened their employers and vandalized the Elliott residence. A number of the workers were injured before the sheriff arrested several of the ringleaders of the disturbance. One or two contractors resolved to hire no worker who made use of "stimulating drink."

With the major stone bridges all finished, Jonathan Knight was able to speed up track laying up the narrow winding valley of the Patapsco River to Ellicotts Mills. By the third week of May 1830, the single track of railroad was completed between Pratt Street and Ellicotts Mills, thirteen miles distant. Passenger service on the newly completed road, to start on Monday, May 24, 1830, was announced in the pages of *Niles' Register:*

> A brigade or train of coaches will leave the company's depot, on Pratt Street, and return, making three trips each day—starting at the following hour precisely, viz—
> Leave Baltimore at 7 A.M. and Ellicotts at 9 A.M.
> Leave Baltimore at 11 A.M. and Ellicotts at 1 P.M.
> Leave Baltimore at 4 P.M. and Ellicotts at 6 P.M.[4]

The cars, still hauled by horses, made the thirteen-mile trip in about an hour and a half. Tickets cost seventy-five cents per person for the round trip of twenty-six miles, and, at the outset, the passengers were required to return in the same coach on the next return trip. The demand for the new service was heavy, and only by late June had enough passenger cars been built to meet the demand for tickets. Four trips a day each way were started on July 5, 1830. This horse-powered limited operation was the first regular rail passenger service in the United States. Freight cars to haul to market the produce of the flour mills at the end of the track were not ready until the last weeks of summer. The total receipts that first year (January 1, 1830 to September 30, 1830) were $14,711, with passenger revenue far larger than freight. As the directors rejoiced at the news of their first revenue, they still had to recall that it had taken eighteen months to build a dozen miles of road. At such a rate, it might take forty years to reach the Ohio River.

There were only minor changes in the officers and the board of directors as the *Fourth Annual Report* was prepared in September 1830. The twelve stockholder board members serving during 1830 were identical to the original twelve elected in the spring of 1827, except for Alexander Fridge who had replaced Thomas Ellicott, and Patrick Macaulay who replaced Talbot Jones. Ellicott had resigned late in 1827, and Jones left the board early in 1829. During 1829 and 1830, the two directors representing Baltimore were Hugh McElderry and Fielding Lucas. In the spring of 1829, Richard Magruder and Virgil Maxcy were named state directors to represent the interests of the state of Maryland. In 1830 Philip Thomas was still president and George Brown was still treasurer. *Niles' Register,* late in July 1829, listed eleven of the largest individual stockholders, men who had subscribed for 400 or more shares of stock. The total holdings of the eleven amounted to $572,000, or more than one-sixth of the stock held by individuals. Naturally several board members were included in the list: George Hoffman, Alexander Brown, Robert Oliver, William Patterson, Philip Thomas, and Charles Carroll. George Hoffman, along with his brothers, was listed as having the most stock (1067 shares), while President Thomas had 474 shares and Charles Carroll, 412 shares.

The crowded passenger cars going back and forth between Pratt Street and Ellicotts Mills were still being pulled by horses in the summer of 1830. There were still a number of "experts" who were arguing that steam locomotives should be used. But the news concerning steam power which filtered into Baltimore in 1829–30 was mixed. News of the easy victory of the Stephenson *Rocket* at the Rainhill locomotive competition in England in October 1829, seemed to assure the success of steam locomotion. On the other hand, when Horatio Allen, resident engineer of the Delaware and Hudson Canal and Railroad, had tried the English-built locomotive *Stourbridge Lion* on his road in 1829, he soon found the engine to be too heavy and rigid for American track. Most who rode over the abrupt curves of the B&O line out to Ellicotts Mills doubted if English-built engines could be used successfully.

Two other experiments in motive power appeared in 1830–31. One was a sailing car invented by Evan Thomas, the brother of the company president. Years later John H. B. Latrobe, the long-time general counsel for the B&O, recalled the experiment: "This was a sailing vehicle. . . . It required a good gale to drive it, and would only run when the wind was what sailors call abaft or on the quarter. Head winds were fatal to it, and Mr. Thomas was afraid to trust a strong side wind lest the *Meteor* might upset. . . . It was an amusing toy—nothing more."[5] Later a horse-powered treadmill car was built with the inventor, a Mr. Stimpson, claiming that speeds of fifteen miles per hour were possible. On a trial run in mid-June 1831, the front passenger car, carrying eight passengers including an editor, ran into a cow upsetting the car and sending it down an embankment. None of the passengers were seriously injured, but the errant cow was killed. Clearly the B&O was ready for the steam locomotive.

Steam motive power first came to the Baltimore and Ohio because Peter Cooper, manufacturer, merchant, part-time inventor, and later a philanthropist, became interested in Baltimore. After making a modest fortune as a manufacturer of glue in New York City, Cooper, along with two partners, purchased 3,000 acres of land on the Baltimore waterfront and erected the Canton Iron Works. It was important to Cooper and his iron works that the new railroad should succeed, and when he heard doubts about the feasibility of using locomotives on a road of such tight curves, he met with the board of directors, telling them that he could build a locomotive in six weeks that would pull trains at the rate of ten miles an hour.

Cooper did not meet his time schedule, but he did build an experimental locomotive. Working in the B&O Mount Clare shops with help from Ross Winans and James Millholland, he constructed a small engine made from borrowed wheels, scrap iron, and a tiny vertical boiler with musket barrels for boiler tubes. Named the *Tom Thumb,* but sometimes called the Teakettle, the little one-ton locomotive used anthracite coal for fuel. In the summer of 1830, it carried the B&O directors on a run of thirteen miles

PETER COOPER'S "TOM THUMB" 1829-30 BALTIMORE & OHIO R.R.

Peter Cooper's *Tom Thumb*. This replica was built for the Centenary Pageant of 1927. *(Courtesy, Association of American Railroads)*

in the good time of fifty-seven minutes. Later, the small engine lost its famous race with a gray mare on a return trip from Ellicotts Mills. However, the speed and general practicability of the *Tom Thumb* convinced President Thomas and his fellow directors that they should turn to steam.

In January 1831, the directors announced a prize of $4,000 for the best four-wheel 3-1/2-ton coal-burning locomotive to be delivered by June 1, 1831. Only five entries competed for the prize with the winner being the *York*, built by Phineas Davis, a one-time watch-maker turned inventor-machinist of York, Pennsylvania. Davis also built the 6-1/2-ton *Atlantic*. Later Davis-built engines had a grasshopper look because of the four vertical rods moving up and down to power all four wheels. These Grasshopper four-wheel vertical boiler engines were ideal for the sharp curves of the B&O and became the standard motive power by the mid-1830s.

Horses, and later the early steam locomotives, pulled a variety of passenger cars in the early thirties. The first horse-drawn cars were little more than wooden boxes mounted on four flanged wheels with the seats arranged along the sides of the car. In August 1830, Richard Imlay of Philadelphia produced several improved cars for the B&O which were much like enlarged four-wheeled stage coaches with additional seating on the roof of the car. A dozen passengers were accommodated in the coach proper and an equal number could ride on top. Later, changes in passenger equipment were made by Ross Winans, a farmer with a bent for invention. Winans had sold some horses to the Baltimore and Ohio in 1828, and a year or two later became an assistant to the chief engineer. Winans sold the B&O on the idea of having the car axles move with the wheels, with the axles rolling on bearings placed outside of the wheels. He also was one of several inventors who introduced four-wheel trucks for railway cars. In 1831 Winans built the *Columbus*, an experimental passenger car, much longer than the Imlay cars and placed on two four-wheel trucks. By the mid-1830s, such cars, with a capacity of thirty-six to forty passengers in seats along either side of a central aisle, were becoming standard on the Baltimore and Ohio. This type of coach, very different from those used in England, soon became common in America. Baggage cars were added to Baltimore and Ohio passenger trains by 1833–34.

The construction of the line west of Ellicotts Mills progressed much faster in 1830 and 1831 than many observers had expected. The line followed the banks of the winding Patapsco up to the foot of Parr's Spring Ridge, about forty miles west of Baltimore, where the steepness of the ascent far exceeded the ruling grade of 0.6 percent earlier established by Colonel Long and Jonathan Knight. At this point, Knight had two inclined planes built on the east side of the ridge and two more down the western slope. The grade of the inclined planes, something more than 2 percent, required extra horses. West of the ridge, the line descended Buck Creek to cross the Monocacy River and continue toward Point of Rocks on the Potomac, with a 3-1/2-mile branch line north to Frederick. The road was double track from Baltimore to the Monocacy.

As construction neared Frederick the citizens of that city became enthusiastic about the nearly completed railroad. A local Frederick newspaper printed this tribute to Philip Thomas, B&O president: "He is a financier and engineer, mechanic and artist; he can direct the drilling of the laborers or a blast in a rock—ever fruitful in expedients and indefatigable in the application of them. In the language of a friend, he is '*up to everything*,' and if it were not for his straight coat, he would make an excellent commanding general of an army."[6] The line was opened to Frederick, sixty-one miles west of Baltimore, on December 1, 1831, with a special train carrying railroad officials, the mayor of Baltimore, and the governor of Maryland seated in his barouche firmly fastened to a flat car. The citizens of Frederick welcomed the train with bells and band

The *Atlantic* built by Phineas Davis in 1832. Shown is a replica built for the 1927 Fair of the Iron Horse. *(Courtesy, Baltimore and Ohio Railroad)*

music. The Great Western Stages, which gave service on west to the National Road, announced they would deposit their east-bound passengers at Frederick for the rail journey on to Baltimore. Eighteen months later, Andrew Jackson gave up the stage for rail travel when on June 6, 1833, he became the first American president to travel by rail—on the B&O between Ellicotts Mills and Baltimore.

The regular schedule of the horse-drawn trains to Frederick called for an eight hour trip, including meal stops, with horses changed at twelve points along the route. When the 6-1/2-ton *Atlantic* came into service in the late summer of 1832, steam power replaced horses for the trip out to the foot of the first inclined plane just east of Parrs Ridge. By 1834 it was discovered, quite by accident almost, that a Grasshopper steam locomotive could ascend the inclined planes pulling a moderate load. The event really ended the use of *horse* power on the Baltimore and Ohio.

Meanwhile, the Baltimore City Council had relented and in mid-1831 gave permission to lay tracks from the Mount Clare Station along Pratt Street to the city harbor a mile to the east. The city also donated some land near the waterfront for terminal facilities and the railroad built a depot at Pratt and Charles Streets. At the western end of the line, the track was built to Point of Rocks on the Potomac River on April 1, 1832. Including the branch to Frederick, this gave a total of 72 miles in service with a total of 130 miles of track, including double track and sidings. Reaching the Potomac meant that considerable river-borne farm produce shifted to the railroad at Point of Rocks to reach the Baltimore market.

Progress beyond Point of Rocks was halted because of a bitter controversy with the Chesapeake and Ohio Canal. Both the railroad and the canal, in their earliest planning, had proposed to follow the north bank of the Potomac, probably as far as Cumberland. At Point of Rocks, the eastern wall of Catoctin Mountain crowded so close to the waters of the Potomac that there was hardly room on the riverbank for one internal improvement, let alone two. Upriver there were other tight spots along the twelve-mile route to Harpers Ferry. The canal company obtained an injunction against the railroad and in 1832 won a long drawn out court battle. Casper Wever, who had purchased some riverfront property in the area, helped the B&O by forcing the canal to sue him for their desired right-of-way.

Eventually the Maryland legislature, which was helping finance both the canal and the railroad, stepped in and forced a compromise agreement. By the agreement, made in the spring of 1833, the narrow ledge was to be shared with the canal provided with a forty- to fifty-foot width, and the railroad confined to a twenty-foot single track right-of-way. The canal was to build the railroad road-bed in the three most difficult passes, with the cost to be paid by the B&O. Furthermore, the B&O would be required to leave the north side of the river to the canal upriver from Harpers Ferry.

The line was finished to the Maryland side of the Potomac opposite Harpers Ferry on December 1, 1834. Building a bridge across the Potomac at Harpers Ferry took longer than the construction of twelve miles of track from Point of Rocks. Benjamin H. Latrobe, brother of John H. B. Latrobe and a member of Knight's engineering corps, designed and built a six span 800-foot covered wooden bridge wide enough to accommodate a single railroad track and a wagon roadway. The bridge was opened in January 1837, and the B&O was soon exchanging freight with the newly completed thirty-two-mile Winchester and Potomac Railroad, which served the lower valley of the Shenandoah.

During the months of controversy over the Point of Rocks and the line to Harpers Ferry, a branch line south to the nation's capital was being built. Almost from the very beginning, many railroad supporters in Baltimore had argued for a line south to Washington City, as it was then often called. The rival turnpike companies were naturally opposed to all rail competition. In his *Fifth Annual Report*, dated October 1, 1831, President Thomas commented favorably on the idea of a branch to Washington and noted that company engineers were making preliminary surveys for such a road. By the end of 1832, Benjamin Latrobe had surveyed several alternate routes from Relay to the nation's capital. The two Latrobe brothers—John H. B. and Benjamin H.—were the remarkable sons of Benjamin H. Latrobe, Sr. (1764–1820) an architect who had planned much of the nation's capital. John H. B. (1803–91) was trained as an engineer at West Point, but became a lawyer. Benjamin H. (1806–78) began life as a lawyer but became a civil engineer, long employed by the B&O. Chief engineer Jonathan Knight by 1833 had decided upon one of Benjamin Latrobe's surveys—a thirty-two-mile route from Relay, running slightly east of the Baltimore to Washington turnpike. It was a good route with low grades and easy curves which, through the years, permitted high speed plus low operating and maintenance costs.

The state of Maryland chartered the route to Washington as the Washington branch of the Baltimore and Ohio Railroad on March 9, 1833. The state subscribed to $500,000 of Washington

An early train into Frederick, Maryland. From a painting by H. D. Stitt. *(Courtesy, Baltimore and Ohio Railroad)*

branch stock with several conditions: (1) that $1 million should be subscribed by others; (2) that the state directors of the B&O should be increased from two to four members; and (3) that the Washington branch should pay the state 20 percent of the annual passenger revenues plus the normal declared dividends. To make it easier for the B&O to pay this 20 percent tax, the law also set the one way fare between Washington and Baltimore at $2.50—a rather high fare in a day when the average worker's wage was little more than a dollar a day. This special tax on passenger fares on the Washington branch was not repealed until the early 1870s.

Construction of the Washington branch began in October 1833. The road was graded, including all cuts and bridges, for two tracks, but only a single track was laid between Relay and Washington. As the workers laid the track, the mistakes made on the main line to Harpers Ferry were not repeated. No stone roadbed or strap rail was used. Instead "T" rails, a type of rail earlier designed by Robert L. Stevens, president of the Camden and Amboy Railroad, were placed on longitudinal wooden stringers which were placed on cross ties. The iron, weighing forty pounds to the yard, was imported from England.

The greatest single construction project on the Washington branch was the Thomas Viaduct, a huge stone structure named for the B&O president, and carrying the curving track across the Patapsco from Relay to Elk Ridge. Designed by Benjamin Latrobe, with construction supervised by Casper Wever, the giant bridge was over 600 feet in length and consisted of eight handsome sixty-foot arches built of Patapsco granite. The Thomas Viaduct was so well built that it easily handles the much heavier traffic of today. The line to Washington was officially opened on August 25, 1835, with four special trains from Baltimore pulled by new Grasshopper engines—the *Thomas Jefferson, James Madison, James Monroe,* and *J. Q. Adams*—all built for the new service by Phineas Davis. The new Washington depot was located at Pennsylvania Avenue and Second Street, just west of the capital. Passenger travel on the new branch was brisk, and at $2.50 per trip, also quite profitable. During the fiscal year 1836 (October 1, 1835 to September 30, 1836), the Washington branch produced a passenger revenue of $176,149 from a total of 75,416 passengers and a freight revenue of $11,563 from 5,662 tons of freight. After paying Maryland one-fifth of the gross passenger revenue and paying all transportation, repair, and track maintenance expenses, the Baltimore and Ohio had a remaining net revenue of $88,772 in 1836 for the Washington branch.

Traffic on the Main Stem, Baltimore to Harpers Ferry, had been growing in the thirties, but was not as profitable as the Washington branch. In the early 1830s, the *Niles' Register* frequently referred to the growing traffic on the new road. In July 1831, the paper noted that during the past spring the average passenger traffic between Baltimore and Ellicotts Mills was 400 travelers a day while the average transportation of freight was twenty-six tons a day. Traffic greatly increased when the line was open to Frederick. In mid-January 1832, just a few weeks after the completion of the road, the *Frederick Herald* reported that 4,000 barrels of flour had been shipped to Baltimore in an eleven-day period at a savings of fifty cents a barrel over the cost of wagon freight. In the spring of 1833 the *Niles' Register* described the erection of a machine at the Frederick depot which could lift loaded wagons weighing over two tons onto railroad cars for shipment to Baltimore. Railroad backers were proud of the fact that the new service was year-round and not closed down in the winter as were canals. Four days before Christmas 1833, a heavy snowfall, eighteen inches deep at Frederick, only delayed the train's arrival in Baltimore by an hour and a half.

TABLE 2. Baltimore and Ohio Traffic and Financial Growth of Main Stem 1830–36

Year	Miles of Road	Passenger Receipts	Freight Receipts	Total Receipts	Expenses	Net Receipts
1830	13	—	—	$ 14,711	$ 11,985	$ 2,726
1831	61	$ 27,250	$ 4,155	31,405	10,995	20,410
1832	72	67,910	69,027	136,937	75,673	61,264
1833	72	83,233	112,447	195,680	138,495	57,185
1834	84	89,182	116,255	205,437	138,402	67,035
1835	84	93,540	169,828	263,368	161,216	102,152
1836	84	128,126	153,186	281,312	212,937	68,375

The freight traffic and revenue quickly became more important than the passenger. Both passenger and freight traffic were much lower in the winter than in the rest of the year. The peak of passenger traffic came in midsummer while the largest freight revenues were in the fall. Flour was by far the most important item of freight moving to Baltimore, making up nearly half the total in the midthirties. Both the passenger fares and the freight rates charged by the B&O were lower than those of many other early American railroads.

The *Tenth Annual Report* listed operating expenses of the Main Stem for the year 1836 which included $128,000 for transportation, $53,000 for repair of the road, $26,000 for repair of machin-

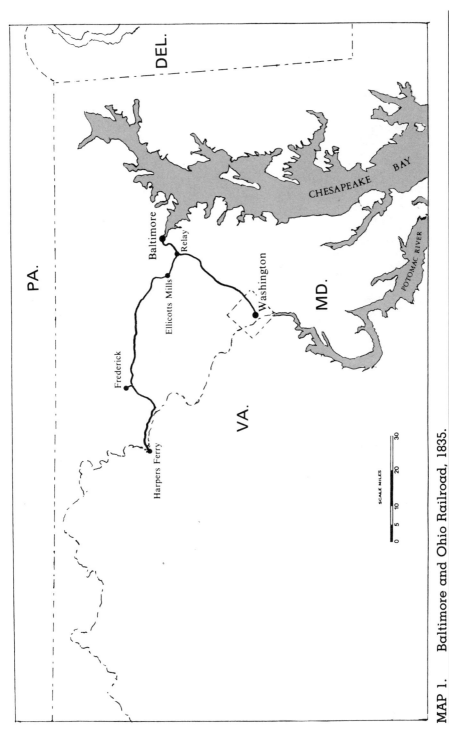

MAP 1.   Baltimore and Ohio Railroad, 1835.

The B&O reached Ellicotts Mills in 1830, Frederick late in 1831, the vicinity of Harpers Ferry in 1834, and Washing- ton in 1835. The railroad bridge across the Potomac at Harpers Ferry was opened in January 1837.

Joseph W. Patterson, president, 1836.
(Courtesy, Baltimore and Ohio Railroad)

ery and cars, and $5,000 for salaries and office expense. Railroad officials figured that one of their locomotives cost about $13 per day to operate, including $7.50 for coal (1-1/4 tons at $6 per ton), $2.00 for the wages of the engineer, and $1.50 for the firemen. The roster of equipment in 1836, for use on the Main Stem and the Washington branch consisted of 12 locomotives, 1,062 burden or freight cars, and 46 passenger cars. More than 90 percent of the freight cars were small short cars with only four wheels. The B&O also owned 173 horses and 60 mules. About one-third of the horses were required for the streets of Baltimore, since steam locomotives were not permitted on the Pratt Street extension into the center of town.

The *Tenth Annual Report* for the year 1836 was different in that it carried the signature of a new president, Joseph W. Patterson. Philip E. Thomas had considered giving up the presidency for some time, and he resigned on June 30, 1836, due to ill health and the pressure of private affairs. The board passed appropriate resolutions moving "that the most unfeigned and cordial thanks of this Board are due to Mr. Thomas for the long, faithful, and valuable services rendered by him to this Company."[7] The board then elected Joseph W. Patterson as president protem. Patterson had been a member of the board only since April 1835, when he was elected to fill the vacancy caused by the death of his father, William Patterson, one of the original directors. Another of the original directors, Alexander Brown, had died in the spring of 1834 and was succeeded by his son, George Brown.

Under the years of the Thomas leadership, the Baltimore and Ohio had faced a multitude of unique engineering problems and by 1836 had built and had in operation 115 miles of line. The decade of railroad development experienced by the B&O was so important that D. Kimball Minor, the editor of the *American Rail-road Journal,* in 1835 wrote of the Baltimore and Ohio as the Railroad University of the United States. Even so, the B&O in 1836 was close to bankruptcy. The costly masonry bridges, the low rates, and the relatively unpopulated area it served had all resulted in meager profits and low financial returns. In 1836 it seemed to many observers that if the road was ever to reach Ohio both new leadership and new money would be required.

Chapter IV

• • • • • • • • • • • • • •

Cumberland— But No Further

WHEN THE BALTIMORE AND OHIO BOARD OF DIRECTORS learned of the contemplated resignation of President Thomas, they anxiously started to seek a competent successor—someone who could retain the confidence of both Baltimore and Maryland and one who also had a knowledge of European finance. By the early summer of 1836, they were in active correspondence with Louis McLane, a former United States senator, cabinet officer, and diplomat. Joseph W. Patterson was only an interim president until Louis McLane could leave New York City, where he was president of the Morris Canal and Banking Company. When McLane was formally elected president on December 27, 1836, his salary was fixed at $4,000 which was modestly increased once he was in office. The new president brought a vast breadth of experience to his new position. Born in Delaware in 1786, at the age of twelve he became a midshipman in the United States Navy, cruising for a year under Como. Stephen Decatur. He left the navy in 1801, attended college, studied law and was admitted to the bar in 1807. From 1817 to 1829, he represented Delaware in both houses of the United States Congress. Between 1829 and 1834 he served President Andrew Jackson in turn as minister to England, secretary of the treasury, and secretary of state. McLane often found it difficult to cooperate with fellow workers, but he proved to be a capable executive who was orderly, efficient, and a strong enemy of waste.

Louis McLane, president, 1836–48.
(Courtesy, Baltimore and Ohio Railroad)

In many ways, a new team of officials came in with Louis Mc-Lane in 1836. The twelve men elected (as directors representing individual stockholders) on October 9, 1836, included only two men, Philip Thomas and William Steuart, who had been on the original board selected in 1827. Philip Thomas had been a director as well as president during his years of leadership. In contrast, Louis McLane and his successors were normally not members of the board of directors. By 1837 the numbers of "city" and "state" directors had increased to eight each. All the directors came from Maryland and most, of course, from Baltimore.

There were some other administrative changes in the mid-1830s. Jonathan Knight continued as chief engineer. Benjamin Latrobe had left the Baltimore and Ohio in 1835 to become the chief engineer of the Baltimore and Port Deposit Railroad, but returned to the B&O in 1836 when he was placed in charge of surveying the line west of Harpers Ferry to Cumberland. His brother, John H. B. Latrobe, continued as general counsel of the B&O, a position he would hold for another half century. George Brown, the first B&O treasurer, had resigned that position in the spring of 1834 to take a place on the board of directors upon the death of his father, Alexander Brown. The new treasurer was William H. Murray. The first secretary of the railroad, John N. Brown (no relation to Alexander or George Brown), was replaced by Joshua I. Atkinson in October 1835.

During his nine year presidency, Philip Thomas had built about 114 miles of road, west to Harpers Ferry and south to Washington. During the dozen years that Louis McLane headed the railroad, the line was pushed ninety-seven miles further west to Cumberland. Not only did the new mileage west of Harpers Ferry lie through more difficult terrain than the earlier construction, but there was general agreement that the original line in 1836 needed major repair and considerable rebuilding. In fact, there were reports that the new president, after his first examination of his property, tersely called it a "wreck." McLane was a bit more judicious in his language when he described the problem of necessary reconstruction in his first annual report in October 1837:

> Although the original construction, under the circumstances, and with the knowledge then possessed, may have been the best, the subsequent experience upon this road, and the progress of improvement elsewhere have shown, that a different mode should now be adopted. It has become obvious, moreover, that to continue the repairs of the road, upon the present plan of construction, will expose both the road, and the machinery employed upon it to even greater dilapidation.[1]

President McLane first turned to the construction of a new route suitable for locomotives that would bypass the inclined planes at Parr's Ridge. While locomotives had managed on occasion to climb the inclined planes, horse and mule power were still regularly being employed to get over the ridge. Surveys for a new route sightly to the north and crossing the summit of the ridge at Mount Airy had been started in 1836. The new double track, 5-1/2-mile bypass route, which required a fifty-foot cut at the summit, was completed by 1838. The grade of just under 1.6 percent, while less steep than the original inclined planes, still required helper engines for all heavier trains.

Next the new president had Benjamin Latrobe and his work crews straighten out some of the sharpest hairpin curves in the Patapsco Valley. One of the worst of the sharp curves was near Elysville, about five miles upstream from Ellicotts Mills. Here Latrobe moved the track to the north side of the river by building two new wooden-truss covered bridges, each about 300 feet in length. By 1838 both bridges had been built, and five or six miles of the sharper curves had been eliminated. Even with these improvements, nearly half of the Main Stem from Baltimore to Harpers Ferry still consisted of curved track rather than tangents. At least the grades were low, rarely being above 0.7 percent, except for the new line at Mount Airy.

Everyone agreed that the major flaw in the B&O line was the iron strap rail which was on the entire eighty-one miles from Baltimore to Harpers Ferry. Such track was adequate for light horse-drawn cars, but heavier locomotives and cars had a tendency to make the thin iron strips bend upwards, breaking them loose from the stringers below. A piece of loose strap rail was called a "snakehead." A twenty-foot "snakehead" could derail an engine and wreck a train. Or, if it broke through the floor of moving passenger coach, it could cause the most unbelieveable injury and havoc. Late in 1837, President McLane sent Jonathan Knight and Benjamin Latrobe to visit several northeastern lines, in order to study their experience with different types of track. Knight and Latrobe returned convinced that the entire B&O route should be relaid with iron T-rail. Certainly the engineering staff was well pleased with the T-rail earlier laid on the Washington branch. Of almost equal importance was the realization that all of the track laid on stone blocks and stringers—most of which was located on the twenty-three miles between Relay and Sykesville—needed to be replaced with a wooden substructure.

The new track over Parr's Ridge and the relocation work in the Patapsco Valley had already strained the financial resources of the road. This condition was made worse by the relative decline in traffic and revenue caused by the general depression prevailing in tha nation in the late 1830s. Clearly the Baltimore and Ohio could not afford to replace all the strap rail with T-rail and also do away with the stone track structure. One favorable factor was the realization, after a decade of actual operation, that the B&O did not really need a double track along the entire length of the Main Stem.

The solution to the problem had to be one of compromise and patch work. All of the stone roadbed was replaced with wood, but only small portions of the line received T-rail. Eleven miles of T-rail were laid on the double track, 5-1/2-mile new route over Parr's Ridge at Mount Airy. T-rail was also laid on one of the two tracks from Mount Clare to Relay. Nearly all of the Main Stem from Ellicotts Mills to Harpers Ferry was reduced to a single track, with the best strap rail relaid and the worst discarded. Most of the Baltimore and Ohio line was to remain laid with strap rail until the late 1840s. This long usage of strap rail during these years was made possible in part by the type of motive power used on the B&O. The small and light weight Grasshopper locomotives, with their geared drive and small wheels, were relatively easy on this type of track. Double track still existed on the line from Baltimore to Ellicotts Mills, and also on the new route near Parr's Ridge.

In commenting on the reconstruction program of the late thirties, President McLane in his annual report for 1840 wrote: ". . .by the first of December next, the whole [line] will be substantially renewed, and in the condition of greater efficiency and durability than at any previous period."[2] The directors were no doubt glad that the extra expenses of the rebuilding program were now past. The late 1830s, during and after the Panic of 1837, had been difficult years for the railroad. Where the banks of Baltimore, like those in New York and Philadephia, had suspended specie payments during the financial crisis, they began the issuance of fractional paper money often called "shinplasters." Soon the Baltimore and Ohio followed suit and issued "shinplasters," in amounts ranging from 12-1/2 cents to $100, which quickly had a wide circulation in Maryland and Virginia. With the railroad in such financial straits, no doubt some directors felt that the president's salary might again be reduced to $4,000 a year.

But the major accomplishment during the McLane years was the extension of the road west of Harpers Ferry on to Cumberland. At the time of McLane's acceptance of the presidency, the railroad itself did not possess the resources to finance the estimated cost of $4,500,000 to build the line west to Cumberland. Certainly the original capital stock had been exhausted in building the Main Stem, since the construction cost of the road to Harpers Ferry, about $3,600,000, was $200,000 more than the company had received from the stockholders. It was true that the sum of $450,000, or $15 per share was still due and callable from the original stockholders, but this would provide only a small portion of the funds required for the western extension. As of 1836, it seemed quite unlikely that private capital would be able to make up the difference. Again the Baltimore and Ohio had to ask the city of Baltimore and the state of Maryland for financial assistance.

During the summer of 1836, the railroad received the promise of additional substantial support from both the city and the state. In June 1836, the Maryland legislature agreed to an additional stock subscription of $3 million and at about the same time the city of Baltimore decided to make a new stock subscription of equal size. Railroad officials received the Maryland subscription for 30,000 new shares from the state treasurer on September 23, 1836, and a subscription also for 30,000 shares from the mayor of Baltimore on September 27, 1836. The Maryland legislation also extended the time for the completion of the road from 1838 to 1843, and also allowed the railroad to increase its passenger fare on the Main Stem from three cents to four cents per mile.

Unfortunately, there were difficulties and delays in obtaining the financial support offered by the city and the state. In the case of Baltimore, the funds from the city could only be used for the actual construction of the line west of Harpers Ferry, and they were to be payable at the rate of no more than one million dollars a year. In the depression years of 1838, 1839, and 1840, the city of Baltimore found it quite difficult to meet its commitments to the railroad. The railroad did not receive full payment from the city of Baltimore for the 30,000 shares of new stock until 1842–43. There were also problems with the stock subscription. The railroad was unhappy when the state insisted that its 30,000 shares of new stock must be considered as "preferred stock." Maryland forced the railroad to pledge to pay 6 percent interest on the 30,000 shares of stock, beginning three years after the date of receipt. These payments had to be made before any dividend could be declared. In order to raise the required $3 million, the state first tried to sell state currency bonds. When the bad financial market conditions of the late 1830s made such sales impossible, the state shifted to 5 percent sterling bonds, the principal and interest payable in London. President McLane went to Europe in an effort to place the bonds on the European market. Eventually he was successful in getting the Baring Brothers of London to take the bonds and also advance construction credits to the Baltimore and Ohio. A substantial portion of the credits were used for the purchase of English iron rail to be laid on the extension to Cumberland.

As the first surveys were being made west of Harpers Ferry toward Cumberland, both Pittsburgh and Wheeling on the upper Ohio expressed an interest in being connected with Cumberland by railroad. Wheeling promised financial aid to the B&O, but later Pennsylvania refused permission for the B&O to build to Pittsburgh or even to cross the state enroute on Wheeling. Since the original Virginia charter of 1827 had required that any construction in that state must be completed by 1838, new legislation by Virginia was necessary before the road could be extended to Cumberland. After some difficulty, Virginia, in 1838, passed legislation giving the Baltimore and Ohio an additional five years in which to complete the road. However, Virginia insisted that the route from Harpers Ferry to Cumberland, Maryland, must remain in Virginia to a point only five or six miles below Cumberland. The legislation promised a stock subscription of about $300,000 but also required that Wheeling must be one of the termini of the road as it was built to the Ohio River.

During the many months of legislative and financial activity, Benjamin Latrobe and his surveying crews had mapped out several alternate routes between Harpers Ferry and Cumberland. The action of Virginia, of course, meant that nearly all of the line would be located south of the Potomac in Virginia. The final route selected left the Potomac valley at Harpers Ferry going in a northwesterly direction via Martinsburg for about thirty miles until it again entered the Potomac valley ten miles downstream from Hancock. The route stayed on the southern or Virginia side of the Potomac until within five or six miles of Cumberland where it crossed the river into Maryland. The terrain was far from difficult compared to the region west of Cumberland, but even so three tunnels were necessary: two short ones of 90 and 250 feet, and a longer 1,200-foot bore at Doe Gulley. The maximum grade in the ninety-seven-mile route was less than 1 percent. Even though only one track was to be laid, the entire route, including bridges, was graded and built to the width of double track. Ten wooden bridges, plus one of stone, for a total length of 3,690 feet, were required in the extension to Cumberland.

Benjamin Latrobe first had to find a feasible route out of Harpers Ferry. There were only two possible routes: (1) obtaining the right to use the tracks of the Winchester and Potomac along the Shenandoah river for a short distance or (2) following the south shore of the Potomac by obtaining a narrow right-of-way through the grounds of the United States arsenal at Harpers Ferry. The Winchester and Potomac refused to grant trackage rights to the B&O, but, fortunately, perhaps because of Louis McLane's influence in Washington, the secretary of war gave Latrobe permission to lay his tracks on a trestle along the edge of the arsenal property next to the Potomac. This did not solve the problem, however, since the trestle alignment along the river intersected the south end of the new B&O bridge over the Potomac at almost a right angle. This six-span bridge, which had just been completed by Latrobe, had been built to connect head-on with the Winchester and Potomac, not to lead upriver along the Potomac. Latrobe had to rebuild the southern end of the new bridge, placing a junction switch 265 feet out from the south shore, with a sharply curved new span to carry the tracks to the trestle along the arsenal property. This awkward arrangement proved very durable and was not replaced with an easier curve for several decades.

Construction contracts were finally let, and construction west of Harpers Ferry started in 1839. At the height of the construction, nearly 1,500 men and more than 450 horses were employed in the project. Iron T-rail, weighing fifty-one pounds to the yard, and requiring eighty tons of rail per mile, was laid on wooden ties resting on a bed of broken stone one foot deep. The nearly 8,000 tons of iron required for the single track to Cumberland was imported from England and arrived at the docks in Baltimore in ships carrying rail cargoes of 500 to 700 tons each. The road was completed on June 1, 1842, to a point in Virginia just across the Potomac from Hancock, Maryland, forty-one miles from Harpers Ferry and 122 miles west of Baltimore. Track laying increased in the summer and fall months of 1842. The *American Railroad Journal* later that summer reported that "four extensive brick buildings are now under construction at the Depot of the Baltimore and Ohio Railroad at Cumberland. They are severally intended for forwarding and commission merchants."[3] A few weeks later, on November 5, 1842, the Baltimore and Ohio Railroad was opened to Cumberland, fifty-six miles west of Hancock.

Cumberland was 178 miles west of Baltimore. In the fifteen years since the chartering of the B&O in 1827, Jonathan Knight and Benjamin Latrobe had pushed the B&O nearly halfway to the Ohio River. Latrobe would have to finish the job, since Knight had resigned as chief engineer back on March 31, 1842, to be succeeded by Latrobe. At Cumberland the B&O was able to take over much of the wagon and stagecoach traffic of the National Road which had its eastern terminal at that point. Certainly rail travel was faster than that of the turnpike coach. On December 5, 1842, just a month after the completion of construction, a special locomotive running out of Washington, had carried a copy of President Tyler's message to Congress out to Cumberland, a distance of 200 miles, in the record time of five hours and forty minutes. More profitable to the Baltimore and Ohio was the increased traffic in coal from the growing number of mines in the hills surrounding Cumberland. President McLane seemed well satisfied with the extension, writing in 1843: ". . . The operations of the road between Baltimore and Cumberland since the 5th of November, 1842, have been altogether encouraging, fully warranting the expectations which urged its completion to that point; and calculated to inspire the stockholders and board with renewed zeal in their future exertions to carry it forward."[4] However, the "renewed zeal" was not sufficient in the mid or late forties to push the road on to the Ohio. Almost a decade would pass before the B&O would reach that river.

During the dozen years of the McLane presidency there were vast changes in motive power and rolling stock. The types of locomotives greatly increased, as did the number of locomotives from twelve in 1836 to fifty-seven in 1848. Many of the first B&O locomotives had been built by Phineas Davis in the company shops at Mount Clare. Davis was killed while riding one of his engines on the newly opened Washington branch in September 1835. Ross Winans and George Gillingham took over the operation of the Mount Clare shop and continued to manufacture engines and cars for the B&O. The shop turned out the small, four-wheeled Grasshopper locomotives until 1837. In 1838 Winans built two engines, the *Isaac McKim* and the *Mazeppa*, called Crabs, which were basically Grasshoppers with horizontal cylinders.

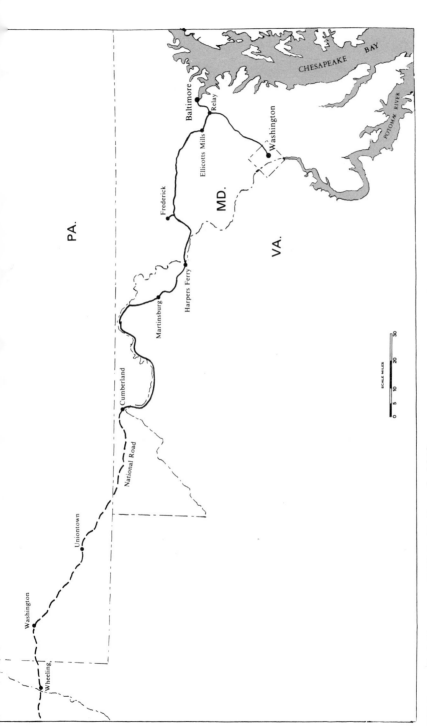

MAP 2.   Baltimore and Ohio Railroad, 1842.

Between 1839 and November 1842, the B&O was built westward from Harpers Ferry to Cumberland. At Cumberland the new railroad captured the wagon and stagecoach traffic of the National Road (— — —) which ran westward through Pennsylvania to Wheeling and beyond.

The *William Galloway* is an exact reproduction of the earlier *Lafayette*. The *Lafayette*, one of the first B&O engines with a horizontal boiler, was purchased in the late 1830s. *(Courtesy, Baltimore and Ohio Railroad)*

President McLane had not been in office long before he decided to purchase some locomotives made by commercial builders outside of Baltimore. McLane was becoming increasingly dissatisfied with the small Grasshopper. Between 1837 and 1839, McLane bought from the Norris Locomotive Works several engines with horizontal boilers and a 4-2-0 wheel design (pony truck in front plus two drivers). These new engines, several of which were used on the Washington branch, were often called "One Armed Billys" for their single drivers and their maker, William Norris. Half a dozen years later Ross Winans, who set up his own locomotive works in the early 1840s, produced an engine with a very different wheel design, 0-8-0, weighing about 23 tons with a horizontal boiler powered by eight rather small drivers. The new engines were soon known as "Mud Diggers" because of their propensity for derailing on the sharp curves of the Main Stem. However, they were great for pulling heavy freight trains, and between 1844 and 1847 McLane added a dozen "Mud Diggers" to his motive power roster.

In 1848 Winans built his first "Camel" locomotive, a hulking engine weighing twenty-two to twenty-four tons with eight small drivers (0-8-0) and a huge cab located on top of the boiler. Winans built over one hundred Camels for the Baltimore and Ohio by 1857. By 1848 the railroad had also purchased from various manufacturers several American type locomotives (4-4-0), with a pony truck under the stack, four drivers, and no trailing wheels under the cab. One of these American type engines was the *Philip E.Thomas*, named for the first president and built in 1838 by William Norris. The fifty-seven engines on the motive power roster in 1848 all had names, including American political figures, B&O officials, animals, rivers, and numerous mythical figures. After 1851, as the B&O locomotive fleet started a rapid expansion, locomotive names were all replaced by numbers. In 1848 the locomotives of the Baltimore and Ohio were divided into four classes, according to weight:

TABLE 3. Locomotives of the B&O 1848

Class	Weight	Number in Class	When Placed on Road	Usage
1	19-1/2–23-1/2 tons	18	1844–48	Freight only
2	16–17 tons	4	1840–48	Freight only
3	14-1/2–15-1/2 tons	15	1838–48	Freight & Passenger
4	10–11 tons	20	1834–39	Freight & Passenger

Most new locomotives purchased in the 1840s cost between $7,000 and $9,500. A majority of the first B&O engines were coal burners, but by 1848 many of the locomotives on the line were burning wood. In 1848 the B&O purchased 17,700 cords of wood for $36,632 and 12,700 tons of coal for $18,458. A few years later, most roads were paying far more than $2 for a cord of wood and $1.50 for a ton of coal.

In his dual capacity as chief engineer and general superintendent (since February 1847), Benjamin Latrobe reported that during 1848 the fifty-seven locomotives ran for a total of 1,039,000 miles (Main Stem plus Washington branch) or an average of about 18,200 miles per engine, or roughly sixty miles per working day. This was quite good daily mileage for that date considering the relatively low train speeds of that time plus the fact that about 70 percent of all engine mileage was freight. Some locomotives were well above the average annual mileage. The *Buffaloe* (all freight service acquired in 1844, and class 1) was operated 23,968 miles in 1848. The *Atlas* (99 percent freight, 1839, class 3) ran for 28,330 miles, while the *Mercury* (all passenger, 1842, class 3) ran for a total of 40,950 miles during the year. Latrobe figured that locomotive repairs on his road for the year 1848 averaged about $1,070 per engine. During the year about 82 percent of the motive power was in daily use.

Latrobe's roster of cars in 1848 included 1,201 freight or "burden" cars. The great bulk of the cars were box or "house" cars, but also included were 240 coal cars, 49 stock cars, and 6 express cars. The roster of freight equipment had grown only modestly since 1836 when 1,062 cars had been in use, but the cars of 1848 had a greater average carrying capacity and the great majority had eight wheels. The eight-wheel cars of 1848 had a capacity of six to eight tons. The four-wheel cars, which made up 90 percent of the car roster in 1836 but only 12 percent in 1848, carried a load of only two or three tons. The passenger car roster of 1848 consisted of sixty-five cars as compared to forty-six cars a dozen years earlier. In the 1848 roster, forty-six cars operated on the Main Stem, while nineteen were used on the Washington branch. The sixty-five cars consisted of twenty-seven thoroughfare cars, twelve excursion cars, nine ladies cars, three smoking cars, nine baggage cars, and five mail cars.

"Twenty Minutes for Dinner," a typical railway scene of the 1840s. From a painting by H. D. Stitt. *(Courtesy, Baltimore and Ohio Railroad)*

Almost from the beginning, railroads were used for United States mail service, with the South Carolina Railroad in 1831 probably the first to do so. The Baltimore and Ohio carried mail on its Washington branch soon after its completion, but the service did not always satisfy the postmaster general. Like other railroads between Washington, D.C., and Boston, the Baltimore and Ohio insisted on rates that seemed high to the post office department: $250 per mile of road per year. Federal legislation in 1838 made all railroads "post roads," but the legislation did not cut the costs of rail postal service. In 1839 Congress permitted the postmaster general to pay as much as $300 per mile per year. In the middle 1840s, the Baltimore and Ohio was receiving about $43,000 a year for carrying the United States mail over the 178 mile Main Stem. In the first years of mail via railway, it was all "closed pouch" service, with a postmaster at one point sending sacks of mail to other postmasters. The practice of sorting or "working" the mail enroute in railway post office cars did not start until the early 1860s.

The B&O may not have been the first railroad to carry the mail, but it was the first to have a telegraph line and service along its right-of-way. Samuel F. B. Morse, a Yankee-born painter who had studied in Europe, found upon his return to America that while his countrymen liked his portraits, his income was still meager and irregular. In 1837 he gave up painting to perfect his electro-magnetic telegraph for which he had just received a patent. Morse decided a railway right-of-way would be a good place to install his first telegraph line, but he was turned down by the New Jersey Railroad since the officials of the company felt that their patrons would conduct their business by wire instead of by traveling.

Morse turned to Maryland where he obtained a charter for his magnetic telegraph company. In 1843 the United States Congress voted to pay $30,000 for an experimental line from Baltimore to Washington. Both Benjamin Latrobe and John H. B. Latrobe endorsed the project, the B&O board of directors approved, and in the fall of 1843, Morse contracted with Ezra Cornell, a New York millwright and mechanic, to lay the line underground along the Washington branch. A special plow was perfected in the Mount Clare shops to dig a trench two inches wide and two feet deep beside the B&O track. By the time the copper wire, placed in lead pipe, had reached Relay, serious problems of inadequate insulation had developed. Even though more than half the government appropriation had already been spent, Morse did not give up. He quickly had the copper wire removed from the pipe and was soon stringing it on poles placed along the track. More than half the line had been put in place by May 1, 1844. Later that day the success of the telegraph was fully proven when the news of Henry Clay's presidential nomination by the Whig Convention in Baltimore was transmitted to the basement of the nation's capitol by the combined efforts of a B&O train and the partially completed telegraph line. Three and a half weeks later, the words "What hath God wrought!" were transmitted over the completed line running from the Pratt Street Depot in Baltimore to the Supreme Court chamber in the capitol building in Washington. By agreement with Morse the B&O had full and free use of the telegraph line upon its completion. For some reason neither Morse nor the top officials of the B&O realized in 1844 the natural affinity of the railroad and the telegraph. Already in the early forties the railroads of England and France were using the telegraph for train dispatching and control. In the United States this did not happen until September 1851, when Charles Minot, superintendent of the New York and Erie, first used the telegraph for such purposes.

Naturally Baltimore and Ohio traffic increased during the dozen years of the McLane term.

TABLE 4. Growth in Main Stem Traffic 1837–48

Years	Miles of Road	Passenger Receipts	Freight Receipts	Total Receipts	Expense	Net Receipts
1837	84	$145,625	$155,676	$ 301,301	$289,125	$ 12,176
1838	84	166,694	198,530	365,224	271,581	93,643
1839	84	173,860	233,487	407,347	312,700	94,647
1840	84	177,035	255,848	432,883	275,189	157,694
1841	84	179,616	211,454	391,070	239,622	151,448
1842	125	181,177	245,315	426,492	216,715	209,777
1843	181	274,617	300,618	575,235	295,833	279,402
1844	181	336,876	321,743	658,619	311,633	346,986
1845	181	369,882	368,721	738,603	363,841	374,762
1846	181	413,341	468,346	881,687	454,840	426,847
1847	181	447,020	654,917	1,101,937	590,829	511,108
1848	181	488,376	725,288	1,213,664	662,108	551,556

During the dozen years total receipts on the Main Stem increased fourfold, with freight receipts growing much faster than passenger revenue. All Main Stem revenue increased in the mid-1840s, even though passenger fares had been cut 25 percent and freight rates 30 percent.

On the Washington branch which had no increased mileage, the revenue growth was slower. Washington branch revenue, which was three-quarters passenger and one-quarter freight, increased from $160,000 in 1837 to $255,000 in 1848. During the decade, many western and northern congressmen had used the Washington branch as they went to or from the nation's capital. In mid-March 1849, Abraham Lincoln returned home to Illinois after the end of a rather undistinguished single term as a United States congressman. He began his trip by purchasing an $8.60 ticket for the twelve-hour, 200-mile trip from Washington to Cumberland on the "Great Western Mail." West of Cumberland he took a stage over the mountains to Wheeling and then an Ohio River packet on to St. Louis. His entire trip took nearly twelve days because so few rail lines had been built in the west—only 575 miles in Ohio, 228 in Indiana, and 111 in Illinois. A dozen years later, in February, 1861, as president-elect, he returned to Washington entirely by rail.

The expanding freight traffic on the Main Stem was increasingly more eastbound than westbound. By 1848 the eastbound tonnage moving toward Baltimore was more than triple the tonnage moving to the West. The tonnage of flour to Baltimore increased in the late 1830s and by 1840 accounted for two-thirds of all tonnage going east. For the year 1848 coal moving to Baltimore—more than 66,000 tons—made up 40 percent of all eastward tonnage. During 1848 flour moving eastward amounted to 45,000 tons. Other heavy eastbound shipments in 1848 were: livestock—13,000 tons; iron—7,000 tons; stone products—6,000 tons; and tobacco—5,000 tons.

During the decade of the 1840s, expenses fortunately grew slower than total receipts allowing the net receipts to increase at a fairly rapid rate. For example, in the year 1844, the total expenses for operating the Main Stem were:

Expenses of transportation, fuel, salaries of superintendents, train crews, agents, etc.	$107,207
Repairs of road, depots, bridges, etc.	110,810
Repairs of locomotives and cars	74,965
Other expenses, salaries, rents, taxes, etc.	18,692
	$311,674

A major portion of all the above consisted of salaries and wages paid the officials and employees of the Baltimore and Ohio. Early in January 1845, the Maryland House of Delegates ordered that "the President of the Baltimore & Ohio Railroad . . . inform the House . . . what amount has been paid the officers of said company."[5] The report sent to the House of Delegates revealed that the top salaries in 1844 were: Louis McLane (president)—$6,000; J. I. Atkinson (secretary)—$2,000; John H. B. Latrobe (counsel)—$1,000: Benjamin Latrobe (chief engineer)—$3,000; James Murray (engineer of machinery & repairs)—$2,000; and Thatcher Perkins (shop foreman)—$1,000. Obviously, President McLane had received a handsome increase since taking office in 1836. The salaries of John and Benjamin Latrobe were a far cry from the time twenty years earlier when the two brothers were poverty stricken roommates at Saint Mary's College. Between them they owned only one pair of black silk dress stockings, which were wearing so thin that to keep up a good appearance they put black ink on their legs.

In 1844 depot agents along the Main Stem had annual salaries ranging from $240 to $1,200. Most clerks received $500 yearly, while supervisors of road repair were paid $540 to $600 a year. The pay of a master carpenter was $600, while several resident engineers who had helped Benjamin Latrobe complete the extension to Cumberland in 1842 were paid from $450 to $890 a year. In the early forties, locomotive engineers received $2 a day, firemen $35 a month, brakemen $30 a month, and ordinary labor 75¢ to $1.00 a day. The request from the Maryland House of Delegates also asked for a list of all persons who were given passes for free travel on the railroad. In 1844 the Baltimore and Ohio gave such passes to the B&O president, directors, secretary and their families, to other top B&O officials, to the proprietors of the Good Intent and National Road stage lines, to the president of the Chesapeake and Ohio Canal, and the presidents of seven nearby or connecting railroads.

Traffic on the road during the 1840s was heavy enough to permit modest dividends in several years. Very small dividends, ranging from .375 percent to .75 percent had been paid yearly from 1830 to 1833 and another of 1.125 percent in 1835. In 1840, when the net receipts had grown to $157,000, a dividend of 2 percent ($80,000) was declared, and in 1841 another 2 percent ($130,000) was also paid. No dividends were paid in 1842, but cash dividends were resumed in 1843, when 2 percent ($140,000) was paid, and again in 1844 a 2.5 percent ($175,000) dividend was declared. No dividends were paid in 1845. In 1846 a 3 percent dividend ($210,000) consisted of $1 in cash and $2 in new bonds. In 1847 another 3 percent dividend ($210,000) was paid entirely in new bonds. A stock dividend of 3.5 percent was paid in 1848.

During the presidency of McLane, many changes occurred in the board of directors. Both Joseph Patterson and Philip E. Thomas left the board in 1838. As the financial support of both Baltimore and Maryland increased, so did the number of city and state directors. By 1846 the thirty-member board consisted of twelve stockholder-directors, eight city directors, and ten state directors. Important additions to the stockholders group in 1847 were Johns Hopkins, a wealthy Baltimore Commission merchant and banker, and Thomas Swann, a Baltimore businessman. In the six years since the completion of the road to Cumberland, little had effectively been done to push the road further westward. In the words of John H. B. Latrobe: "The public and the stockholders had become dissatisfied, the road stopped at Cumberland, and the same circumstances that operated to remove Mr. Thomas and make McLane President, now bore upon Mr. McLane."[6] Being aware of the opposition, Louis McLane resigned the presidency, effective October 9, 1848. At the annual meeting on October 11, 1848, Thomas Swann was unanimously elected president of the Baltimore and Ohio.

Chapter V

. . . .

On to the Ohio River

BY THE LATE SUMMER OF 1848, THERE HAD SEEMED TO BE A widespread feeling of discouragement concerning the railroad's efforts to reach the Ohio River. The stock of the B&O, which had sold for $48–$49 in the mid-1840s, had declined to $28, against a par value of $100. In the fall of 1848, the election of Thomas Swann to succeed Louis McLane gave new life and vigor to the Baltimore and Ohio. President Swann, some twenty years younger than McLane, had studied law with his father in Washington, D.C., and had served as a secretary to a diplomatic commission during the Andrew Jackson years before becoming a Baltimore businessman.

Where Louis McLane was often abrupt and abrasive, Thomas Swann was generally suave and diplomatic. He was a well-rounded politician and found it easy to influence and work with people. When Swann joined the board of directors, he was a friend of McLane and supported the president loyally up to McLane's resignation. Swann served McLane in lobbying efforts with the Virginia legislators at Richmond and chaired a committee appointed in January 1848, which was charged with actively pushing the extension of the Main Stem to the Ohio. During the year 1848, a series of letters favoring the extension had appeared in the *Baltimore Patriot*. Signed by "A Large Stockholder," the letters were generally believed to have been written by Thomas Swann. When Swann became president of the Baltimore and Ohio in October 1848, he had the full support and goodwill of his board of directors, the city of Baltimore, and the state of Maryland.

Thomas Swann, president, 1848–53.
(Courtesy, Baltimore and Ohio Railroad)

Even before Mc-Lane left the Baltimore and Ohio presidency, the legal problems concerning the extension to the Ohio had been worked out with Virginia and Pennsylvania. Virginia had been slow in cooperating with the Baltimore and Ohio and its desire to push its line west of Cumberland. Several times in the mid-1840s, a Baltimore and Ohio bill was passed by the Virginia legislature, but each time the bill included difficult restrictions and qualifications. It almost seemed that the Virginia lawmakers still resented the fact that the B&O served Baltimore and the upper Potomac, rather than the Virginia capital of Richmond and the valley of the James River. In the spring of 1845, the *American Railroad Journal* summarized the problem when it noted: "The chief obstacle which prevents the extension of the road, is the unwillingness of Virginia to grant the right of way through her territory upon terms at all practicable without great sacrifice."[1]

By the mid-1840s, the surveying teams of Benjamin Latrobe had decided upon three possible routes from Cumberland to three different points on the Ohio: (1) northwestward through Pennsylvania to Pittsburgh; (2) westward up the Potomac into Virginia, and then northwest to Wheeling; and (3) westward up the Potomac and continuing westward to Parkersburg, a small settlement on the Ohio well downstream from Wheeling. The route to Pittsburgh was the shortest, the easiest to build, and would end at the most important city of the three. Wheeling was much smaller than Pittsburgh, but it was the junction of the Ohio and the National Road from the west. While Parkersburg was a town of little importance, it was located on the most direct route from Baltimore to the growing and important cities of Cincinnati and St. Louis. At

the outset, McLane, Latrobe, and other B&O officials had no preference among the three routes, but none could be built without
the approval of Virginia or Pennsylvania.

In the late winter of 1846–47, the Virginia legislature passed
a Baltimore and Ohio bill which was acceptable to the railroad. The
act, finally passed on March 6, 1847, contained terms acceptable to
the directors and officials of the B&O largely because of the persua-
siveness and persistence of the affable Thomas Swann, the lobbyist
earlier sent to Richmond by Louis McLane. In 1846–47 Swann did
not yet have a seat on the B&O board, but he was already a firm
supporter of the railroad. In the 1847 act, Virginia gave the B&O
twelve more years, or until March 6, 1859, to complete its route
across Virginia to the Ohio. The act designated Wheeling as the
terminal on the Ohio and insisted that the railroad should reach the
Ohio no further south than the mouth of Fish Creek, a few miles
downstream from Wheeling. Virginia insisted upon Wheeling as
the terminal, not only because of the large political influence that
western city had in Richmond, but also because such a terminal
would keep the B&O line well north of any possible Norfolk and
Richmond rail route later built to the west. The earlier pledge of
Virginia to subscribe to one million dollars of B&O stock, as contained in the law of 1838, was annulled, but Wheeling was authorized to subscribe a similar amount in B&O stock. Virginia reserved
the right to tax the railroad, and other later railroad lines were
given the right to cross or connect with the B&O line. By the time
the law was passed, the B&O officials had decided that Parkersburg was really their choice for a terminal on the Ohio River, but
they reluctantly approved the Virginia act since a line to Wheeling
was preferable to retaining Cumberland as their western railhead.

For a short time in 1846, it also seemed possible that the
Baltimore and Ohio might be extended to Pittsburgh. When Pennsylvania affirmed the original B&O charter in 1828, it had allowed
the company fifteen years to extend its line across a portion of the
state to the Ohio River. Since this right had expired in 1843, new
legislation would be necessary if the B&O were to reach Pittsburgh. Certainly, the business interests in Pittsburgh were anxious
to have a rail connection with Baltimore since they were thoroughly dissatisfied with the inadequacies of the state's Main Line of
canals and inclined planes. In 1845 and 1846, Pittsburgh renewed
its interest in the Pittsburgh and Connellsville, a road projected
towards Cumberland and originally chartered in 1837. Many businessmen in Baltimore, including the wholesale grocery firm of
Robert Garrett and Sons, were anxious to see the Pittsburgh and
Connellsville project succeed.

In the spring of 1846, two railroad bills were passed by the seventieth session of the Pennsylvania legislature meeting in Harrisburg. A number of influential business interests from Philadelphia supported an act signed by Gov. Francis R. Shunk on April 13, 1846, which granted a charter to the Pennsylvania Railroad. This newly chartered line could use the state rail system east of Harrisburg and also build a new road west to Pittsburgh. The Pittsburgh interests and Louis McLane's lobbyists in Harrisburg were equally happy a week later when Governor Shunk, on April 21, 1846, signed a bill giving the Baltimore and Ohio the right to build a line from Cumberland to Pittsburgh. For a while it seemed that Pittsburgh might soon have two rail routes to the East. However, some conditions and amendments added to the B&O act were going to cause trouble. The B&O act was not to be effective until July 30, 1847. Also, if within those fifteen months, should the Pennsylvania Railroad obtain $3 million in stock subscriptions, with $1 million paid in to the company treasury and have fifteen miles of road at the Pittsburgh end of the line under contract, then the entire B&O act would be null and void. Helped by a house-to-house stock subscription campaign in Philadelphia, the Pennsylvania Railroad met all the above conditions, and on August 2, 1847, Governor Shunk issued a proclamation ending the rights of the B&O to build to Pittsburgh. Thus, twenty years after Baltimore had chosen to build a railroad, the Quaker city of Philadelphia followed suit.

Even though McLane was president of the Baltimore and Ohio more than a year after the passage of the Virginia B&O legislation in the spring of 1847, he did not vigorously push the construction toward Wheeling. However, in the spring of 1848, President McLane did add a second daily passenger train (both ways between Baltimore and Cumberland) to connect with the twice daily coach service over the National Road between Cumberland and Wheeling. But it remained for the younger and more aggressive Thomas Swann to get the construction project to Wheeling underway. When Swann became president in the fall of 1848, his views favoring the speedy construction of the railroad to Wheeling were well known. In 1849 Swann estimated the total cost of the 200-mile extension to the Ohio to be about $6 million, which was very close to the actual cost upon completion late in 1852. Early in 1849, he addressed the board of directors concerning the importance of the westward extension and stressed that the B&O should start at once to build the *whole* extension instead of a *part* of the route which had originally been proposed. Upon the conclusion of his stirring address, George Brown, one of the founders of

the road and a state director since 1841, moved the following resolution: "Resolved, That the Chief Engineer be directed to proceed
to arrange to put the whole line to the Ohio River under contract as
speedily as practicable."[2] The resolution was at once unanimously
adopted.

One of the first things facing Swann was the problem of the
Chesapeake and Ohio Canal. The waterway was hopelessly in debt
and would not be completed to Cumberland until 1850, but it still
had some vague rights to the north bank of the north branch of the
Potomac upstream from Cumberland. In the early months of 1849,
President Swann worked out a compromise with the C&O which
he summarized in the railroad's 1849 *Annual Report*: "With the
same spirit of accommodation, the Chesapeake and Ohio Canal
Company, in response to an application from the President of this
Company directed . . . a permanent location of their work, under
their claim of priority, thus removing all ground for future misun-
derstanding between the two Companies."[3] One of Swann's advantages over his predecessor was his complete dedication to the
B&O, as illustrated by the long hours of labor he spent on behalf of
the railroad. During the day he worked in his office or in the offices
of officials or directors of the line—at night he found time to use his
powers of persuasion to convince the general public and the patrons of the B&O that the railroad would soon be constructed to
Wheeling and the Ohio River.

Very early in his presidency, Thomas Swann faced the problem of financing the 200 miles of difficult construction between
Cumberland and Wheeling. Shortly after taking office, Thomas
Swann began to correspond with George Peabody, a London
banker who had been in the wholesale dry goods business in Baltimore between 1814 and 1837. After a lengthy correspondence,
George Peabody helped arrange to have the Baring Brothers of
London buy £200,000 of the 5 percent sterling bonds earlier issued
by the state of Maryland. Some of the proceeds of this sale had
already been expended by the late summer of 1850 when President
Swann prepared the *Annual Report* for 1850. As of September 30,
1850, the president reported that something over five million dollars had been expended or was available for the western extension.

To meet the difference of about $1,125,000 between the
total and the estimated total cost of $6,278,000, Swann proposed
that the Baltimore and Ohio issue a series of coupon bonds.

During the fiscal year 1849, Swann and Benjamin Latrobe
had let out contracts for 103 miles of road between Cumberland
and the Ohio River. Latrobe had earlier decided that the maximum
grade for the 200-mile route through Maryland and Virginia should

TABLE 5. Western Extension Finances

Money expended to date, exclusive of bonds given for iron rails	$ 934,713.56
Balance of cash on hand from sale of £200,000 5 percent bonds	476,650.00
Value of 5 percent Sterling bonds unsold, £507,500, estimated at market value	2,172,908.06
Bonds issued for iron rails purchased by Baring Brothers	566,666.67
Revenue from B&O during the progress of the construction	500,000.00
Subscription of the city of Wheeling, guaranteed by the state of Virginia	500,000.00
Total expended and available	$5,150,938.29

be 116 feet, or 2.2 percent per mile. Included in the mileage were eleven tunnels with a total length of 11,156 feet, the three longest being 4,100 feet, 2,350 feet, and 1,250 feet respectively.

It took more than two years to complete the 4,100-foot Kingwood Tunnel, located 261 miles west of Baltimore at an elevation of about 1,800 feet. Late in 1850, some three hundred workers were using hand drills, black powder, and horse-drawn carts at five different locations to blast the tunnel through the mountain. Most of the workers lived at a new town of Greigville, which soon boasted eighty houses, two churches, two schools, seven stores, and a police force of a dozen men. While the tedious digging was taking place, Latrobe had a temporary track laid over the mountaintop, using "Y" switches and steep tangents with a grade of 500 feet per mile, or nearly 10 percent. Powerful Camel locomotives could push one or two cars at a time up the steep grades. Between Cumberland and Wheeling, 113 bridges were built with a total length of 7,003 feet with spans ranging from 12 to 215 feet. Most were built of wood but a few were of iron. Stone or masonry bridges were both too expensive and too slow to build. One of the longest bridges was the three-span iron bridge over the Monongahela River.

By the late summer of 1850, some 3,500 men and 700 horses were working up and down 167 miles of western extension. Rail was laid on the eastern portion of the new route in the spring of 1851, and by early July 1851, the road was opened to the Piedmont Station, twenty-eight miles southwest of Cumberland. At Piedmont, the surveyed route left the valley of the North Potomac and headed west up a long seventeen-mile steady ascent—much of it at the maximum grade—to the 2,626-foot summit near Altamont. This high ridge divided the watershed of the Potomac from that of the Ohio. At Piedmont they soon built a sixteen-stall engine-house for the locomotives that would pull B&O trains up the long grade. President Swann wrote in this *Twenty-fifth Annual Report* (1851): "It is gratifying to the Board to be able to announce, that the maximum grade of 116 feet, is now being worked daily, with heavy trains, at rates varying from twelve to twenty miles an hour—both ascending and descending, with the utmost ease and regularity."[4]

Once over the ridge at Altamont, the route continued through western Maryland until it entered Virginia at Corinth. The winding route to the west crossed successive ridges and streams, all tributary to the upper Ohio. At Grafton, 101 miles west of Cumberland, the route turned to the northwest, crossed the Monongahela at Fairmont, skirted the southwestern corner of Pennsylvania, and descended into the valley of Grave Creek to Moundsville on the Ohio, eleven miles downstream from Wheeling. In the spring of 1850, President Swann and the stockholders of the B&O had acquiesced when the citizens of Wheeling urged that Grave Creek, a few miles north of Fish Creek, be the route used to enter the valley of the Ohio.

By the fall of 1851, up to 5,000 men and 1,250 horses were employed to push the construction toward completion. Monthly construction payrolls often reached $200,000. Generally the workers were paid promptly, but sometimes they were not. Benjamin Latrobe worked out in the field to keep up both the work schedule and the morale of the track crews. In Baltimore President Swann maintained the enthusiasm of the owners at the same time that he was arranging fresh 6 percent loans, often sold at a discount. As the grading of the roadbed was completed, the pace of track laying increased. The 200 miles of new line west of Cumberland, plus the necessary sidings and yards required 22,000 tons of iron rail, nearly all of it imported from England at $40 per ton.

The line was completed to Fairmont, on the Monongahela River, 124 miles west of Cumberland, and 77 miles from Wheeling, on June 22, 1852. The regular operation of trains to Cumberland and Baltimore was started at once. President Swann had promised the people of Wheeling that the road would be finished by New Year's Day, 1853. The last rails were laid and the last spike driven on Christmas Eve, 1852, at Roseby's Rock in a narrow valley eighteen miles southeast of Wheeling. Near the track closing was a huge glacial rock, named for Roseby Carr, the superintendent for laying rails for that portion of the line.

Even before the line was finished, the B&O was using the partially completed road to vie for the traffic to the Ohio and beyond. At Grafton, 279 miles west of Baltimore and where the route turned northward toward Wheeling, connecting stage lines ran west to Parkersburg. In the summer of 1852, B&O officials were offering a sixteen dollar through ticket to Cincinnati, by rail to Grafton, stage to the Ohio River, and steamboat on to Cincinnati. That same summer, plans were being made in Wheeling for the Union Line of steamboats to run from Wheeling to Louisville with service to start once the railroad reached Wheeling. Back in the company shops in Baltimore, many workers in the fall of 1852, were busy building iron bridges to be placed over streams between Fairmont and Wheeling, while others were completing new locomotives and cars for the expected growth in traffic.

The celebration in Wheeling was delayed until early January 1853, in order to allow the burghers of Wheeling to prepare a proper celebration. Some 500 citizens of Baltimore journeyed west to Wheeling making the 379-mile trip in eighteen hours. Speeches by President Swann, both of the Latrobe brothers, the venerable George Brown, and the governors of Maryland and Virginia were followed by major banquets in the two dining rooms of the McLure House. It was high time to celebrate since nearly twenty-six years had passed since two dozen of the leading men in Baltimore, meeting in the residence of George Brown, had planned the building of a railroad to the Ohio.

As Latrobe was pushing his construction crews to complete the tunnels and iron tracks through and over the green ridges of Western Virginia, the iron roads connecting New York and Phila-

The levee at Wheeling, Virginia, in the mid 1850s.
(Courtesy, Baltimore and Ohio Railroad)

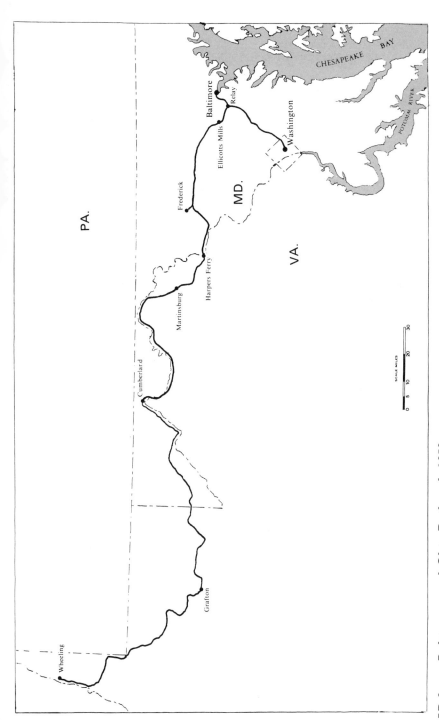

MAP 3.   Baltimore and Ohio Railroad, 1853.

Service west of Cumberland to Grafton, Virginia, was started   Baltimore to Wheeling was officially opened in January 1853.
in the summer of 1852, and the entire 379-mile route from

delphia with the Great Lakes and the Ohio River were also being completed. This competition among the rival seaport cities was noted in the spring of 1850 when the *Baltimore American* was quoted in the pages of the *American Railroad Journal*: "We see Philadelphia hurrying forward to reach Pittsburgh, and New York to reach Dunkirk, if they can, before we reach Wheeling; and we see Ohio and the states north and west of her, and indeed the whole Mississippi valley, stimulated to the highest enthusiasm in the railway race by that which is now running between the Atlantic Cities."[5]

Rail service between the Hudson River and Lake Erie had been available since the early 1840s. Ten little roads connecting Albany and Buffalo and strung for 290 miles along the Mohawk Valley and Erie Canal were known as the "Central Line" long before they were merged into the New York Central in 1853. Erastus Corning, the crippled iron merchant and long-time president of the seventy-eight-mile Utica and Schenectady, was the first president of the New York Central. Even before the 1853 creation of the New York Central, the connecting lines were giving economical rail service along the "water level" route from Buffalo to Albany and New York City.

A second rail route across New York state was available by May 1851, when the broad six-foot gauge Erie Railroad was completed from Piermont-on-Hudson to Dunkirk on Lake Erie, a few miles west of Buffalo. New York City saluted the 460-mile Erie as "the Work of the Age" and was happy when President Benjamin Loder, a wealthy New York dry goods merchant, insisted on a special celebration to mark his line's completion. Two special excursion trains took two days to make the run to Dunkirk carrying 300 guests, including top railroad brass, President Millard Fillmore, several members of his cabinet, and such presidential hopefuls as Sen. Stephen A. Douglas, former Gov. William H. Seward, and Secretary of State Daniel Webster. The aging Webster insisted on seeing all the scenery and found himself placed in a rocking chair firmly fastened on a flatcar at the end of the second train. Covered with a warm steamer rug, Webster had a jug of high quality Medford rum for company between stops for making speeches. In spite of the resplendent celebration in May 1851, Benjamin Loder's Erie Railroad would be a much less serious competitor for the western trade than Corning's, and later Vanderbilt's, New York Central.

Closer home, the Baltimore and Ohio even lost to the Pennsylvania Railroad in their race to be first to reach the Ohio River. The business interests of Philadelphia had been slow in accepting iron rails as a way to capture the western trade, but once aroused they were quick to build their railroad. Incorporated in April 1846, the Pennsylvania Railroad by the spring of 1847 had elected Samuel V. Merrick, a Yankee from Maine and a manufacturer of fire engines, as their first president. Merrick selected J. Edgar Thomson, who had had extensive railroad experience in New Jersey and Georgia, as chief engineer to plan and supervise the construction of the 248-mile road from Harrisburg to Pittsburgh. By early December 1852, Thomson, now the president of the line, had completed the Pennsylvania Railroad to Pittsburgh, but was still using the inclined planes of the Portage Railroad to cross the highest mountain ridges between Hollidaysburg and Johnstown. Two years later, the inclined planes were retired, and the entire 355-mile trip from Philadelphia to Pittsburgh was being made by locomotive drawn trains.

The Baltimore and Ohio may have been edged out in the race to the Ohio River, but the completion of the western extension was good for the railroad. Traffic on the railroad increased substantially during the short five-year (October 1848 to April 1853) presidency of Thomas Swann, the years in which the 200-mile extension to Wheeling was built. The Main Stem revenue of $1,213,000 in 1848 climbed to $2,033,000 in 1853, and to $2,645,000 in fiscal 1854, the first full year in which the 379-mile line was in operation. Passenger traffic during the five years increased from 12 million passenger-miles in 1848 to 19 million passenger-miles in 1854. Freight traffic expanded even more rapidly, growing from 30 million ton-miles to 82 million ton-miles in the same five year period. Stockholders and financial circles appreciated these increases, shown in the growing market value of B&O capital stock. Shares which had sold for no more than $28 when Swann was elected president, had climbed to $40 by the early summer of 1849, and two years later, in July 1851, were up to $75. In June 1852, shares were bringing $83, and by November of that year, as the road was nearing Wheeling, some were selling as high as $99.

The reality of the completed road to the Ohio in 1852 and the dream held by two dozen men in George Brown's residence a quarter of a century earlier were not identical. The Browns and the two Thomas brothers, along with their friends, had estimated the distance to the Ohio at 290 miles; the completed road was 379 miles in length. The 1827 estimate of cost had been $5 million; the actual cost of the original construction, not counting necessary reconstruction, was nearly $15 million. The early planners of the B&O had hoped the completed road would yield $750,000 in annual revenue. The actual revenue for the year 1853 (October 1, 1852 to October 1, 1853) was just over $2·million.

During the five-year tenure of Thomas Swann, the railroad also spent considerable money for the repairing and upgrading of the line from Cumberland east to Baltimore. This was especially necessary because of the increasingly heavy traffic from the coal mines in the Cumberland area. Between 1847 and 1849, more than $600,000 was spent on roadbed improvement, the reduction of sharp curves, and the laying of heavier rail. The *Annual Report* for 1849 claimed that, except for three points along the line, no curves of less than 600 feet in radius were in use. President Swann in the same report wrote: "Before the winter sets in, the Company will have a continuous track of heavy rail in complete order from Baltimore to Cumberland."[6] Some of the new "heavy" fifty-one-pound rail, which replaced the fifteen-pound strap rail, was of domestic manufacture, being produced either at Mount Savage near Cumberland or in the Baltimore area.

Two major improvements in the Baltimore area were also completed, or at least started, during the Swann years. The increasing coal traffic required a water terminal better than that available in the relatively shallow inner harbor of downtown Baltimore. Late in the McLane presidency, the board of directors selected Locust Point as the spot for the new deep-water terminal. This was a flat area located on the north side of the peninsula upon which Fort McHenry was situated. To reach the new terminal, a branch had to be built leaving the original line near Gwynns Run, a short distance southwest of Mount Clare Station. The new branch skirted the north end of the middle branch and crossed some marshy land south of the city to a loop of new track serving the piers to be built at Locust Point. The *American Railroad Journal* late in July 1849, reported that the completed Locust Point harbor facility had 2,600 feet of waterfront with a water depth of twenty-two feet and was currently serving several ships of 750-ton capacity. As of October 1849, the railroad had spent $176,000 on the project, three-fifths of which had been paid for with bonds. Later Locust Point would serve as a major grain and merchandise terminal in addition to its traffic in coal.

With the near completion of the line to Wheeling, Swann and his directors realized the B&O would soon need passenger station facilities better than the nearly obsolete station on Pratt Street. In June 1852, the B&O purchased a four-block area southwest of the center of the city south of Camden Street and east of Howard Street. Since the site was just seven blocks north of the branch line to Locust Point, it could easily be reached by a spur from the Locust Point line. A temporary passenger facility was constructed, but in 1856 work was started on the permanent Camden Station, a large three-story brick structure made distinctive by its three tall towers. These new passenger and freight terminals would reduce, but not end, the horse-drawn rail traffic along Pratt Street.

By midcentury it was also time to build a new station in Washington. When the Washington branch was opened in 1835, the B&O was both short of money and irritated that the United States Congress had given no financial assistance in the construction of the new railroad. As a makeshift solution to the problem, Philip Thomas and his fellow officials had purchased a narrow three-story brick boarding house located at Pennsylvania Avenue and Second Street Northwest. By 1850 this facility had clearly been outgrown by the expanding passenger traffic. Also a major change was required since the grade of all streets in that area was about to be raised. After some delay, the B&O purchased a new location to the northwest, at New Jersey Avenue and C Street. Between 1850 and 1852, a new station was built, 106 feet by 68 feet in size, with a front built of "Connecticut brown stone," a 100-foot clock tower, and an ample two-track "car house" or train shed.

The Baltimore and Ohio ordered much new motive power and rolling stock between 1850 and 1852 in order to meet the new traffic that would appear once their road reached the Ohio. The *Annual Report* for 1852 listed seventy-six new locomotives, most built by Ross Winans, at an average cost of $9,700 per locomotive. Samuel J. Hayes, long time employee and master of machinery since early 1851, estimated that of the roster of 140 locomotives, old and new, about 65 percent would be used on the line west of Cumberland. The locomotive roster of 1852 was more than twice the roster of fifty-seven engines available in 1848. Between 1848 and 1852, the number of freight cars had grown from 1,201 to 2,290. The average cost of the 1,348 cars acquired since 1850 was about $475 per car. The passenger car equipment in 1852 numbered well over one hundred cars, with the thirty-nine cars added since 1850 costing an average of $1,650 a car.

Naturally the capital structure of the railroad had also increased greatly during the years of Swann's leadership. Joshua I. Atkinson, secretary and treasurer of the B&O from 1847 until his death in 1869, reported the total investment in the road to be $13,136,940.85 as of October 1, 1848. Four years later, on October 1, 1852, this figure had grown to $18,074,909.37. The major items included in this amount were: (1) capital stock and scrip— $9,200,000; (2) state of Maryland 5 percent sterling bonds—

William G. Harrison, president, 1853–55.
(Courtesy, Baltimore and Ohio Railroad)

$3,200,000; and (3) five separate 6 percent loans—just over $4,000,000. Since not all of the costs of the Wheeling extension had yet been paid in the fall of 1852, the total investment in the road would climb to more than $22 million by the fall of 1853. The practice of issuing stock dividends, started with a 3.5 percent dividend in 1848, was continued during the Swann years. A stock dividend of 5 percent was paid in 1849 and was increased to 7 percent in each of the three years, 1850, 1851, and 1852.

With the road completed to Wheeling, Thomas Swann decided he deserved a rest from the strenuous life of a railroad president. At the April 1953 meeting of the board of directors, he resigned the presidency and was succeeded by William G. Harrison, a Baltimore merchant and a board member for only a year. Shortly after resigning, Swann went abroad for a tour of Europe. Upon his return, he became president of the Northwestern Virginia Railroad for three years before going into politics. In turn Swann was mayor of Baltimore (1856–60), governor of Maryland (1866–69), and a member of Congress (1869–77). Swann was an important political servant of his city and state, but no doubt his greatest contribution was the completion of the Baltimore and Ohio to the Ohio River. Swann was thinking of Baltimore's long delayed dream as he concluded the *Twenty-sixth Annual Report* in the fall of 1852: "The rich prize is within her grasp. The Union of the Ohio and the Chesapeake, by the favorite highway which nature has indicated, is no longer among the probabilities of the future; and the City of Baltimore, so long retarded in her progress . . . will look with renewed pride upon the enterprise and public spirit of a people whose indomitable courage has achieved the lasting glory of binding together these remote extremes of our Union."[7]

Chapter VI

• • • • • • • • • • • • • •

Railroad Operations in the Fifties

DURING THE 1850S, FOUR DIFFERENT PRESIDENTS DIRECTED the destiny of the Baltimore and Ohio: Thomas Swann, who resigned in April 1853; William G. Harrison, president from April 13, 1853, to November 14, 1855; Chauncy Brooks, in office from November 14, 1855, to November 17, 1858; and John W. Garrett, elected on November 17, 1858, and in office until his death in 1884. While the length of time in office for the four men split the decade into rather equal parts, the contributions of the four were quite unequal. Thomas Swann left office in a blaze of glory, having finally completed the road to the Ohio. In contrast, neither Harrison nor Brooks made major contributions to their railroad during their short tenures. Neither was a serious railroader, and neither man fully solved the several problems facing the B&O. The last of the four, John W. Garrett, had some weaknesses, but he was a very dedicated railroad executive and remained in office more than 25 years, a record surpassed only by Daniel Willard in the first half of the twentieth century.

Probably the two most important leaders of the Baltimore and Ohio during the late fifties and the decade of the sixties were John W. Garrett and Johns Hopkins. Both Garrett and Hopkins were important businessmen in Baltimore. John Work Garrett was the second son of Robert Garrett, a Scotch-Irish farmboy who had moved from Pennsylvania to Baltimore where he soon had a prosperous produce and commission house. Born in 1820, the younger

Chauncy Brooks, president, 1855-58.
(Courtesy, Baltimore and Ohio Railroad)

Garrett soon joined his father and brother in disposing of western farm produce, selling butter in the West Indies and flour in Boston, while importing fish from New England and coffee from Haiti. As the company prospered, the Garretts moved into banking and finance and by midcentury held a number of B&O shares. John's brother, Henry, was a director in 1852–53, and John became a board member in 1855, helping elect his friend Chauncy Brooks to the presidency a few weeks later.

Johns Hopkins, twenty-five years older than John W. Garrett, was born on a tobacco plantation in Anne Arundel County, just south of Baltimore. At the age of twelve, he left school to work on the plantation when his devout Quaker parents freed their slaves. When he was seventeen, Johns Hopkins moved to Baltimore to live with an uncle, a wholesale grocer and commission merchant. The young Hopkins proved adept at the trade but quarreled with his uncle when the nephew wished to accommodate country customers who desired to pay for their goods with whiskey. The uncle refused "to sell souls into perdition."[1] Johns Hopkins set up his own commission business and resold the whiskey as "Hopkins Best," even though he was, for a time, "turned out of meeting" by the Society of Friends. His company prospered, and he later expanded his business interests to include banking and finance. By the 1840s he was a major stockholder in the Baltimore and Ohio and became a director in 1847, a position he held until his death in 1873. In 1855 he became the chairman of the finance committee. He helped the railroad weather the financial difficulties during the panics of 1857 and 1873. Hopkins was generally considered the largest holder of B&O stock after the state of Maryland and the city of Baltimore and at his death owned 15,000 shares.

The major new B&O construction project completed in the decade came during the years of Presidents Swann, Harrison, and Brooks. Even as the road to Wheeling was nearing completion, the board of directors was not fully convinced that that city was the proper or best Ohio River terminal. Many of the directors, both in public and private, were asking, Why Wheeling? It was true that Wheeling, being on the National Road, provided the B&O with a fair amount of wagon traffic. But as an Ohio River port, it left much to be desired. The upper Ohio in the midnineteenth century, long before the appearance of the improved navigation that came with dams and locks, was often a temperamental waterway. Frequently, for weeks and even months, the water level at Wheeling would be too low for river craft of any major size to reach the city. Also, the B&O officials had been looking further westward to the trade and commerce of Cincinnati and St. Louis. Many of the railroad officials had long viewed Parkersburg, more than ninety miles downstream from Wheeling, as a preferable Ohio River terminal for the B&O. When the Ohio River was not navigable at Wheeling, it often was at Parkersburg, and Parkersburg was also on a nearly direct line westward to Cincinnati and St. Louis.

During the winter of 1850–51, President Swann managed to convince the Virginia general assembly to charter a second rail branch from the B&O to the Ohio River. On February 14, 1851, the Northwestern Virginia Railroad was chartered as an independent company to build a line from the Baltimore and Ohio, at or near the mouth of Three Forks Creek in Taylor County, westward to Parkersburg. To protect their earlier commitment to Wheeling, the Virginia lawmakers included in the charter a provision that "the North-Western Road shall not be opened for trade or travel, until twelve months after the completion of the road to the City of Wheeling."[2]

Even though the projected line was an "independent" line, the basic financing of the road was largely by B&O interests. In his annual report for 1852, President Swann reported that his road would "contribute, not less than $1,000,000."[3] In addition, the city of Baltimore subscribed $1,500,000 towards the stock, with another $500,000 provided by individual stock subscribers. Virginia gentlemen from the Parkersburg area dominated the first board of directors of the Northwestern Virginia, but quite soon Baltimore and Ohio men were in control. Benjamin Latrobe became the chief engineer and had completed his basic survey of the route to the Ohio by 1852. From 1853 to 1856, Thomas Swann, now returned from his European tour, served as president of the new road.

Even though the first construction was started late in 1852, the building and completion of the Northwestern Virginia was far from rapid. The terrain of the new line was much less difficult than that east of the junction point toward Cumberland. The newly created town of Grafton, at the junction point, had an elevation of one thousand feet, hundreds of feet lower than the hills and mountains which the line had crossed on its way west from Cumberland. Even though the route to Parkersburg (elevation of 641 feet) was generally downhill, several ridges still had to be crossed. The 104-mile route included numerous trestles and bridges and more than twenty tunnels, most of them quite short. The maximum grade on the new road was 1 percent, and the curves were generally more moderate than those between Grafton and Wheeling. Most of the track was laid during 1856, and the road was finally opened on May 1, 1857. Monthly payrolls had exceeded $100,000 in some of the final months, and the total cost of the more than four years of construction came to $5.4 million, well above the earlier estimates. In December 1856, the Baltimore and Ohio leased the Northwestern Virginia Railroad for a period of five years. As Chauncy Brooks and his fellow officials took possession of the new line to Parkersburg they found "the road . . . much more unfinished than statements presented to this Company had indicated."[4]

Both the Wheeling and the Parkersburg terminals on the Ohio had connections across the river with new railroads in Ohio. At Wheeling the connection was with the Central Ohio Railroad, and at Parkersburg service westward was over the Marietta and Cincinnati. During the 1850s, the five states of the Old Northwest built thousands of miles of new railroad. Ohio, in 1850, claimed 575 miles of railroad and ranked fifth among the states of the nation. During the fifties, the Buckeye State laid down 2,371 miles of new iron, and her 1860 total of 2,946 miles placed her first in mileage in the country. Most of the Ohio mileage was built in the "Ohio gauge" of 4 feet 10 inches rather than the standard gauge of 4 feet 8-1/2 inches. This odd gauge had been adopted when the first locomotive in the state, the *Sandusky*, happened to be built in that gauge. In the 1850s, the Central Ohio was in the "Ohio gauge," while the Marietta and Cincinnati was built in standard gauge, the same as that of the B&O. It was possible for "compromise cars," with extra wide, 5-inch wheel treads, to run over tracks both of standard and "Ohio gauge."

The Central Ohio received a charter from the state in February 1847, some five years before the B&O would complete its first terminal on the Ohio. The road was projected from Columbus to Bellaire on the Ohio, a few miles downstream from Wheeling.

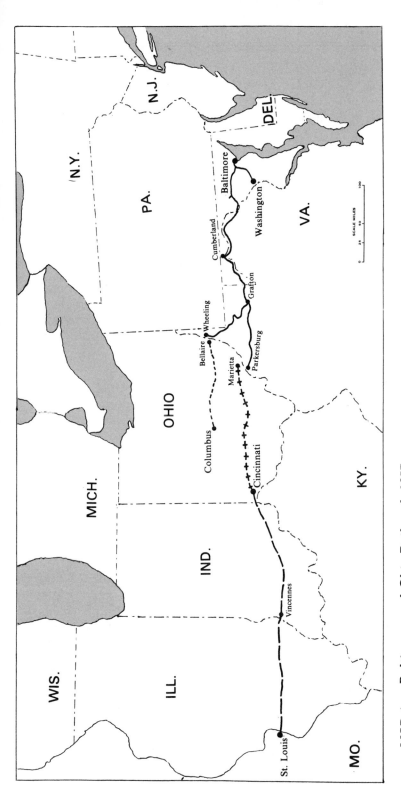

MAP 4. Baltimore and Ohio Railroad, 1857.

By 1857 the B&O had completed (and leased) the 104-mile Northwestern Virginia from Grafton to Parkersburg. Service west of Parkersburg was over the Marietta and Cincinnati (+ + + +) and the Ohio and Mississippi (———) on to St. Louis. West of Wheeling, the Central Ohio (–––––) gave service to Columbus.

In 1852 construction started in the center of the line, and by the end of 1853, track was laid from Columbus to Zanesville, a distance of fifty-nine miles. During 1854 the road was built seventy-eight miles on to Bellaire. There a 1000-ton train ferry, large enough to carry a passenger train or half a freight train, gave service across the Ohio to Benwood, on the B&O line, and four miles downstream from Wheeling. In March of 1854, J. H. Sullivan, the Central Ohio president, wrote that the ferry service "almost entirely obviates all the anxiety which has heretofore been felt for a Railroad bridge."[5] Certainly in the midfifties, most railroad officials shied away from any thought of a railroad bridge at Wheeling. They all remembered the 1,000-foot suspension bridge built by Charles Ellet to carry the National Road over the Ohio at Wheeling. Ellet's bridge had collapsed in a heavy windstorm in mid-May 1854. In the 1850s, the Central Ohio was never sufficiently prosperous to pay any dividends. The Panic of 1857 brought receivership to the road in 1859. Several years later, the reorganized road was leased to the Baltimore and Ohio which later took over full control.

The Marietta and Cincinnati, which connected at Parkersburg with the Northwestern Virginia, was the second east-west line across Ohio which would eventually come under the control of the B&O. The Marietta and Cincinnati was an 1851 consolidation of two earlier projected roads, the Belpre and Cincinnati (chartered in 1847) and the Franklin and Ohio. The merged road was to run eastward from Cincinnati to the Ohio River. A Marietta landowner, politician, and future Republican congressman, William Parker Cutler was the president of the Marietta and Cincinnati during the 1850s. Cutler, by 1854, had managed to secure stock subscriptions from individuals, towns, and counties in southern Ohio totalling nearly $3 million. Hoping that the line might be extended northward to Wheeling, the Pennsylvania Railroad was also thinking about a major stock subscription. President Cutler found that building a railway through the hills of southern Ohio was not easy, especially since his surveying engineer kept insisting upon a maximum grade of no more than fifty-two feet to the mile. During 1855, a line of 100 miles was constructed from Loveland, twenty-three miles east of Cincinnati, to Byers. Service from Loveland into Cincinnati was over the tracks of the connecting Little Miami. During 1856 and the first months of 1857, the line was pushed seventy-three miles further eastward from Byers through Athens to Marietta, where a nine-mile ferriage connected with the Parkersburg branch across the Ohio River. In October 1857, Chauncy Brooks, president of the B&O, was able to write: "The interchange of business with the Marietta and Cincinnati road, has commenced during the past three months, and a large increase may be anticipated during the coming year."6

West of Cincinnati, the longer Ohio and Mississippi Railroad was projected to give rail service to East St. Louis. The 340-mile broad-gauge Ohio and Mississippi was chartered at midcentury in three states: in Indiana on February 14, 1848; in Ohio on March 15, 1849; and in Illinois on February 12, 1851. Included among the early sponsors of the road were Alphonso Taft, Cincinnati lawyer and father of a later American president; Judge Abner T. Ellis of Vincennes, an early advocate of river traffic; and John O'Fallon, soldier-merchant of St. Louis and nephew of George Rogers Clark. Cincinnati, with a population of 115,000 and the largest city in Ohio, was quite eager to build a rail line westward to the Mississippi and St. Louis. In 1849 the citizens of the city voted to have Cincinnati subscribe to $1 million of stock in the O&M, and later individual sponsors of the road subscribed in a single hour to $80,000 of stock. The organization of the Ohio and Indiana portions of the road was completed in 1850 with Judge Ellis of Vincennes as the first president. By 1851, $2 million of capital stock was subscribed and the first construction contracts were let.

Ormsby M. Mitchel, West Point graduate and classmate of Robert E. Lee and later a professor of mathematics and astronomy at the academy, was the chief engineer for the Ohio and Mississippi from 1848 to 1853. His survey indicated that the entire line could be built for just over $5 million with grades of no more than 40 feet to the mile. After completing his surveys, Mitchel went to London, where he sold several million dollars of O&M securities, most of them to the American banker George Peabody. Even with this new financial backing, construction was slow. The first segments of the road were completed in 1854, twenty-seven miles west of Cincinnati plus a sixty-one-mile segment in southwestern Illinois. The first shipments of rail, costing eight pounds, five shillings per ton and weighing sixty pounds per yard, were imported from Cardiff, Wales, and arrived via the St. Lawrence, the Great Lakes, and canal or railroad through Ohio. During 1855 an even 100 miles of line were built in Indiana and another eighty-seven miles completed in Illinois. Early in 1857 the final sixty-five-mile segment in Indiana was built, from Mitchell west to Vincennes, and the entire road to the Mississippi was finished.

The 340-rail mileage from Cincinnati west to East St. Louis was about one half the river-steamer distance via the Ohio and Mississippi. The completed road had cost over $17 million, more than triple the original estimates made by Mitchel. The financial problems of the road had become so onerous by the midfifties that the O&M was divided into two parts, the eastern division (Ohio and Indiana) and the Illinois division. In the summer of 1857, Joseph Alsop of New York City was elected president of the eastern division, and Thomas Brown of St. Louis became president of the Illinois division. Even in completion, the Ohio and Mississippi was a far from ideal western connection for the Baltimore and Ohio. In 1857 there was no rail connection across the city of Cincinnati, with the Little Miami (connecting with the Marietta and Cincinnati) having a depot on the eastern edge of the city while the terminal of the O&M was on the western side. Even when tracks were finally laid, ending the extensive horse-drawn cartage, there remained the problem of gauge—the Little Miami was built in a four-foot-ten-inch gauge, while the track of the Ohio and Mississippi was the broad six-foot gauge! No "compromise cars" could bridge such a difference.

But such small matters as difference in gauge were not going to keep Chauncy Brooks, president of the Baltimore and Ohio, from having a celebration. He and the top officials of the Marietta and Cincinnati and the Ohio and Mississippi had already agreed to call the newly completed rail route of some 920 miles connecting Baltimore and St. Louis as the "American Central Route." The guest lists, special trains, and fancy banquets, all planned by Brooks, were quite reminiscent of the big party the Erie had thrown six years earlier in 1851. President Brooks planned a much larger celebration than the one Thomas Swann had given when the line had been completed to Wheeling. Hundreds of invitations for a special week-long excursion from Baltimore to St. Louis were sent out by Brooks and his fellow railroad presidents. President James Buchanan was unable to attend, but Secretary of State Lewis Cass, Henry Ward Beecher, George Bancroft, and two former B&O presidents, Philip E. Thomas and Thomas Swann, now mayor of Baltimore, all came. When the excursion left Baltimore early on Monday morning, June 1, 1857, hundreds of men, women, and children were crowded into the special train. At Piedmont, where the heavy gradient started, the long train was divided into two parts, each behind a heavy locomotive.

After a long day's journey, the trains reached Grafton where it was discovered that in the new railroad hotel there was room only for the ladies and the more elderly gentlemen. The rest of the group was relegated to crude sleeping cars on some side tracks of the line. At each of the stopping places—Parkersburg, Marietta, Chillicothe, and Cincinnati—there were innumerable speeches. At Marietta, the governor of Ohio, Salmon P. Chase, welcomed the excursion party, and spoke of "the Railroad, the Locomotive,

and the Telegraph—iron, steam, and lightning—the three mighty
genie of modern civilization."[7] The next day at Cincinnati, Mayor
Swann of Baltimore and former president of the B&O, predicted
that, "at no distant day, the voice of the steam whistle, sounding
along the line of this great national highway, shall be lost amidst
the distant roar of the Pacific."[8] The stay at Cincinnati consisted of
banquets, marching bands, and other entertainment. Included was
a demonstration of the new equipment of the Steam Fire Department, the pride of the citizens of Cincinnati. A carriage containing
Gen. Lewis Cass, Governor Chase, and other dignitaries was
moved up near the center of activity. Somehow an errant fire crew
threw "an irreverent stream . . . into the party, and showered them
plentifully. General Cass took the accident kindly, rising to let the
water drip off, and returning the shout of the crowd with a good-
natured smile."[9] There were reports that the fine silk hat of Secretary of State Cass rolled down into a Cincinnati gutter.

Most of the party continued on westward over the broad-
gauged tracks of the Ohio and Mississippi to St. Louis. There they
enjoyed more entertainment, fireworks, banquets, and the shriek-
ing of the whistles of many steamboats tied up along the St. Louis
riverfront. Many of these riverboats were soon to lose some of their
traffic and commerce to the oncoming railroad. About six weeks
later, western excursionists from St. Louis, Cincinnati, Louisville,
and other western cities would respond to the first celebration by

Hotel and station at Grafton, Virginia, in the late 1850s. Grafton
was the junction point for the B&O and the Northwestern Virginia.
(Courtesy, Baltimore and Ohio Railroad)

traveling eastward over the same rail lines on their way to Baltimore. Baltimore easily matched the earlier hospitality shown in June by the western cities. The guests visited Fort McHenry, viewed a parade which included many military units, and listened to more speeches. Baltimore kept its fire department safely in the background. Perhaps the high point was the final banquet held at the Maryland Institute where the guests, upon entering the dining hall, viewed a giant decorated canvas which read "A Hearty Welcome from Baltimore to the West." The menu that evening included four varieties of fish, eight relishes, eleven different entrées, and twenty-five kinds of desserts.

But the completion of the "American Central Route," which had engendered the great celebration of 1857, did not immediately bring any great increase in traffic and prosperity to the Baltimore and Ohio. The new route was plagued with trouble spots and weak connections. The B&O leased the Northwestern of Virginia in 1856 only to discover that extensive and expensive work would be needed on the tunnels and roadbed before any great volume of traffic could move over the newly acquired line. At Parkersburg, a long and tedious nine-mile steamer trip was required to reach the tracks of the Marietta and Cincinnati at Marietta. Marietta, which had a strong voice in the management of the M&C, for several years resisted efforts to extend the M&C tracks to Belpre, a rivertown much closer to Parkersburg. The same kind of problem had earlier appeared ninety miles upstream at the Central Ohio–B&O connection near Wheeling. The city of Wheeling objected to the railroad ferry crossing between Bellaire, Ohio and Benwood, Virginia, four miles downstream from Wheeling. Contending that it was deprived of its legal terminal facilities, the city of Wheeling obtained an injunction against the B&O and the downstream river crossing. The Baltimore and Ohio eventually had the injunction dissolved, but only after two years of expensive and troublesome litigation. Further west at Cincinnati, as earlier mentioned, the connection with the Ohio and Mississippi was troubled both by the difference in gauge and the delays caused by drayage through the streets of the Queen City.

Of the four trunk lines serving New York City, Philadelphia, and Baltimore, the B&O had the smallest number of branch lines serving its main route. In New York State, both the Erie and the New York Central had several tributary lines bringing in extra traffic as their routes moved across the state. In Pennsylvania, J. Edgar Thomson, by the end of the fifties, had either acquired, or had good working relations with, more than half a dozen branch lines between Pittsburgh and Philadelphia. In contrast, between

Baltimore and Parkersburg, the B&O had only three branch lines of any importance: (1) the Washington branch going south at Relay; (2) the Winchester and Potomac south of Harpers Ferry; and (3) the line to Wheeling and the Ohio River at Grafton. By the late 1850s, both the New York Central and the Pennsylvania had better connections west of Buffalo and Pittsburgh than those possessed by the B&O on the Ohio River.

Even though the Baltimore and Ohio Railroad in the antebellum fifties did not prosper to the same degree as Thomson's Pennsylvania or Erastus Corning's New York Central, the traffic and revenue figures grew during the decade.

TABLE 6. Baltimore and Ohio Traffic and Financial Growth of Main Stem 1849–60

Year	Miles of Road	Passenger Receipts	Freight Recepits	Total Receipts	Expenses	Net Receipts
1849	181	$394,497	$ 846,708	$1,241,205	$ 644,634	$ 596,571
1850	181	438,375	905,430	1,343,805	609,589	734,216
1851	181	406,796	942,427	1,349,223	695,919	653,304
1852	302	314,914	1,010,649	1,325,563	710,179	615,384
1853	379	464,245	1,569,175	2,033,420	1,235,277	798,143
1854	379	569,091	3,076,518	3,645,609	2,026,211	1,619,398
1855	379	608,299	3,103,155	3,711,454	2,110,363	1,601,091
1856	379	672,999	3,712,952	4,385,951	2,384,779	2,001,172
1857	379	732,262	3,884,736	4,616,998	2,760,785	1,856,213
1858	379	–	–	3,856,485	2,531,199	1,325,286
1859	379	690,207	2,928,411	3,618,618	1,654,998	1,963,620
1860	379	697,735	3,224,467	3,922,202	1,616,616	2,305,586

Freight traffic during the 1850s grew much more rapidly than the passenger traffic. Freight revenue in the late 1840s was a bit more than double that of the passenger service. By 1856 and 1857, it was more than five times the volume of the passenger revenue. During the decade there were great changes in the kind of freight carried, with coal from the mines of Virginia and western Maryland making the major gains. In 1848, 157,000 tons of freight moved eastward over the lines of the B&O including coal—66,000 tons; flour—45,0000 tons; and livestock—13,000 tons. Eight years later, the 703,000 tons of eastbound freight transported included coal—446,000 tons; flour—91,000 tons; provisions—35,000 tons; grain—27,000 tons; and livestock—26,000 tons.

The increase in coal traffic in the 1850s was not surprising. By the midnineteenth century, coal was becoming much more important in the American economy both as a fuel and as a source of power. The growth of the American rail network from 9,000 to 30,000 miles during the 1850s greatly expanded the use of coal across the nation. In his essay entitled *Wealth*, Ralph Waldo Emerson described coal as a "portable climate" which made it possible for those living in Canada to be as warm as the people of Calcutta. The increased rail transport of coal allowed it to become portable power, allowing factories to be located some distance away from rapid streams and waterfalls.

The bulk of the coal moving over the Baltimore and Ohio in the 1850s and 1860s came from the coal mines located in western Virginia, from counties that in 1863 would become the new state of West Virginia. The bituminous coal fields of this area were a major portion of the great Appalachian coal region stretching from western Pennsylvania and eastern Ohio through western Virginia into eastern Kentucky and eastern Tennessee. The coal deposits discovered in West Virginia after the Civil War were even richer. Mining engineers estimated that the vast deposits in a single mountain county could supply world needs for hundreds of years. On the eve of the Civil War, the only railroads operating in western Virginia were the Baltimore and Ohio and the Northwestern Virginia, which was controlled by the B&O.

Both President Thomas Swann in 1852 and President William G. Harrison in 1855 had stressed the importance of the growing coal traffic in furthering the prosperity of Baltimore and the railroad which served the city. The optimism of the two men was justified, and soon thousands of tons of soft coal were moving eastward over the B&O Main Line to the recently completed new waterfront loading docks at Locust Point. In these antebellum years, nearly all of the B&O coal traffic moved eastward.

TABLE 7. Coal Moving Eastward over the B&O to Baltimore (in tons)

1849	72,000
1850	132,000
1851	139,000
1852	132,000
1853	309,000
1854	445,000
1855	452,000
1856	446,000

The Panic of 1857 caused a drop in the B&O coal traffic, but by 1860 B&O coal revenues were nearly as high as those of the midfifties. In 1860 B&O revenue from the movement of coal was just over $1 million, or about one-third of the total freight revenue. In the fall of 1859, the Baltimore and Ohio Main Stem and the Northwestern Virginia together had 3,272 freight cars, with 1,290 employed in the transportation of coal.

Even though the growth of passenger traffic was slower than freight traffic, the passenger traffic by 1856 had increased to 10 million passenger-miles on the Washington branch and 28 million passenger-miles on the Main Stem. Of the Main Stem passenger traffic, about one-third was through traffic and two-thirds local traffic. Of the nearly 18 million passenger-miles of local traffic on the Main Stem, Baltimore generated over 7,500,000 passenger-miles with Wheeling accounting for 2,480,000; Washington Junction 1,930,000; Cumberland 925,000; Martinsburg 820,000; and Frederick 612,000.

For its length, the thirty-one-mile Washington branch, from Washington Junction, or Relay, south to the nation's capital, was a very busy and productive line. Throughout the 1850s, as earlier, the line produced roughly three times as much passenger revenue as freight. Even though the passenger fare between Baltimore and Washington was reduced in 1853 from $1.80 to $1.25, the total yearly revenue for the short branch line increased from $274,832 in 1849 to $402,635 in 1855 and $469,422 in 1858. Throughout the decade, the Washington branch paid annual dividends ranging from 6 percent to 8 percent. The branch to Parkersburg, which the B&O had leased in 1856, was much less productive. During 1858 the total revenues for the 104-mile branch line were $248,000 while the expenses were $253,000.

The completion of the two lines to the Ohio River, plus the general increase of traffic during the decade, naturally created a need for additional equipment. By the fall of 1857, the total equipment roster consisted of 236 locomotives, 3,668 freight cars, and 124 passenger cars, many of which were painted yellow. More than three-quarters of the locomotives were quite new having been placed on the road during the 1850s. More than half of the engines had been built by Ross Winans, most of them the heavy Camel freight locomotives. The Camels with their eight drivers were not handsome engines but had been excellent performers in moving coal and freight over the mountain grades west of Cumberland. Both wood and coal were used as fuel; in mid-1858, the inventory of locomotive fuel included 2,000 tons of coal and 16,000 cords of wood. Some of the best looking locomotives were the American type (4-4-0) engines built for the B&O passenger service by William Mason, a Yankee who had built textile machinery before turning to the building of locomotives. Mason was once reported to have said that locomotives should look somewhat better than cookstoves on wheels.

The 1857 locomotive roster also included a few "Camels" not produced by Ross Winans. These maverick Camels retained the cab on top of the drivers but were 4-6-0 in wheel arrangement instead of 0-8-0. The new type of Camel was known as a Hayes Ten-Wheeler since it had been designed by Samuel J. Hayes, master of machinery from 1851 to 1856. Hayes contended that the addition of a leading truck would reduce the tendency of the Camel to derail. When Henry Tyson succeeded Hayes as master of machinery in 1856, he decided to order ten more of the 4-6-0 Camels. In the process, he became entangled in a quarrel with Ross Winans, the inventor of the original Camel. In the bitter feud between Tyson and Winans, lengthy pamphlets were published along with numerous letters in the local press. The B&O board naturally sided with their master of machinery, and Ross Winans built no more locomotives for the Baltimore and Ohio.

Camel locomotive No. 65, one of many built by Ross Winans in the years prior to the Civil War. *(Courtesy, Baltimore and Ohio Railroad)*

The *William Mason*, passenger locomotive, built in 1856. *(Courtesy, Association of American Railroads)*

Earlier in the decade, Charles Grafton Page, a Yankee physician more interested in electrical experiments than the practice of medicine, built an electrical locomotive that was neither handsome nor practical. While working for the United States Patent Office he obtained a small congressional appropriation to finance his experiment with an electric locomotive. Late in April 1851, the crude engine, powered with huge storage batteries, managed to run from the Washington depot out to Bladensburg, six miles north of Washingon, and back. The great weight and expense of the batteries, plus the trouble of recharging them, made the experiment far from practical in the midnineteenth century . Even so, the Baltimore and Ohio could claim that within a space of only seven years they had played a role in the first telegraph line and the first electrically operated locomotive.

The balance sheet of the railroad had also grown during the decade of the fifties. The statement of liabilities and assets of the Baltimore and Ohio Railroad shown in the 1856 *Annual Report* revealed a total investment of $26,900,000. The principle items shown as liabilities in the 1856 balance sheet were: common stock, $10,108,000; preferred stock (Maryland 5 percent sterling bonds), $3,000,000; loans, $9,755,000; and profit and loss, $3,833,000. The common stock was held by four different groups: (1) individuals— 54,233 shares ($5,423,300); (2) city of Baltimore—35,000 shares ($3,500,000); (3) state of Maryland—6,855 shares ($685,500); and (4) city of Wheeling—5,000 shares ($500,000). While individuals held a slight majority of the total stock, they elected only twelve of the thirty members of the board of directors. The city of Baltimore appointed eight board members while the state of Maryland had ten members to represent its common stock plus its preferred shares (sterling bonds).

More than one-third of the liabilities of the B&O in 1856 were in the form of loans—about $9,755,000. Of this amount, nearly $6 million was in the form of earlier loans, obtained to finance the construction and completion of the road to Wheeling. The loans were due at various dates, ranging from 1857 to 1885, with about 90 percent not due until 1867 or later. Even with the completion of this road, the Baltimore and Ohio in 1853 was hard pressed for working capital. Late in 1853, the railroad received a new $5 million loan from the city of Baltimore which was intended to (1) meet the most pressing debts of the railroad, (2) pay for needed side tracks and additional double tracking, and (3) line the major tunnels west of Cumberland to guard against the collapse of tunnel ceilings. Not all of this $5 million loan was immediately available, but by the fall of 1856, $3,831,000 had been received from the city.

John W. Garrett, president, 1858–84.
(Courtesy, Baltimore and Ohio Railroad)

In the early midfifties, when the Baltimore and Ohio always seemed to be short of working capital, a growing number of the individual stockholders became discontented with the growing evidence of some financial mismanagement in the company and with the relative scarcity of dividends. President Harrison convinced his board of directors to omit dividends in 1854 and 1855. In 1854 John W. Garrett played a leading role in stockholder committees concerned with these problems. By the time Garrett became a director in July 1855, a growing division was appearing in the thirty-member board, basically between the private stockholder group of twelve directors and the eighteen directors who represented the city of Baltimore and the state of Maryland. The private interests saw the B&O as a railroad that should have freight rates high enough to produce a profit that could permit dividends. The city and state interests felt that rates should be low enough to bring prosperity to the city and state, with dividends being only of secondary importance.

Once the railroad reached the Ohio River, this private versus public dispute rapidly came to a head. With John Garrett and Johns Hopkins both on the board and Chauncy Brooks in the president's chair, the private interests were ready for battle. While the private interest group held only twelve seats on the board, frequently some of the eighteen public directors were absent from board meetings. Also three or four of the city directors often voted with the dozen directors who represented the individual stockholders. In any event, the private interests soon managed to vote a freight rate increase of fifty cents per ton of coal. The private interests gained another victory in December 1856, when by a vote of seventeen to twelve, they voted a 30 percent stock dividend, payable after January 12, 1857, in certificates of debt paying 6 percent

which were convertible into stock after five years. The city of Baltimore and the state of Maryland responded with lawsuits and in-
junctions. The lengthy litigation was not finally resolved until 1860
when the courts approved the 30 percent stock dividend. By 1862
the debt certificates of 1857 could be converted into new stock.
During this litigation, John W. Garrett was elected president on
November 17, 1858, by a vote of sixteen to fourteen at an annual
salary of $4,000. During the mid- and late-fifties Baltimore and
Ohio stock certificates rarely reached the high levels of the fall of
1852 when President Swann's road was nearing Wheeling. In May
1854, the stock was listed at 62; at 69 in March 1857; and at 56 in
January 1859.

A railroad with more than 500 miles of line representing a
total investment of over $26 million naturally had a large number of
employees. William Prescott Smith, the assistant master of transportation in the midfifties, estimated that during 1857 the "full
time" roster of employees was very close to 4,500 persons: 1,420 in
the transportation department; 1,200 in the machinery department; and 1,850 in the road department. Included in the roster of
the transportation department were 254 conductors, 246 engineers, 272 brakemen, 260 firemen, 210 watchmen, and 34 telegraph operators. Also included in this department were all of the
agents necessary to man the 85 freight and passenger stations in
the system. The *Annual Report* for 1857 reveals that the total expenses of these three departments were: transportation—
$1,032,000; machinery—$879,000; and road—$778,000. The rela-
tively heavier expenses per employee in the transportation and
machinery departments were due both to the larger material costs
(fuel plus parts for engine and car repair) and also to the higher
wages paid train crews and machine shop workers. In contrast, the
workers in section gangs and bridge repair crews were at the low
end of the wage scale.

The number of B&O employees per mile of road—more
than eight per mile—seems a little high for the decade. In 1853 the
Central of Georgia with 257 miles of road, had 927 workers, while
in 1856, the number employed on the 705-mile Illinois Central was
3,581. However, the gross revenue of the B&O in 1857 was nearly
double that of the larger Illinois Central in 1856. The general wage
scales for the B&O employees in 1857 did not differ greatly from
those earlier described for the work force of 1844.

As the American rail network expanded during the fifties—
from some 9,000 miles of line to more than 30,000 miles—there
naturally was an increase in railroad accidents and fatalities. Early
in 1856, the *American Railroad Journal* reported 142 major rail-

road accidents during the preceding year causing death or injury to more than 650 people. Railroad accidents were so common in the 1850s that a humor magazine of the day made fun of railroad directors and officials who were often afraid to ride in their own passenger trains. In general, far more crew members and employees were killed or injured than were passengers. But passengers also were often accident victims. Charles R. Weld, an Englishman touring America in 1855, was a passenger on a B&O train which jumped the track between Cumberland and Harpers Ferry because an overzealous crew was trying to make up lost time on the winding track along the Potomac. The uninjured but shaken Englishman observed, "Accidents on railways are thought so little of in America it is useless to remonstrate."[10]

The hundreds of B&O employees, especially the train crews in the transportation department, were required to follow a number of rules, all found in the book of rules. Such items as: "a red flag by day and a lantern by night"; "one-half mile or more apart"; "in all cases of doubt, take the side of safety"; and "entire sobriety" were all intended to ensure the safe and orderly operation of trains.[11] Even so, some serious accidents could not be avoided. Thirty-five fatal accidents during the fiscal year, 1854–55, are described in the appendix of the *Annual Report* for 1855. Of

A halt for pictures. A group of journalists and photographers made a trip over the B&O Main Stem in the summer of 1857. (*Courtesy, Baltimore and Ohio Railroad*)

the thirty-five victims, only two were passengers, about a dozen were neither passengers nor employees (often in fact trespassers on railroad property), and the remainder were Baltimore and Ohio employees. (Of the two passengers, one was trying to avoid paying his fare, and both were injured as they were jumping on or off a moving train.) Eleven of the employees killed were brakemen, of whom several were killed as they "fell between the cars." Across the nation, freight train crews had to work on the tops of moving cars, often in inclement weather. All the cars were equipped with the link-and-pin coupler, which much increased the hazards of a brakeman's life. Both the automatic coupler and the air brake would not appear until the 1870s and the 1880s.

During the decade, the Baltimore and Ohio Railroad, in reaching Wheeling and the Ohio River, had finally achieved the dreams of the commercial leaders of Baltimore. In the long generation since 1827, the city fathers of Baltimore had been generous with the financial support given to the railroad. And the city had prospered and grown since the laying of the first stone in 1828. In population Baltimore had increased each decade: 62,000 in 1820; 80,000 in 1830; 102,000 in 1840; 169,000 in 1850; and 212,000 in 1860. The leaders of the B&O did not forget the city on the Chesapeake. Thomas Swann, the president who completed the line to the Ohio, was later mayor of Baltimore from 1856 to 1860, and Johns Hopkins, one of the largest stockholders in the railroad, would leave the bulk of his fortune for the establishment of a university and a hospital in Baltimore.

In the early 1850s, four major lines—the Erie, the New York Central, the Pennsylvania, and the Baltimore and Ohio—had each reached either the Great Lakes or the Ohio River, and soon connecting lines were being built on into the Old Northwest. The men of commerce and business in New York City, Philadelphia, and Baltimore, no longer preoccupied with foreign trade, were increasingly shifting their attention from dock and wharf to the railroad depot and the freight yard. During the 1850s, an east-west axis of domestic trade was being forged between the Middle Atlantic states and the Old Northwest. By the mid-1850s, there was also a growing political alliance between the western states north of the Ohio and the Northeast that would help determine loyalties during the Civil War. Because of its geographic location in a border state near the Mason-Dixon Line, the Baltimore and Ohio in the coming decade was destined to experience far more than its share of violence and destruction in that war.

Chapter VII

• • • • • • • • • • • • • •

A Railroad at War

THE VIOLENCE OF ARMED CONFLICT CAME TO THE BALTI-more and Ohio Railroad eighteen months before the firing on Fort Sumter. Early on the morning of October 17, 1859, A. J. Phelps, the conductor of the Night Express, eastbound from Wheeling to Baltimore, sent this wire to William Prescott Smith, the B&O master of transportation in Baltimore:

Monocacy, 7:05 a.m. Oct. 17, 1859

W. P. Smith
Baltimore

Express train bound east under my charge was stopped this morning at Harpers Ferry by armed abolitionists. They have possession of the bridges and of the arms and armory of the United States. Myself and the baggage master have been fired at and Hayward, the colored porter, is wounded very severely. . . . The doctor says he cannot survive. They are headed by a man named Anderson and number about 150 strong. They say they have come to free the slaves, and intend to do it at all hazards. . . . The telegraph wires are cut east and west of Harpers Ferry and this is the first station I could send a despatch from.

A. J. Phelps[1]

99

Conductor Phelps, in his excitement, had greatly overestimated the number of raiders who had come down out of the hills above the Potomac to raid and capture the United States Arsenal at Harpers Ferry. Mr. Smith found it hard to believe the wire from the excited conductor, and it took a second telegram from Phelps before the master of transportation alerted President Garrett. Garrett's wire to Secretary of War John B. Floyd brought a detachment of United States Marines under Col. Robert E. Lee to Harpers Ferry. Once there, the marines quickly subdued John Brown (not Anderson) and the remnants of his little band of eighteen raiders.

John Brown had chosen to make his raid in a border slave state not far south of the Mason-Dixon Line, the very region through which the Baltimore and Ohio Railroad ran. As the threat of disunion, secession, and armed conflict grew in the long winter and spring of 1860–61, the B&O was threatened with trouble and violence ranging from the halted train and cut telegraph wires of John Brown's raid in 1859, to seizure, blockade, and complete destruction during the four war years. The railroad was in an unenviable position with her origin and ownership in a slave state, but much of her traffic moving to and from free states. As the war began, the Wheeling *Intelligence* wrote of the B&O as being like "the amphibious animal that could not live on land, and died in water."[2]

United States arsenal at Harpers Ferry, Virginia, on the eve of the Civil War. *(Courtesy, Baltimore and Ohio Railroad)*

As secession and war came closer in 1860 and 1861, both the state of Maryland and President Garrett's railroad had to make difficult choices. Both the state and the railroad would have preferred compromise and neutrality. In the fall of 1859, President Garrett turned down the request for a northern excursion train to Harpers Ferry during John Brown's trial, and early in 1860, he spoke of the Baltimore and Ohio as a *Southern* railroad. The Garrett family had long been Southern Democrats, and certainly the rise of the Republican party and the election of Lincoln were disturbing developments. But Garrett was far from being a fire-eating sort of Southerner. In the election of 1860, he probably preferred Douglas to Breckenridge.

But in spite of the southern flavor found in Baltimore and the existence of slavery in Maryland, the commercial life of Baltimore for half a century had been bound to the North and the West, regions that in 1860 clearly favored the Union. Before the decade of the fifties, the political and commercial orientation of the West may well have looked southward along the commercial axis of the north-south Mississippi riverboat traffic. But by 1860, the four major rail track lines of the Middle Atlantic states, plus their connecting roads built in Ohio, Indiana, and Illinois, had clearly moved the West toward a new commercial and political alliance with the North and the Union. Not the tobacco from southern plantations, but the flour from the West had made Baltimore prosperous. The B&O hopper cars filled with Cumberland coal did not go south, but rather north to power the plants and factories of New England. John W. Garrett might claim that the B&O was a Southern line, but in his heart he knew that both the prosperity and the future of his railroad lay with the North, the West, and the Union, rather than the South.

The Baltimore and Ohio and the city of Baltimore played minor roles in two events as the nation neared armed conflict in the early months of 1861. In mid-February, Abraham Lincoln had embarked upon a leisurely and indirect twelve-day rail trip from Springfield to Washington, D.C., 2,000 miles through eight states, a dozen major cities, and hundreds of towns and villages. At Harrisburg, Pennsylvania, Lincoln learned of a change in travel plans—a proposal to pass through Baltimore quietly at night because of rumors of possible trouble in that pro-Southern city. Accordingly, a special train carried Lincoln to Philadelphia. Accompanied only by his long time friend, Col. Ward H. Lamon and Detective Allan Pinkerton, Lincoln's sleeping car left Philadelphia and arrived in Baltimore at the President Street Station of the

Philadelphia, Wilmington and Baltimore Railroad about 3 A.M. on February 23. A team of horses pulled the car along Pratt Street to the B&O Camden Station where a waiting train quickly left for Washington. The president-elect arrived safe, but unannounced, in Washington at 6 A.M. Saturday morning.

During the four-year Civil War, many new weapons and military techniques were used for the first time. Trench warfare, wire entanglements, the repeating rifle, incendiary shells, and aerial observation were all introduced during the long conflict. While railroads had been used in a very modest way in supporting both the Mexican War and the Crimean War, the Civil War was the first war in which the railroad was used extensively. During the war, the iron rails of both the Union and the Confederacy became a new weapon in tactics, logistics, and strategy. Very often the offensive actions that ignored available railroads, or used them poorly, were not successful.

On April 19, six days after the surrender of Fort Sumter and four days after President Lincoln had made his call for 75,000 militia from the Northern states, the Sixth Massachusetts Infantry was enroute by rail to Washington in answer to the president's call for

President-elect Lincoln arrives in Washington, February 23, 1861. From a painting by H. D. Stitt. *(Courtesy, Baltimore and Ohio Railroad)*

troops. As the horse-drawn cars carried the troops along Pratt Street from the Philadelphia, Wilmington and Baltimore depot toward the B&O Camden Station, they were met by a noisy Baltimore mob carrying not only Confederate flags but also stones and bricks. Violence came to Pratt Street when the soldiers finally answered a shower of brickbats with gunfire. Casualty figures included four dead soldiers, nine civilians, and dozens of wounded and injured. The Massachusetts regiment finally reached Washington, but Baltimore, for a time, ceased to provide a rail connection between Washington and the Northern states. For several weeks, Lincoln and the War Department were forced to bypass Baltimore as Northern troops reached Washington using Chesapeake Bay steamers from the mouth of the Susquehanna down to a railhead at Annapolis.

In the troubled days of late April and early May, John W. Garrett and his railroad were suspected both by the Union and the Confederacy. Just after the Baltimore riot of April 19, Garrett received an anonymous note from Marylanders favoring the South which read: "One hundred of us, firm, respectable, resolute men—have determined & sworn to each other to destroy 'every' bridge & tear up your track on both lines of your road (the Main & the Branch) between this city & their head points—If you carry another soldier over either line of your road after April 20th."[3] But at almost the same time, there was a critical report in the pro-Union Wheeling *Intelligence* that Garrett's road was willing to transport rebel Virginia and Maryland troops. And Secretary of War Simon Cameron, a Pennsylvania Republican with large financial interests in the rival Northern Central Railroad, notified the B&O president that if his railroad carried any "rebel troops," it would be considered a treasonable act. At one point, J. Edgar Thomson, president of the rival Pennsylvania Railroad, urged Secretary Cameron to destroy the bridges of the B&O east of Harpers Ferry.

Federal troops helped tip the city of Baltimore and its railroad out of their state of indecision. On May 5, 1861, Union troops under Gen. Benjamin F. Butler occupied Relay House, nine miles west of Baltimore, where the general could inspect and stop any further freight headed for the military forces of Virginia. A week later, on May 13, General Butler moved troops into Baltimore, occupied Federal Hill, and started to arrest citizens known for their open Confederate support. Included among those arrested was Ross Winans, long-time inventor and locomotive builder. More and more of the citizens of the city forgot their secessionist fervor, and most businessmen remembered that their commercial and financial ties were really with the North. Very shortly regular rail service from the North was again moving through Baltimore down to Washington. Before the end of the month, the Confederates, under Col. Thomas J. Jackson, a former obscure and quiet professor at the Virginia Military Institute, would be causing real trouble at Harpers Ferry.

The attitude of President Garrett had changed during the late winter and spring months of 1861. In the early weeks of the growing crisis, when he was speaking of his line as a "Southern" railroad, he often called the Confederate leaders "Our Southern Friends." Later, as the crisis deepened and he came under increasing pressure from both sides, these same men were spoken of as "misguided" friends. After Colonel Jackson had occupied and destroyed much of the B&O at Harpers Ferry and to the west, the word "rebel" was added to the president's vocabulary. Since Garrett was outspoken and rarely minced words, he may on occasion have used some strong adjectives to lend stress to "rebel."[4]

Back on April 18, 1861, a detachment of Federal troops guarding the arsenal at Harpers Ferry set fire to the arsenal building and left the town. Within a few hours, Virginia militia from Charlestown and Winchester occupied the town. B&O trains continued to run, with many interruptions and only with the consent of Virginia. Late in April, Colonel Jackson was placed in command of the Virginia troops in the Harpers Ferry area. During early May, dozens of heavy coal and freight trains were moving daily over the double-track line in the Harpers Ferry area. Colonel Jackson knew that the heavily laden trains were helping to build up the supplies for the forthcoming Northern war effort. About the middle of May 1861, Colonel Jackson informed President Garrett that the noisy night railroad traffic was disturbing the sleep of his soldiers and that, henceforth, all freight traffic could move through Harpers Ferry only during daylight hours. Within a few days, he further demanded that freight traffic could move through Harpers Ferry only between the hours of 11 A.M. and 1 P.M. President Garrett and his master of transportation, William P. Smith, knew they were in no position to defy the God-fearing Confederate colonel.

Once the new midday traffic pattern was established, the crafty Jackson sprang his trap. On May 23, 1861, Confederate forces at Point of Rocks, twelve miles east of Harpers Ferry, and at Cherry Run, thirty-two miles west of Harpers Ferry, were ordered to close down the line at the end of the busy noontime traffic. The forty-four-mile double-track line was filled with dozens of wrathy, impatient locomotive engineers wondering what was causing the tie up. Jackson's haul of railroad equipment that day included 56 locomotives and more than 300 freight cars, most of them coal cars. Four of the lighter weight B&O locomotives were run down the line of the Winchester and Potomac where they were taken off the track and dragged behind dozens of horses over the valley turnpike twenty miles south to Strasburg on the Manassas Gap Railway. The tracks of the Manassas Gap, like the B&O and most of the Virginia lines, were built in standard gauge. Most of the remaining captured rolling stock was soon concentrated in Martinsburg.

When Federal forces from the North threatened Harpers Ferry in early June 1861, Jackson started to destroy the railroad itself. Early on the morning of June 14, the seven-span, 800-foot combined highway-railroad bridge at Harpers Ferry was blown up with gunpowder and totally destroyed. Earlier, other important bridges west of Harpers Ferry had been put to the torch. With this dramatic action, the main line of the B&O was to be effectively closed down for nearly ten months.

A few days later, Jackson, now a brigadier general, received orders to destroy all the B&O railroad property at Martinsburg. On June 23, 1861, the dutiful general followed his order with a vengeance. Nearly 400 cars and 42 engines were put to the torch; shops, depots, and machinery at Martinsburg were destroyed; and blazing coal cars were pushed onto wooden bridges which soon fell into the streams below. Of his work, the general later wrote his

B&O Camel captured and destroyed by General Stonewall Jackson in 1861. The Martinsburg, Virginia, youngsters in their Union blue uniforms seem undisturbed by the destruction. *(Courtesy, Baltimore and Ohio Railroad)*

wife: ". . . It was a sad work; but I had my orders and my duty was to obey."[5] A few weeks later, Jackson realized that some of the burnt locomotives of Martinsburg might still be of use to the Confederacy. Ten of the best engines made the thirty-eight-mile trek to Strasburg and the Confederate rail network, each locomotive pulled by forty of the strongest farm horses in the region. During the last weeks of the summer of 1861, the Confederate forces west of Harpers Ferry actually tore up some of the B&O track and sent it south. In the *Annual Report* for 1861 master of the road, John L. Wilson reported: "Aug. & Sept. '61. Thirty-six and a half miles track torn up between Harpers Ferry and Paxton's Cut, and the iron and several thousand ties and track fixtures were being transported by animal power to Southern roads."[6] With such destruction and abuse of *his* railroad, it was quite easy for President Garrett in the summer of 1861 to be certain of his loyalty to the Union. Increasingly he thought of the Confederate forces as the rebel enemy.

President Garrett later wrote a summary of the effect of the Confederate action against the B&O in his *Annual Report* for 1861:

> On May 28, 1861, general possession was taken by the Confederate forces of more than one hundred miles of the Main Stem, embroiling chiefly the region between Point of Rocks and Cumberland. Occassional movements were also made, accompanied by considerable destruction upon the roads between Cumberland and Wheeling, and Grafton and Parkersburg, during the fiscal year.
>
> The Protection of the Government was not restored throughout the line until March, 1862, when the reconstruction was pressed with great energy, and the line reopened on the 29th of that month[7]

The 1861 *Annual Report* listed as destroyed some 26 bridges (127 spans with a total length of 4,713 feet), 102 miles of telegraph line, plus two water stations. This was in addition to all the rolling stock lost and burnt at Martinsburg.

During 1861 and the remaining years of the conflict, the Confederate occupation and destruction was much more common on the eastern slopes of the Alleghenies than on the western. This was natural, since pro-Confederate feelings were fairly rare in the western counties of Virginia. In the spring of 1861, Gen. Robert E. Lee had experienced a notable failure in his efforts to recruit volunteers for the Confederacy in the western counties of his native state. During the early weeks of the summer of 1861, Federal forces, under the overall command of Gen. George B. McClellan occupied the B&O lines west and north of Grafton. McClellan had earlier been chief engineer and vice president of the Illinois Central before becoming president of the Ohio and Mississippi in 1860. The Federal move into western Virginia was welcomed both by the B&O officials and the pro-Union citizenry of the region. The pro-Union sentiment in the western counties eventually, in 1863, resulted in the creation and admission of West Virginia as the thirty-fifth state in June 1863.

Whenever the Confederate forces were pushed well south of the Main Stem, the work crews of John L. Wilson moved in to repair and restore the broken road. Considerable bridge repair work had been accomplished by the end of the summer of 1861. Almost at once, much of the repair work was destroyed by heavy rains during the last days of September. Especially hard hit was the new trestle work across the Potomac at Harpers Ferry. During the summer and fall of 1861, the indifference of Simon Cameron and the War Department to the plight of the Baltimore and Ohio was sufficient to make many recall that the problems of the B&O were helping increase the profits of the Pennsylvania Railroad and the Northern Central, in which Cameron had a major interest. Fortunately for the B&O, Simon Cameron left the War Department early in 1862 to become the United States minister to Russia. His successor was Edwin M. Stanton, a pro-Union Democrat and a critic of Lincoln, but a man who honestly and efficiently ran the War Department. This was good news for the Baltimore and Ohio. Stanton and Garrett were not only friends, but Stanton had earlier been general counsel for the Ohio Central, the line that connected with the Baltimore and Ohio at Wheeling.

The War Department under Stanton definitely took more interest in the plight of the Baltimore and Ohio, and by early March 1862, the entire middle section of the Main Stem from Harpers Ferry west was again under Federal control. Wilson's work crews of bridge builders and track men were busy the entire month of March, sometimes even working extra shifts at night. A new wooden bridge at Harpers Ferry was rushed to completion, and by March 30, 1862, the entire line was open from Baltimore to the Ohio. Unfortunately, heavy rains and high water on the Potomac washed out the Harpers Ferry bridge late in April. In May, General Jackson pushed the Federal troops north of the Potomac for a few days, destroying a few railroad bridges near Martinsburg. It seemed that Wilson and his top assistants, W. C. Quincy and W. E. Porter, were constantly repairing or rebuilding bridges. During the fiscal year 1862—October 1, 1861 to September 30, 1862—Wilson reported the expenditure of over $140,000, more than half of it on the building and rebuilding of the Harpers Ferry bridge.

Early in September 1862, the gray-clad troops of Robert E. Lee again moved north across the Potomac River and the tracks of the Baltimore and Ohio. Again the Confederates were hard on the bridges of the B&O including the wooden trestle at Harpers Ferry and the iron bridge over the Monocacy River near Frederick. Of the destruction of the Monocacy bridge, master of road John L. Wilson wrote in the 1862 *Annual Report:* "September 8 [1862], The splendid iron suspension bridge at Monocacy blown up by the enemy. This bridge consisted of three spans of 115 feet each. The water station at Monocacy, including pump house and engine house, also burned,"[8] General Lee had broken the Main Stem of the B&O once more, but he had not broken the pro-Union spirit of western Maryland. The prudent farmers of the western counties of the state were more impressed by the ragged uniforms of the Confederate veterans as they marched toward Antietam than they were by Lee's invitation to throw off the foreign Union yoke. It was the harvest season in the rich Maryland Piedmont, and the lush orchards and sweet corn of the region were tempting to the tired Southern soldiers. In fact, Robert E. Lee probably lost more deserters than he gained in new recruits as he marched through Maryland.

As the Confederate forces retreated from Antietam in the autumn days of 1862, they brought more destruction to B&O property at Martinsburg and the line of the Main Stem. Of the destruc-

President Lincoln, Gen. George B. McClellan, and John W. Garrett at Antietam shortly after the 1862 battle. *(Courtesy, Baltimore and Ohio Railroad)*

tion at Martinsburg in mid-October 1862, Wilson wrote in the *Annual Report* for 1863:

> October 19-20, 1862: Great destruction of company's property at Martinsburg. The polygonal engine house, the half round engine house, the large and costly machine shops, warehouse, ticket and telegraph offices, the company's hotel and dining and wash house, coalbins, sand houses, blacksmith shop and tool houses, pumping engine for water station and connecting pipes were all destroyed. The destruction of tracks also commenced and continued . . . making a total of 37 1/2 miles of track [destroyed].[9]

This time Jackson's men did not move the torn-up iron south for use on their own lines, but rather heated it over bonfires of ties and fence posts, twisting the heated rails around trees or poles, leaving it to cool in fantastic shapes. One Baltimore and Ohio official wrote President Garrett that the route of the railroad could be traced "by a continuous line of fires."[10] The damage to the B&O also affected the connecting line west of Wheeling, the Central Ohio. In mid-November 1862, Hugh J. Jewett, president of the Central Ohio, wrote John Garrett: "Can you advise me of about the time when your road will be open. We are suffering terribly for want of it."[11]

In some ways, 1863 was a repeat of the previous year. Late in April 1863, the railroad suffered at the hands of two Confederate generals, William E. "Grumble" Jones and John D. Imboden, who led raids into western Maryland and western Virginia. The two raiding generals led more than 5,000 men in a joint effort to wreck the B&O, overthrow the "loyal" West Virginia government at Wheeling, and find fresh recruits plus supplies for the Confederacy. They captured a loaded B&O livestock train for their own use, destroyed several bridges, caused a locomotive to crash into a river, tore up track, and destroyed other B&O property. Finally returning south, General Jones reported to Lee that his men had destroyed two trains, sixteen railroad bridges, and one railroad tunnel; had captured several hundred Federal prisoners; and had seized for Confederate use 1,200 horses and 1,000 cattle.

Far more serious was General Lee's second invasion of Maryland and the North. Lee's advance forces crossed the Potomac at several places in mid-June 1863 and, before long, controlled the B&O Railroad for roughly 150 miles, from Sykesville thirty-two miles west of Baltimore to Rawling's water station, a few miles west of Cumberland. Stonewall Jackson was not with the invading forces this time, having been mortally wounded six weeks before at Chancellorsville, but his successors were equally skillful in the art of destruction. All the B&O bridges from Harpers Ferry west to Cumberland were again destroyed. Rolling stock, telegraph lines, toolsheds, engine houses, machinery, and several miles of track met the same fate.

Before returning from Gettysburg to Virginia in mid-July, Lee's army had destroyed twenty-seven miles of track and ninety-two miles of telegraph line. However, the repair crews of John Wilson had also learned a great deal in two years of war. Every attack, broken bridge, or torn up rail line had taught the construction workers new ways and methods of speedy repair. John Wilson was able to report after days and weeks of hectic work: "Aug. 10th, 1863. Road fully reopened, and trains running through. Track layers restoring sidings in Martinsburg."[12] Three months later, in mid-November 1863, Abraham Lincoln rode over the Washington branch and passed through Baltimore on his way to Gettysburg and the consecration of the battlefield cemetery. The enthusiastic reception given the president as his horse-drawn railway car moved up Howard Street to the Northern Central Bolton Station was far different than his passage through Baltimore back in late February 1861.

In the early autumn of 1863, the Baltimore and Ohio played a major role in a massive movement of Union troops. In September 1863, a Union army, under Gen. William Rosecrans, moved into northwestern Georgia and at Chickamauga was badly defeated by a Confederate army led by Gen. Braxton Bragg. Secretary of War Stanton realized that a relief force should, if possible, be sent to aid Rosecrans and his army of the Cumberland. On the evening of September 23, Stanton proposed to Lincoln's inner cabinet that the War Department should send by railroad some 25,000 men— the Eleventh and Twelfth Corps of the Army of the Potomac located in northern Virginia—to break the seige of Chattanooga. Stanton estimated that the total move could be made in five days. President Lincoln was so skeptical that he said to Stanton: "I will bet that if the order is given tonight the troops could not be got to Washington in five days."[13]

On September 24, War Department orders were given for the Eleventh and Twelfth Corps to get ready to move. That same day, Edwin Stanton summoned President Garrett, Vice President Tom Scott of the Pennsylvania, and President Samuel M. Felton of the Philadelphia, Wilmington and Baltimore to Washington to help plan the massive rail movement. Garrett and Scott, long time railroad adversaries, forgot their rivalry as Stanton gave them the chief responsibility for the unique operations. Garrett was to direct the movement from Washington, D.C., to Jeffersonville, Indiana, and Scott from the Ohio River and Louisville south to Bridgeport, Alabama, the nearest railroad to Chattanooga. Aided by the highest military authority, Garrett started to assemble in the Baltimore area hundreds of passenger cars plus freight cars outfitted with crude seats. By September 28, the two Corps, under the command of Gen. Joseph Hooker, with all their equipment, artillery and horses, had left Virginia for the long 1,200 mile trek to Alabama.

The route was via the Baltimore and Ohio from Washington, D.C., to Harpers Ferry, Grafton, and Wheeling. President Garrett, aided by William P. Smith, had ordered the construction of a pontoon bridge across the low water of the Ohio at Benwood, and the crude structure was completed in two days. West of the Ohio, the troops boarded the trains of the Ohio Central, continuing on via Columbus, Indianapolis, Jeffersonville, Louisville, and Nashville to Bridgeport in northeastern Alabama. The last of the more than thirty trains, with about 700 cars carrying some 23,000 troops, arrived in Alabama by the end of the first week in October. In the next few days, freight trains of flatcars and stock cars arrived carrying army baggage, heavy guns, and hundreds of army mules. Secretary Stanton had proven to be nearer right than President Lincoln in guessing the time needed for the rail movement.

After Gettysburg pressure on the B&O from the Confederate forces relaxed a bit as the center of the conflict in the East moved into southern Virginia. For about eleven months—August 1863 to July 1864—the Main Stem operated without any serious halt in service. However, in July 1864, the Confederate troops of

Union troops guard B&O bridge over Monongahela River at Fairmont, West Virginia. *(Courtesy, Baltimore and Ohio Railroad)*

Gen. Jubal Early moved out of the Shenandoah Valley to raid the B&O at several places between Cumberland and Harpers Ferry. Later they struck east of Harpers Ferry at Monocacy Junction and on July 12, 1864, cavalry troops even briefly struck the Washington branch at Beltsville, only a dozen miles north of Washington, D.C. The Main Stem remained out of operation most of July, August, and early September. In mid-September 1864, Gen. Philip Sheridan defeated the Confederate forces at Winchester. Within ten days the Main Stem was again in operation.

However in mid-October 1864, Col. John Singleton Mosby, whose troops of Partisan Rangers were very active in northern and eastern Virginia in the last two years of the war, hit the B&O with what became known as the "Greenback Raid." Early on the morning of October 14, Mosby's men pulled up some rails in a cut at Quincy's Siding, eleven miles west of Harpers Ferry and derailed the eight-car Western Express, four hours out of Baltimore. The two hundred sleepy passengers were quickly relieved of jewelry and more than $20,000 in cash. But the biggest haul came with the capture of $168,000 in crisp greenbacks taken from Major Moore, an army paymaster enroute to give Union soldiers a payday. Before departing, Mosby's men burnt the train down to the tracks and metal work. Few other raids were made against the B&O in the remaining months of the war. In the spring of 1865, the bridge crews of John L. Wilson were replacing bridges taken out by "spring freshets" rather than by gray-clad Confederates.

Even with the end of destruction along the Main Stem, financial problems remained in the early months of 1865. The B&O, along with most northern lines that had carried federal troops and war material, found the War Department often tardy in making payment for the service. In late February 1865, Hugh Jewett of the Central Ohio, wired John Garrett: ". . . I was led to believe I could rely on forty six thousand more from the Quarter Master two weeks since, but it fails me here and I sent Gen'l Wright to Washington to try and arrange it."[14]

Even during the difficult war years, President Garrett was trying to expand the mileage of the Baltimore and Ohio. On the eve of the Civil War, the B&O president had been looking toward the control of the Northern Central which ran from Baltimore north to Harrisburg. During a financial crisis in Baltimore late in 1860, Garrett was forced to sell much of his recently acquired stock in the Northern Central, most of which was purchased by J. Edgar Thomson and Tom Scott of the Pennsylvania. Despite the best efforts of Garrett in the early war years, the Northern Central was soon fully controlled by the Pennsylvania.

During the Civil War, Garrett was no more successful in his efforts to extend the Pittsburgh and Connellsville road ninety-five miles eastward to a connection with the B&O at Cumberland. In the early war years, it seemed probable that the B&O would finally succeed in achieving its long sought connection to Pittsburgh—the B&O owned 17,000 shares of stock in the Pittsburgh and Connellsville, Garrett was willing to loan the road $1 million, and Benjamin Latrobe was president of the P&C. But the P&C was located in Pennsylvania, the home ground of the crafty Tom Scott, vice president of the Pennsylvania. Tom Scott successfully managed to control both the courts and the legislature in Pennsylvania. After Scott had maneuvered legislation through both houses of the legislature at Harrisburg—legislation which completely tied the hands of John Garrett—it was reported that one senator rose from his seat to say: "Mr. Speaker, may we now go Scott free?"[15] Garrett would not achieve his Pittsburgh connection until six years after Appomattox.

Garrett's efforts for expansion away from the Keystone State were more successful. The Northwestern Virginia Railroad from Grafton west to Parkersburg had been leased and operated by the B&O since 1856. But the line was a financial disappointment, always near bankruptcy, and in such a sad state of repair in 1863 that Garrett reported that patrons in passenger cars needed to put up umbrellas to keep dry in a hard rain. Nevertheless, it was part of the direct route to Cincinnati and St. Louis. Garrett convinced his board of directors to reorganize the line and to assume the first mortgage from the city of Baltimore. In the summer of 1864, Garrett completed the agreement with Peter Godwin Van Winkle, president of the Northwestern Virginia and the United States senator from the newly formed state of West Virginia. The B&O became the major stockholder of the line, which after January 1, 1865, was known as the Parkersburg branch. About the same time, Garrett also acquired a major control over the Central Ohio, the Ohio line connecting Bellaire, across the Ohio from Wheeling, with Columbus.

With the secession of Virginia, that state could no longer oppose the bridging of the upper Ohio. Despite the opposition of Tom Scott, Garrett managed to obtain federal legislation which approved the bridging of the Ohio both at Benwood, to connect with the Ohio Central, and at Parkersburg, to connect with the Marietta and Cincinnati. By 1865, both bridge projects were well along in the planning stage, and Garrett was ready to order stone from nearby quarries. In the late war years, Garrett was making his first moves with railroads west of Columbus, Ohio, looking toward a connecting rail service to Chicago. During 1865 Garrett was also making plans and starting surveys for two branch lines at the eastern end of the Main Stem. The shortest of the two new lines was the branch to Hagerstown, twenty-five miles north of Harpers Ferry. This line, opened late in 1867 and known for a time as the Washington County Railway, was a defensive effort against the Western Maryland Railroad. The second new route was the Metropolitan branch, which would connect Washington with the Main Stem at Point of Rocks. The Metropolitan branch would not be completed until early in the next decade.

Fortunately, both for the Baltimore and Ohio and the Union war effort, the Washington branch remained in operation throughout the four years of the Civil War. The forty-mile Washington branch made up more than one-sixth of the vital 225-mile rail route from New York City to Washington. Like its connecting lines to the north, the Washington branch saw a great increase in traffic, both freight and passenger, during the four-year conflict. In the late fifties, often a single daily B&O freight train of no more than ten cars satisfied the rail freight needs of the nation's capital. After the coming of war, there was a tremendous increase, with some days seeing as many as 200 freight cars arriving in Washington. The annual freight revenue on the Washington branch increased from $101,000 in 1860 to $334,000 in 1862. Between 1861 and 1865, the passenger revenue on the forty-mile route more than doubled, climbing from $327,000 to $747,000.

Naturally there were late trains, slow deliveries, and missed connections. As the complaints increased, it was easy for congressmen and other federal officials to listen, since so many of them frequently used the rail route in and out of Washington. During the four years, several efforts were made to have the government build a new "air line" route from Washington to New York City. When the first such proposals were made, Simon Cameron, no friend of John Garrett, was among the early advocates. Garrett pointed out that such a new railroad would take years to build and could not be completed before the end of the conflict. Garrett and the other railroad presidents to the northeast promised to double-track the entire route and to improve and increase the equipment available. The B&O yards at Relay were enlarged and the entire Washington branch had double track before the end of 1864. None of the bills to build a new rail route to New York were approved and private ownership prevailed. In January 1865, President Lincoln himself wrote Garrett concerning the delivery of more coal to Washington: "It is said we shall soon be all in the dark here, unless *you can* bring coal to make gas. . . . I only write now to say *it is very important to us*; and not to say you must *stop* supplying the army to make room to carry coal. Do all you can for us in *both matters.*"16 The B&O president managed to get some coal down to Washington. Garrett was buying coal for B&O locomotives at the mine for eighty-five cents per ton, while retail coal delivered in Baltimore sometimes sold for as much as ten dollars to twelve dollars per ton.

John Garrett had some fairly serious problems during the war right in Baltimore. In the fall of 1862, John Lee Chapman was elected mayor of Baltimore and reelected twice for a total tenure of six years. Chapman represented the "public interests" in the continuing struggle for dominance between the private and public stockholders and the directors of the B&O. Representing the citizens of Baltimore who resented the growing transportation monopoly which the B&O had in the city and the state, Chapman often favored the small and struggling Western Maryland over the older and larger line. Chapman and Garrett also had some political differences. Chapman was an unconditional Unionist in sympathy with radical Republican doctrines, while Garrett was a former Democrat who had only recently become a conservative Unionist. Chapman's appointees on the B&O board frequently desired stronger loyalty oaths for B&O employees than those set up by Garrett. Chapman also sided with Tom Scott in the matter of the Pittsburgh and Connellsville. In 1865, the mayor charged Garrett with financial mismanagement, charges which the B&O president successfully answered.

In 1862 the B&O 30 percent extra dividend certificates, which had been issued earlier, matured giving the city of Baltimore more than 10,000 additional shares of stock. This gave the city four additional directors for a total of twelve. The dozen city directors plus the ten from the state outnumbered the twelve private directors by nearly two to one. President Garrett stayed calm, retained the general support of most board members, and was reelected president each year. During 1864 and 1865, the railroad succeeded in having most of the 10,000 shares of extra dividend stock held by the city placed on the open market, much of it being purchased by the Garrett family. By 1866 the board members representing Baltimore had dropped back to the earlier number of eight.

The Civil War brought prosperity as well as destruction to the Baltimore and Ohio. Both passenger and freight revenue greatly increased between 1861 and 1865, passenger receipts increasing more than fourfold in the four years and freight revenue climbing nearly threefold. However, the 1861 revenue, partly because of the destruction caused by Stonewall Jackson, was much below that of the previous years. During each of the seven years, 1854 through 1860, the B&O revenue was higher than that of 1861. In fact, the total 1862 revenue was slightly below that of the best year of the fifties, 1857. The drop in traffic was in freight rather than passenger. The 1861 passenger revenue set an all time record, but not until 1863 did the B&O freight revenue top the record year of 1857. As noted earlier, the traffic and revenue on the Washington branch also greatly expanded during the war. On the 104-mile Northwestern Virginia Railroad, the total annual revenue more than doubled during the war, climbing from $350,000 in 1861 to $759,000 in 1865. Each year the revenue was slightly higher than the operating expenses.

TABLE 8. Baltimore and Ohio Traffic and Financial Growth of Main Stem 1861–65

Year	Passenger Receipts	Freight Receipts	Total Receipts	Expenses	Net Receipts
1861	$ 887,159	$2,324,267	$ 3,211,426	$1,391,095	$1,820,331
1862	1,769,497	2,712,362	4,481,859	1,427,206	3,054,653
1863	2,332,806	4,177,139	6,509,945	1,965,847	4,544,098
1864	3,250,307	5,327,385	8,577,692	3,270,509	5,307,183
1865	3,997,642	6,099,064	10,096,706	5,658,722	4,437,984

The net receipts on the Main Stem were sufficient for the B&O to declare dividends each of the war years. Dividends of 6 percent per year were paid in 1861, 1862, and 1863. They were increased to 7 percent in 1864 and 8 percent for 1865. The balance sheets of liabilities and assets during the war years indicated a marked increase in the total investment in the B&O, climbing from $31,639,000 in 1861 to $43,083,000 in 1865. Much of this increase was caused by the 30 percent stock dividend which had been made in 1862 and investments in the securities of other railroads made by President Garrett during the Civil War years.

Certainly not all of the great increase in traffic and revenue between 1861 and 1865 was caused just by the war. Poor crops in Europe in the early sixties increased the demand for western farm produce, providing extra traffic for all the trunk lines. Part of the revenue increase was, of course, caused by wartime inflation. During the war years, civilian travel increased at the same time that troop mobilization created increased passenger traffic. Troop movements were heavy on many lines, but, overall, military passengers made up a small percentage of the total passenger traffic. An exception to this would, of course, be the heavy troop traffic over the Washington branch. Probably the heaviest troop movement over the B&O was during the weeks of demobilization after the collapse of the Confederacy and the national reviews of the armies of Grant and Sherman in Washington, D.C., in the last days of May 1865. In the weeks after these mammoth parades, a daily average of more than 4,000 troops moved out of Washington over the Washington branch. Record days were 13,943 shipped out on June 5, and 13,935 on June 7. In seven weeks, over 208,000 troops traveled over the Baltimore and Ohio. The passenger revenue on the Washington branch for June 1865, was a record $101,232, about twice a normal month in 1865.

Early in the war, the Baltimore and Ohio charged the government 3.75 cents per mile for troop movement and between 5 and 8 cents per ton-mile for freight. As expected, Secretary of War Cameron claimed that such rates were excessive. In February 1862, the Baltimore and Ohio was one of six railroads which presented transportation bills to the government in excess of $100,000. During the course of the war, the fares and rates were changed, but the general trend was upward. Between 1860 and 1865, freight rates on the trunk lines moved up about 50 percent, along with the general wartime inflation.

John Garrett's railroad was one of the first to play a major role in the four-year long conflict. Even though the line's location in slave states near the battle front caused her to be frequently under attack, her strategic position meant that she was of immense value throughout the war to the Union cause. As the war ended, the optimistic President Garrett was looking more to the future than to the problems of the past. He was thinking of new routes to the west and of the four first-class steamers purchased from the government which would allow the inauguration of ocean service between Baltimore and Liverpool. His reference to the four-year conflict in the last paragraph of the 1865 *Annual Report* was one of understatement: "The Board again acknowledge with satisfaction their appreciation of the vigor, skill, and fidelity of the officers and men in each department of the service, by which the business of the Company was successfully conducted during periods of frequent danger and embarrassment."[17]

Chapter VIII

• • • • • • • • • • • • • • •

President Garrett Faces Postwar Problems

AT THE END OF THE CIVIL WAR, PRESIDENT JOHN WORK Garrett was firmly in control of his railroad. In the late fall of 1865, Garrett was reelected for the seventh time to the presidency of the Baltimore and Ohio. In this election, one of the city directors nominated John Lee Chapman, long time political foe of Garrett, for the presidency. Garrett easily won the election, with only one vote cast in opposition. In subsequent years, Garrett was returned to office, generally by a unanimous vote. His long tenure in the president's chair—nearly twenty-six years—until his death at the age of sixty-four on September 26, 1884, was exceeded only by the thirty-one years of Daniel Willard, 1910–41.

Garrett had come to the presidency in the fall of 1858 as still a fairly young man of thirty-eight. He knew the Baltimore commission business, and was well versed in the banking and financial affairs of his city, but still much of a neophyte in the management of a large and expanding railway. The difficult years of the Civil War had done much to improve the polish of the railroad president. In the postwar sixties and early seventies, the urbane and portly Garrett was confident of the future of his growing railroad and quite certain of his own political skill both with his subordinates in his

119

company and with the political leaders of his city and state. Physically a large man he generally gave the impression both of a determination and a vigor that were steady and methodical. At times he was autocratic, but those close to him knew him as a kindly and often affectionate man.

During Garrett's more than a quarter of a century in the president's chair, the extent of his railroad greatly increased. In 1858 the gross earnings of the 379-mile Main Stem, with its few short branches, was just over $4 million. In 1884, his last year in office, the B&O, the Main Stem with its branches, produced gross revenues of about $11,500,000. In that year, the total B&O system—lines owned, leased, and operated—amounted to nearly 1,700 miles with gross revenues of $19,400,000 and an operating ratio of just over 60 percent. These years were also years of a very substantial reduction both in freight rates and passenger fares.

Garrett's railroad in 1884 did not match either the New York Central or the Pennsylvania in total revenue or total investment and assets. But this is not surprising. After all, Baltimore was not New York City, the major terminal of the New York Central. Nor was Garrett in any way a match for J. Edgar Thomson and Thomas A. Scott, the masters of the Pennsylvania in these years.

But all three of these major trunk lines, plus most other rail lines as well, were enjoying a golden age of growth and general prosperity in the long generation after the Civil War. In the years before the war, each of the three lines had basically served, and been quite subservient to, one of the three rival Atlantic seaports—Baltimore, Philadelphia, or New York. As each road pushed its subordinate connecting lines well west of the Appalachians to Chicago, St. Louis, and other growing cities of the Midwest, these eastern seaports could no longer expect to fully control the actions and goals of the railways they had earlier sponsored and supported.

The iron network expanded across the nation at a rapid rate, increasing from 35,000 miles in 1865 to 53,000 in 1870, and 93,000 miles in 1880. During the eighties, 71,000 more miles were built, with 1887 seeing an all time high of 12,878 miles of new construction. As traffic grew, more powerful locomotives were built to pull longer trains of heavier and larger cars. A host of technical advances in rail service also appeared in the postwar years. Maj. Eli H. Janney received a patent for his automatic coupler in 1868, and in 1869, George Westinghouse, at the age of twenty-two, applied for a patent for his air brake. Improvements and the general use of these two inventions in subsequent years greatly aided the safety of the work of railroad brakemen. In the same years, steel rail replaced iron, locomotive fuel shifted completely from wood to coal, fast freight lines appeared, and improved signaling increased the safety of all train movement. In the decade of the 1880s, "standard time" was adopted by the railroads of the nation, the last railroads in the country—those in the South—changed their track from five-foot to standard gauge, and the first passenger trains received steam heat and electric lights.

But even during the golden age of railroading after the Civil War, most railroad presidents faced serious and difficult problems in the management and administration of their companies. John W. Garrett was no exception. Throughout the postwar sixties and seventies, the Baltimore and Ohio president faced problems concerning the establishment and maintenance of railroad rates. A second major problem appeared with the decline in revenues caused by the long depression which followed the Panic of 1873. Finally, Garrett was plagued by the violence of the Railroad Strike of 1877 which had started on his own railroad.

The problem of railroad rates and fares was certainly not unique to the Baltimore and Ohio. In the early years of railroading when lines were few and most cities were served by only a single railroad, the presidents and their traffic managers had a rather free hand in the setting of rates. This changed with the rapid rail construction in the 1850s, which soon saw major cities served by two or more competing railroads. Once the major trunk lines to the west had reached the Ohio River or Lake Erie in the early fifties, the four rival lines started to quarrel over feeder lines, freight rates, and the size of their respective traffic regions. The Erie fought with the New York Central for the lake traffic, while the Pennsylvania and the B&O each tried to claim and keep the lion's share of the river traffic on the upper Ohio. The competition for traffic and the rate wars which ensued were basically unregulated, since federal regulation would not appear until late in the century, and state railroad commissions, where they existed, were weak and ineffective.

In the last decades of the nineteenth century, freight rates were perhaps the major source of railroad abuses and difficulties. The very complexity of the subject magnified the problem. One contemporary expert believed there might be as many as 15,000 different principles involved in the total movement of railroad freight across the nation. Such a figure is no doubt an exaggeration, but as one thinks of rail traffic flow consisting of an almost infinite variety of items carried by dozens of different railroads between thousands of towns, any simple solution that would equally satisfy the shipper, the railroad, and the general public seemed to be utterly impossible. By the last decades of the century, a vast array of different theories of rate making had appeared: flat rate by distance, flat rate regardless of distance, cost of the service, what the traffic will bear, value of the commodity, value of the service, keep everybody in business, and the general public interest.

Quite naturally, railroad officials favored charging as much as the traffic would bear. Some rail officials claimed that "charging all they could" still was not enough. Most rates were placed somewhere above the out-of-pocket cost to the carrier and somewhat below the top value of the service to the shipper. Normally, the final rate was determined by the conditions of competition, the value of the commodity, and the importance of the movement to the general public. Many of the railroad rates in effect in the decades after the Civil War seemed unfair, and rate discrimination of at least three types existed: between classes of freight, between places, and between persons. Certainly there was nothing wrong in charging more for some commodities than others—ladies' hats or groceries could easily pay a higher rate, by weight, than goods such as grain, coal, or lumber. Discrimination by place often arose from the fact that nature itself had discriminated by giving the river town the advantages of cheap water transport or by locating one farmer's elevator one thousand miles farther from the Chicago grain market than that of another farmer. Except for lower rates given for quantity shipments, there is no justification for rate discrimination between persons. Such special rates, including rebates, were generally made secretly.

The variety of freight rate schedules far exceeded the number of theories and principles of rate making. Traffic managers who made up freight rates first divided the hundreds of different items moving by rail into major classifications on a basis of the value and bulk of the commodity. Next, rate schedules were prepared for each class of freight between all points of shipment with consideration given both to distance and terminal costs. In the trunk line region, the heaviest traffic was between such western points as St. Louis or Chicago and New York City. Often, the Chicago to New York City rates were drawn up first. Since the rail distance from Chicago to Philadelphia and from Chicago to Baltimore was somewhat shorter than the New York Central and Erie routes to New York City, both the Pennsylvania and the B&O felt that they should be permitted to charge lower rates for freight moving to the seaboard.

The complexity of making freight rates was compounded by the fact that several different railroads were often used in moving freight to its destination. Shippers sending goods from Chicago or

St. Louis to New York City or Baltimore had their choice of several routes of varying lengths. The proper division of the total rate among the two or more lines carrying the freight required that the concerned traffic managers have skill both in mathematics and diplomacy. Rate making in the trunk line region was also faced with the problem of often sharing the traffic with steamers on the Great Lakes or the stern-wheelers of the Ohio River. The basic lower rates of water carriage, plus seasonal variations in the closing of the waterways, naturally led to rate disagreements among the several trunk line railroads.

Even before the Civil War, the four major trunk lines found it necessary to meet together to iron out their differences and disputes concerning freight rates. One of the first trunk line conventions was held at the Saint Nicholas Hotel in New York City in 1854. At that time, several eastern railroad presidents, including William G. Harrison of the Baltimore and Ohio, J. Edgar Thomson of the Pennsylvania, and Erastus Corning of the New York Central, sought to reach an equitable agreement on freight rates. After the Civil War, John W. Garrett represented his railroad at many such meetings. In postwar years, the favorite meeting ground in New York City was the Brevoort House. Other neutral locations for such peace-making sessions were the Girard House in Philadelphia, the International Hotel in Niagara Falls, or the long broad veranda of the United States Hotel at Saratoga in upstate New York.

There were several rate wars among the trunk line railroads in the postwar years, most of them in the dozen years following the Panic of 1873. The rate wars were so frequent in the 1870s that the editors of the *Commericial and Financial Chronicle* claimed that they recurred as often as "small pox or the change of seasons."[1] But the four longest and major rate wars were: (1) January 1874 to December 1875; (2) April 1876 to April 1877; (3) June 1881 to January 1882; and (4) March 1884 to November 1885. An earlier conflict over rates between the B&O and the Pennsylvania occurred in 1867 when J. Edgar Thomson and the Pennsylvania became angered at Garrett's insistence in trying to complete a B&O branch line from Cumberland to Pittsburgh.

Once a rate war started, each road answered its competitor with lower rates of its own. Soon the collapse of rates was nearly total. In 1874 the normal rate from Chicago to New York was forty-five cents for 100 pounds of fourth-class freight. Within two months, the rate had dropped to thirty cents. In a later rate war, the rate was down to twenty cents, and in the mideighties it was as low as ten cents. Chicago to New York passenger fares which were nineteen dollars in 1874 soon dropped to nine dollars, and for a short time in 1884 westbound immigrants could travel the 1,000 miles to the West for as little as one dollar per person. Comparable rate reductions were made by the Baltimore and Ohio and the Pennsylvania for their long-haul traffic in and out of Baltimore and Philadelphia. The Baltimore and Ohio, like other lines, was generally guilty of maintaining, or even boosting, its short-haul local rates during a rate war.

In 1874 the Baltimore and Ohio was completing its branch west to Chicago. The appearance of another trunk line to the East was hailed by the farmers of the upper Midwest, and the B&O was viewed as the Granger's friend. President Garrett declared that once his line to Chicago was open he would, like the biblical Samson, pull down the temple of high freight rates upon the heads of rival carriers. This attitude by the B&O led to retaliation by the other trunk lines carriers, and the result was another rate war. While B&O revenues were hurt by the rate war, Garrett, in his 1875 *Annual Report*, only referred to the conflict as "prolonged attacks of the great trunk lines upon the business and interests of the Baltimore and Ohio Company, during which time rates entirely unremunerative were established for the transportation of freight."[2]

In the competition between the several trunk lines, the New York Central was most reluctant to allow the Pennsylvania or the Baltimore and Ohio to lower the Chicago to seaboard rates simply because Philadelphia and Baltimore were closer to Chicago than was New York City. Commodore Cornelius Vanderbilt and his son, William H., liked to claim that the water level route of the New York Central, with its lower grades and easier curves, easily compensated for the shorter distance claimed by the B&O. In September 1876, John Garrett told his B&O board that the New York Central was overlooking "the fact that on the Baltimore & Ohio line for three hundred miles coal literally crops out immediately on our roads, and thus the company has in the competitive economy of fuel alone a difference which more than compensates for the difference in grades and curves."[3]

Eventually all the rate wars were ended by some conference or new agreement reached by the trunk line presidents, or their agents, at meetings held in New York City at the Brevoort House or upstate at Saratoga. Such agreements or pool arrangements were always fragile things easily broken and violated. Any marked downturn in business was a real temptation for one of the trunk lines to endeavor to gain additional traffic by cutting a rate earlier agreed upon. A new disturbing factor was the Grand Trunk, a fifth trunk line which was a weak road, often on the verge of

Two Perkins ten-wheelers and passenger train near Rowlesburg, West Virginia, in 1875.
(Courtesy, Smithsonian Institution)

insolvency. Any bankrupt line, or one in receivership, could cut rates more readily, since it was relieved, for the time being at least, of paying interest on its bonds and dividends on its stock. The editors of Poor's *Manual of the Railroads of the United States* noted this fact when they wrote: "Railroads, unfortunately, seem to reverse the rule of the 'survival of the fittest' to the 'survival of the unfittest' . . . when they go into the hands of receivers, they are to run so long as operating expenses can be paid."[4]

The most important agreement reached by the trunk line railroads in these years was that reached in the spring of 1877, which resulted in the formation of the group often called the "Trunk Line Association." Col. Albert Fink, for several years the vice president of the Louisville and Nashville and later the general commissioner of the Southern Railway and Steamship Association (a pool of southern railroads), was made the top executive officer of the trunk lines joint executive committee. Colonel Fink served as the final arbiter of disputes and often was spoken of as the "Caesar" or "Napoleon" of the new organization. The general agreement of 1877 did accept the principle that both Philadelphia and Baltimore should be permitted slightly lower rates than New York City for long-haul traffic to and from Chicago. The general provisions of the 1877 rate agreement concerning trunk line traffic were to remain in effect during most of the remaining years of the nineteenth century.

Shippers, farmers, and railroad patrons, in the short run at least, enjoyed the lower freight rates and passenger fares which appeared with every new rate war. But most businessmen were disturbed by the rather constant fluctuation of rates as rate agreements were so quickly followed by new rate wars. However, they did benefit from the fact that after each rate war the new higher stabilized rates were normally down a bit from the "normal" rates which had prevailed before the last rate conflict. In the generation after the Civil War, average freight rates across the nation dropped by more than 50 percent, declining from something over 2 cents a ton-mile at the end of the Civil War to about 0.75 cents per ton-mile by 1900. This reduction was a more rapid decline than the fall of prices in the general price structure. Much of the rate decline was the direct result of the increasing efficiency—steel rail, larger cars, longer trains, and heavier, more powerful engines. While the per ton-mile revenue of the average line was dropping, the total rail traffic was growing much faster than the increase in population. The per capita annual freight service in the nation increased from about 285 ton-miles in 1867 to more than 1,200 ton-miles in 1890. The Baltimore and Ohio experienced the decline in average freight rates, the growth of a new rail efficiency, and also the massive increase in the total freight traffic and revenue.

John Garrett and the B&O were very slow to adopt and use one recent innovation in improved freight service, the "fast freight line." In 1866 Garrett told a committee of the Ohio senate that fast freight lines were injurious to the public and expensive and corrupting to railroad companies. In a fast freight line, a transportation company, separate and apart from any railroad, provided cars which were run over the lines of several railroads with schedules faster than normal. Each participating railroad received either a flat fee or a percentage of the total freight charge. The cars used in such service were often equipped with "compromise" or adjustable wheels allowing them to run over tracks of more than one gauge. While the fast freight service avoided delays at transfer points and arrived at their final destination without breaking bulk, the system was subject to abuses. Often railroad officials formed the fast freight lines, made contracts with themselves, and obtained an extra unfair profit.

The first fast freight lines appeared before the Civil War with the Merchant's Dispatch serving the New York Central, the Great Western Dispatch operating over the Erie, and the Star Union Line running over the tracks of Thomson's Pennsylvania. After the Civil War, many of the earlier abuses were eliminated with the appearance of the cooperative fast freight lines in which several railroads provided the service. Garrett still was slow to provide such a service. Finally, in 1871, the Baltimore and Ohio established the Continental Fast Freight Line, a cooperative line running over the Baltimore and Ohio, the Marietta and Cincinnati, and the Ohio and Mississippi to give direct service between Baltimore and St. Louis. By this time, the new bridge over the Ohio at Parkersburg had been completed, and the Ohio and Mississippi had altered its gauge from six feet to four feet nine inches.

President Garrett was firmly in control of the Baltimore and Ohio policy during the numerous rate wars in the years after the Civil War. Shortly after the end of the conflict, Garrett's brother Henry, two years older than John, died after a short illness of typhoid fever. John had always placed a strong reliance upon his brother and now missed his frequent advice and counsel. Increasingly, the B&O president now turned to the B&O vice president, John King, Jr. King, a cousin of the Garretts, was the first person to occupy this new position, newly created in December 1866. For several years, King had been the general freight agent and company auditor. King was elected a member of the board of directors in 1871, a position he held for ten years. Soon John Garrett was leaving more and more administrative detail to King in order to give his first attention to top company policy.

Garrett's second major problem in the postwar years—the Panic of 1873 and the following depression—had naturally helped trigger much of the rate cutting that appeared in the middle seventies. The Panic of 1873 followed several years of rapid and hectic growth and expansion. Much of the expansion was in railroads. Between 1865 and 1873, the iron and steel network had doubled in extent, growing from 35,000 to 70,000 miles of line. Each postwar year revealed new track laying records with a peak reached in 1871, when more than 7,300 miles of new line were completed. Shippers, farmers, manufacturers, and merchants all were eager for more railroad mileage. But much of the new construction was in the West, out beyond the frontier, where operations on the newly built lines would be carried on with red ink for several years at least. But most Americans saw the railroad—the nation's major consumer of timber, coal, steel, and foreign investments—as the road to prosperity and future growth. Included in the new mileage built in the early postwar years was the nearly 1,800 miles of the two lines to the Pacific, the Union Pacific and the Central Pacific, which celebrated their completion on May 10, 1869, with the driving of the Golden Spike out on the Utah desert.

An attempt to build a second road to the Pacific in the early seventies helped trigger the Panic of 1873. Jay Cooke, the pious and patriotic Philadelphia banker who had helped the Union government finance the Civil War, took over the management of the Northern Pacific Railroad in 1869 and started to finance the construction of the line across the bleak prairies of Minnesota and North Dakota. The nearly 500 miles of line built out to Bismarck, North Dakota, by 1873 strained Cooke's financial resources and his bank closed its doors on September 18, 1873. The news that one of the strongest banks in the nation had failed was so unbelievable that a newsboy hawking an extra about the failure of Jay Cooke was arrested by an incredulous police officer. Other banks also quickly closed their doors. The New York Stock Exchange was closed for ten days. President U. S. Grant, and his Secretary of the Treasury William Adams Richardson, rushed to New York City to confer with Commodore Vanderbilt and other financiers. President Grant remarked that the nation's first need was "a week of Sundays."[5] But more drastic measures than a calendar change were to be required. The federal treasury released 13 million greenbacks for the purchase of government bonds. Bankruptcies became commonplace as factories shut down and business came to a standstill. Before long there were more than 5,000 commercial failures across the nation.

During the long ensuing depression, eighty-nine railways defaulted on their bonds including the Union Pacific, the Kansas Pacific, the Jersey Central, and the Chesapeake and Ohio. However, of the four major trunk lines, only the Erie was forced into receivership.

The financial condition of Garrett's railroad in the early postwar years was generally rated excellent. While the share of the capital structure that was in bonds was higher than for either the Pennsylvania or the New York Central, Garrett had experienced no difficulty at all in promptly selling sterling bonds through the Baring Brothers in London. Baltimore and Ohio stock in the early postwar years was well above the figure of $50 to $60 per share common in the prewar years. By 1867 and 1868, it was ranging from $112 to $130 and went still higher in the early seventies. Annual dividends which were 8 percent after the war rose to 10 percent in 1872 and continued at that level even after the Panic of 1873.

Many financial experts much preferred the "sound" management of Garrett to the stock-watering activities of Commodore Vanderbilt or the railroad piracy of Jay Gould. In the spring of 1871, the editors of the *American Railroad Journal* wrote of the good and honest management of Garrett, and in the fall of 1872, they wrote: "Mr. Garrett has shown that scrupulous regard for his promises for which he is distinguished and which has given him so honorable a position among the great railroad kings of the day." Some Midwestern railroad leaders were not so friendly. William H.Osborn, former sturdy president of the Illinois Central wrote of the B&O and Garrett: "I made up my mind as to John W. Garrett 25 years ago [i.e., the late 1850s] and have given them a wide berth. . . . They will get very cold comfort from this individual."[6]

By the early seventies, the large holdings of B&O stock held by Garrett permitted him to enjoy life a bit more. In addition to his fine town house at 50 Mount Vernon Place, in 1870 Garrett purchased about 1,400 acres of land a few miles northeast of the center of the city, where he built a country home he named Montebello. In addition to the mansion, the estate included gardens, a greenhouse, and barns and stables filled with registered shorthorn cattle and fine Arabian horses. Both of Garrett's sons, Robert and Harry, had graduated from Princeton in the late sixties and were married and well established by the early seventies. Robert, the elder brother, succeeded the Confederate hero, Robert E. Lee, as the president of the Valley Railroad, a short Virginia line controlled by the Baltimore and Ohio. The other brother, Harry, had entered a banking house.

President Garrett was in Europe when the panic started. The long years of busy rail management finally had taken their toll on John Garrett's robust physique. When, in the early months of 1873, the fifty-two-year-old Garrett complained of extreme fatigue and occasional dizziness, his doctors strongly urged an extended trip to Europe to restore the health of the ailing railroad executive. Garrett offered to resign the presidency before his departure, but the board refused, agreeing instead that vice president John King should be president pro tem during Garrett's absence. In July 1873, Garrett, accompanied by his wife and daughter, sailed on the North German Lloyd Steamer *Berlin* for Southhampton. Once in England, Garrett found time to visit London where he easily placed £1 million of B&O 6 percent, three-year bonds at a price of 96-1/2. This was a fortunate event since the loan was completed only three weeks before panic struck American banks.

TABLE 9. Entire Baltimore and Ohio System Traffic and Financial Growth 1866–78

Year	Main Stem			Entire B&O System			
	Total Receipts	Net Revenue	Expenses to Earnings (%)	Miles of Road	Total Receipts	Net Revenue	Expenses to Earnings (%)
1866	$ 7,702,229	$3,222,039	58	521	$ 8,698,425	$3,462,560	60
1867	7,442,684	3,066,418	59	521	8,340,409	3,349,054	60
1868	7,558,645	2,504,196	67	521	8,472,217	2,292,106	73
1869	8,724,916	2,968,809	66	521	9,672,873	3,087,745	68
1870	8,427,728	2,974,268	64	588	10,840,370	3,332,737	69
1871	9,913,390	4,006,502	59	630	12,257,528	4,559,354	63
1872	10,654,472	4,532,072	57	902	13,626,617	5,259,201	61
1873	12,252,844	4,934,796	60	974	15,693,198	5,551,575	65
1874	11,693,955	5,018,060	58	1,166	14,947,090	5,485,438	64
1875	10,514,179	4,643,612	59	1,314	14,444,239	4,535,574	69
1876	9,632,361	4,561,990	56	1,430	15,031,236	5,421,379	64
1877	8,262,045	3,779,931	56	1,473	13,208,860	4,982,805	62
1878	8,563,957	4,039,612	53	1,499	13,765,280	5,995,979	56

In the weeks of September and October 1873, Garrett in Europe and King in Baltimore were in frequent communication by cable and letter. Garrett expressed only modest alarm at the banking crisis back home and felt the stormy financial weather would wreck the weaker lines, while allowing stronger companies to endure. When John King urged his return to Baltimore, Garrett replied: "Reduce purchases to judicious minimum, using materials closely. Cease buying engines. . . . Reduce constructing cars to company's economical capacity. . . . Maintain revenues granting safe indulgences. . . . Panic must be brief country being sound."[7]

Naturally, the absent Garrett was unanimously reelected president with the board strongly urging his acceptance. While resting on the shores of Lake Geneva in Switzerland, Garrett wrote the company's *Annual Report* for 1873. Later the family toured Italy, France, Germany, and Holland before returning to America in the late fall of 1874. The well-rested Garrett would soon face fresh problems at home.

The Panic of 1873 did not bring receivership to the Baltimore and Ohio like that suffered by the Erie in 1874, but nevertheless the railroad suffered substantial losses of traffic and revenue.

The early postwar traffic on the Baltimore and Ohio was much below the level of the last years of the Civil War. The total revenue for the year 1865 exceeded $10 million on the Main Stem and more than $11.7 million for the entire system. For Main Stem traffic, only 1872 through 1875 had revenues larger than those of 1865. There was a gradual pickup in revenue in the late sixties and then a marked increase in 1871, 1872, and 1873. The depression following the Panic of 1873 lasted about five years, but a marked improvement appeared in 1878 with 1879 and 1880 showing still greater gains. The low point in gross revenue for the entire system came in 1877, while the lowest net revenue occurred two years earlier in 1875. Throughout the thirteen years, the bulk of the revenue was developed on the Main Stem. The traffic on the Washington branch also declined with the end of the Civil War; the revenue of $425,000 in 1866 was only about half of that of the previous year. By 1872 annual revenue on the line to Washington rose to about $480,000, but soon declined modestly with the completion of the competing Pennsylvania line into the nation's capital. As in the past, the passenger revenue on the Washington branch was several times as large as that of freight.

TABLE 10. Main Stem Passenger and Freight Revenue 1866–78

	Passenger Revenue	Freight Revenue
1866	$1,635,000	$6,067,000
1867	1,671,000	5,772,000
1868	1,451,000	6,107,000
1869	1,247,000	7,999,000
1870	1,477,000	6,950,000
1871	1,161,000	8,452,000
1872	1,695,000	8,959,000
1873	1,593,000	10,659,000
1874	1,518,000	10,175,000
1875	1,613,000	8,901,000
1876	1,674,000	7,958,000
1877	1,365,000	6,897,000
1878	1,201,000	7,363,000

On the Main Stem and the rest of the system, freight traffic was four to five times as great as passenger. During the postwar years, freight traffic across the nation grew more rapidly than the passenger traffic. This trend had been developing for some time. Back in the 1830s and 1840s, passenger traffic and revenue was larger than that of freight on many railroads. On the 9,000 miles of railway in the nation in 1851, passenger revenue and freight revenue were nearly equal: $19.3 million passenger and $20.2 million freight. By 1877 freight traffic on the 79,000-mile national rail network was well ahead of passenger traffic: $361 million freight and $120 million passenger.

Traffic in all the major items of freight increased on the Main Stem between 1866 and 1878: livestock from 35,000 to 133,000 tons; lumber from 16,000 to 41,000 tons; flour from 640,000 to 778,000 barrels; and coal from 710,000 to 1,129,000 tons. The increase in coal traffic in these years was proportionately less than that for livestock and lumber. This slow growth in the coal traffic was even more surprising since total soft coal production in the nation had nearly tripled, from 13 million tons in 1867 to 36 million tons in 1878. Of course additional coal was also carried over the Pittsburgh and Trans-Ohio divisions. In his *Annual Report* for 1878, John W. Garrett blamed the poor coal traffic on the depression which followed the Panic of 1873.

But there were other reasons for the slow growth of the coal traffic on the Main Stem. In the middle 1870s, the B&O still had the same mileage in West Virginia that it had been operating twenty years earlier—the original line to Wheeling and the second line from Grafton west to Parkersburg. A new coal-bearing line had appeared in West Virginia in the early 1870s, the Chesapeake and Ohio. The first president of the Chesapeake and Ohio was Gen. William C. Wickham, an ex-Confederate cavalry officer from Richmond. Wickham was anxious to build the C&O into West Virginia with an extension running from Covington, Virginia, west to the Ohio River, but he could find no adequate financial backing either in Virginia or in Europe.

Wickham next turned to New York City and was soon negotiating with a group led by the Connecticut Yankee from California, Collis P. Huntington. Fresh from his laurels of building the Central Pacific, Huntington proposed to build and equip the 200-mile extension with $15 million of new capital from the banks of New York City. Huntington soon replaced Wickham as president of the Chesapeake and Ohio. Using money borrowed from the New York banking firm of Fisk and Hatch, Huntington employed up to 7,000 men at a time in pushing the new line across and through the mountains to the new Ohio River town of Huntington, West Virginia. On the way, vast and rich coal deposits were discovered in West Virginia. C&O officials drove the final spike January 29, 1873, completing the 428-mile line from Richmond to Huntington. The cost of building the new transmountain line to the Ohio had been high, but soon much West Virginia coal was moving eastward over the C&O. In 1877 more than half of the 2,154 Chesapeake and Ohio freight cars were used for the haulage of coal. In the same year, Garrett's B&O was operating 2,694 gondola cars and 2,868 coal cars out of a total roster of 11,425 freight cars.

In the postwar years, the B&O traffic men were also soliciting items of freight other than coal, lumber, livestock, and flour. In the spring of 1869, George R. Blanchard, the general freight agent, wrote to Henry du Pont's powder works up in Wilmington, Delaware: "We will receive powder on our cars [carload lots of 16,000 pounds] at Locust Point. . . . The rate Locust Point to Wheeling is one dollar and forty cents per 100 pounds."[8] Later Blanchard cut the rate to $1.25 per hundred pounds.

During the seventies, John Garrett extended his system to Pittsburgh, to Columbus, and then on to Chicago. However, the increased revenue from the extended system was quite modest, and even after the B&O was extended to Chicago, the Main Stem was still producing about two-thirds of the total revenue. Some of the extensions developed very small net revenues, and the Parkersburg branch even had deficits in five years between 1866 and 1878.

Riding over the B&O system in his business car, Garrett was constantly seeking out new ways to cut costs, increase efficiency, and avoid unnecessary expenditures. Once near the western end of the line, he poked his cane through a rotten plank in a depot platform. At once he upbraided the nearby master of transportation about the possibility of a personal injury lawsuit. Garrett's diligent pursuit of economy helped keep the expenses to revenue ratio or "operating ratio" low in these years. Quite naturally the operating ratio on the Main Stem was lower than on the rest of the system. Any reduction in yearly revenue seemed to challenge Garrett to be even more ruthless in his cost cutting. In the five years 1874–78, he managed to further reduce the operating ratio both on the Main Stem and the system at large.

The low operating ratio on his railroad helped Garrett maintain his good dividend record. The 8 percent dividend of the late sixties was increased to 9 percent in 1872 and to 10 percent in 1873. Garrett continued the high rate of 10 percent even though the depression worsened in the middle seventies. In the early summer

Thatcher Perkins, built at Mount Clare Shops for passenger service during the Civil War. *(Courtesy, Association of American Railroads)*

of 1877, Junius Morgan, Garrett's banker in London and the father of J. Pierpont Morgan, urged Garrett to reduce his dividend rate, especially since the Baltimore and Ohio had a large floating debt—reported to be more than $8 million. Garrett ignored the advice from London. There could be no doubt that the debt structure of the B&O had greatly increased during the decade of the seventies. According to *Poor's Manual of Railroads, 1879* the funded debt of the company had increased from $11 million in 1871 to $19 million in 1873, $32 million in 1875, and $39 million in 1877.

Since the amount of common stock—slightly over $13 million worth—remained constant during these years, the expansion of the system, both in mileage and equipment, had resulted in a much larger funded debt. Certainly the equipment used on the Baltimore and Ohio had greatly increased in the long decade. The 1866 roster of equipment—290 locomotives, 164 passenger cars, and 3,846 freight cars (one-third of which were coal cars)—had grown by 1873 to 473 locomotives, 261 passenger cars, and 10,292 freight cars. With the slump in traffic after the panic, there was also a slower increase in the growth of the equipment roster. By 1877 the total B&O system had an equipment roster of 590 locomotives, 307 passenger cars, and 11,521 freight cars.

Many of the new engines built or acquired after the war were of a design different from the Winans Camels which had been the standard engine in the prewar years. Shortly after the end of the war, the Baltimore and Ohio purchased forty-two United States military locomotives from the federal government. Most of these were 4-4-0 American type engines, with twenty-eight units kept on the B&O and eleven others assigned to the Central Ohio Railroad. John C. Davis, who replaced Thatcher Perkins as master of machinery in 1865, built nearly one hundred Davis Camels, a 4-6-0 locomotive similar to the earlier Hayes and Tyson Ten Wheelers. In 1875 Davis built a new heavier engine, the *J.C. Davis*, designed for passenger service over the steep grades west of Cumberland. The *J. C. Davis*, weighing forty-five tons and designed as a Mogul (2-6-0), was not a sucess in passenger service, but later proved quite effective in freight service. Many more Moguls, as well as the larger Consolidations (2-8-0), were added to the B&O locomotive roster in the seventies and eighties.

The third major problem facing John Garrett in the seventies was the labor violence caused by the railroad strikes of 1877, trouble which started with a labor dispute on Garrett's own line in mid-July 1877. In a sense, the strikes and labor violence in the summer of 1877 directly resulted from the earlier rate wars and the long and deep nation-wide depression which had followed the Panic of 1873. Unlike the earlier problems, the labor violence in mid-1877 was of fairly short duration, with most of the striking railways having resumed normal operations by early August. Even so, an editorial in the *Nation* referred to the 1877 labor violence as "the most extensive and deplorable working men's strike" in the history of the United States.[9]

Between May and November in 1876, some 10 million Americans had visited the Centennial Exposition in Philadelphia, viewed Freedom's Torch of the projected Statue of Liberty and the mammoth Corliss engine, and listened to Alexander Graham Bell's first telephone. They also may have seen an early B&O Grasshopper locomotive which was on exhibit at the exposition. Most visitors left the exhibit grounds with pride in their nation's past and great expectations for its future. But the view was far different for the several million Americans either unemployed or underpaid because of the long and deep depression of the midseventies. Railroad wages were not high in 1876. In that year, the average fireman's yearly wage on the B&O was $421, while a brakeman's annual pay was $493. Engineers and conductors did receive more, but train crewmen with little seniority rarely were fully employed throughout the year. The first three of the big four brotherhoods of operating personnel had been organized—engineers in 1863, conductors in 1868, and firemen and enginemen in 1868—but few railroad executives looked with friendly eyes upon the new unions. John Garrett, like most railroad presidents, believed in the law of supply and demand. In 1876 the B&O president had not ony refused to talk to a grievance committee of firemen, but also had all the men involved discharged on the following day. Earlier in 1865, Garrett had requested and received help from United States troops to break up a strike of trackmen.

Despite Garrett's glowing public statements about the sound financial condition of his company, B&O common stock fell drastically during the first half of 1877. When Garrett, early in the summer of 1877, asked his London banker, Junius Morgan, for another loan, the elder Morgan had urged the B&O president to reduce his dividend rate. Morgan wrote Garrett that it was "either that or something far more disastrous. . . . The storm is upon you."[10] But Garrett had a different solution in mind—a cut in wages. That had been a common practice across the nation since the start of the depression in 1873. President Tom Scott, of the Pennsylvania, late in May 1877, announced a general wage reduction of 10 percent, effective on June 1. Soon many other roads, including the Lehigh, the Lackawanna, the Erie, and the New York Central all followed suit. No serious trouble had followed in the wake of these cuts during the weeks of June and early July. Garrett, on July 11 at a regular directors' meeting, received approval for a 10 percent wage cut for all employees earning more than one dollar per day, to be effective Monday, July 16. This was the second 10 percent cut on the B&O in less than a year. The directors adjourned till mid-September, since most would be away on vacation during August.

In his official statement of the wage cut, Garrett explained that all officials would receive comparable reductions and that the action was due to financial necessity. However, some of his workers had recently read the rosy and optimistic reports given to stockholders as another 10 percent dividend was declared. Some B&O workers were being enticed to join the new Trainmens Union, being organized by Robert A. Ammon, recently fired from the Pittsburgh, Fort Wayne and Chicago. More and more B&O trainmen were complaining about reduced crews on longer trains and the lack of overtime pay for Sunday shifts. Wheeling newspapers claimed that many B&O workers felt they were treated as though they were only another freight car or a locomotive. Clearly trouble was brewing for John Garrett.

The unhappy workers knew that Garrett would be quick to bring in strike breakers to man the trains and break the strike. They resolved to seize the trains and yards and scare off the scabs with violence if it were necessary. On Monday, July 16, a hot and sticky day in Baltimore, the trouble started at Camden Junction, two miles out of town. When firemen and other crewmen deserted their freight trains at that yard, Vice President John King at once replaced them with strike breakers on hand. Trouble was not so easily stopped at Martinsburg, a railroad town 100 miles west of Baltimore. There the B&O trainmen were urged on by Dick Zepp, an attractive young B&O brakeman who was eager for trouble. By afternoon, crowds of idle B&O workmen were forming in the yards and around the machine shops at Martinsburg. The crew of a cattle train deserted their posts, and soon a blockade was set up which allowed no freight trains to depart from or pass through the town. The strikers stated that no freight trains would move until the pay cut had been cancelled. Passenger trains were allowed to move through without trouble.

When the town mayor and police could not restore order, the B&O officials at Martinsburg wired Gov. Henry M. Mathews of West Virginia requesting that he send in the state militia to restore order and permit the movement of trains. That same night, a wire to John Garrett up in New York City brought the B&O president back to Baltimore to the bedside of his eighty-five-year-old dying mother. Governor Mathews ordered the Berkeley Light Guards, a Martinsburg militia group commanded by Col. Charles J. Faulkner, Jr., to perserve the peace and prevent any further obstruction of freight train movement. On Tuesday the Berkeley Light Guards managed to start the movement of a freight train operated by a loyal crew, but a scuffle at a switch stand resulted in the fatal wounding of a striker and the wounding of a soldier. The bloodshed stoppped both the train and the effectiveness of the Berkeley Light Guards. More state militia were requested from Governor Mathews. In Baltimore President Garrett, in spite of his mother's death, found time to ask the governor to request the aid of federal troops.

Before asking President Rutherford B. Hayes for troops, Governor Mathews decided to send the sixty-man Wheeling Company of Light Guards to Martinsburg. After a slow journey to the trouble spot, the light guards also proved ineffective in breaking the blockade at Martinsburg, where several dozen engines and about 600 freight cars were now jammed in the train yards. Not wanting to further defy the wishes of John Garrett, Governor Mathews on Wednesday, July 18, requested President Hayes to send in troops to put down the "domestic violence" existing along the line of the B&O in West Virginia. With some reluctance, the president ordered units from Washington, D.C., and Baltimore's Fort McHenry to proceed to West Virginia, and on the morning of July 19, some 300 federal troops arrived in Martinsburg. Federal troops were not much more successful than the state militia in moving freight trains. On Friday, July 20, sixteen freight trains were sent west out of Martinsburg, but only one arrived at Keyser, 100 miles to the west, on that day. The remainder were all stopped at Cumberland, Maryland. The mobs at Cumberland, made up more of idle youths and unemployed canal and rolling mill workers than railroaders, were more violent that those of Martinsburg.

Even greater street violence would soon come to Baltimore. In mid-July the city held not only many unhappy B&O workers, but more than 800 local boxmakers and canmakers striking for higher wages. On the morning of Friday, July 20, President Garrett, upon hearing of blockade and violence at Cumberland, asked John Lee Carroll, the governor of Maryland, to help restore order along the B&O line to the west. Governor Carroll was the great-grandson of Charles Carroll who forty-nine years earlier had laid the first stone on the railroad. After meeting with President Garrett and Vice President John King, the governor called upon the citizens of his state to abstain from all acts of violence and lawlessness. He then ordered Brig. Gen. James R. Herbert to use portions of the fifth and sixth regiments of the Maryland National Guard to restore order in Cumberland. Both of these Baltimore units were to assemble in their armories before marching to the Camden Station where a B&O troop train would carry them west to Cumberland. The news of the order was carried in the evening papers, and the "call to arms," or riot signal, was rung on the large city hall bell at 6:35 P.M., just as hundreds of Baltimore workmen were going home to supper.

Soon the streets were filled with hundreds of people wondering where the excitement might develop. Much of the crowd moved toward the Camden Station. The 250 men of the Fifth Regiment marching toward the station soon reached a hostile crowd that greeted the soldiers with shouts of abuse and some stones and brickbats. The Fifth reached the station in fair order, with some two dozen of the militia slightly injured but no one seriously hurt or killed.

The Sixth Regiment was not so fortunate. The armory of the Sixth was located in a rougher area of town. The mob around the armory, composed of youths, the unemployed, and the underpaid, manhandled some of the soldiers even as they were approaching the armory for assembly. The armory soon seemed almost under seige, but at 7:45 P.M. three companies—a total of 120 men—finally started through the mob toward the Camden Station. Marching into a hail of brickbats and stones, some of the soldiers involuntarily fired into the air. The crowd thought the rifles carried only blanks and replied with a heavier shower of stones. This time some of the soldiers fired directly into the crowd and not with blanks. The march to the station was a long and bloody one. Only fifty-nine of the militia reached the station. Behind were a total of ten dead, more than a score seriously wounded, and several dozen with minor injuries.

The mob of 15,000 around the Camden Station started to tear up some track nearby, and soon three passenger cars were set on fire. Even though the police were helping to quiet the mob, Governor Carroll recalled the Chicago Fire of 1871 as he viewed the fire out in the train yard. He at once wired President Hayes for military aid. Soon troops from Fort McHenry, New York Harbor, and the Washington Navy Yard were on their way to Baltimore. The arrival of 500 federal troops brought peace to Baltimore. While relatively few of those involved in the Baltimore riot were B&O workers, the mob seemed to feel a deep hatred and animosity toward the president of the railroad.

The strike fever spread quickly to Pennsylvania and Tom Scott's Pennsylvania Railroad. The trouble and violence that had appeared along the B&O line was nothing compared to the fury of the mobs as they fought the militia in the Pennsylvania train yards in Pittsburgh. Riots, fire, and violence in that city destroyed property worth at least $5 million. Soon the trouble spread to Buffalo, Chicago, St. Louis, and Omaha. State militia, policemen, regular army units, and even GAR (Grand Army of the Republic) veterans were used to end the violence, nearly 10,000 of them required to finally open the main line of the Pennsylvania. Public opinion seemed to generally favor law and order and several state legislatures began to revise the conspiracy laws to guard against future labor violence.

The violence and fury of the strike began to die away across the nation in late July and early August. A Baltimore and Ohio freight train left Cumberland escorted by United States Army regulars late on July 27 and reached Martinsburg with no trouble. Brief trouble appeared at Keyser, West Virginia, and at Bellaire, Ohio, but soon operations had returned to normal all up and down the line. On the Baltimore and Ohio, as throughout the nation, the strikers realized they had lost the strike.

Even though not all of the strikers regained their jobs, Garrett and his fellow top officials decided it would be wise to make some concessions to the workers and their grievances. Late in the summer of 1877, some reforms for train crewmen were established: crewmen were not called more than an hour before the time of departure, a quarter day's pay was assured when a man was called even if the train was cancelled, and passes home were provided workers during long layovers. Memories of the labor violence of 1877 no doubt also helped bring about the creation of the Baltimore and Ohio Employees Relief Association, set up in 1880.

Naturally the Railroad Strike of 1877 was fully covered in the press of the nation. Like most editors in America, the editors of the *American Railroad Journal* came out strongly for law and order. Under the headline of "Recent Railroad Damages" they wrote: "Neither do we wish to express any opinion relative to the questions involved, one of which is whether the employed receive proper remuneration for their services or not. But we do affirm most plainly and decidedly that all such riotous proceedings by a mob resulting in the damage to property and injury to person should be crushed out at once so firmly and effectively that a repetition will not be likely to take place for at least some time to come."[11] But on the Sunday after the Baltimore riot, July 22, 1877, Rev. Henry Ward Beecher did address the question of "proper remuneratiuon" in his sermon to his congregation of the Plymouth Church in Brooklyn: "It is true that a dollar a day is not enough to support a man and five children, if the man insists on smoking and drinking beer. Is not a dollar a day enough to buy bread? Water costs nothing. Man cannot live by bread alone, it is true, but the man who cannot live on bread and water is not fit to live."[12] Some of those who listened to the sermon, or later read about it, suspected the good Reverend, with his sensational remarks, was trying to get the public mind diverted from their interest in charges that Beecher had recently broken the seventh commandment.

While the public press had carried much about the strike of 1877, John Garrett in his summary of the year in the *Annual Report* for 1877 (October 1877) made no mention at all of the labor trouble. Nor was there any recognition in the *Annual Report* that the Baltimore and Ohio had been formally organized fifty years earlier in April 1827. Certainly the Baltimore and Ohio president himself was well aware that in the first dozen years after the Civil War, his company had experienced serious problems concerning the control of freight rates, the depression which followed the Panic of 1873, and the labor violence in the summer of 1877. Fortunately, he could also recall that the lines of the road and the total traffic carried had both experienced a major growth in those same years.

Chapter IX

. . . .

Garrett Expands His Lines

IN THE POSTWAR DECADES, JOHN WORK GARRETT GREATLY expanded the Baltimore and Ohio system in the same years that he faced problems of rate wars, economic depression, and labor violence. In writing his *Annual Report* for the year of 1865, the forty-five-year-old railroad president was describing the operations of a 520-mile rail network that stretched from Baltimore south to Washington, D.C., and west to Wheeling and Parkersburg on the upper Ohio River. At the time of his death nineteen years later in September 1884, John Garrett was operating a rail network of about 1,700 miles, more than triple the mileage of 1865. The B&O in 1884 had a line south to Lexington, Virginia, was building a road northeast to Philadelphia, had a branch to Pittsburgh, and operated branches west of the Ohio that reached to Columbus, Ohio, Sandusky on Lake Erie, and Chicago on Lake Michigan. After the Civil War, Garrett's B&O had expanded in the eastern states of Pennsylvania, Delaware, and Virginia and in the western states of Ohio, Indiana, and Illinois.

John W. Garrett extended his railroad far more with borrowed money than with new share capital. In the first thirty years of the B&O, the road had been built largely with common and preferred stock. When Chauncey Brooks turned the president's chair over to John Garrett, the capital structure of the B&O consisted of roughly $13 million of common and preferred stock and about $10 million of borrowed money. During the twenty-six-year presidency of Garrett, the share capital increased by less than one-half, while the bonded debt more than tripled. By the 1890s, this trend toward larger and larger debt would greatly contribute to financial crises and receivership.

Much of Garrett's expansion after the Civil War was west and north of the Ohio, but some of the earliest was located in Maryland, Virginia, and Pennsylvania. One of the first programs of new construction was the building of the forty-three-mile metropolitan branch from Washington, D.C., westward to Point of Rocks on the Main Stem. While the citizens of the nation's capital had long had an interest in the construction of a railroad west of their city, the managers of the B&O in the prewar years of the forties and fifties had no interest at all in such a project. Any such railroad would have only helped the commercial rivals of Baltimore, the port cities of Georgetown and Alexandria on the Potomac. The businessmen of Baltimore were happy to let their rivals to the south continue to rely upon the Chesapeake and Ohio Canal, which finally reached Cumberland in 1850. Once at Cumberland, the C&O Canal did move tonnages of Cumberland coal which modestly expanded until peaking in 1875. But the C&O Canal did not satisfy the businessmen of Georgetown and Montgomery County. In 1853 these interests organized the Metropolitan Railroad, which was projected to run from Washington to the B&O Main Stem near Frederick Junction. The projected road made engineering surveys during 1854, but lack of capital stalled any significant construction during the 1850s.

By the conclusion of the Civil War, John Garrett began to fear that if the B&O did not build a line west out of Washington, some other competing road would probably come forward to undertake the project. The federal government, after experiencing periods of almost total isolation during the Civil War, definitely favored the construction of such a line. Furthermore, the growth of Washington, plus Garrett's desire to expand to Pittsburgh and Chicago, were other arguments for the sponsorship of such a line. Accordingly, Garrett acquired the charter of the Metropolitan Railroad in 1865 and by 1866 had run surveys for the start of construction out of Washington. The route could not follow the Potomac since the C&O Canal already occupied the best route along the course of the river. Diverted into the interior north of the river, the B&O engineers soon found that any possible inland route would have to consist of numerous cuts, fills, and bridges as the line ran across the hills and valleys of the Piedmont region. Like the original line west of Baltimore, the road west of Washington had a number of grades, but had far fewer curves since the route followed no major streams.

Construction crews started to build the metropolitan branch in 1866 at Barnesville, a few miles east of Point of Rocks. Garrett did not push construction, and little mileage had been completed by 1868. However, when the Pennsylvania started to build its road from Baltimore to Washington, Garrett resumed work on the metropolitan branch, and the last rails on the forty-three-mile route were laid in February 1873. Service began on the line on May 25, 1873. In his *Annual Report* for 1873, President Garrett admitted that the "costly line" with its "very bold" engineering had cost $3,583,000 to complete, or an average of about $83,000 per mile.[1] Included in the cost was the construction of a red brick two-story Victorian station, complete with tall spire, located in the Point of Rocks wye between the old main line and the new road to Washington.

Once the new Metropolitan branch was in service most B&O through passenger and mail trains to the west used the new line instead of the older route out of Baltimore up the valley of the Patapsco. Coal and freight trains soon made up most of the traffic on the original line west out of Baltimore. A few years later, in the decade of the eighties, an active suburban development sprang up along the new branch between Washington and Rockville. Because of the popularity of the new suburbs, by the late 1880s the line was gradually double-tracked out to Gaithersburg, twenty-one miles west of Washington.

Even while the Baltimore and Ohio was planning and building its new line west of Washington, John Garrett was suffering a defeat as the Pennsylvania Railroad successfully challenged the longtime monopoly held over Washington traffic by the Washington branch. During the Civil War, Garrett had managed to defeat several efforts to construct a rival "air line" between Washington and New York City. Early in 1866, Thaddeus Stevens, the vindictive but able radical Republican congressman from Pennsylvania introduced another air line bill in the first postwar session of Congress. Aided by such Pennsylvania Railroad stalwarts as Tom Scott, Edgar Thomson, and Simon Cameron, the Stevens air-line bill passed the lower house in the summer of 1866. Garrett and his allies managed to stop the bill in the United States Senate, but Scott and Thomson quickly adopted a new approach in their effort to build into Washington. They were eager to reach that city since the B&O had never been cooperative in providing through service south of Baltimore for the Northern Central, a Pennsylvania controlled road which entered Baltimore from the north.

The Pennsylvania officials discovered that back in 1853 the Maryland legislature had granted to some tobacco planters of southern Maryland a charter for the Baltimore and Potomac Railroad to run from Baltimore to Popes Creek, some thirty miles south of Washington. The charter also allowed the construction of lateral branches up to twenty miles in length—sufficient to reach to the District of Columbia. In August 1866, the Pennsylvania officials arranged for George Washington Cass, nephew of the longtime Democratic political leader Lewis Cass and former head of the Fort Wayne, Pittsburgh and Chicago, along with other parties friendly to the Pennsylvania, to make a contract to finance and build the Baltimore and Potomac. Despite the best efforts of the Garrett forces, the United States Congress agreed in February 1867, to permit the Baltimore and Potomac to enter the District of Columbia. The Pennsylvania officials quietly took over the Cass contract and by the end of 1868 had built thirty-five miles of their new road toward Washington. Garrett managed several delaying law suits, but the new Pennsylvania line from Baltimore to Washington was opened early in July 1872. Satisfactory service between the Northern Central and the new Baltimore and Potomac was made possible only after the Pennsylvania Railroad finally obtained permission from the Baltimore city council to construct a tunnel 1.4 miles in length with tracks laid twenty to fifty feet under street level connecting the two depots. The chagrin suffered by John Garrett had been made even greater when Congress, in 1870, permitted the Pennsylvania to make a connection with the railroads of Virginia over the Long Bridge across the Potomac, a bridge earlier controlled for some years by the Baltimore and Ohio.

However, during the same years that Thomson and Scott were finally achieving entry into Washington, John Garrett's railroad pushed the tracks of the Baltimore and Ohio system up to Pittsburgh. The Baltimore and Ohio had long had an interest in the Pittsburgh and Connellsville Railroad, a road originally chartered in 1837 and completed from Pittsburgh to Connellsville by the beginning of the Civil War. During the Civil War, Garrett had high hopes of completing the road on to Cumberland—the B&O held 17,000 shares of P&C stock, was willing to loan the road $1 million, and Benjamin Latrobe sat in the president's chair. But in 1864, Tom Scott, vice president of the Pennsylvania and fully in control of the legislature of the Keystone State, had stopped Garrett cold by getting legislation passed which allowed the P&C to be taken over by a newly formed company controlled by the Pennsylvania Railroad. A new president replaced Latrobe who was soon demoted to become chief engineer of the line.

After the Civil War, Garrett and his allies in Baltimore sued in the courts for relief from the action of Tom Scott and the Pennsylvania legislature. Federal Courts twice found in favor of Garrett and the Pittsburgh and Connellsville. In 1868 the Pennsylvania Supreme Court finally found the Scott-inspired law of 1864 to be unconstitutional. Shortly thereafter, the Pennsylvania legislature repealed their action of 1864, restoring the Pittsburgh and Connellsville to the control of Garrett and the Baltimore and Ohio. In the meantime, fresh financial support both from Baltimore and Pittsburgh bankers assured the completion of a ninety-five-mile extension from Connellsville to Cumberland. Track crews, including a number of Negro and Canadian workers, pushed the grading and track laying through and over the high Allegheny ridges between Connellsville and Cumberland on the upper Potomac. Benjamin Latrobe helped drive the "Golden Spike" near Fort Hill, thirty-three miles southeast of Connellsville and just a few miles north of the Pennsylvania-Maryland border, on April 10, 1871.

The completed 150-mile road, renamed the Pittsburgh, Washington and Baltimore, was opened for through traffic in May 1871. President Garrett, commenting on the newly completed line to Pittsburgh in the 1871 *Annual Report* wrote: "The road is being supplied with additional locomotives and cars, and it is believed that the sanguine expectations entertained regarding the results of that important line, will ultimately be realized."[2] No doubt Garrett's success in extending his road into the very heart and center of a traffic monopoly long held exclusively by the Pennsylvania was another reason for the stubborn insistence by Thomson and Scott that they had to extend their own road south into Washington, D.C.

In the early postwar years, the Baltimore and Ohio also extended its lines and influence southward into Virginia. Shortly after the B&O had reached Harpers Ferry late in 1834, it had gained the tributary traffic of the Winchester and Potomac Railroad. The Winchester and Potomac, chartered in 1831 to serve the needs of the farmers and merchants of the lower Shenandoah Valley, built its thirty-two miles of line from Harpers Ferry to Winchester between 1833 and 1836. Thirty years later, on July 1, 1867, it was leased for twenty years by the B&O for a yearly rental of $27,000. The Winchester and Potomac was the first link in a chain of short connecting roads that would bring rail service to the valley of Virginia. The Winchester and Strasburg Railroad, chartered in 1860, was built on up the valley from Winchester to Strasburg and opened in 1870. This road was at once leased for seventeen years by the B&O for an annual rental of only $5,229. In 1870 John King, Jr., vice president of the B&O, was the president of the short nineteen-mile line. The Virginia Midland Railroad opened its recently completed Harrison branch, running further up the Shenandoah Valley from Strasburg to Harrisonburg, in 1873–74. This fifty-two-mile line was leased to the Baltimore and Ohio on September 1, 1873, for ninety-nine years at an annual rental of $89,250.

John W. Garrett had even more ambitious dreams for the extension of his road in Virginia. On February 23, 1866, Baltimore and Ohio interests had obtained a charter for the Valley Railroad, a line proposed to connect Harrisonburg and Salem, Virginia, 113 miles to the southwest. By 1869 the city of Baltimore made a million dollar stock subscription to the proposed line, matching an earlier stock subscription made by Garrett's B&O. In the same year, Gen. Robert E. Lee became interested in the possibilities of getting a railroad to Lexington, where he was serving as the president of Washington College. Lexington was certainly isolated, reached only by a long canal or a twenty-three-mile rough mountain road. Once when a visitor to the town asked Lee the best way to return to Washington, the General replied: "It makes but little difference, for whichever route you select you will wish you had taken the other."[3]

General Lee's enthusiasm for the new railroad helped obtain stock subscriptions, and on August 30, 1870, he was elected president of the Valley Railroad, succeeding Col. M. J. Harmon. The Confederate hero died only six weeks after his election, without seeing a single rail laid in the projected line. Robert Garrett, son of the B&O president, succeeded General Lee a few days later. The construction of the Valley Railroad was very slow. Staunton, twenty-six miles from Harrisonburg, was not reached until 1874, and Lexington only in 1883. The several connecting lines southwest of Harpers Ferry in the valley of Virginia were operated as branches of the Main Stem.

Long before 1883, John Garrett had really given up his dream of a southern rail system. The hard times following the Panic of 1873, plus the stiff competition from both the Pennsylvania Railroad and the aggressive stance of the Atlantic, Mississippi and Ohio Railroad, made Garrett hesitate. The Atlantic, Mississippi and Ohio was the 1867 merger of three short Virginia lines running from Norfolk westward to Bristol, Tennessee. The president of the 400-mile road was William Mahone, a former Con-

federate major general. The merger and creation of the AM&O by
Mahone had been partially upon the advice of J. Edgar Thomson,
president of the Pennsylvania. The poker-playing Mahone soon
was known as the "railroad Bismarck" of Virginia. Critics of his
unprecedented annual salary of $25,000 claimed that AM&O really
meant "All Mine and Otelia's." (The maiden name of Mrs. Mahone
was Otelia Butler.) Even though the Panic of 1873 soon brought
Mahone to grief, John Garrett soon realized his best chances for
expansion were in the states west of the Ohio River.

Garrett also realized that any significant expansion of rail
traffic beyond the Ohio depended upon replacing the car ferries at
Wheeling and Parkersburg with bridges across the Ohio. Plans and
specifications for bridges at both points were pushed early in the
postwar years. The first stone of the Wheeling bridge, which was
actually located at Benwood, four miles south of Wheeling, was
laid on May 2, 1868. Construction of the bridge at Parkersburg
began fourteen months later on July 9, 1869. By the end of 1868,
the Baltimore and Ohio had already spent $364,000 on the plan-
ning, materials, and early construction of the two bridges. By October 1, 1869, this figure had risen to $648,000. The planning and
construction of the bridges was under the supervision of chief engineer James L. Randolph, who had held that position since 1863,
and John L. Wilson, master of road.

The Wheeling bridge, which crossed the Ohio from Benwood, West Virginia to Bellaire, Ohio, and the Central Ohio was
completed and opened to traffic on June 21, 1871. Its total length
between abutments was 3,916 feet, including approaches it was
8,566 feet. The track was elevated forty feet above low water to
allow for the passage of river traffic below. The Parkersburg
bridge, which was built a little more rapidly, was opened to traffic
on January 7, 1871. This bridge, which crossed the Ohio to Belpre,
and the Marietta and Cincinnati Railroad, was 4,397 feet in length,
between abutments, and 7,140 feet including approaches. John
Garrett reported in October 1871, that during the year $647,000
had been spent to complete the two bridges. The total combined
cost, from early planning to final opening of the two wrought iron
truss bridges was $2,237,000.

In 1871, the same year that the two Ohio River bridges
were opened, the Baltimore and Ohio also acquired a line east of
Wheeling. The Hempfield Railroad was chartered in 1850, and by
the Civil War had built a thirty-two-mile line from Wheeling east
to Washington, Pennsylvania. After foreclosure this road was reorganized as the Wheeling, Pittsburgh and Baltimore and sold to the
Baltimore and Ohio on May 1, 1871. During 1872 the short line

had a total revenue of just over $48,000. John Garrett hoped to push the line on eastward to connect with the Pittsburgh and Connellsville a few miles north of Connellsville, but no construction was achieved during the 1870s. Instead, the B&O eventually reached Pittsburgh from the west by purchasing, in 1883, the Pittsburgh Southern Railroad, a thirty-seven-mile narrow gauge line running from Pittsburgh to Washington. The B&O rebuilt the line in standard gauge, laying down sixty-pound steel rail.

West of the new bridges over the Ohio the Baltimore and Ohio connected with two Ohio lines, the Central Ohio and the Marietta and Cincinnati. The Central Ohio Railroad had been chartered by the state of Ohio in 1847 and by 1854 had been built from Columbus east to Bellaire. Hugh J. Jewett, a Zanesville banker, lawyer, and Democratic member of the state legislature, became a director of the Central Ohio in 1855, vice president in 1856, and president in 1857. The 137-mile Central Ohio had a large funded debt and had never been sufficiently prosperous to declare any dividends. The Panic of 1857 increased its financial problems, and in 1859 Jewett was appointed receiver of the line. After a lengthy receivership, the Central Ohio was reorganized in 1865 and on November 21, 1866, was leased to the Baltimore and Ohio for twenty years at an annual rental of 35 percent of the gross revenues for the first five years and 40 percent thereafter. The leased line was known as the Central Ohio Division of the B&O. In 1868 Hugh Jewett was again president and the leased road had gross revenue of just over $1 million, sufficient to pay a 6 percent dividend. When the Wheeling bridge was opened in 1871, the gauge of the Central Ohio was shifted from the Ohio gauge of four feet ten inches to standard gauge long used on the Baltimore and Ohio.

West of Parkersburg, the tracks of the Marietta and Cincinnati did not need to be changed since they had been built originally in standard gauge. This 173-mile road had been built in 1855, 1856, and 1857 from Loveland, twenty-three miles east of Cincinnati, eastward to Marietta, nine miles upstream from Parkersburg. Later the line was extended downstream to Belpre, where the Ohio River bridge to Parkersburg was to be built. Service from Loveland into Cincinnati was over the tracks of the connecting Little Miami. By the spring of 1857, the B&O thus had a connecting rail route west of Parkersburg to Cincinnati and St. Louis. The Marietta and Cincinnati had stiff competition from the riverboats on the Ohio and soon was compelled to lower its freight rates. In 1868 the 200-mile road with an employee roster of just over 1,400 workers had gross revenues of over $1,300,000. In 1868 John King

B&O bridge over the Ohio River between Benwood, West Virginia, and Bellaire, Ohio.
(*Courtesy, Baltimore and Ohio Railroad*)

of the B&O was president of the M&C while William Parker Cutler was vice president and general superintendent. During the postwar years, the B&O had a growing financial interest in the railroad. In the early 1880s, the B&O acquired the Marietta and Cincinnati which in 1889 was reorganized as the Baltimore and Ohio Southwestern Railroad.

The Sandusky, Mansfield and Newark was a third Ohio line acquired by the Baltimore and Ohio during the Garrett years. Merged from four earlier lines, the Sandusky, Mansfield and Newark was constructed between 1848 and 1851 from Newark on the Central Ohio north through Mansfield up to Sandusky. The 116-mile line was originally built in the non-standard gauge of five feet four inches, but within a few years had shifted to the Ohio gauge of four feet ten inches. In February 1869, the road was leased to the Central Ohio for seventeen years and five months from July 1, 1869, for an annual rental of $174,350. Since the B&O had earlier leased the Central Ohio, the 1869 lease of the SM&N was guaranteed by the B&O, who also operated the line to Sandusky as the Lake Erie Division. By 1882 the board of directors of the Sandusky, Mansfield and Ohio included two men from Baltimore, Robert Garrett and Samuel Spencer, both of whom would later be presidents of the Baltimore and Ohio. South of Newark the Newark, Somerset and Straitsville Railroad had been organized in 1867 and built forty-four miles south to Shawnee, Ohio by 1871. This line was leased by the Sandusky, Mansfield and Newark on January 1, 1872, for fourteen years, the road to be equipped and operated by the Baltimore and Ohio, for an annual rental of 30 percent of the gross earnings.

West of Ohio, Garrett had long had an ambition to reach Chicago, as well as to increase the traffic over the connecting line west of Cincinnati, the Ohio and Mississippi. During the postwar years, the railroad from Cincinnati to St. Louis was never strong enough to make Garrett desire to acquire the connecting western road. The 340-mile line had been difficult to construct and complete in the 1850s and was quite top heavy with financial obligations. "Extraordinary repairs" on the road seemed to be required year after year. The postwar president of the O&M, William D. Griswold, contended in 1867 that his road through the state of Indiana was "as compared to other western roads" in excellent order.[4] However, several disastrous floods along the Ohio just west of Cincinnati caused much new damage in the late 1860s. Revenues and income never seemed to match expenses and outgo. The fact was that the area traversed by the O&M—southern Indiana and southern Illinois—was quite thinly populated and unable to produce heavy traffic. As a consequence, the Ohio and Mississippi twice suffered long receiverships in the twenty years after the Civil War.

The shifting of the track in 1871 from the broad gauge six feet to four feet nine inches did not seem to materially increase traffic. Neither did the fifty-three-mile Louisville branch, opened earlier in 1869 from North Vernon, Indiana to Jeffersonville, nor the 1875 purchase of the 225-mile Springfield division, running across Illinois from Shawneetown to Beardstown, bring in much additional revenue. As a result, the B&O officials during the seventies had no real interest in acquiring the road. Early in 1874, Vice President John King wrote to Garrett that he did not favor a lease of the Ohio and Mississippi and continued: ". . . That road will have quite as much as it can accomplish to earn interest on its mortgage debt, more than it can do to earn dividends on the preferred stock. The management is feeble."[5] Four years later, late in 1877 when he was receiver for the Ohio and Mississippi, John King tried to sound more optimistic as he explained to Drexel Morgan and Company that he could not pay the coupons due January 1, 1878, because of "constant rains and the condition of the country roads." Continuing, King wrote: ". . . There are immense quantities of corn west of the Mississippi River and upon the line of our road. . . . If we should have freezing weather for a week, we will have demand for every car we can control at very good prices."[6] John W. Garrett had no intention of acquiring a road that had to depend upon freezing weather to pay its bond coupons. The B&O did not acquire the Ohio and Mississippi until several years after Garrett's death.

President Garrett was much more positive and optimistic concerning the acquisition of a line from northern Ohio across Indiana to Chicago. Shortly after the Civil War, Garrett started to look eagerly toward this growing rail terminal with its expanding manufacturing and increasing agricultural and industrial traffic. In his *Annual Report* for 1871 Garrett wrote: "It's expected that the construction of the Baltimore, Pittsburgh and Chicago Rail Road, fraught as the enterprise will be with such vast advantages to all the extensive and varied interests with which it is connected, will be rapidly effected."[7] A year later, in the fall of 1872, he reported that the 260-mile line from a point on the Lake Erie division ninety miles north of Newark west to Chicago had been entirely located with low grades. In the 1873 *Annual Report*, Garrett reported that the new line to Chicago would be only 795 miles from Baltimore, while the Chicago to Philadelphia route (via the Pennsylvania) was 899 miles and the Chicago to New York City route (via the New York Central) was 980 miles.

During 1873 most of the track was laid between Chicago Junction on the Lake Erie division and Deshler, Ohio, sixty-three miles to the west. The remaining 200 miles of line, west from Deshler to Baltimore Junction, Illinois, was completed during 1874. The route from Chicago Junction to the southern end of Lake Michigan was nearly a direct air line, including more than 240 miles of tangent track. The grades along the 263-mile route were very slight with only eleven miles having grades as steep as twenty-six feet to the mile. The track was laid with iron and steel rails from the B&O rolling mill at Cumberland, weighing sixty-four pounds to the yard.

The Baltimore and Ohio route to Chicago entered that city over the Illinois Central line, with that road building an extra track from Hyde Park into downtown Chicago. B&O passenger trains used the IC lakefront depot, while a new 600 foot brick freight depot was built for the new eastern trunk line. Final track on the line was laid on November 15, 1874, and traffic between Deshler and Chicago was opened on November 23. The new route to the West, officially called the Baltimore, Pittsburgh and Chicago, but soon known as the Chicago division, had cost $7,800,000 to complete. During its first year of traffic, late November 1874, to October 1875, the Chicago division had revenue of $959,000, but showed a deficit of nearly $126,000. The following year saw revenues on the Chicago division increase to $1,232,000 with net earnings of nearly $167,000. Garrett concluded his annual report that year by claiming that "the Chicago Division . . . has already demonstrated its power and usefulness."[8]

With his own or connecting lines giving service both to Chicago and St. Louis in the West, John Garrett next turned his interest to railroad service to the northeast of Baltimore. For many years, rail service between Washington and New York City had been via the Washington branch from Washington to Baltimore, the ninety-five-mile main line of the Philadelphia, Wilmington and Baltimore from Baltimore to Philadelphia, and the lines of the United New Jersey Railroad and Canal Company for service on to Jersey City and the Hudson River. Garrett and the B&O were not happy with two events occurring in the early seventies: (1) leasing by the Pennsylvania Railroad in 1871 of the United New Jersey Railroad and Canal Company for 999 years and (2) the completion in 1872 of the Pennsylvania line south from Baltimore to Washington, D.C. Quite suddenly, on December 1, 1880, President Garrett announced that all B&O service east of Philadelphia would soon be routed to Jersey City over the tracks of the Delaware and Bound Brook Railroad (leased to the Philadelphia and Reading) and the Central Railroad of New Jersey.

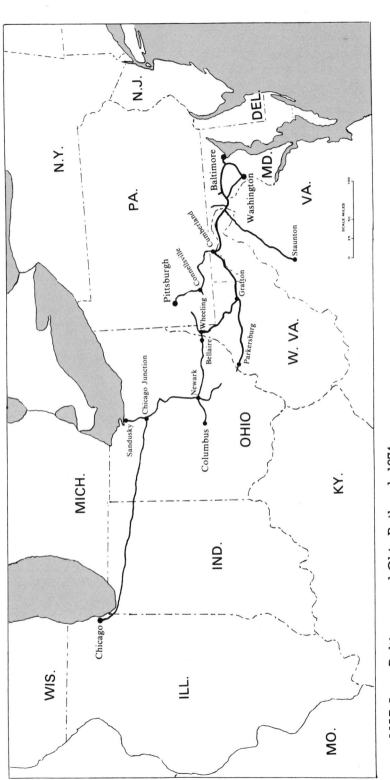

MAP 5.   Baltimore and Ohio Railroad, 1874.

Major additions to the B&O after the Civil War included the leases of the Central Ohio in 1868 and the Sandusky, Mansfield, and Newark in 1869. The road from Cumberland to Pittsburgh was completed in 1871 and a line from Washington to Point of Rocks in 1873. Late in 1874, the 263-mile line from Chicago was opened for traffic.

Hearing reports that Jay Gould, recently elected to the board of the Central Railroad of New Jersey, might be trying to build a new line from Philadelphia to Baltimore, the Boston owners of the Philadelphia, Wilmington and Baltimore decided it might be a good time to sell an interest in their own line to the promoters of the rival road. Soon a group including John Garrett, Jay Gould, Russell Sage, August Belmont, and John Jacob Astor were actively negotiating with Nathaniel Thayer, a Boston investment banker, who represented the stockholders of the PW&B Railroad. By about February 17, 1881, the Garrett syndicate had agreed to purchase 120,000 shares of the PW&B stock at seventy dollars per share. Shortly thereafter Vice President Alexander J. Cassatt of the Pennsylvania was offered a one-third interest in the syndicate purchase, but he refused. Feeling secure of the agreement, John Garrett found it difficult to keep quiet. There were reports that on a wintry day in early March he even boasted of his coup to George B. Roberts, president of the Pennsylvania. At that same time, the Thayer group was beginning to believe that seventy dollars per share was too low a price for their stock. Within a few days, Cassatt and Roberts had offered seventy-eight dollars per share and eventually paid just over $17 million for nearly 218,000 shares of PW&B stock, more than 90 percent of the outstanding shares of the railroad.

Having been thoroughly outmaneuvered by Roberts and Cassatt of the Pennsylvania, John Garrett on March 23, 1881, announced that he had bought control of the Delaware Western, a company with a charter but no completed track, from Col. Henry S. McComb. McComb was a Wilmington capitalist who, as a southern railroad carpetbagger, had recently lost control of a Cairo to New Orleans line to the Illinois Central. Garrett planned to use the Delaware Western to start the construction of a line from Baltimore to Philadelphia. The rate wars of the early 1880s delayed the project, and the new line to Philadelphia was not mentioned in Garrett's annual reports until 1883. The Philadelphia, Wilmington and Baltimore continued to let the B&O use its tracks until October 1884, just shortly after John Garrett's death. The new line to Philadelphia was not fully in operation until September 1886.

Even with some defeats and disappointments, Garrett's railroad continued to have a growing traffic and revenue in the late 1870s and early 1880s.

The B&O's growth from 1879 to 1884 was nearly as rapid as that of the Pennsylvania Railroad and somewhat greater than that of the New York Central. Of the several branches other than the Main Stem, the Chicago branch and the Pittsburgh branch (Cumberland to Pittsburgh) had the heaviest traffic by far. The growth of the net revenue during the six years permitted a substantial increase in the dividends paid the stockholders. The 7 percent dividend paid in 1878 rose to 8 percent in 1879 and 1880 and to 10 percent for the years 1881–84. As in previous years, passenger revenue was much less than freight, generally producing only from one-seventh to one-fifth of the total annual revenues. Between 1879 and 1884 the increase of through merchandise (east and west) increased from 1,425,000 tons to 2,275,000 tons. The tonnage of coal moving over the line from the mines of Maryland and West Virginia increased from 1,213,000 tons in 1879 to 2,828,000 tons in 1884.

TABLE 11. Entire Baltimore and Ohio System Traffic and Financial Growth 1879–84

Year	Main Stem			Entire B&O System			
	Total Receipts	*Net Revenues*	*Expenses to Earnings (%)*	*Miles of Road*	*Total Receipts*	*Net Revenues*	*Expenses to Earnings (%)*
1879	$ 8,864,827	$4,341,245	51	1,449	$14,193,981	$6,502,385	54
1880	11,229,881	5,172,981	54	1,449	18,317,740	7,986,370	56
1881	11,122,259	4,846,616	56	1,495	18,463,877	7,073,398	62
1882	10,556,570	4,572,944	57	1,509	18,383,876	7,454,662	59
1883	11,579,839	5,432,183	53	1,584	19,739,838	8,705,823	56
1884	11,506,958	5,237,742	54	1,711	19,436,607	7,760,300	60

In 1884, the last year of John Garrett's presidency, the balance sheet of the Baltimore and Ohio showed liabilities and assets each amounting to just over $93 million. This was a figure slightly more than three times the comparable figure for 1858, the first year of Garrett's leadership. Included among the liabilities were $14,793,000 of capital stock, $5,000,000 of preferred stock, $23,960,000 of funded debt and debentures, and $47,704,000 of profit and loss. Included among the assets were $36,015,000 for Main Stem and branches, $17,311,000 for rolling stock, and $21,787,000 in the stocks and bonds of other railroads, much of which was in the securities of connecting or leased lines west of the original B&O system.

In the years since the end of the Civil War, John Garrett had accomplished much more than just tripling the size of his balance sheet and expanding his rail empire. In the 1870s, Garrett finally succeeded in ridding the Washington branch of the onerous 20 percent tax due the state of Maryland on all passenger fares between Baltimore and Washington, D.C. This clause in the original charter of the Washington branch in 1832 was held by the courts to be constitutional since the charter gave the B&O an exclusive franchise for rail passenger service between the two cities. When the Pennsylvania started to build its parallel line to Washington breaking the exclusive franchise, Garrett filed suit to end the 20 percent tax. However, on May 3, 1875, the Supreme Court of the United States upheld the constitutionality of the capitation tax and ordered the B&O to pay Maryland back taxes amounting to $424,230. Garrett and his lawyers appealed to the General Assembly of Maryland, and finally an act of that body on March 27, 1878, ended the 20 percent capitation tax as of July 1, 1873.

During the 1870s, the Baltimore and Ohio also expanded its chain of resort hotels in Maryland and further west. In 1872 the Queen City station hotel was built at Cumberland and the next year a resort hotel was built at Deer Park, located in western Maryland near the crest of the B&O tracks as they crossed the Alleghenies. Another such hotel was built in 1875 at nearby Oakland and along the route of the new Chicago line at Newark, Ohio, and Chicago Junction (later renamed Willard), Ohio. During the mid-seventies, John Garrett was purchasing at a good discount from Harper Brothers and J. B. Lippincott, the works of Charles Dickens, Charles Darwin, Edward Gibbon, and Mark Twain; all of these books were placed in the libraries of the new hotels. The resort hotels, which offered horseback riding, tennis, croquet, and a scenic environment, made modest profits even in the midst of the depression years of the seventies. Within a few years, they were so popular that the hotels at Deer Park and Oakland were doubled in size during 1881–82.

John Garrett made a number of additional improvements on his railroad at this time. A rolling mill plant, a facility capable of turning out iron and steel rails as well as other heavy iron products, was opened at Cumberland in 1872. Between 1880 and 1888, the B&O built and operated its own sleeping cars and also organized its own independent telegraph organization. In 1880, when Baltimore celebrated its one hundred fiftieth anniversary, the B&O contributed a procession of several thousand workers, ten bands, and thirty wagons and tableaux. As prosperity returned to the railroad in the early 1880s, a new tobacco warehouse was built at Baltimore, another 1,800,000-bushel grain elevator was constructed at Locust Point, and the railroad assisted in organizing the Baltimore Stock Yard Company to aid in the transportation and marketing of additional livestock. The B&O also cooperated in the dredging of the channel of the inner harbor of Baltimore to a depth of twenty-seven feet at mean low water. In 1880 and 1881, Garrett led in the planning and construction of a new brick, seven-story central office building located at the corner of Baltimore and Calvert streets. The fire-proof building had giant burglar proof vaults and included "all the latest improvements and conveniences for the transaction of business and ready intercommunication of the officers who will occupy it: such as safe and speedy elevators, electric annunciators and calls, pneumatic tubes and message drops upon each floor."[9]

But President Garrett also had interests in his railroad which went beyond stone, concrete, steel, and new equipment. In 1880, three years after the labor violence of 1877, Garrett recommended to his board that the B&O should establish the Baltimore and Ohio Railroad Employees' Relief Association for the purpose of "protecting and promoting the interests of the employees of the Baltimore and Ohio Company and of their families in cases of accident, sickness and death."[10] The plan, which called for an annual

Locust Point in Baltimore Harbor. From a painting by H. D. Stitt.
(Courtesy, Baltimore and Ohio Railroad)

contribution of $6,000 by the B&O plus modest dues paid by the workers, had been prepared and organized by Garrett's son, Robert, who had been the third vice president of the line since October 1879. By the fall of 1881, the relief association had an active membership of 14,673 workers and during the first eighteen months of its existence had paid out $163,929 for 6,239 claims and 1,269 medical bills. By 1884 the contribution of the B&O to the plan had been increased to $20,000 a year. In March 1884, Robert Garrett, who had been first vice president since August 1881, wrote his father that the relief association really needed an annual gift of $25,000 and then added: "Now I beg to suggest that if you are unwilling that the Railway Company shall go beyond the $20,000, that you, yourself individually give $5,000 per annum so that your supplement to the amount given by the Railway Co. will

B&O headquarters building, built by John W. Garrett in the early 1880s. *(Courtesy, Baltimore and Ohio Railroad)*

make the amount at command of the fund $25,000—the amount required."[11] The relief association continued to expand its activities in the years after 1884.

During the Garrett years, vast improvements had been achieved in the equipment and rolling stock of the railroad. In the twenty-five years between 1859 and 1884, the number of locomotives on the B&O had increased from 235 to 662, passenger cars from 126 to 466, and freight cars from 3,432 to 21,096. The new engines were bigger and more powerful. During the year 1881, the Mount Clare shops built thirty-five new engines at a total cost of $301,000 or $8,600 per locomotive. Included were twenty-two Consolidation (2-8-0) freight engines weighing fifty-one tons each, twelve American (4-4-0) passenger engines weighing forty-two tons each, and one thirty-three-ton switch engine. Garrett also used more and more steel rails in place of iron in the postwar years. In 1871 some 9,118 tons of steel rails were laid down replacing the older iron, bring steel track up to a total of 256 miles. By 1884 almost half of the total line, 762 miles, was laid with steel rail. In that year, the typical steel rail weighed sixty-seven pounds to the yard with iron rail in use ranging from sixty to eighty pounds per yard.

In the postwar seventies and eighties, the B&O also started to use the several types of automatic car couplers made available by such inventors as Ezra Miller and Eli Janney. George Westinghouse's improvements in the air brakes were also made available for the locomotives and cars of the B&O. The eventual adoption of the new couplers and brakes made life much easier for the railroad trainmen, especially for the freight brakemen. Earlier, when the locomotive engineer's whistle for "down brakes" had sent the brakemen up to the top of the moving cars, the risk to life and limb was made greater when the work was being done in snow, ice, or darkness.

Another innovation in rail operations appeared late in the Garrett regime with the introduction of standard time at noon, on Sunday, November 18, 1883. Before the adoption of standard time, nearly every town had its own local "sun time" and the variety across the nation was almost infinite. In the early 1880s, Indiana had twenty-three different local times and there were twenty-seven in Illinois. However, most railroads used the local times of major division points as the official times for their train operation. The Baltimore and Ohio used Baltimore time for westbound trains out of Baltimore, Columbus time for trains in Ohio, and Vincennes time for those moving west of Cincinnati. During the 1870s and early 1880s, the General Time Convention, an organization of railroad superintendents from across the nation, was considering the adoption of some type of standard time. By 1883 they had decided upon a system of four time zones: eastern time centered on the 75th meridian, central time of the 90th, mountain time on the 105th, and pacific on the 120th.

When this new time went into effect on November 18, 1883, all B&O operations were either on eastern time (Maryland, Virginia, Delaware, New Jersey, and the eastern two thirds of West Virginia) or central time (Ohio, Indiana, and Illinois). When the change occurred, the clocks in Baltimore were set ahead about five minutes, while those west of Pennsylvania and east of the 90th meridian were set back—Columbus twenty-eight minutes; Cincinnati twenty-two minutes; Vincennes ten minutes; and Chicago nine minutes. Seven months after the adoption of standard time, the Baltimore and Ohio set a speed record for fast passenger train travel between Chicago and Washington, D.C. After the nomination of James G. Blaine for United States president by the Republican National Convention in Chicago in early June 1884, a group of Washington reporters desired to return to the capital as soon as possible. They turned to the B&O which arranged for a special train consisting of a combination car, a diner, two sleeping cars, and a Mann boudoir car. The train made the 812-mile trip to Washington in twenty-two hours and thirty minutes, a record for 1884.

"B&O Bosses," taken by a local photographer in Grafton, West Virginia, in 1871. (*Courtesy, Baltimore and Ohio Railroad*)

John Garrett had certainly prospered during his long tenure as president of the Baltimore and Ohio. In mid-1867 the Garrett family owned 14,500 shares of B&O stock with a value of more than $1,700,000. Other securities brought the family wealth to nearly $2 million in 1867, a total which continued to grow in later years. While Garrett's attitude toward labor, as revealed in the strike of 1877, was generally tough and unbending, he was frequently a generous man with gifts to his church, Lafayette College, the YMCA, and other worthy projects. Garrett's long tenure as B&O president—extending well past that of his early rivals, Commodore Vanderbilt and J. Edgar Thomson—had made his name a household word in much of the nation by the mid-1870s. In the late seventies, a new brand of cigars was named for the B&O president, and in West Virginia a company of militia volunteers was named "the Garrett Rifles." Along the line of the B&O, both in 1872 and again in 1876, a number of local newspapers suggested that the Democratic party should nominate Garrett for president. In 1881 his name was also suggested as one who could represent Maryland in the United States Senate.

Throughout the postwar years, John Garrett found time to travel. He made several trips to Europe, including the extended trip of 1873–74, and shorter trips in the late summer of 1878 and the spring of 1881. In the spring of 1876, he also made a trip out to

"B&O Workmen," taken by a local photographer in Grafton, West Virginia, in 1885. *(Courtesy, Baltimore and Ohio Railroad)*

the Pacific Coast, accompanied by his wife, daughter Mary, and a single servant. The family passed through sixteen states in their two month, 7,200-mile railroad trip to and from San Francisco. Returning from that city, they stopped for five days at "Yo Semite" valley and four days at Salt Lake City.

By the early eighties, the veteran railroad president was beginning to slow down. He increasingly preferred to conduct company business at home, either in his town house at Mount Vernon Square or at Montebello, rather than in the fine headquarters in downtown Baltimore. At his home office, he could read every important dispatch, send orders, and quickly call needed subordinates since a telegrapher was in constant attendance during the business day. More and more, Garrett preferred to be with his wife, Rachel Ann, who often was a buffer between the tiring president and the outside business world. On November 16, 1883, Mrs. Garrett was fatally injured in a carriage accident. The sixty-three-year-old Garrett never really recovered from his wife's death and soon lost all interest in life. Within a few months, his son Robert became acting president of the railroad. John Garrett died at his cottage at Deer Park, Maryland, on September 26, 1884.

The B&O board of directors, meeting later that same day, passed a resolution concerning Garrett which concluded with the words: ". . . he devoted all the powers of a great intelligence and a persistent energy which, deterred by no obstacle, had but one purpose, the giving to Baltimore the unequalled advantages of its geographical position . . . as one of the greatest entrepots of the world."[12] A week later, the *Railroad Gazette* endorsed the same point of view when the editors wrote of the B&O president: "No man in Baltimore has been so closely or so extensively identified with the progress of the city as has Mr. John W. Garrett."[13] It was true that John Garrett would be remembered for these things, but a decade later he would also be remembered as the man who had expanded his railroad system largely with borrowed money. The receivership which faced the B&O a dozen years after Garrett's death was, in part, a direct result of this excessive borrowing.

Chapter X

• • • • • • • • • • • • • •

Many Presidents and a Receivership

IN THE THIRTY-ONE YEARS BETWEEN THE FOUNDING OF THE railroad in 1827 and the first election of John W. Garrett in 1858, six different presidents had directed the destinies of the Baltimore and Ohio as it reached the Ohio River and achieved connections to the West. In the twenty-six-year presidency of Garrett, the railroad had greatly expanded and modestly prospered. During the next twenty-six years, 1884–1910, six different men would sit in the president's chair in the headquarters building of the B&O and control the trunk road as it neared and entered a new century.

In the decade and a half between 1884 and the turn of the century, four different men were president of the Baltimore and Ohio: Robert Garrett (1884–87), Samuel Spencer (1887–88), Charles F. Mayer (1888–96), and John K. Cowen (1896–1901). During these years, the earnings of the total B&O system tripled, the mileage more than doubled, and the employees far more than doubled in number. As the earnings, mileage, and work force grew, the B&O faced a variety of growing pains. In 1887, with the creation of the Interstate Commerce Commission, the Baltimore and Ohio, along with all the nation's railways, experienced its first regulation and supervision by the federal government. The growth of traffic enjoyed under Robert Garrett and Samuel Spencer dropped off in the presidency of Charles Mayer during the panic and depression of 1893. As a result, the Baltimore and Ohio was placed in the hands of receivers on March 1, 1896.

Robert Garrett, president, 1884-87.
(*Courtesy, Baltimore and Ohio Railroad*)

Robert Garrett succeeded his father as president of the Baltimore and Ohio, being elected on November 20, 1884, at the age of thirty-seven, a year younger than his father had been in 1858. Robert had received his early education in Baltimore and Providence. At the age of sixteen, he ran away from home in an effort to join Gen. Robert E. Lee in the valley of Virginia, but the senior Garrett persuaded him to forget the war, return home, and enter Princeton College where he graduated in 1867. After college he briefly worked in the family bank, Robert Garrett and Sons. In 1870 he succeeded Robert E. Lee as president of the projected Valley Railroad and remained in that position for several years. On October 8, 1879, he was appointed to the newly created position of third vice president of the Baltimore and Ohio and two years later, on August 1, 1881, elevated to first vice president. During his father's illness in 1884, he became acting president, and signed the 1884 *Annual Report* as "President pro tem." He had been a member of the board of directors since April 1881, a position he relinquished before being elected president.

Robert Garrett was not the dominant, forceful, and aggressive figure that his father had been. John Work Garrett had served a long and useful apprenticeship under the stern eyes of the first Robert Garrett in the 1830s and 1840s. The younger Robert had had too much given to him and really earned very few of the several advancements presented to him in the 1870s and early 1880s. As a result, he leaned heavily on others during his three-year presidency. The two subordinates upon whom he leaned most heavily were John K. Cowen and Samuel Spencer. Spencer had followed Robert up the vice presidential ladder in the early eighties, in turn being third vice president, 1881–82; second vice president,

1882–84; and first vice president 1884–87. Robert Garrett also depended greatly on John Cowen, Robert's Princeton classmate and the dominate figure in the B&O legal department in the middle 1880s. No doubt Robert Garrett would have been a stronger president had he not suffered from ill health much of the time he held the presidency.

During the presidency of Robert Garrett, a growing rupture occurred between the Baltimore and Ohio and the Democratic party in the state of Maryland. During the long tenure of John Garrett, there had been generally good relations between the Baltimore and Ohio and the Gorman-Rasin dominated Democratic party. As a youth, Arthur Pue Gorman had been a page in the House of Representatives in Washington and was befriended by Stephen A. Douglas. During the 1870s, he became a power in the Maryland legislature and president of the Chesapeake and Ohio Canal, which gave him control over substantial patronage. He served in the United States Senate from 1881 to 1899 and from 1903 until his death in 1906. Isaac Freeman Rasin, from an old eastern shore family and the Democratic political boss of Baltimore since the early 1870s, was a natural partner for the rural based Gorman.

Robert Garrett had little political know-how, and his close friend and advisor, John K. Cowen, was a reform Democrat who had little use for the Gorman-Rasin machine. As a result, the earlier cooperation between the railroad and the Democratic party began to deteriorate. The long time influence of the B&O on the Maryland General Assembly was greatly diminished after the death of the elder Garrett. It seemed to Robert Garrett and his fellow B&O officials that the Maryland General Assembly gave special privileges to the rival Pennsylvania while increasing taxes on the B&O. Often it appeared that the Baltimore city- and Maryland state-appointed directors on the board were reflecting the views of the Gorman-Rasin machine. This problem would become less serious in the early 1890s when the city and state representation on the board was greatly reduced.

During the Robert Garrett years, the first major expansion in B&O mileage was the completion of the 111-mile Philadelphia division from Baltimore to Philadelphia. This project had been started by John W. Garrett in the early 1880s after his failure to acquire the majority stock in the existing Philadelphia, Wilmington and Baltimore Railroad. Son Robert seemed determined to complete this project which his father had started. During his presidency, Robert Garrett also insisted on continuing a costly rate war with the Pennsylvania. The construction of the new line to Philadelphia was slow and delayed by the necessity of building and completing major bridges over the Brandywine River at Wilmington, the Susquehanna River near Havre de Grace, and the Schuylkill River in Philadelphia. By far the most difficult and costly to build was the nine-span steel and iron bridge across the broad Susquehanna—a bridge 6,346 feet in total length with the track ninety-four feet above mean low tide.

Less costly in money but more difficult in time, effort, and final success, was getting permission from the Philadelphia city fathers—fully controlled by the Pennsylvania Railroad—to bring the B&O into the heart of the city. Early in the legal struggle, John K.Cowen, top legal counsel for the B&O, had written a pamphlet, *Here and There, or a Tale of Two Cities*, in which he had raised the question, "Is Philadelphia finished, and ready to be fenced in [by the Pennsylvania R.R.]?" Cowen asked the city officials: "Are times so good and labor so actively employed as to justify this deliberate perfection of a Dog in the Manger policy?"[1] Eventually, entry by the B&O into the city for a connection with the Philadelphia and Reading was given by Philadelphia. The line was finally completed with freight service opened on July 11, 1886, and passenger service on September 19,1886. The line to Philadelphia had not been cheap to build. When the bills for the completed construction, not including any rolling stock, were added up in 1888, the total bill was $15,764,000, all of it being paid for by two new issues of bonds. There were some reports that the final cost of the new division was closer to $20,000,000. The first full year of use, 1886–87, showed the new Philadelphia division with revenue of $719,000, expenses of $795,000, and a deficit of $76,000. Revenues did, of course, increase. Five years later, the year 1891–92 (July 1 to June 30) showed gross earnings of $1,966,000, expenses of $1,389,000, and net earnings of $577,000. Even so, it had been an expensive venture which may well have contributed to the later receivership.

In 1885 the Baltimore and Ohio purchased a controlling share of the capital stock of the Staten Island Rapid Transit Railway. By 1885 the B&O already had running rights over the Philadelphia and Reading and the Central of New Jersey, which had been leased to the Philadelphia and Reading in 1883. By 1887 the B&O had built a truss bridge over Arthur Kill, which separated Staten Island from the mainland of New Jersey. With the bridge completion, the B&O had a connecting service of sorts into the lower harbor of New York City. Also in 1885, the completion of the Columbus and Cincinnati Midland Railroad out in Ohio gave the B&O a new connection between Columbus and the Marietta and Cincinnati line a few miles east of Cincinnati. The B&O would later lease the Columbus and Cincinnati Midland in 1890.

Samuel Spencer, president, 1887–88.
(Courtesy, Baltimore and Ohio Railroad)

Robert Garrett's health became worse, and late in July 1887, he left Baltimore for a trip to Europe. While there, upon his physician s advice, he resigned the presidency of the B&O, effective on October 12, 1887, writing to the board of directors: "It is well known to many of you that it has been for some time my fixed desire and intention to withdraw when I properly could from . . . my position as President of the Baltimore & Ohio."[2] On the same day, William F. Burns, a board member since 1880, and son of Francis Burns who was a director from 1854 to 1880, was elected president pro tem. William Burns completed and signed the *Annual Report* for 1887 and remained in office until the election of Samuel Spencer on December 10, 1887.

Samuel Spencer, the forty-year-old first vice president of the B&O, was born in Georgia and as a sixteen-year-old youth in 1863, enlisted in the Confederate army as a cavalry private, first in the "Nelson Rangers" and later under Nathan Bedford Forrest. After the war, he obtained a B.A. degree from the University of Georgia and a civil engineering degree from the University of Virginia. During the 1870s, Spencer worked for several northern lines including the Baltimore and Ohio. In 1877 he was appointed superintendent of the Long Island Railroad at a salary of $5,000 per year. Spencer soon gained the attention of J. Pierpont Morgan, whose bank held many of the securities of the Long Island Railroad. Morgan soon came to rely upon Spencer's tact and general railroad knowledge. After only eighteen months with the Long Island, Spencer was called back to the Baltimore and Ohio to become assistant to President John W. Garrett. Soon Spencer started to follow Robert Garrett up the vice presidential ladder.

Certainly the Baltimore and Ohio directors thought highly of their newly elected top executive. A few days after Spencer's election, the *Railroad Gazette* reported that, "it is said that President Spencer will receive $25,000 a year, which is 6 1/4 times the salary of his predecessor."[3] Through his twenty-six-year tenure as president, John Garrett, and son Robert, had refused to take more than $4,000 as annual salary. Of course, both men received far more than that as major holders of stock which paid good annual dividends.

In the early fall of 1887, while President Robert Garrett was in England, First Vice President Samuel Spencer had started to negotiate with J. P. Morgan and other bankers for the addition of fresh capital to the B&O. It was soon rumored that the Morgan interests might require some share in the selection of B&O executive officers. When Robert Garrett heard the rumors while in London, he became quite disturbed at the possibility of his losing the presidency. Spencer made a public statement which quieted Robert Garrett, but did not soften his feelings toward Morgan. It seems probable that the controversy over the Morgan-Spencer negotiations, more than his poor health, was the major factor in Robert Garrett's resignation in mid-October 1887.

Samuel Spencer, in his single year in the president's chair, was a forceful and active railroad executive. He was unhappy that the B&O had a floating debt of more than $8,769,000 and decided to reduce it. Spencer felt that the B&O's own private express, telegraph, and sleeping car services were costly and inefficient. In the fall of 1887, the sale of the B&O telegraph system to the Western Union Telegraph Company had been completed, and in June 1888, the B&O sold its sleeping and parlor car equipment to the Pullman Palace Car Company. These newly available funds helped him reduce the floating debt of the B&O to only $3,478,000 as of September 30, 1888. Spencer also considered the B&O balance sheet to be in error with the continued valuation of ancient and nearly obsolete locomotives figured at their original cost. He estimated that such figures were at least 30 percent too high. As a result, the value of B&O rolling stock which was listed as $18,270,000 in the 1887 *Annual Report* of Robert Garrett was reduced to only $14,532,000 in Spencer's *Annual Report* for 1888. Spencer also felt that many securities of other roads held by the B&O were vastly over-valued. After he had made appropriate reductions in these valuations, the "profit and loss" figure in the balance sheet dropped from $48,083,000 in 1887 to $23,465,000 in 1888.

When the *Annual Report* for 1888 appeared, the *Railroad Gazette* was pleased with the fiscal reforms achieved by Spencer. The editors of the *Gazette* wrote:

> For the first time in many years we are given a straightforward account of the conditions of the Baltimore & Ohio R.R. The showing is in some respects good, in others bad. It is good as indicating a desire on the part of the management to deal honestly with the public. . . . The report does credit to President Spencer's management. But it shows even more clearly that the conditions of the property a year ago was much worse than was supposed at the time. Not only were the securities over valued . . . but the apparent earnings of the company were exaggerated by tricks of book-keeping.[4]

There is little doubt that the "book-keeping" during the years of John Garrett's leadership did not always meet the standards typical of the best accounting practices. Referring to the statistics to be shown in the forthcoming 1873 *Annual Report*, Vice President John King had written to John Garrett in Europe: "These improvements [on Ohio roads], which are properly Construction, you understand, are in conformity with our practice, since leasing Central Ohio, charged to Repairs. . . . Iron from Cumberland Mill is charged at $90 per ton, which price can be reduced if you think proper."[5] Certainly in the postwar years, many railroad executives were following the same rather flexible practices in their accounting.

Spencer's year as president of the Baltimore and Ohio was also the first year of federal regulation of railroads by the new Interstate Commerce Commission. In his concluding comments in the 1888 *Annual Report*, Spencer urged that all railroad managers should follow "conservative and businesslike methods" and that a failure to do so might "provoke additional legislation under which it will be even more difficult to make adequate returns upon invested capital."[6] The *Railroad Gazette* had earlier urged railroad managers to give the Interstate Commerce Commission a fair trial concluding that "the only way to get rid of obnoxious legislation is by making people see the hardship it involves."[7]

Many of the twenty-three members of the B&O board of directors were not as enthusiastic about Spencer's drastic reform measures as were the editors of the *Railroad Gazette*. This was especially true of the seven Baltimore and the four Maryland state directors. A growing number in the total membership seemed fearful that Drexel, Morgan and Company was hoping to gain control of the B&O through Samuel Spencer. Some of them recalled that Morgan, back in the 1870s, had often been critical of John Garrett's leadership. Board members and stockholders favorable to the Garrett family naturally were unhappy with Spencer's annual report and wished to stifle any further investigation. When the new board was elected on November 18, 1888, only five of the twelve stockholder directors were retained. Among those dropped were several who had favored the Spencer reforms.

The new board clearly was supportive of the Garrett faction and critical of Spencer. Finding that board support was lacking for his reforms, President Spencer on December 19, 1888, tendered his resignation, which was quickly accepted. He had been in the president's chair just one year and nine days. The board's suspicion of Spencer's close ties with the New York banking house seemed justified, for in March 1889, he was appointed the railroad expert for Drexel, Morgan and Company. Late in 1890, he became a partner in the banking house and in 1893 was named one of the receivers for the failing Richmond Terminal system. When the Southern Railway was created in 1894, Spencer became its president, a position he held until his death in 1906. From the outset, the new road was known for its conservative and efficient management. During Spencer's tenure as president, the Southern Railway nearly doubled its mileage and increased its passenger and freight traffic more than fourfold.

In retrospect, the Baltimore and Ohio should have embraced and continued most of the reforms and changes that Spencer introduced in his short tenure as president. If such a program had been accepted, it seems quite probable that the B&O could have escaped the receivership and reorganization of the late 1890s.

On the same day that Spencer resigned, the board of directors elected Charles F. Mayer the tenth president of the Baltimore and Ohio Railroad. The fifty-six-year-old Mayer was a native of Baltimore and, after a public school education, worked for an uncle, Frederick Koenig, a Baltimore importing merchant. In 1865 he left the importing business and helped organize the Despard Coal Company. In 1877 he became president of the Consolidation Coal Company which owned 21,000 acres of West Virginia coal lands and several short-line railroads. Mayer had been elected to the B&O board of directors in November 1887, just a year before his election to the presidency. After his elevation to the president's chair, the *Railroad Gazette* described Mayer as a man of action rather than words with an above average ability in the compilation of statistics.

The seven-year presidency of Charles Mayer was a period of contrasts. During his years in office, he added a new route to Chicago and significant new mileage in Pennsylvania, Ohio, and West Virginia. He added an entrance into Chicago, including a new station, and built a tunnel under downtown Baltimore to improve service to Philadelphia. The new president almost completely removed state and city interference from the B&O board of

Charles F. Mayer, president, 1888–96.
(Courtesy, Baltimore and Ohio Railroad)

directors. The seven years were years of record earnings and even greater increases in operating expense. Total tonnage figures expanded, but these were also years in which both the Chesapeake and Ohio and the Norfolk and Western were gaining on the Baltimore and Ohio in the hauling of coal. Finally, Mayer ended his tenure with his road in receivership, but a receivership no doubt caused more by the imperfect management of earlier presidents than by errors in judgment made by Mayer himself.

Between 1890 and 1892, the Baltimore and Ohio acquired control of the West Virginia and Pittsburgh Railroad which, by 1893, had 160 miles of branch lines south of Clarksburg on the Parkersburg Branch. The new lines served an undeveloped area of West Virginia rich in timber and minerals. A little later, Mayer acquired the Fairmont, Morgantown and Pittsburgh Railroad, a sixty-three-mile line connecting Fairmont, West Virginia, with Connellsville, Pennsylvania. By 1890 President Mayer had succeeded in purchasing a controlling interest in the Valley Railway of Ohio, a seventy-five-mile line extending from Cleveland southward through Akron to Valley Junction, Ohio. During the early 1890s, the B&O also acquired a controlling interest in the Pittsburgh and Western. This 328-mile line, including its branches, ran from Allegheny City, just north of Pittsburgh, to Akron, Ohio, and also north to Fairport, a port on Lake Erie several miles east of Cleveland. During 1890 and 1891, B&O construction crews had built the seventy-three-mile Akron and Chicago Junction Railroad, westward from Akron to Chicago Junction on the original B&O route to Chicago. Freight service was opened on this new line in August 1891. Through passenger service from Baltimore to Chicago via the new route did not start until May 1893. The new superior route was via the Main Line to Cumberland, the Pittsburgh and Connellsville to Pittsburgh, the Pittsburgh and Western Railway to Akron, the Akron and Chicago Junction to Chicago Junction, and the Baltimore and Ohio and Chicago into Chicago.

Even before the new route to Chicago was opened, the Baltimore and Ohio had built a new station in Chicago. After nearly two decades of sharing the Illinois Central Station, located near the lakefront at Randolph Street, the B&O decided it needed a larger terminal. The Illinois Central in fact was moving its main passenger terminal a mile south to a new station located near Twelfth Street (Roosevelt Road), in order to be ready for the crowds expected for the World's Fair of 1893. The Baltimore and Ohio obtained permanent trackage rights over the Rock Island Line to enter downtown Chicago southwest of the Loop with a new terminal, the Grand Central Station, located at the corner of Harrison and Wells streets. The new four-story station with its tall, corner clock tower was opened for traffic on December 1, 1891. A few years later, an electric sign on top of the tower flashed out the letters, "B&O" for the benefit of nighttime travelers. Separate freight and switching yards were located south of the new station and just east of the south branch of the Chicago River. President Mayer was certain that the new Chicago facilities "cannot fail, in the immediate future, to materially increase the business . . . west of the [Ohio] river."[8]

A much more difficult and time-consuming terminal project was taking place in Baltimore in the same years. By 1880 it had been decided that the difficult and irritating transfer of passenger trains along Pratt Street between the B&O and the Philadelphia, Wilmington and Baltimore Railroad would have to end. Instead, the through passenger trains, headed for Philadelphia and beyond, were routed to Locust Point where they used a carferry to cross the Inner Harbor to Canton and the tracks of the PW&B. The new carferry, the "Canton" was a 324-foot sidewheeler with a thirty-six-foot beam and a capacity of ten passenger cars or twenty-seven freight cars. After the Pennsylvania cut off further B&O passenger traffic on the PW&B, the B&O still used the carferry to get its trains to the tracks of the new line it was building to Philadelphia. As traffic increased, President Mayer and his fellow B&O officials realized they were at an increasing disadvantage with the Pennsylvania which more than a dozen years earlier had crossed under the growing city of Baltimore by building a tunnel.

By the fall of 1889, both the top B&O officials and the citizenry of Baltimore were in agreement that some sort of connecting line should be built across Baltimore to replace the carferry to Canton. But no one had much enthusiasm for a possible crosstown

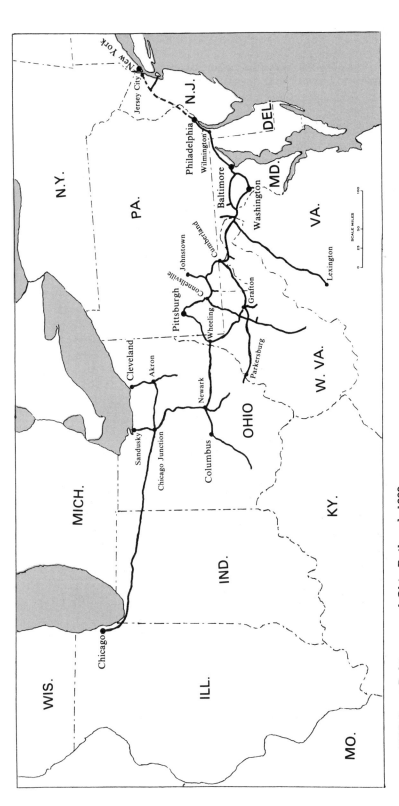

MAP 6.   Baltimore and Ohio Railroad, 1890.

Major extensions in the 1880s included the line from Baltimore to Philadelphia, lines to Cleveland and Akron, and additional mileage in Pennsylvania and West Virginia. The B&O also had trackage rights (– –) over the Philadelphia and Reading and the Central of New Jersey to Jersey City, just across the Hudson from New York City.

elevated railroad like those already in use up in New York City. When another tunnel was suggested, the people of Baltimore could only remember the smoked-filled, badly ventilated Pennsylvania tunnel built under the streets of the city. John K. Cowen, B&O general counsel, and his fellow railroad lawyers had already organized the Baltimore Belt Railroad out of two earlier projected lines. In 1889 President Mayer enticed Samuel Rea, a young "principal assistant engineer" on the Pennsylvania Railroad to move to Baltimore as the chief engineer of the Baltimore Belt Railroad.

By December 1889, early surveys had been completed for a seven-mile connecting double-track line running north from Camden Station via a tunnel under Howard Street and then eastward to a Bay View connection with the line to Philadelphia. The B&O announced that the smoke and ventilation problem in the tunnel would be solved by the use of electric, not steam, locomotives. Illness prevented Rea from finishing the project, and by 1892 he again was with the Pennsylvania. Early in the twentieth century, Rea was in charge of the tunnel project under the Hudson River and the building of the new Pennsylvania Station in midtown Manhattan. In 1912 he became the ninth president of the Pennsylvania.

An electric locomotive pulls a train through the tunnel to Mount Royal Station in Baltimore. *(Courtesy, Smithsonian Institution)*

All the contracts for the seven-mile project were let by September 1890, and in 1891 work started on the 7,341-foot Howard Street Tunnel. Seven shafts were sunk along the route so that several construction gangs could work simultaneously. The double-track tunnel ranged from fifty to sixty-five feet under the surface of the pavement above, and had a width of twenty-seven feet and an extreme height of twenty-one feet three inches. Throughout the length of the tunnel, the track ascended to the north at a constant grade of 0.8 percent. When the tunnel was completed in 1895, it was equipped with electric lights, and power to the electric locomotive was supplied from a suspended lightweight rail. A few years later, it was discovered that the power pick-up was improved by using a third rail system. The first electric locomotive, known as "No. 1," weighed ninety-six tons, was thirty-five feet long, had a drawbar pull of 56,000 pounds, and was referred to as a "giant" by the local press. The press also estimated that the entire belt line would cost about $5 million to build. The Howard Street Tunnel alone cost more than $2,400,000. The first passenger train used the new tunnel and the Baltimore belt route on May 1, 1895. Sixteen months later, on September 1, 1896, the new Mount Royal Station, located uptown at the northern end of the tunnel, was opened for passenger use. With both passenger and freight trains using the Howard Street Tunnel, the water transfer by carferry from Locust Point to Canton was abandoned.

During the construction of the Baltimore Belt Railroad, the Baltimore and Ohio had played a role in the 1893 World's Columbian Exposition at Chicago. In the spring of 1893, an "exposition line" branch was laid from the B&O main line in Chicago to the exposition grounds, both for the delivery of building materials and later for the movement of visitors to the exposition. The B&O also prepared an extensive exhibit of locomotives and railway equipment, including not only its own equipment, but many models of famous engines and cars from around the world. The man chiefly responsible for the exhibit was "Major" J. G. Pangborn, former drummer boy in the Civil War, world traveler, and a traffic officer on the B&O much interested in the early history of railroading. The newest locomotive in the popular exhibit was the B&O *Director General*, an 1893 Baldwin built 4-4-0 weighing sixty-two tons with seventy-eight inch drivers, which had recently made a speed record of ninety-six miles per hour.

Certainly very few of the 860 locomotives (in 1892) on the entire B&O system were capable of the speed of the *Director General*. But the passenger locomotives and the 650 passenger train cars were giving an extensive passenger service in 1893. The six-teen pages of B&O passenger train schedules in the 1893 *Traveler's Official Guide* could not match the sixty-five-page spread of the Pennsylvania System, but the B&O did provide more than twenty daily trains between New York, Philadelphia, Baltimore, and Washington. The best of these trains was the all-Pullman *Royal Blue* which, since 1890, had been giving deluxe service between Washington and New York City. Painted a deep blue with Royal Saxon gold striping, each of the cars was identified with an emblazoned state crest. The fastest B&O schedule between the two cities in 1893 was five hours, including a twelve-minute ferry boat trip across the Hudson River to the foot of Liberty Street. The Pennsylvania also had to rely on a ferryboat crossing until the completion of their tunnel under the Hudson in 1910. In 1893 dozens of other B&O trains were giving service west to Pittsburgh, Cleveland, Columbus, and Chicago, while connecting service was also available to Cincinnati and St. Louis. In 1893 the best B&O trains had vestibule "anti telescoping" cars heated by steam and lighted by Pintsch gas. Twenty-five years earlier, the first issue of the *Traveler's Official Guide* (June 1868) had included only three pages listing less than two dozen trains on a much smaller B&O system.

In the summer of 1890, President Mayer achieved a change in the management and direction of his railroad every bit as important as terminal improvements made in Chicago and Baltimore. For nearly seventy-five years, the B&O board of directors had been something of a hybrid, having nearly as many public directors as directors representing the private sector. For a number of years, the board had consisted of twelve stockholder directors, seven city directors representing the city of Baltimore, and four state directors representing Maryland. On July 16, 1890, President Mayer reported to the board that the city of Baltimore had sold its B&O stock and that the seven city directors would soon be leaving the board; at about the same time, the state of Maryland disposed of its preferred stock and withdrew two of its four directors. Thus, with the new fiscal year of 1890–91, the B&O board consisted of only fourteen members, twelve representing private stockholders and two representing the state of Maryland, which retained its Washington branch stock until it was finally sold in the spring of 1906.

The B&O board, regardless of its size, had seen many changes in the dozen years covering the tenures of three presidents: Robert Garrett, Samuel Spencer, and Charles Mayer. Samuel Spencer, in his summary for the year of 1888, had not only enlarged the page size of the *Annual Report*, but had changed the entire format. No longer was the old Main Stem given the prominence it had known for so many decades. Figures and statistics replaced the earlier, wordy paragraphs of John and Robert Garrett. On the first page, Spencer pointed out that "interest, rentals, taxes and other charges" for the year amounted to $6,246,553. This left a balance so small that no dividends on common stock could be paid that year. In 1892 the fiscal year for the B&O was changed to end on June 30 rather than September 30. Thus the *Annual Report* for 1892 covered only nine months, from October 1, 1891 to June 30, 1892.

Other changes also came during 1891. On November 11, 1891, the board of directors declared a special 20 percent common stock dividend payable on December 31, 1891. They justified the dividend by pointing out the absence of dividends on the common stock during the years of 1889, 1890, and 1891. In the same resolution, the board provided for the issuance of $5,096,600 of new common stock. The effect of the large stock dividend plus the newly issued stock resulted in the growth of B&O common stock from $14,784,600 in 1891 to $24,995,700 in 1892. The total bonded indebtedness of the company in 1892 was very close to $75,000,000. In the dozen years, the total receipts of the Baltimore and Ohio had increased about 44 percent while the freight revenue had climbed slightly less than one-third. In the years since 1885, the total annual freight tonnage carried on the entire system had climbed from 8,422,000 tons to 17,861,000 tons. Since in the same

TABLE 12. Entire Baltimore and Ohio System Traffic and Financial Growth 1885–96

Year	Miles of Road	Freight Receipts	Total Receipts	Net Earnings	Expenses to Earnings (%)	Dividends on Common Stock (%)
1885	1,695	$12,825,715	$16,616,641	$5,643,057	66	10
1886	1,808	14,146,073	18,422,437	6,306,695	65	10
1887	1,821	15,780,460	20,659,035	6,538,904	68	8
1888	1,774	14,309,773	20,353,491	6,152,930	69	—
1889	1,790	14,669,447	21,303,002	6,492,158	69	—
1890	1,845	16,991,647	24,412,096	7,445,226	69	—
1891	1,902	16,813,020	24,530,395	7,452,162	69	—
1892 (9 mo.)	1,983	13,100,441	18,927,574	5,060,996	73	1.25 +20*
1892–93	2,053	17,561,996	26,214,807	7,172,825	72	2.5
1893–94	2,065	13,916,476	22,502,662	6,941,973	69	2.5
1894–95	2,094	15,591,062	22,817,182	7,016,138	69	—
1895–96	2,095	16,818,672	23,944,781	6,361,361	73	—

*20% stock dividend

years average freight rates had declined somewhat, the annual dollar revenue did not climb as fast as did the tonnage figures. During the late 1880s and the early 1890s, operating expenses on the B&O climbed faster than did the total revenue. The ratio of expenses to earnings, which averaged 67.7 percent from 1885 through 1890, climbed to an average of just under 71 percent in the years 1891 through 1896.

The rate of revenue growth on the B&O for the years 1885–96 was quite comparable to the rate of revenue increase on the two rival trunk lines to the north, the Pennsylvania and the New York Central. But in one respect, the B&O was a much weaker road than the two rivals to the north. The relative size of the funded debt was much larger on the B&O than on either the New York Central or the Pennsylvania. In 1896, the year of receivership, the B&O had capital stock of $30 million—$5 million preferred, and $25 million common. However, its total funded debt by 1896 was just under $90 million, or three times the size of its capital stock. The various loans and bonds listed in the 1896 report consisted of sixteen different issues, paying interest of from 4 to 7 percent a year, with most of the rates being either 5 or 6 percent. The total annual interest due in 1896 was $4,552,000. In contrast, the nation's railroads, as a whole in 1896, had an investment almost equally divided between stock and bonds ($5,373,000,000 capital stock and $5,461,000,000 bonded debt). On the New York Central in 1896, the total capital stock was roughly one-third larger than the bonded debt, and on the Pennsylvania the ratio of stock to bonds was even higher.

Charles Mayer had growing financial problems throughout his seven year one month tenure as president. The younger Garrett somehow had managed to maintain a dividend policy for common stock quite reminiscent of the years of the elder Garrett. Up to 1887, no general apprehension was felt by investors because of the generally high prestige enjoyed by the B&O. Certainly no dividends on the common stock were possible in 1888, the year of Spencer's stern leadership and strict accounting methods. The *Annual Report* for 1888 revealed that the money paid out for "interest, rentals, taxes and other charges" was a bit larger than the net earnings from operations. Even though both total receipts and net earnings increased in his first three years in office, Mayer was not able to pay any dividend on the common stock in 1889, 1890, or 1891. Baltimore and Ohio stock, which had been selling at 150 or higher, had dropped to 85 by January 1889.

Charles Mayer soon found that he was losing the support of two banking houses long allied with the Baltimore and Ohio. Early in the Mayer presidency, it became apparent that Drexel, Morgan and Company, where former president Spencer was now employed, was no longer friendly with the Baltimore and Ohio. The second shoe dropped in November 1890, with the failure of the Baring Brothers of London, a banking house that had been supportive of the financial needs of the Baltimore and Ohio for many years. Even before the failure of the Baring Brothers, the Garrett family was favoring a syndicate scheme which would control a major share of all B&O stock in order to improve traffic conditions between eastern and western roads. In June 1890, Mr. E. R. Bacon formed a syndicate to control a large portion of all B&O stock. Participating in the syndicate, in addition to the Garrett family, were capitalists from New York, Philadelphia, Baltimore, and Pittsburgh representing the Richmond Terminal, the Pittsburgh and Western, the Reading, and the Northern Pacific systems. Participants in the syndicate were required to pool their stock for three years with an unlimited proxy given to Charles Mayer for the same length of time.

The presence of Northern Pacific interests in the new syndicate was later to help the B&O officials in the early 1890s as they obtained new terminal facilities in Chicago just before the 1893 Worlds Fair. The amount of stock in the new pool increased when the syndicate purchased 32,500 shares of common stock from the city of Baltimore and 9,686 shares of preferred stock from the state of Maryland, both purchases being made in 1890. An incidental advantage of these sales was the removal of several city and state members from the board of directors. Later, the syndicate exchanged the newly acquired preferred stock for common stock held by Johns Hopkins University. The total stock held by the syndicate now amounted to nearly 90,000 shares.

The 1890 syndicate failed to bring any marked improvement in the financial problems facing President Mayer. Dividends of 1.25 percent were paid on the common stock for the short nine month year, October 1, 1891 to June 30, 1892, and the rate was raised to 2.5 percent for both 1892–93 and 1893–94. No dividends on the common stock were paid in 1894–95 or after. Certainly there was little money for repairs or improvements. After President Benjamin Harrison signed the Railroad Safety Appliance Act on March 2, 1893, a B&O director complained that compliance with the automatic coupler bill might cost the B&O several million dollars. Enemies of the railroad were claiming the B&O floating debt was so large that the railroad could not afford to repaint fading passenger cars and that oil lamps were still used on some passenger trains. Certainly Charles Mayer worked hard to stem the tide of bad financial news, spending long hours at his office checking traffic contracts and personally approving requisitions of any size. He found it difficult to delegate tasks to others. Once, when a wheel chair was required at Camden Station, President Mayer in person purchased one on Howard Street.

There was no improvement in the financial picture in 1895. As he concluded the *Annual Report* in the fall of 1895, Charles Mayer wrote of "the continued depression . . . and the extreme low rates of freight . . . rendered it proper . . . to exercise every economy."[9] But these efforts were not sufficient. Even earlier it had been decided by the board to again appeal to top banking interests for help in reorganizing the finances of the company. The bankers agreed, but insisted that in the November 1895 election of directors, they should be well represented in the twelve-man board. Accordingly, in the board election on November 18, four new names appeared on the board: (1) Louis Fitzgerald, president of the Mercantile Trust Company of New York and an ally of J. P. Morgan; (2) William A. Read of Vermilye Brothers; (3) Eugene Delano of Brown Brothers; and (4) Howland Davis of Blake, Bossevaine and Company of London. Two months later, on January 24, 1896, upon the resignation of George Jenkins, Edward R. Bacon, president of the Baltimore and Ohio Southwestern and member of the 1890 syndicate, was also added to the board. The twelve-member board, as it existed in the winter of 1895–96, continued in office through the receivership years without change.

In mid-December 1895, Charles Mayer resigned the presidency effective upon the selection of his successor. He gave his wife's declining health as the reason for his departure, but there was little doubt that the board was glad to have him leave office. On the first day of January, there were growing rumors concerning the possible receivership, and these reports soon affected the market for B&O stock. In the early 1880s, when the operating ratio of the road had normally been well below 60 percent and stockholders received 10 percent dividends each year, B&O stock was selling at 200 or more. Such quotations were ancient history by the 1890s, and late in January 1896, the price had dropped to 42 1/2. In mid-January, as the board was looking for Mayer's successor, there were rumors that they were offering the job to a vice president from the Santa Fe. The rumor was proven false, for on January 24, 1896, John K. Cowen, long time general counsel of the Baltimore and Ohio, was elected the eleventh president of the railroad to succeed Charles Mayer.

John Kissig Cowen was born in Ohio in 1844 and, after graduating from Princeton and studying law at the University of Michi-

John K. Cowen, president, 1896–1901.
(Courtesy, Baltimore and Ohio Railroad)

gan, practiced law in Ohio from 1868 to 1872. The broadshouldered, six-foot, red-haired young lawyer with an amiable disposition joined the legal department of the Baltimore and Ohio in 1872 and four years later was made general counsel. Robert Garrett, during his short presidency, leaned heavily upon his old Princeton classmate for advice and support. Cowen had a magnetic personality and a great capacity for work. He had a remarkable memory and was an excellent after dinner speaker. As a "sound money" Democrat, Cowen entered politics in the early 1890s and was elected to a two-year term in Congress in 1894. Once in the president's chair, he had little time for politics.

In the weeks of January and February 1896, President Cowen frantically sought new funds from New York City bankers while at the same time he tried to appease and resist the persistent B&O creditors and bill collectors. Cowen even started the process of obtaining a mortgage on the B&O central headquarters building at Calvert and Baltimore streets. In the meantime, the market for B&O stock drifted lower and lower, being quoted at 21-1/2 in late February. Cowen received some help from Oscar G. Murray, a veteran traffic manager on several western railroads, who, on February 19, 1896, was elected first vice president of the Baltimore and Ohio. In the last days of February, Cowen gave top priority to obtaining sufficient cash that would permit him to pay $404,000 interest on bonds and equipment trusts that were going to fall due on March 1, 1896. On Saturday, February 29 (1896 was a leap year), Louis Fitzgerald, president of the Mercantile Trust, the bank to which the interest was due on March 1, called John Cowen and Edward R. Bacon to New York City. Fitzgerald told Cowen and Bacon a receivership could not be avoided.

Returning back to Baltimore, Cowen and Bacon hurried to the office of Judge Goff of the United States Circuit Court, where Oscar Murray soon joined them. The necessary papers were soon signed, and Judge Goff appointed John Cowen and Oscar Murray as receivers for the Baltimore and Ohio Railroad. With the signature of the judge, the authority of Cowen as the B&O president amounted to very little, but the new power of Cowen and Murray, as newly appointed federal officials, was quite great. In the next two years, the two receivers would rebuild and greatly reform both the finances and the physical structure of the Baltimore and Ohio.

Several factors contributed to the insolvency and receivership which befell the Baltimore and Ohio in 1896. Probably the main one was the line's excessive dependency upon borrowed money rather than share capital to finance the expansion of the system. This increase in the fixed charges of large annual interest costs gave the B&O a basically weak financial structure. During the mid-1890s, the Baltimore and Ohio was not the only road to face receivership. Between 1894 and 1898, more than 40,000 miles of line—almost one-quarter of the national rail network—were in financial trouble. Seven major lines—the B&O, Erie, Northern Pacific, Reading, Richmond and Danville, Santa Fe, and Union Pacific—all had reorganizations between 1893 and 1898. All seven roads had heavy bonded indebtedness, ranging from 41 percent to 80 percent (and averaging 66 percent) of their capital structures. This was at a time when the national average was about 50 percent.

Early B&O roundhouse at Piedmont, West Virginia.
(Courtesy, Smithsonian Institution)

The seven lines in financial trouble paid from 24 percent to 46 percent (and averaging 35 percent) of their gross income in fixed charges in 1893. Seven other major roads that escaped reorganization in the decade paid average annual fixed charges that were 22 percent of their gross income in 1893.

Of course, there were additional causes of the B&O receivership. The deficiencies in accounting and bookkeeping—weaknesses that had continued for many years—compounded the bad financial structure. The failure of the B&O board in the late 1880s to heed and follow the warnings and reforms of Samuel Spencer indicated the line was drifting toward serious financial trouble. Finally, the hard economic years of the depression 1890s only compounded and deepened the financial woes of the railroad.

The shock waves of the receivership in Baltimore were quite severe. During the first week in March 1896, B&O common stock dropped to a record low of 13. But for many observers, the fact of a B&O receivership came as no great surprise. Six days after the appointment of the two receivers, the *Railroad Gazette* wrote: ". . . The weakness of its finances for years, and specifically, the heavy burdens of debt which the company was attempting to carry have been well known, so that insolvency had been pretty well discounted among all interests which could be affected. . . . For many months the stock exchange values of securities have been falling."[10] In the last weeks of 1896, B&O shareholders could read in the latest annual report about the condition of their insolvent railroad. Nearly 70 years had passed since that February night in 1827 when the business leaders of Baltimore had first dreamed about a railway to the Ohio River. But already two hard working receivers were beginning to rebuild and strengthen their railroad.

Chapter XI

. . . .

A Reorganized
Railroad Faces
a New Century

IN THE SHORT DECADE AND A HALF BETWEEN THE
receivership suffered in 1896 and the election of Daniel Willard to
the presidency in 1910, many changes came to the Baltimore and
Ohio Railroad. Three different presidents served the road during
the fourteen years: John K. Cowen, 1896–1901; Leonor F. Loree,
1901–4; and Oscar G. Murray, 1904–10. The second of the three
presidents, Leonor F. Loree, was in office as a direct result of the
fact that the Pennsylvania Railroad had, at the turn of the century,
gradually purchased a dominant portion of the capital stock of the
B&O. During the fourteen years, the Baltimore and Ohio expanded greatly both in mileage and in total revenue. The mileage
of the B&O system increased from 2,095 miles in 1895–96 to 4,434
miles by the year 1909–10. Total revenues had climbed even more
rapidly, increasing from just under $24 million in 1895–96 to $90
million for the year 1909–10. During the first decade of the new
century, Presidents Loree and Murray saw the appearance of new
modes of transport—the electric interurban, the automobile, and
the airplane—new competitors for rail passenger and freight traffic
that would be of growing concern to Daniel Willard and later presidents. Of more immediate concern to Loree and Murray were the

new efforts to further regulate railroads. Both the Elkins Act of
1903 and the Hepburn Act of 1906, passed during the presidency
of Theodore Roosevelt, greatly increased the powers of the Interstate Commerce Commission.

Some writers of railroad history in the twentieth century
have referred to the B&O receivership in 1896 as being the result
of a scandal of bad management. In fact, the financial history of the
Baltimore and Ohio in the postwar decades was little different than
that of dozens of other American railways in those years. The general financial policies and practices of the B&O in the seventies and
eighties were no better and no worse than those of most other
railroads across the nation. The general reaction at the news of the
receivership was more one of surprise than shocked disapproval.
The severe panic of 1893 and the following depression pushed
dozens of lines into default, and by the mid-1890s, nearly one
quarter of the railroads in America, representing more than 40,000
miles and $2,500,000,000 of capital, were in the hands of receivers.

The joint-receivers of the B&O, John K. Cowen and Oscar
G. Murray, were very different in background, but had strengths
and abilities which complemented each other. Cowen, longtime
general counsel and elected president just five weeks before becoming one of the two receivers, was an expert both in law and
finance. Murray, on the other hand, was a genial, friendly man
who knew railroading and was an expert at obtaining traffic. Born
in Connecticut in 1847, he moved to the Southwest to start his
railroad career. For the fifteen years prior to his coming to the
B&O as vice president early in 1896, Murray had served as traffic
manager of such lines as the Missouri Pacific, the Big Four, and the
Chesapeake and Ohio. Murray was in his position as first vice president on the B&O for only ten days before the receivership elevated him to be a joint-receiver with Cowen. Murray, who never
married, soon became known in Baltimore as a *bon vivant* noted
for his immaculate apparel, fancy carriages, and generous tips to
the employees of the Stafford Hotel where he had a large suite.

In the spring of 1896, with the property of the B&O in the
hands of the courts, there was an opportunity to bring about the
kind of reforms that Samuel Spencer had sought during his short
presidency in the late 1880s. The bankers who had been added to
the board before the receivership had insisted on a complete audit
of the B&O books in order to see the extent of the problem. Stephen Little, an expert accountant and comptroller of the Denver
and Rio Grande, had been employed to make the financial inventory. When Little's final report was released in December 1896, it
charged that over a period of years the B&O management had

been guilty of overstating net income, making mischarges of worn-out equipment to profit and loss, paying unearned dividends, and making an understatement of liabilities. While these charges generally supported the earlier point of view of Samuel Spencer, there was no universal acceptance of the Little figures by the business press of the day. The *Railroad Gazette* supported Little, while the *Commercial and Financial Chronicle* held that, in several instances, Little had been too critical of the B&O accounting practices. In the early months of the receivership, there was no more agreement among the several rival reorganization committees. But eventually, a reorganization committee was formed with whom were deposited the bulk of the shares from the Garrett family plus those of the Philadelphia, Morgan, and New York interests. For a while, Johns Hopkins University attempted to maintain that its B&O preferred stock had rights superior even to B&O bonds. It was hoped to avoid a formal foreclosure, and legislation was passed by the Maryland legislature which permitted a new company to succeed, after a reorganization plan had been accepted, to the property of the B&O.

Long before a reorganization plan had been achieved, the two receivers were busy with a vigorous program of rebuilding the railroad. In the spring of 1896, the *Railroad Gazette* revealed that Cowen and Murray would each be paid a monthly salary of $2,300 as joint receivers. Both men earned their pay as they rebuilt the railroad. In May 1896, they let contracts for 5,000 new freight cars and seventy-five locomotives, all to be financed by receivers' certificates. Shop workers earlier laid off, or working only on a part-time basis, were recalled at the Mount Clare shops as well as at shop centers at Cumberland, Wheeling, and other western points. Soon, more than 4,000 shopmen throughout the B&O system were working full time.

The *Commercial and Financial Chronical* reported that during the entire receivership the receivers added 216 locomotives and more than 28,000 freight cars to the equipment roster, as well as 123,000 tons of new rails. Cowen and Murray were fortunate in being able to purchase some new steel rails at the record low price of only seventeen dollars per ton. Almost at once, the price began to rise so high that later the receivers were able to sell some old rail for as much as the cost of the new. New bridges, new ties and ballast, extra marine equipment, and improved terminal facilities were all added during the period of the receivership. The extensive track improvement work during the period of the receivership resulted in an extra bonus. In August 1898, as trackmen were working on the line running into the Mount Clare shops, they uncovered at a depth of several feet, the original first stone which had been laid by Charles Carroll on that Independence Day more than seventy years before. The forgotten stone was raised to the surface, placed on a granite base and enclosed with a strong steel cage. Half a century later it would be given a place of honor in the B&O Transportation Museum in Baltimore.

John Moody, the financial analyst, later reported that the rebuilt Baltimore and Ohio at the end of the receivership "was in splendid condition to take advantage of the tide of commercial and industrial prosperity which was just beginning to flow."[1] On June 30, 1899, the renewed roster of B&O equipment consisted of 950 steam and 4 electric locomotives, 671 passenger cars, 44,087 freight cars (including 22,000 box and 20,000 gondola or hopper cars), 1,006 service cars, and marine equipment including 11 steamers, tugs and lighters, 56 barges and floats, and 45 canal boats. The 1899 balance sheet valued the rolling stock at $22,224,000 and the marine equipment at $583,000.

As the receivers rebuilt and renewed the property of the Baltimore and Ohio between 1896 and 1898, they were following some of the unheeded advice of an earlier president, Samuel Spencer. The reorganized B&O at the turn of the century was much more like the railroad Spencer had wanted the B&O to become

In 1900 two official photographers snap a picture of the approaching *Royal Blue*. (*Courtesy, Smithsonian Institution*)

when he was president in 1887–88. A short decade later, in 1906, when Spencer died in a train wreck on his own railroad, it was Oscar G. Murray, as president of the B&O, who ordered the flag on the new headquarters building to be flown at half-mast.

By April 1898, the B&O reorganization plan was complete, but it was not made public for two months because of the threatened war with Spain. The plan of June 22, 1898, called for new bond and stock issues as follows: 3.5 percent prior lien gold bonds—$70,000,000; 4 percent first mortgage bonds—$50,000,000; 4 percent non-cumulative preferred stock—$35,000,000; and common stock—$35,000,000. The exchange of bonds was based on the principle of retiring high interest old bonds for a slightly increased volume of new bonds paying lower rates. Some of the old bondholders also received modest issues of the new preferred stock with its lower rate of return. The cash required in the plan of reorganization was estimated at about $36 million for arrears of interest, receiver's certificates, and new working capital. This was to be raised by stock assessments ranging from two dollars to twenty dollars per share and by the sale of portions of the new securities to the syndicate. Both the common and the preferred stock was to be vested in five trustees for five years, with the trustees having the discretionary power to deliver the stock at an earlier date.

The great bulk of the old share and bond holders readily accepted the reorganization plan, and the receivers officially surrendered control of the B&O on July 1, 1899. President Cowen, in a public address before the Maryland Bar Association, claimed that all bondholders had been paid in full and that all floating debt creditors had also received all that was due them. Only a modest reduction in fixed charges had been achieved, but this proved to be sufficient since company traffic and earnings were to grow rapidly in the years following the receivership. The success of the reorganization was, in fact, greatly aided by the general prosperity enjoyed by the nation in the late 1890s as America looked toward the new century.

The general balance sheet of the Baltimore and Ohio, as it was relieved of its receivership on June 30, 1899, listed securities of $35,000,000 of common stock, $39,228,000 of 4 percent preferred stock, $76,733,000 of prior lien 3.5 percent bonds, and $57,500,000 of first mortgage 4 percent bonds, for a total of $208,461,000 of issued capital liabilities. The *Annual Report* for 1898–99 also revealed that traffic revenue on the B&O had substantially increased during the receivership. Much of this increase was the result of the good work of Oscar Murray, who was to regain his position as first vice president in charge of traffic on July 1, 1899. The gross revenue of 1898–99 was $28,405,000, or an increase of nearly 19 percent over the revenue of $23,945,000 for the year 1895–96. Freight tonnage moving over the system had increased from 17,862,000 tons to 25,057,000 tons during the three years. During the same years, the gross revenue of the Pennsylvania had climbed only 17 percent, while that of the New York Central had increased only 3 percent.

With the acceptance of the reorganization plan, it was only natural that new names and faces began to appear in the active control of the railroad. In September 1898, Philip D. Armour, Marshall Field, and Norman D. Ream, all from Chicago and the executors of the George Pullman estate, purchased a large block of B&O stock. James J. Hill, who controlled the Great Northern and the Northern Pacific, also became a heavy investor in the Baltimore and Ohio. Receiver Cowen welcomed the new money from the West and said: "The recent transaction has been the realization of my hopes about the future of the road."[2] Since Hill had invested his money in the B&O, he proceeded to advise both Cowen and Murray that they should rebuild parts of the line and obtain lower grades to help with the heavy haulage of coal. Hill also helped persuade Frederick D. Underwood to leave the Soo to become second vice president and general manager on the Baltimore and Ohio. When Underwood left the Soo for his two years (1899–1901) on the B&O, he took one of his division superintendents, Daniel Willard, with him to become assistant general manager. In New York City, J.P. Morgan was happy to see Jim Hill become interested in the Baltimore and Ohio, and declared "Your connection with the B&O would remove a long standing irritating element in the railroad situation in this country."[3]

The B&O board of directors had been left unchanged during the receivership, but the board elected on April 11, 1899, had many new men added. From the old group of twelve shareholder directors, only two men were reelected in April 1899: Edward R. Bacon, president of the Baltimore and Ohio Southwestern, and Louis Fitzgerald, a New York banker. Among the new directors were James J. Hill; Jacob H. Schiff, head of the New York bank of Kuhn, Loeb and Co.; Norman B. Ream, Chicago grain and beef speculator and ally of J. P. Morgan; James Stillman; William Salomon; and Edward H. Harriman, a major investor in the Illinois Central and future antagonist of Jim Hill. Hill was a member of the board for only two years, while two others with western interests, Ream and Harriman, remained on the board until their deaths. By the time of Hill's resignation in the spring of 1901, there were four

B&O board members who also had strong interests in the Pennsylvania Railroad. The receivership and the new directors caused a radical shift in the geographic location of the board members. During the Garrett era, nearly all the directors came from Baltimore and Maryland. In the year 1886–87, all of the directors elected by the shareholders came from Baltimore. By 1901–2 seven came from New York City, two from Philadelphia, and one each from Chicago, Pittsburgh, and Baltimore.

With the reorganization complete on July 1, 1899, John Cowen became president in fact as well as in name, and Oscar Murray was reelected first vice president. The major expansion of B&O mileage during the Cowen years was the formal acquisition of the 922-mile Baltimore and Ohio Southwestern Railroad which was operated by the B&O after July 1, 1900. The Baltimore and Ohio Southwestern was essentially a combination of two lines, the Marietta and Cincinnati and the Ohio and Mississippi, which, back in 1857, had given the B&O service west to the Mississippi River and St. Louis. This route had become more useful with the narrowing of the broad gauge (six foot) O&M to standard gauge during the morning and early afternoon hours of Sunday, July 13, 1871. The completion of the bridge across the Mississippi at St. Louis, built by Capt. James B. Eads between 1869 and 1874, also improved the service. In 1882 John Garrett and the B&O had provided some financing necessary to help the Marietta and Cincinnati be reorganized as the Cincinnati, Washington and Baltimore Railway. In 1893 this road, now known as the Baltimore and Ohio Southwestern Railroad, was consolidated with the Ohio and Mississippi into the Baltimore and Ohio Southwestern Railway. By 1893 the B&O held a major share of the stock in the company and also was a guarantor of $11 million of first mortgage bonds of the newly consolidated line. However, the B&O and the western route to St. Louis continued to be operated as separate roads until 1900. The *Annual Report* for 1899–1900 consolidated the accounts of the two roads for the first time. As of July 1, 1900, the total mileage operated by the B&O system came to 3,199 miles.

In 1900 the 922-mile Baltimore and Ohio Southwestern consisted of a 532-mile main line from Belpre, Ohio, to East St. Louis; a 228-mile Springfield division from Beardstown, Illinois to Shawneetown, Illinois; plus several branches. Both principal branches ran south to the Ohio River, a 55-mile line to Portsmouth, Ohio, and a 53-mile line to Jeffersonville, Indiana. The gross earnings for the B&OSW for 1899–1900 amounted to $7,227,000, including $4,693,000 for freight traffic and $1,791,000 for passenger traffic. This amounted to roughly one-sixth of the total revenue on the combined 3,200-mile B&O system for 1899–1900. As of July 1, 1900, the equipment roster of the smaller B&OSW consisted of 228 locomotives, 203 passenger cars, and 12,448 freight cars. With the addition of the new line to the West, new securities were naturally added to the B&O capital structure. As of July 1, 1900, the B&O capital stock was $104 million ($74 million in 1899) and the funded debt had risen to $187 million ($134 million).

The summer the Baltimore and Ohio Southwestern merged with the B&O was also the summer that Cowen's railroad first tried to streamline a passenger train. Frederick U. Adams, a Denver newspaperman, had obtained a patent for a streamlined train, and by 1900 had convinced the B&O officials to give his design a test on the Baltimore to Washington route. A train of several wooden passenger cars was "streamlined" with shrouding, and the rear car was lengthened with a pointed end. The "streamlined" train operated for a number of trips between the two cities in May and June of 1900. The new service seemed to have no great public appeal and was soon discontinued. A year later, the special cars were dismantled and returned to regular service. However, the basic design proposed by Adams would be followed a long generation later when the American public gladly accepted the streamlined trains of the 1930s.

Adam's experimental streamlined train of 1900. (*Courtesy, Association of American Railroads*)

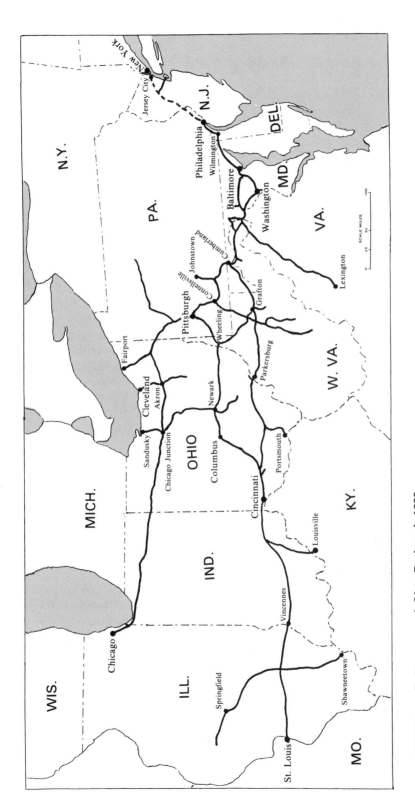

MAP 7.   Baltimore and Ohio Railroad, 1900.

Major extensions during the 1890s included new lines in Ohio and Pennsylvania. However, the most important addition was the

922-mile Baltimore Ohio Southwestern, which provided a route west of Parkersburg to Cincinnati and St. Louis.

Unfortunately, John Cowen was to have only a short time in which to enjoy the operation of a rebuilt 3,000-mile railroad. In 1899, the same year that the B&O came out of receivership, the Pennsylvania Railroad elected Alexander J. Cassatt to be its seventh president. Cassatt was an efficient railroad man with skills both in engineering and administration. He firmly believed that the freight rates of the late 1890s were abnormally low because large shippers, such as the Standard Oil Company and the Carnegie Steel Company, could demand, and obtain, substantial rebates. Cassatt sought to curtail the rebate practice by proposing to the top officials of the New York Central that that road and the Pennsylvania join together in a "community of interest" plan. The New York Central officials agreed to cooperate in a plan for the two trunk lines to purchase substantial amounts of the stock of the smaller and weaker trunk lines. The New York Central made a large investment in the Reading, while the Pennsylvania bought stock in the Chesapeake and Ohio, the Norfolk and Western, and the Baltimore and Ohio. Later, the Baltimore and Ohio purchased a large block of Reading stock. Working together the trunk lines managed to reduce to some degree the practice of rebates. President Cassatt's "community of interest" plan hardly endeared him to either John D. Rockefeller or Andrew Carnegie, but it did result in an increase in average freight rates. Between 1899 and 1901, average freight rates on the Pennsylvania rose from .47 cents per ton-mile to .58 cents. On the B&O, the .39 cents per ton-mile rate of 1898–99 increased to .49 cents in 1900–1901.

Another result of Cassatt's "community of interest" plan was the joint control by several roads, through a holding company, of the rail route south of Washington to Richmond, Virginia. At the turn of the century, the Seaboard Air Line was projecting a line of its own from Richmond to Washington. Certainly Cassatt had much to do with the creation of the Richmond-Washington Company, incorporated in New Jersey in 1901, a holding company which acquired all the share capital of the thirty-two mile Washington Southern and the majority of the stock of the Richmond, Fredericksburg and Potomac, an eighty-five mile road running from Richmond north to Quantico. The control of the Richmond-Washington Company was shared equally by six railroads—the Pennsylvania, the Baltimore and Ohio, the Southern, the Atlantic Coast Line, the Seaboard Air Line, and the Chesapeake and Ohio. This scheme assured each of the six lines of an entry into Washington and helped the later planning of a new Washington Union Station.

Cassatt had purchased his first B&O stock in November 1899, when he acquired 100,000 shares of preferred stock for just over $8,400,000. More stock was purchased in 1900, and in 1901 most of the B&O stock belonging to James J. Hill and his Chicago associates was also acquired by the Pennsylvania. Hill and the Chicago group made a big profit, probably more that doubling their money in less than three years. By the end of 1902, Cassatt's Pennsylvania Railroad had more than $65 million invested in Baltimore and Ohio stock. Naturally the heavy stock purchases resulted in a growing Pennsylvania representation on the Baltimore and Ohio board of directors. The board of twelve stockholder directors elected on November 19,1900, included two Pennsylvania men, John D. Green and Sutherland Prevost, both of whom were members of the Pennsylvania board and also company vice presidents. Six months later, in May 1901, Charles H. Tweed, chairman of the Southern Pacific, resigned from the B&O board to be replaced by James McCrea, while Jim Hill was replaced by Samuel Rea. Both men were Pennsylvania vice presidents and both would later become Pennsylvania Railroad presidents, McCrea succeeding Cassatt in 1907, and Rea following McCrea in 1913. By the spring of 1901, the four Pennsylvanians on the B&O board gave the northern rival effective control of the Baltimore and Ohio.

Not surprisingly, the masters of the Pennsylvania Railroad in their Broad Street office in Philadelphia decided that since they had effective stock control of the B&O, they should also have direct management of the 3,000-mile rail system. One morning in May 1901, President Cowen in his office was brought a letter from a high official of the Pennsylvania. Cowen was shocked to read that while the high official regretted the decision, the rulers of the Pennsylvania had decided that the B&O should be run by an operating man rather than a lawyer. The request for his resignation was accompanied by words of praise for his ability and also the offer of his old job as general counsel of the B&O at the same salary he had received as president. Cowen read and reread the letter in disbelief. He left his office that night never to return to his presidential desk. Cowen was elected to the board of directors and he also accepted the general counsel position, retaining it until his death, but he was a broken man, in spirit and soon in health. He traveled extensively in South America and Europe, but never regained his health, dying on April 26, 1904.

Leonor F. Loree succeeded Cowen on June 1, 1901, and remained president of the railroad for exactly thirty-one months, resigning on January 1, 1904. Born in Illinois in 1858, Loree graduated from Rutgers College in 1877 with a degree in civil engineering and at once entered the service of the Pennsylvania Railroad as a rodman. In 1879 he left that company for other railroads, but

Leonor F. Loree, president, 1901–4.
(Courtesy, Baltimore and Ohio Railroad)

returned to the Pennsylvania in 1883. He quickly advanced, becoming a division superintendent in 1889, and fourth vice president of the Pennsylvania lines west of Pittsburgh on January 1, 1901. Loree was an Anglophile and, with his wing collar and close-clipped beard, might easily have been taken for an English gentleman.

Commenting on the sudden elevation of Loree to the B&O presidency, the editor of the *Railroad Gazette* wrote: ". . . This event means that the Baltimore and Ohio is now to be practically a part of the Pennsylvania system."[4] The sudden appearance of an outsider from a rival line to manage the Baltimore and Ohio was hard for many of the older company officials to accept, but Loree was an excellent railroader who had big plans for the B&O. Quite soon he had prepared a twenty-year program of expansion and improvement for the entire system. His stay on the B&O was too brief for him to complete the program, but he made an excellent start in several directions. Loree's first concern was to further improve terminal facilities and to generally upgrade major portions of the line.

New interchange freight yards were built at Connellsville and New Castle in Pennsylvania, at Keyser and Fairmont in West Virginia, and at Holloway in Ohio. New yards were also built at Pittsburgh and a large locomotive repair shop was installed at Wheeling. Extensive track work was pushed in all parts of the system. Many curves were reduced on the Main Stem in Maryland, and grades in West Virginia were generally reduced to a maximun of 0.3 percent. A new cut-off south of Cumberland, plus a new 4,000-foot tunnel, reduced by more than ten miles the main line between Baltimore and Cincinnati. More than 125 new miles of double-track were laid on the Connellsville, Pittsburgh, and

Chicago divisions. In the single year 1902–3, President Loree pushed $9 million of construction and betterments on the fifteen different divisions of the system with the Cumberland, Connellsville, and New Castle divisions together spending more than half of the total. In the same year, 1,291,000 new crossties were put in place, 578 miles of line ballasted, and 56,000 tons of new steel rail (85 and 100 pounds to the yard) laid.

President Loree not only improved the B&O route, but also the motive power. It was Loree who ordered America's first articulated, or Mallet, engine, a steam locomotive with two sets of drivers powered by a single firebox and boiler. This locomotive type had first been designed twenty years earlier by Anatole Mallet of France. Reportedly, President Loree gave his general manager, Clifford S. Sims, only twenty-four hours to obtain background details on the new type of motive power. John E. Muhlfeld, general superintendent of motive power, designed the new locomotive and had it built by the American Locomotive Company. The giant 0-6-6-0 engine had twelve fifty-six-inch drivers, weighed 334,500 pounds, and had an impressive tractive power of 71,500 pounds. The locomotive was completed in 1904, shortly after Loree's departure from the B&O. The engine carried the number "2400," but since it was often balky, it was frequently called "Old Maude" after a comic strip mule of that day. The engine was exhibited at the 1904 St. Louis World's Fair before being put in service on a stiff grade on the Pittsburgh division. In later years, the Baltimore and Ohio would build dozens of additional articulated engines.

First articulated, or Mallet, locomotive on the B&O. This 167-ton 0-6-6-0 engine was powerful, but called "Old Maude" because of its balky behavior. *(Courtesy, Baltimore and Ohio Railroad)*

Many other improvements appeared during the two and one-half year tenure of the hard working Loree. The number of freight cars owned by the B&O increased by one-third during the Loree years, most with a larger capacity. He introduced the upper quadrant system of semaphore signalling and set up a new system of disbursement accounting which was soon adopted by other railroads. For years the B&O had been noted for the low salaries paid company officials. When Oscar Murray came to head the traffic department in the mid-1890s, he had insisted on a general salary increase for his department. Loree soon raised other departmental salaries to match the traffic department. Between 1901 and 1904, many clerks in the general offices saw their pay climb from sixty-five dollars to ninety dollars per month. A number of labor saving machines were introduced to improve office efficiency.

The rail system operated by the B&O increased from 3,220 to 3,986 miles between 1901 and 1904. The B&O also acquired some control over several short "affiliated lines." Included in all this new mileage were many short branch lines and several longer ones. Cowen had started, and Loree completed, the purchase of the 223-mile Ohio River Railroad which followed the southern bank of the Ohio River from Wheeling through Parkersburg and on south to Huntington, West Virginia. This line, which had been built in the 1880s, carried a heavy traffic in oil and petroleum products. Loree's B&O had also acquired greater control over the Cleveland, Lorain and Wheeling, a 192-mile Ohio line organized and built in the 1870s, running from the Ohio River across from Wheeling, northwest to Cleveland and Lorain on Lake Erie. Another acquisition was the seventy-four mile Ohio and Little Kanawha, which ran from Marietta to Zanesville, Ohio. All of these new properties increased both the revenue and the balance sheet of the Baltimore and Ohio. Between 1901 and 1904, the annual revenues of Loree's road increased from $47 million to $65 million, while the balance sheet total climbed from $338 million to $460 million.

President Loree even had plans for a new union station for Baltimore and the possible elimination of the Howard Street Tunnel. However, these plans never passed beyond the drawing board, for fresh challenges from the west seemed more appealing to Leonor Loree. Late in December 1903, he resigned the Baltimore and Ohio presidency, effective January 1, 1904, to become the president of the Chicago Rock Island and Pacific Railway. In 1907 Loree returned east to be president of the Delaware and Hudson, a postion he retained for thirty years. He served on the B&O board of directors from 1908 to 1922.

Oscar G. Murray, president, 1904–10.
(Courtesy, Baltimore and Ohio Railroad)

With the departure of Loree, Oscar G. Murray, the fifty-six-year-old vice president in charge of traffic, was elected president on December 29, 1903, effective January 1, 1904. In the twenty years since the death of the elder Garrett, the president's chair in the B&O central headquarters had been filled, in turn, by a great variety of men: a son trying to take his father's place, a fiscal reformer, a converted coal merchant, a brilliant lawyer, and a tireless engineer. Now in 1904, a picturesque traffic genius, perhaps without a peer in the country, was going to manage and direct the B&O. There were even stories that some major shippers waited in Murray's outer office for the opportunity to talk to the affable president and give him more traffic for his railroad.

There was no doubt about Murray's popularity with his subordinates and fellow workers at the Baltimore and Ohio. Even though the Pennsylvania still controlled the B&O, Murray was much easier to work for than the departed Leonor Loree. Early in the Murray presidency, the Pennsylvania control over the B&O was considerably reduced. In 1906 shortly before the death of Alexander Cassatt, the Pennsylvania Railroad sold about half of its Baltimore and Ohio common and preferred stock to Edwin H. Harriman's Union Pacific Railroad. There were several reasons for the decision to sell the stock: (1) Congress in 1903 had passed the Elkins Act curbing rebates; (2) in 1904 the United States Supreme Court had ordered the dissolution of the Northern Securities Company (which controlled three large western lines); and (3) the dynamic Theodore Roosevelt was becoming very critical of huge railroad consolidations. In the same year, 1906, the last two board members representing the state of Maryland left the board after the state sold its last 5,500 shares of B&O stock to the Maryland

Trust Company. After the spring of 1906, the B&O board consisted only of directors representing non-governmental stockholders.

The Pennsylvania Railroad continued to hold the remainder of its B&O stock, with a par value of more than $40 million, for another half dozen years. In 1912 the United States Supreme Court ordered the Union Pacific to dispose of its holdings of Southern Pacific stock. In 1913 the Union Pacific traded a substantial block of Southern Pacific stock to the Pennsylvania for that company's remaining holdings of B&O common and preferred stock. The Union Pacific then distributed to its own stockholders on a pro rata basis its recently acquired B&O stock. With this action, the B&O stock roster was increased by several thousand new individ-

B&O headquarters after great Baltimore fire of 1904.
(Courtesy, Baltimore and Ohio Railroad)

ual shareholders. In 1913 Samuel Rea and John Green, the remaining representatives of the Pennsylvania, resigned from the B&O board of directors.

The first major crisis to face President Murray came after he had been in office only five weeks. On a quiet Sunday morning, February 7, 1904, a fire broke out in downtown Baltimore which was not stopped until the following evening. Before being subdued, the conflagration had destroyed the center of the Baltimore business section including more than a thousand buildings. Included in the destruction was the B&O central headquarters at Baltimore and Calvert streets, completed in 1881–82 and the pride and joy of John W. Garrett. Of the building's loss, Oscar Murray wrote: "The general books of the Company and many other valuable papers were removed, but it was impossible to save all the records, and there was considerable loss in the way of detail. No serious interruption to the business occurred, as the situation was met by prompt and energetic effort on the part of officers and employees."[5] The total loss to the company was estimated at $1 million. Temporary quarters were promptly secured and plans were started at once for a new headquarters office building. Needing a larger building than the one destroyed, a new site two blocks to the west at the corner of Baltimore and Charles streets was selected. The new thirteen-story building of structural steel had a granite base for the three lower floors and Indiana limestone for the upper stories. The new building was completed in mid-1906 and occupied on September 30, 1906. Next to the fine new president's office, with its private dining room, was the larger "boardroom" with its great table. The board of directors rarely met in this room, however, since they were now normally meeting in New York City.

The year 1905–6 marked the twenty-fifth anniversary of the Baltimore and Ohio Railroad Employees Relief Association, which John Garrett had established in 1880–81. From the outset, this had been largely financed by the contributions from the workers with a modest financial support coming from the company. Participation in the plan naturally grew with the growth of the railroad—14,000 members in 1881, 22,000 in 1887, 26,000 in 1899, and 52,000 in 1905. Quite soon the association provided three separate services: relief (insurance for accidents, disablement, and death), savings, and pensions. In the mid-1880s, these payments were quite modest. The average payment for accidental death (460 between 1880 and 1888) was $1,030 while that for natural death (889 between 1880 and 1888) was $373. The schedules for medical charges were also low: fifty cents for ordinary office consultation, twenty-five dollars for the amputation of a leg, and five dollars for reducing and dressing the fracture of an arm. Nor were the amounts paid for full hospital care high a short century ago. The weekly charges for hospital care including food and nursing ranged from four dollars per week at both the Maryland University Hospital in Baltimore and the Wheeling Hospital to six dollars per week at the Mercy Hospital in Chicago.

Both the savings and the pension activity of the association grew with the passing years. By 1904 more than 4,000 B&O employees had $2,800,000 on deposit with the B&O relief department. Loans, secured by first mortgages, were made to employees

B&O employee takes pride in his new uniform.
(*Courtesy, Smithsonian Institution*)

B&O baggage master poses for official photograph.
(*Courtesy, Smithsonian Institution*)

who requested aid in the purchase of homes. The pension program, started in 1884, later was entirely financed by the company rather than by the workers. In 1887 there were 165 pensioners drawing average pensions of $125 a year. By 1895 the 218 retired workers were receiving average yearly payments of $159. In 1904 an average annual pension of $190 was paid to each of 354 pensioners. At the turn of the century, many Civil War pensions ranged from $10 to $15 a month. In the twenty years since the start of the program, 830 former employees had benefited from the pension program. During the year 1903–4, the company had contributed $75,000 to the program, and the total assets of the pension fund on June 30, 1904, stood at $304,000.

In the early twentieth century, both Loree and Murray were to be faced with the beginnings of new modes of transport, which later would seriously compete with their railroad and also with new tougher federal regulation coming out of Washington, D.C. The new regulation was by far the more serious problem in the first decade of the new century. The revival of new and more stringent federal regulation of the railroads came with the appearance of the Progressive Movement in the United States. By the first years of the new century, the majority of Americans believed that the nation's railways required a more stringent form of public control. They had come to realize that the Interstate Commerce Commission, created in 1887, had achieved very little real control over the nation's rail system. The railroads had successfully challenged the ICC in the courts. Between 1887 and 1905, sixteen cases had reached the United States Supreme Court. In fifteen of the cases, the court had decided in favor of the railroad. The public read what Charles A. Prouty, a member of the ICC, had to say about the railroad and regulation. In an interview in the Chicago *Record-Herald* he had said: "The railroads own many of our courts and other public bodies. . . . If the Interstate Commerce Commission were worth buying, the railroads would try to buy it. . . . The only reason they have not tried to purchase the Commission is that this body is valueless in its ability to correct railroad abuses."[6]

The American public was unhappy when they read of the manipulations of rail securities by the big bankers of Wall Street. They fully supported an amendment to the ICC Act of 1887, introduced in 1903 by Stephen B. Elkins, a Republican senator from West Virginia. The Elkins Act, which was intended to end all rebating by making both the railroads and shippers receiving special rates liable to prosecution, was passed by Congress in 1903, almost without opposition. Public reaction had also been favorable when, in 1901, the energetic president, Theodore Roosevelt, ordered Attorney General Philander C. Knox to begin a suit, under the Sherman Act, against the Northern Securities Company, a giant railroad holding company created by James J. Hill. The Supreme Court outlawed the holding company in 1904, and later that year, Roosevelt was easily elected for a second full term over a conservative Democrat.

President Roosevelt soon asked Congress to further increase the power of the ICC to establish reasonable freight rates. Such action was favored by such congressional leaders as Sen. Jonathan Dolliver of Iowa, Sen. Robert M. LaFollette of Wisconsin, and Rep. William P. Hepburn of Iowa. In June 1906, the Hepburn Act was passed with only seven negative votes in the House and three in the Senate. This act enlarged the commission to seven members and extended the authority of the ICC to such common carriers as sleeping car, express, and pipeline companies. The legislation also forbade the issuance of free railroad passes, except to company employees, the clergy, and certain charity cases, and strengthened the law against rebates. But the most important provision of the Hepburn Act gave the commission the power to establish "just and reasonable" maximum rates. Shippers were soon taking advantage of the new act. Within two years of the passage of the Hepburn Act, more rate complaints, about 1500, were filed with the ICC, more than had been made in the past twenty years.

William Howard Taft, Roosevelt's hand-picked successor in the White House, generally viewed the railroads as monopolies run by a handful of high-handed men. Many of the Progressives desired still more rigorous rail regulation than that of the Hepburn Act, and it was not difficult to pass the Mann-Elkins Act in June 1910. This new legislation strengthened an earlier provision against long-and-short-hauls, gave the Commission the power to change rates upon its own initiative, and suspended new rates proposed by railways for as long as ten months. Further, the burden of proof that the newly proposed rates were reasonable was placed upon the railroads. Thus, in the first dozen years of the twentieth century, the railroads of the nation had become increasingly regulated by a comprehensive system of governmental controls. It soon appeared to Oscar Murray, and his successor Daniel Willard, that the new ICC directed freight rates were so restricted that they could not assure a progressive management plus a satisfactory supply of new capital into the railroad industry.

The new competitive modes of transport which appeared in the early years of the new century were of no great worry to Presidents Loree and Murray. Two weeks before Loree gave up his presidency, Orville and Wilbur Wright had made history with their small, homemade airplane at Kitty Hawk, North Carolina. That same year, the Ford Motor Company was founded, and Ransom E. Olds was building hundreds of "curved dash" Oldsmobiles. At the turn of the century, John D. Rockefeller already controlled an oil pipeline network of perhaps 40,000 miles.

The electric interurban was one of the first new modes of transport to appear. Between 1901 and 1908, more than 9,000 miles of interurban lines were built in the United States, and dozens of small lines were dreaming of capturing a share of the railroad passenger traffic. There was little interurban mileage in either Maryland or West Virginia, but Ohio and Indiana were first and second in interurban mileage in the nation. By the 1920s, the automobile quickly caused a great decline in electric interurban traffic.

In the early years of the new century, the horeseless carriage was viewed by many Americans as a rich man's toy. In 1905 Teddy Roosevelt wrote that two auto rides were all he desired, and two years later Woodrow Wilson was telling his Princeton students that the snobbery of motoring was causing the spread of socialistic feelings. Henry Ford was soon to change this view of the automobile. In 1908 he brought out his first Model T, which sold for as little as $825, and six years later, he was producing cars on the assembly line. By 1917 Ford was selling 500,000 cars a year, and Americans were driving more than 5 million motor vehicles, including 400,000 trucks. By this time, the expanded pipeline system of the nation was carrying 21 billion ton-miles of liquid freight, or over 4 percent of the total intercity freight moving in the nation. In the next year, 1918, airmail service would be started between New York City and Washington, D.C. These new modes of transport were of little consequence to Leonor Loree or Oscar Murray, but Daniel Willard and his successors would find much to worry about in the new competition from highways, pipelines, and airways. Thus, in the first decade of the twentieth century, American railroads not only suffered much new stringent regulation, but also faced the beginnings of several competitive modes of transport. To many it seemed that the golden age of American railroading was about to draw to a close.

But such problems did not keep the railroads of the nation from planning and building several quite elaborate and even luxurious union stations and giant terminal facilities in the twenty years prior to World War I. The giant St. Louis Union Station completed in 1894 had a train shed of several acres which boasted forty-two stub tracks serving eighteen different railways. For a brief period, it was the largest depot in the world. The new South Station in

Boston, opened in 1898, was nearly as large. A decade later, New York City was the location of the two largest rail terminals. During the presidency of Alexander Cassatt, his Pennsylvania Railroad started a major project of extending the end of the line in New Jersey, via a tunnel under the Hudson River, into the heart of midtown New York City. The immense new Pennsylvania Station, when opened in 1910, had cost more than $100 million to complete. A rival of the new Pennsylvania terminal was the New York Central's Grand Central Terminal, opened in 1913 and located a few blocks to the northeast. Oscar Murray's Baltimore and Ohio had shared in this creation of giant new stations with the completion in 1907 of the beautiful Union Station in Washington, D.C.

By the turn of the century, the Baltimore and Ohio was greatly in need of new and larger terminal facilities in the nation's capital. The station on New Jersey and C streets, located about two blocks north of the United States Capitol, had been in use for half a century, having been opened in April 1851. The dominant external feature of the depot, built largely of brick in the Italian style of architecture, was a tall tower containing both a clock and a bell. It soon became the custom to ring the bell prior to the departure of each train. The station had been originally built for eight trains a day, in and out.

The Civil War, of course, quickly increased an activity in the B&O New Jersey Avenue terminal. It was soon almost over-

B&O station in Washington, D.C., as it appeared about 1905.
(Courtesy, Association of American Railroads)

whelmed by the movement of troop trains and military freight. Incoming freight increased from an average of eight cars per day in 1860, to more than 400 cars per day in the winter of 1861–62. With peace in 1865, rail traffic became a bit more normal. Even so, eighteen B&O passenger trains were scheduled each day in and out of the station in 1868. The population of the District of Columbia had climbed 2-1/2 times between 1850 and 1870. In 1873 city officials decided to fill in the low lying area around the station, and both New Jersey Avenue and C Street were raised about fifteen feet, leaving the station and tracks well below the new street level. The Baltimore and Ohio built a large, two-story brick addition on the south side of the depot in 1889. The city of Washington continued to grow, and by 1893 the New Jersey Avenue station was handling ninety-eight arriving and departing trains a day. The bell in the clock tower was seldom quiet.

The other major railroad depot in Washington in the years after the Civil War was the Pennsylvania station located at Sixth and B streets, N.W., a few blocks west of the B&O station. When the Pennsylvania entered Washington in the early 1870s, its line had approached from the southeast close to Virginia Avenue before crossing the Mall from the south. The Pennsylvania had built a rather ornate station with the yard tracks crossing the Mall not quite halfway between the west front of the Captiol and the Washington Monument, still unfinished in the 1870s. By the 1880s, the city officials began to pressure the Pennsylvania and more especially the Baltimore and Ohio to eliminate the numerous grade crossings near the center of the growing city. By the late 1890s, both the Baltimore and Ohio and the Pennsylvania were seriously considering the construction of new, larger, and separate stations to serve the nation's capital.

At the turn of the century, there was a growing sentiment in the 100-year-old city that the nation's capital should be the "city beautiful." There were reports that the new occupant of the White House, Theodore Roosevelt, was enraged when he saw how the Pennsylvania station bulked so large in the Mall just to the west of Capitol Hill. In 1901 Congress passed bills which specified that as the two railroads built new stations they must start a general program of grade crossing removal. Soon, the commission planning the beautification of Washington, a group dominated by such architects as Daniel H. Burnham and Charles F. McKim, decided that the only solution to the city's railroad terminal problem was to have a single union station at a location chosen by the commission. On February 3, 1903, Congress passed legislation providing for a single union station with appropriations of $1,500,000 to each of the two railroads to help with the financing of the project. When the 1903 bill was passed, the B&O was firmly under the control of the Pennsylvania and Alexander Cassatt, a man not adverse to the construction of monumental stations.

The site selected for the new station, on Delaware Avenue just north of Massachusetts Avenue, was about one-half mile north and slightly east of the Capitol. The selected site, in 1903, was largely a boggy swamp at roughly tide water level and to many seemed to present an impossible engineering problem. But millions of cubic yards of dirt were dumped into the swampy area raising it to the existing street level. Most of the fill material came from the new railroad tunnel running south of the new station, east

Frock-coated conductor sends signal to K Tower at Washington Union Station that *Royal Blue* will depart in two minutes.
(*Courtesy, Smithsonian Institution*)

and south of the Capitol before connecting with existing Pennsylvania lines headed for the crossing of the Potomac. The new station, designed by Daniel H. Burnham, was a monumental structure 660 feet long and 210 feet wide built of white marble and granite and when completed became a fitting entrance to the capital of the nation. Original estimates of the building's cost were a modest $4 million, but the entire project required a total expenditure of more than $20 million, with the B&O and the Pennsylvania making roughly equal contributions. The new Washington Union Station was opened for rail traffic late in October 1907.

During the six years of Murray's presidency, an active program of "construction and betterment" was pushed through the

Interlocking devices in K Tower in yards at Washington.
(Courtesy, Smithsonian Institution)

several divisions of the B&O system. Several of these programs
were continued from projects started by the preceding president,
Leonor Loree. During the six years (1903–4 through 1908–9), a
total of about $50 million had been spent on these programs, rang-
ing from a low of $4.8 million in 1908–9 to a high of $11.5 million in
1903–4. The great majority of the money required to pay for the
numerous improvements came from new capital.

The most important acquisition of new mileage made during the Murray years resulted from the negotiations permitting the
eventual control of the Cincinnati, Hamilton and Dayton, a line
serving western Ohio as well as the coal districts in the southern
part of the state. This road had been chartered originally as the
Cincinnati and Hamilton in 1846 and eventually built a sixty-mile
line from Cincinnati to Dayton. During the Civil War, it leased the
Dayton and Michigan, a 142-mile road running from Dayton north
to Toledo. In the late 1860s, the Cincinnati, Hamilton and Dayton
had the dubious distinction of having one of its trains robbed by the
Reno Gang, a band of Hoosier train robbers who earlier had successfully robbed the Ohio and Mississippi in southern Indiana. In
the last decades of the nineteenth century, the CH&D expanded
its holdings, but was not too prosperous. J. P. Morgan placed the
road in receivership and then urged the B&O to take over the
road. A committee from the B&O board, including the director,
E.H. Harriman, finally decided the B&O should acquire the line.
President Murray described the decision in his 1908–9 *Annual
Report:*

> "Negotiations pending during the year have concluded recently
> and made effective July 1, 1909, whereby your Company will
> acquire, at the expiration of seven years, at a price then to be
> agreed upon or determined by arbitration, the controlling stock
> of the Cincinnati, Hamilton and Dayton Railway Company. . . .
> It is expected the closer relations of the Companies will be pro-
> ductive of results mutually beneficial."[7]

By the middle teens, Daniel Willard would officially take over
much of the Cincinnati, Hamilton and Dayton.

During the half-dozen years of Oscar Murray's presidency,
there were few increases in overall mileage of the B&O system.
Throughout these years, the B&O did control 350 to 400 miles of
roads known as "affiliated lines." In the Murray years, the operations of these lines were not fully included in the B&O system of
accounting. In 1910, with the coming of Daniel Willard to the
presidency, such lines were fully added to the mileage of the Baltimore and Ohio.

TABLE 13. Baltimore and Ohio System Traffic and Financial Growth 1896–1909 (Excluding affiliated lines)

Year	Miles of Road	Total Revenue	Net Earnings	Expenses to Earnings (%)	Average Passenger Fare (cents per mile)	Average Freight Rate (cents per ton-mile)	Dividends on Common Stock (%)
1896–7	2,041	$25,582,122	$5,570,028	78	1.75	.52	—
1897–8	2,042	27,722,788	7,446,696	73	1.71	.46	—
1898–9	2,042	29,260,211	7,476,888	76	1.74	.39	—
1899–1900	2,273	42,117,405	14,473,276	66	1.82	.45	2
1900–1	3,216	47,114,430	16,068,200	66	1.97	.50	4
1901–2	3,233	51,178,060	18,289,497	64	2.02	.51	4
1902–3	3,935	63,449,633	23,879,669	62	2.00	.56	4
1903–4	3,986	65,071,080	21,442,217	67	2.00	.58	4
1904–5	4,025	67,689,997	22,979,393	66	1.96	.57	4.5
1905–6	4,029	77,392,056	27,876,835	64	2.00	.56	5.5
1906–7	4,006	82,243,291	27,363,830	67	1.96	.57	6
1907–8	3,992	73,608,781	19,457,901	74	1.89	.57	6
1908–9	4,003	71,043,519	23,491,543	67	1.89	.58	6

Throughout the thirteen years, the ratio of freight traffic to passenger continued about 3.5 to 1, a pattern that had been true for some time. Freight traffic was a bit more important on the B&O than on the typical line in the nation. Since the freight rates for coal haulage were low and the B&O was an important carrier of coal, the B&O average ton-mile rates during these years was somewhat below the national average of .75 cents per ton-mile. The B&O passenger fares for the period were very close to the national average.

Of freight commodities carried on the B&O in 1901, about 9 percent were products of agriculture; 1.5 percent were products of animals; 6 percent were products of forests; 14 percent were manufactures; 8.5 percent were miscellaneous; and 61 percent were products of mines. Of the products of mines carried on the Baltimore and Ohio, about two-thirds were bituminous or soft coal, one-sixth was coke, and a twentieth was anthracite coal. A majority of the soft coal moving over the tracks of the B&O was mined in West Virginia, but some also came from Ohio and western Pennsylvania. By 1900 the B&O had built or acquired much new mileage in western Pennsylvania and also in central West Virginia.

The production of soft coal in the United States had expanded rapidly in the second half of the nineteenth century: 3 million tons in 1850, 20 million tons in 1870, 111 million tons in 1890, 212 million tons in 1900, and 417 million tons in 1910. The average value of soft coal at the mine had declined somewhat as production had boomed, being $1.25 per ton in 1880, 99 cents per ton in 1890, 86 cents per ton in 1895, and $1.04 in 1900. The volume of soft coal moved by the Baltimore and Ohio had increased from about 3 million tons in 1878, to 9 million tons in 1899, 22 million tons in 1906, and 30 million tons in 1912. The average B&O freight rate for soft coal in 1899 was only .26 cents per ton-mile, but by 1912 this had increased to .41 cents per ton-mile. In the early years of the twentieth century, the average distance the B&O carried soft coal was 190 miles.

The Baltimore and Ohio had been sharing the coal traffic of West Virginia with the Chesapeake and Ohio for some years. In the 1880s and early 1890s, President Charles F. Mayer was facing new competition from the Norfolk and Western for the coal traffic of West Virginia. The Norfolk and Western had been reorganized out of William Mahone's Atlantic, Mississippi and Ohio in the early 1880s. Frederick J. Kimball, a Philadelphia banker, was the dominant figure in the Norfolk and Western in the 1880s and 1890s. Kimball was liberal on the matter of labor unions, believed that those who owned coal properties should actively develop them, and favored pooling devices among coal carriers in order to maintain coal prices and avoid unrestricted competition. Several pooling efforts among such lines as the Pennsylvania, Baltimore and Ohio, Chesapeake and Ohio, and the Norfolk and Western were tried without any notable success in the 1880s and 1890s.

At the turn of the century, the B&O had 28,000 coal cars out of a roster of 62,000 freight cars. The C&O owned 7,500 coal cars out of a roster of 17,000 freight cars, and the Norfolk and Western had 10,000 coal cars out of 18,000 freight cars. Many of the coal cars by 1900 were built of iron and steel instead of wood and had a capacity of 25 tons or more as compared to the wooden cars of Civil War days. During the year 1899, the Chesapeake and Ohio moved a total of 4,117,000 tons of coal while the Norfolk and Western carried 4,447,000 tons. The two roads together had a total coal traffic nearly equal to that of the Baltimore and Ohio. By the turn of the century, all three roads were moving much of their West Virginia coal to westward or interior markets instead of the Eastern seacoast.

During the period, B&O revenues roughly tripled, while the mileage of the system only doubled. The decline in revenue appearing in 1907–8 was the result of the general downturn in business following the Panic of 1907. Freight tonnage during the year declined about 9 million tons, caused, as Oscar Murray described it, by "the wide spread depression which has marked all branches of industry and trade."[8] The downturn in traffic did result in a definite increase in the operating ratio of expenses to earnings, but did not affect dividends, which continued at the 6 percent rate. Actually, in the prewar teens, the operating ratio for most American railways was going to move from an average of 65 percent to 70 percent up toward 75 percent. The new regulations of the Progressive Era made it difficult to increase freight rates and passenger fares even though most railroad costs and expenses continued to climb. Between 1896 and 1909, the cost of living had increased more than 20 percent, along with the wages of rail workers. Tax accruals, the cost of fuel, and other operating costs had also risen.

The total investment in the Baltimore and Ohio had also greatly grown in the first decade of the twentieth century. The balance sheet figures of assets and liabilities had grown from a total of $226 million in 1899 to $523 million in 1909. In the decade, the preferred stock had increased from $39 million to $60 million while the common stock had climbed from $35 million in 1899 to $152 million in 1909. The total funded debt had nearly doubled from $134 million to $257 million. All of the bonds in 1909 paid annual interest of either 3.5 or 4 percent. The amount of bonds and stocks held by the trustees of the B&O had increased from $61 million in 1899 to $182 million in 1909. The total cost of the road in the decade had gone from $88 million up to $175 million by 1909. Finally, the value placed upon rolling stock and equipment had increased from $23 million to $48 million by 1909.

Between 1899 and 1909, the number of locomotives on the B&O system had doubled, increasing from 954 to 1,906. In the same years, passenger train cars had grown from 671 to 1,161, while freight cars had climbed from 44,087 to 81,978. Much of the equipment growth resulted from the acquisition and use of hundreds of cars and engines owned by companies and lines taken over by the B&O during the decade. The capacity of the average freight car had grown in the decade. By 1908 the average B&O freight car load was 22.4 tons with the average train consisting of twenty-eight cars (eighteen loaded and ten empty). About two-thirds of the locomotive fleet were in freight service, about one-fifth in passenger service, with the remainder being switch engines. During the decade, many new Consolidations (2-8-0) were ordered for freight service, while new Atlantics (4-4-2) and a few Pacifics (4-6-2) were replacing many of the older American (4-4-0) type locomotives.

As the year 1909 drew to a close, Oscar G. Murray decided that six years as president of the Baltimore and Ohio was enough. He was sixty-two years of age and wished to retire. His resignation as president was accepted on January 4, 1910, and on the same day he was elected to the board of directors. Murray stepped down as president on January 14, 1910, and the next day was elected chairman of the board, a position he retained until his death on March 14, 1917.

Chapter XII

• • • • • • • • • • • • • • •

Daniel Willard
Comes Aboard

MURRAY'S SUCCESSOR WAS DANIEL WILLARD, WHO BECAME the fourteenth president of the Baltimore and Ohio on January 15, 1910. Willard was destined to serve the railroad until June 1, 1941, over thirty-one years, and five years longer than the tenure of John W. Garrett. In those three decades, Willard would face and solve the railroad's problems with war, prosperity, and depression. In the same years, he also served his state and nation in a number of governmental and civic assignments. Certainly a variety of individuals had filled the presidency of the B&O in the quarter of a century prior to 1910. The new president had most of the strengths of his predecessors and few of their weaknesses. The forty-nine-year-old Willard brought three decades of varied railroad experience to his new office in 1910.

Daniel Willard was born on January 28, 1861, in North Hartland, Vermont. His father, the prosperous owner of a large, 250-acre farm, came from English farm folks who had migrated to New England in the midseventeenth century. After country schooling, the youth graduated from high school in 1878 and attended the Massachusetts State Agricultural College at Amherst for a few months before eye trouble forced him to return to his father's farm. Though he was a hardworking farm youth, Daniel had never become enthusiastic about the life of a farmer. He was far more fascinated by the Vermont Central Railroad, which ran

215

Daniel Willard, president, 1910–41.
(Courtesy, Baltimore and Ohio Railroad)

across the family acres, and was further inclined in that direction by the fact that several cousins worked for the railroad. In April 1879, he took a job—one dollar for a ten hour day—as a section hand on the Vermont Central, starting a rail career that would last for more than sixty years. Within a few months, he was a fireman, and before he was twenty, he had been promoted to locomotive engineer. Because of higher wages paid on western lines, Willard moved to northern Indiana and later to the Minneapolis-St. Paul, Sault Ste. Marie, and Atlantic Railroad (Soo Line) in northern Wisconsin. Willard worked for the Soo for fifteen years serving, in turn, as brakeman, conductor, operator, agent, fireman, engineer, roundhouse foreman, trainmaster, assistant superintendent, and division superintendent. During these years, he married a Vermont girl, Miss Bertha Elkins, and moved to Minneapolis where two sons were born: Harold in 1890 and Daniel Junior in 1894.

As Daniel Willard moved up through the ranks of lower and middle management on the Soo, he came to the attention of the road's general manager, Frederick D. Underwood. When Underwood moved to the Baltimore and Ohio in 1899 as general manager and second vice president, he took Willard with him as the assistant general manager. Underwood gave his assistant direct supervision over major purchases, and Willard soon had a growing knowledge of both the personnel and the physical characteristics of the B&O. When Underwood was elected president of the Erie Railroad in 1901, Daniel Willard was at once offered the position of the B&O's general manager by John Cowen. However, Willard preferred to follow Underwood to the Erie where he was soon elected general manager and first vice president. The Erie, in 1901, was far different from the line earlier run by Gould, Fisk, and Drew, but rumor had it that when Willard opened a drawer of Jim Fisk's ancient desk, he found the uptown address of Josie Mansfield, Fisk's mistress.

James J. Hill had a major financial interest in the Erie, and the "Empire Builder" soon became aware of Willard's ability. Shortly after he acquired the Chicago, Burlington and Quincy, Hill succeeded in getting Willard to move to the Burlington as the operating vice president at the handsome salary of $50,000 a year plus a bonus. During his six years (1904–10) at the Burlington, Willard brought that line to a high level of operating excellence. When Daniel Willard was offered the presidency of the B&O in the last weeks of 1909, Jim Hill unsuccessfully tried to retain his services by offering him the presidency of the Burlington.

By 1910 Willard had been away from Vermont for three decades, but he still retained the old Vermont traits of independence, self-reliance, and honesty. As one who had experienced the labor of laying track and shovelling coal into the fire-box of a locomotive, the new president was noted for his ability to work with subordinates without friction. At the same time, his fellow workers soon learned that while he rarely gave direct orders, Willard expected that his suggestions would be performed and completed. He had an insatiable curiosity, a passion for exact information, and was a great reader. In commenting favorably upon his election to head the B&O, the editors of the *Railroad Gazette* in January 1910, wrote that Willard: ". . . not only works hard, but works fast . . . he has been a student all his life."[1]

In a sense, coming to Baltimore in 1910 was for Willard like going back home. The B&O was not a "new" railroad since he had spent nearly two years there in 1899–1901. During those busy months under Frederick Underwood, he had spent much of his time out on the road, viewing main line and branches by the train, by horseback, and even by foot. When Willard had first been approached about the new position in the late fall of 1909, it had clearly been understood that the owners of the railroad wanted the B&O "thoroughly rebuilt." This might seem strange, since Cowen and Murray, as co-receivers, and then Loree and Murray, as presidents, had only recently spent millions of dollars in doing just that. But during the Murray years, the man in the president's office had, first of all, been a traffic man. The B&O had plenty of business, but often there were blockades of cars and trains, especially in the snowy, winter months.

Robert Scott Lovett, B&O director, confidant of E. H. Harriman, and later the president of both the Union Pacific and Southern Pacific, insisted that Murray's successor must improve B&O

service for the coal operators in the hills of West Virginia. In his first *Annual Report*, that of 1909–10, President Willard wrote: ". . . it became evident during the year, that in order to handle satisfactorily the business already offered, it was essential to make immediate provision for additional equipment and other facilities."[2] During the year, Willard's board had approved the expenditure of $23 million for the purchase of 284 locomotives and 15,000 freight cars plus another $20 million for various other improvements in the road.

One of the first things Willard did as president of the Baltimore and Ohio was to cancel all advertising with respect to passenger service. He would not advertise a service unworthy of his line. The president said: "We are not going to advertise until we have something worthwhile to advertise. Some day we are going to have fast and handsome passenger trains, but we shall not have them until we have good track and good engineers and good cars—tracks and engines and cars equal to the very best in American railroad practice."[3]

On the Burlington, Daniel Willard had favored the Prairie type (2-6-2) locomotive, and on one occasion had convinced Jim Hill to approve the purchase of a hundred engines of that type, even though the older man would have preferred a heavier engine. On the Baltimore and Ohio, Willard realized the hills of Maryland, West Virginia, and Pennsylvania required a heavier locomotive and decided on the Mikado type (2-8-2), an engine having one pair of drivers more than the Prairie. During 1911 Willard ordered 150 Mikados from the Baldwin Locomotive Works in Philadelphia since he had decided to give up the policy of having the B&O build its own engines. The new locomotives weighed nearly 140 tons, had 64-inch drivers, 205 pounds of steam pressure, and provided 50,000 pounds of tractive power.

Eventually, Willard had about 600 Mikados on his equipment roster. Willard ordered many of the "Mikes" from his good friend Samuel M. Vauclain, a top salesman for the Baldwin Works, and president of the company from 1919 to 1929. Once, when Willard and Vauclain were discussing an order of twenty-five Mikados for the B&O, the two men were $250 apart on the price of each engine. After a long discussion, they tossed a quarter to decide the issue, and Willard lost. Willard, something of a horse trader, was convinced the Baldwin engines were worth the higher price, but still hoped for a better bargain. Vauclain once said of the B&O president: "Daniel Willard always is a square man with whom to do business. . . . He will plague you and toy with you, but he will never, not in a million years, deceive you."[4]

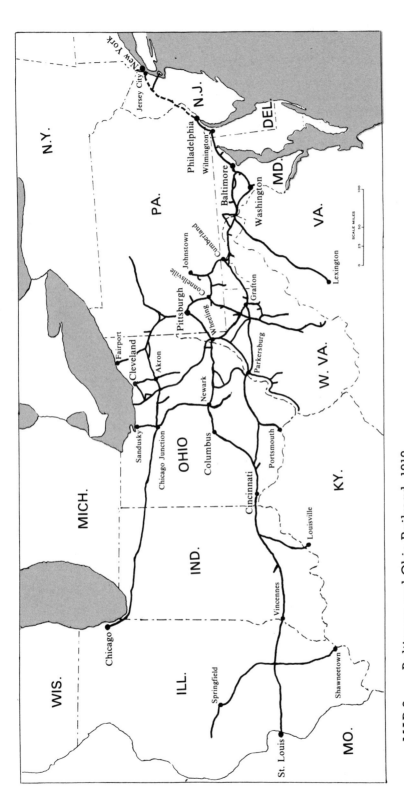

MAP 8. Baltimore and Ohio Railroad, 1910.

Most of the new mileage acquired during the first decade of the twentieth century consisted of branch lines in Penn- sylvania, Ohio, and West Virginia.

Willard was soon spending millions of dollars to rebuild vital parts of his main line. Northeast of Baltimore, the single track, high-set, multi-span bridge over the lower Susquehanna was replaced with a new, double-track bridge. West of Baltimore there was a bad bottleneck for traffic between Cherry Run (a few miles west of Martinsburg) and Patterson Creek, just east of Cumberland. One of the worst places along the fifty-mile stretch was the Doe Gully Tunnel. A million dollars was spent to blast off the roof of the Doe Gully Tunnel and lower the grade. More dollars were spent to increase the double track between Cumberland and Cherry Run to three and even four parallel tracks. West and north of Cumberland, the single track Kingwood and Sand Patch tunnels were both replaced with new double-track bores. Soon Willard had completed plans to double track the entire main route from Philadelphia and Baltimore, via Washington and Pittsburgh, to Chicago. In October 1913, Willard, in his *Annual Report*, was able to write of the newly-opened Sand Patch Tunnel in Pennsylvania: "The completion of their work gives a double track line between Philadelphia, Pa. and Chicago, Ill., with the exception of about 31 miles on the Chicago Division."[5]

Small boys inspect railroad ties in classification yards at Baltimore in 1910. *(Courtesy, Smithsonian Institution)*

The engineer responsible for directing much of the rebuilding of the B&O in the early Willard years was Arthur W. Thompson, a thirty-five-year-old who, since 1907, had been chief engineer, maintenance of way. It had been Thompson who had built the new double-track bridge over the Susquehanna, and later he built a double track, 800-foot bridge over the Monongahela in the record time of only ninety days. Dan Willard liked the energy of the young man and soon made him chief engineer of the road. Later Thompson became general manager and by 1912 was elevated to third vice president. In the fall of 1913, President Willard was able to report that since July 1, 1909, there had been added to the B&O equipment roster 512 locomotives, 150 passenger cars, and 27,438 freight cars. During the four years, the locomotive roster had climbed 16 percent, the total tractive power 35 percent, and the total freight car capacity in tons 27 percent.

Between 1909 and 1913, there had been no increase in mileage in the B&O system, but a vast improvement in route, roadbed, and track. In 1909 only 794 miles of line had been laid with steel rail weighing 90 or 100 pounds per yard. By 1913 the figure had been tripled to a total of 2,427 miles of such rail. During 1910, 1911, and 1912, more than 150,000 tons of new steel rail, costing about $29 a ton, had been laid along with 5,600,000 new crossties costing an average of about sixty-six cents per tie. These major improvements had cost millions of dollars, and Daniel Willard had frequently gone to Wall Street bankers, chiefly Kuhn, Loeb and Company, for the money. In the eight years between January 1, 1910, and December 31, 1917, the B&O spent $139 million for additions, betterments, extensions, and new equipment.

Daniel Willard paid attention to details, and that meant that as his 4,000-mile rail system was upgraded, he spent many days and nights out on the road inspecting and supervising the improvement projects. Some weeks found him out on the road two days for every day spent in his presidential office. His business car, "No. 99,"—the same number he used out on the Burlington—was always ready for use and parked at the Camden Station. When out on the road, Willard spent most of his nights in the comfortable bed of the "No. 99," but he had favorite hotels whenever he spent any time in either New York or Chicago. In New York, he nearly always had the same corner suite in an upper floor of the Biltmore, and in Chicago, he nearly always stayed in the Congress Hotel on Michigan Avenue. The "99" was in reality a "rolling office" filled with maps, files, and company records, and the car steward and

Baltimore's Camden Station (built in 1853) in the early twentieth century. *(Courtesy, Association of American Railroads)*

galley chef always left the car fully stocked with food and supplies for any length of trip.

One of the longest and most serious trips of the "99" started on a Sunday evening late in March 1913, when Willard left Baltimore for a stricken flood area west of the mountains. After hitting eastern Nebraska, an early spring tornado had moved on across the Missouri and Mississippi rivers to bring torrential rains to Illinois, Indiana, Ohio, and Pennsylvania. In the five days from March 23 through March 27, five to ten inches of rain had fallen on Indiana and Ohio. Much of the ground was still frozen, and the deluge quickly filled all the streams and rivers in the area. Such rivers as the Muskingum, Hocking, Licking, Scioto, White, and Wabash in Ohio and Indiana became so swollen that they exceeded by four to six feet the record flood stage of 1884. Hundreds of lives were lost along with millions of dollars of property. Business came to a halt for ten days in much of the upper and middle valley of the Ohio. All the railroads in western Pennsylvania and all of Ohio and Indiana were ravaged by the violent water. For several days, only one through rail route between New York City and Chicago was in operation.

Only three days before leaving Baltimore for the flood area, Willard, who liked a good cigar, had given up smoking for a month. This was an annual habit he followed to maintain his self-discipline. During the long flood emergency, many of his co-workers offered Willard a cigar. But the president just smiled, refused every offer, and kept his self-made pledge. As Willard moved slowly through the flooded area directing operations, the toll of destruction seemed ever to increase—in Wheeling, Zanesville, Columbus, Marietta, and Cincinnati. Eleven major bridges were quickly destroyed and seven more were seriously damaged. Some 170 miles of main line track was washed out, and 405 miles, for a time, were under water. The line was broken in many places and effective restoration was often delayed for several days. The line between Parkersburg and Cincinnati was closed for twelve days, and the road west of Cincinnati to St. Louis was closed for a month. Communication along the entire line was difficult since the flood had destroyed more than 3,500 telegraph poles. Total property damage on the B&O was over $3 million, while the loss in traffic because of the flood was at least $1,500,000. Weeks and months of hard work were required to fully restore the flooded and soggy western lines of the railroad. The top officials of the B&O decided to recognize the hard work and valiant efforts of the work crews in the flooded area. Third Vice President Arthur Thompson promised: "Instructions have been issued to give credit on the service record of every employee who assisted in restoring the road to normal conditions,

Crest of 1913 flood, Zanesville, Ohio.
(Courtesy, Baltimore and Ohio Railroad)

such notation to be made in red ink so that it will stand out as a work of conspicious service."[6]

The *Baltimore and Ohio Employees Magazine*, a new publication started in the fall of 1912, carried details of the tragic flood. The magazine contained short stories, poetry, puzzles, and housekeeping hints, but mainly it was concerned with news of the company and its employees. The news was indeed varied. During the big flood in Chillicothe, a B&O engineer, Fred Dean, had found a boat to rescue his marooned family after going hand-over-hand across a telephone cable to dry land. In the winter of 1912–13, the B&O had established a new record by loading 7,574 tons of coal into a ship at the Baltimore pier in only four hours and fifty-five minutes. In his New Year's greeting to the 60,000 B&O employees, President Willard stressed "Safety First." A later issue pointed out that each month ten B&O employees were injured by kicking car couplers. Out on the Chicago division, 500 members had signed up in the new "Water Wagon Club," an organization dedicated to temperance. In the summer of 1915, a B&O Men's Glee Club of fifty voices sang before a Baltimore audience of a thousand at their first annual concert and dance. The November 1916 issue of the magazine reported that the typical B&O freight car carried an average load of 29.4 tons, and moved 27.5 miles per day, being in motion only one day in eight.

The last year before America entered World War I, 1916, in some ways was a record year for American railroads. The year saw rail mileage in the United States reach a record high of 254,037 miles. After 1916, except for a brief reversal in the late 1920s, each year saw a decline in rail mileage in the nation. In 1916 the Baltimore and Ohio with about 4,500 miles of road and 60,000 employees had a total revenue of $117 million. In the entire nation, the total rail system of 254,000 miles employed 1,701,000 workers and generated national rail revenues of $3,691,000,000. Being a trunk line in the populated northeastern corner of the country meant that the B&O was relatively a busier line than the typical railroad. The B&O, for example, had 13.4 employees per mile of line while the national average was only 6.6 workers per mile. The total revenue per mile of road was more than $25,000 on the B&O while the average for the entire country was about $14,500 per mile.

Passenger service on the Baltimore and Ohio had greatly changed, both in quantity and quality, since the depression days of the early 1890s. In the twenty-three years since 1893, the *Official Guide of Railways* had grown from an 896-page book to a volume of 1,600 pages. In the same years, the B&O portion of the giant schedule book had increased from sixteen to thirty-two pages,

New Class S Santa Fe (2-10-2) pulls a long coal drag up Cranberry Grade in 1915.
(*Courtesy, Smithsonian Institution*)

while that of the Pennsylvania had grown from sixty-five to ninety pages. The B&O could not match the two northern rivals in either the number of trains or in speed over the major routes. The top Pennsylvania train in 1916, the *Broadway Limited*, made the 909-mile trip from New York to Chicago in twenty hours, or just over forty-five miles per hour. The New York Central's the *Twentieth Century Limited* had identical departure and arrival times but, with its longer water level route of 978 miles, had an average speed of just under forty-nine miles per hour. The Baltimore and Ohio train from New York to Chicago, the *Chicago Limited*, needed twenty-five hours and fifty-five minutes for its 954-mile trip, or just under thirty-seven miles per hour.

Certainly the passenger equipment on the Baltimore and Ohio had been improved in recent years. As recently as the early years of the twentieth century, most of the B&O passenger cars were still built of wood. The Pennsylvania Railroad had started to use steel passenger cars in 1898, but few such cars were seen on the B&O until Daniel Willard became president. In 1911–12, Willard purchased seventy-eight steel passenger cars, and many more were added to the passenger car roster. By 1917 nearly three-quarters of all B&O passenger traffic moved in steel cars. In 1916 all first class passenger trains were described in the *Official Guide* as "Electric-lighted vestibuled Steel Trains." In 1916 the B&O was quite self-conscious about its lack of a passenger terminal in New York City. Passengers, to reach a B&O train to the west, were still required to take a ferry across the Hudson to Jersey City. In the June 1916 *Official Guide*, the B&O took a full page advertisement headed:

ROYAL BLUE LINE
PRACTICALLY A UNION STATION
AT NEW YORK CITY

The ad continued:

> "The Jersey City Station of the Baltimore & Ohio, the Reading and New Jersey Central Railroads has all the convenience of a Union Station. . . . The most magnificent view of New York City is that of its skyline, and it cannot be seen in any other way than by the ferry ride from Jersey City.[7]

It was true that Pennsylvania passengers could not view the skyline of New York while passing through the tunnel under the Hudson River, and few New York Central passengers saw the skyscrapers of the city as they came in from the North. But most travelers clearly preferred the convenience of the midtown terminals to the slow and often windy ferry trip across the lower Hudson.

Ten-wheeler pulls the *New York Express* through Maryland coun-tryside early in the twentieth century. *(Courtesy, Smithsonian Institution)*

Daniel Willard increased the mileage of his system very little in the first half dozen years of his presidency. Finally, in the sum-mer of 1917, the B&O acquired the Toledo and Cincinnati Railroad, which in February 1916, had been reorganized from the former Cincinnati, Hamilton and Dayton, the line President Oscar Murray had agreed to eventually purchase back in 1909. In years following the 1909 agreement, the Cincinnati, Hamilton and Dayton had not prospered and eventually was forced into receivership. The mort-gage bonds and capital obligations assumed by the B&O as they took over the Toledo and Cincinnati on July 19, 1917, only amounted to $28,276,000, with a fixed interest charge of $1,278,000 a year. The 403-mile Toledo and Cincinnati consisted of a line from Cincinnati via Dayton to Toledo, plus minor branches. The new acquisition was operated as the Toledo division of the B&O. In the two years follow-ing this addition, criticism of the acquisition was made by several B&O stockholders, especially by Isaac M. Cate of Baltimore. Cate claimed that the newly acquired road had been badly mismanaged by J. P Morgan in much the same way that he earlier had treated the Boston and Maine and the New Haven lines. In his 1919 pamphlet, Cate wrote: "The Morgans sold the stock of the financial wreck [the D. & T.] to the Balt. & Ohio after it had been rejected by the Erie, and after President Underwood had been deceived."[8] Willard

This turn-of-the-century B&O diner offered terrapin and canvas-back on its dollar dinner. *(Courtesy, Smithsonian Institution)*

clearly believed the new addition strengthened the Baltimore and Ohio. Of the new line, Willard had written in the summer of 1918: "Since July 19, 1917, the property has been operated as part of the Baltimore & Ohio System, and the operating figures show a higher ton mile density, a higher revenue train load and larger gross earnings per mile on that part of the line than on the Baltimore & Ohio proper."[9] Also in 1917, the B&O acquired the Coal and Coke Railway Company which operated a 197-mile line in West Virginia from Elkins to Charleston. As America entered the war, the B&O consisted of 4,948 miles.

When world war started in Europe in the late summer of 1914, the United States, as a neutral nation thousands of miles removed from the muddy trenches of France, did not seem greatly concerned. But soon, a Europe fighting a total war began to seek more and more food and military supplies from a productive America. As factory after factory received orders of staggering size, American railroads soon felt the increase of traffic. The ton-mileage for the year 1916 was 30 percent larger than the 1914–15 figure, and rail revenue increased in a like amount. The increased factory orders and railroad traffic soon caused growing labor shortages both in manufacturing and transportation. The extra boards on most railroads, including the Baltimore and Ohio, soon grew short of names. Retired railroaders on a pension came back to swing a brakeman's lantern, punch tickets, or pound a telegraph key. By the winter of 1916–17, America was getting closer to full involvement in the conflict.

Daniel Willard was also becoming directly involved in the defense activity of the nation. On August 29, 1916, the Army Appropriation Act was passed including a provision which established the Council of National Defense. The council consisted of six cabinet officers plus an advisory commission composed of industrial leaders of the nation. When the advisory commission was appointed by President Woodrow Wilson late in October 1916, it included business leaders Daniel Willard, Walter S. Gifford of the American Telephone and Telegraph and Julius Rosenwald, head of the mail order house of Sears Roebuck. As a patriotic American who believed in a strong national defense, Willard cheerfully accepted the Wilson appointment. Willard obtained living quarters in the Willard Hotel in Washington and was soon spending more time in consideration of such subjects as price fixing, wartime food control, conscription, and daylight-savings time than he was in the day-to-day direction of his own railroad. In March 1917, he was elected chairman of the advisory commission.

American railroad labor felt in a strong position in 1916. They were enjoying full employment, and some elements of the railroad work force were well organized. This was true of locomotive engineers, firemen, conductors, brakemen, and shop employees, all of whom had strong and effective labor unions. The average annual wage for all rail workers of $567 in 1900 had climbed to $825 per year by 1915. This increase of about 45 percent was well above the increase in the cost of living which had gone up about 30 percent in the decade and a half. This fairly rapid wage increase had resulted in a rise of total labor costs, going from 39 percent of all operating revenue in 1900 to 43 percent in 1915. Even though their position had improved, the four operating brotherhoods of engineers, firemen, conductors, and trainmen did not propose to let an opportunity for further action be lost. During the teens, American labor was anxious for the complete acceptance of the eight-hour day. Early in 1916, the four operating brotherhoods made demands for an eight-hour work day to replace the ten-hour day then in effect. They also requested that they be paid time and a half for all overtime work. Since the actual hours of train service could hardly be shortened, the demand of the four unions was really for a major boost in pay. The Baltimore and Ohio and all other lines rejected these demands, and subsequent efforts to resolve the dispute were not successful. Feeling their position was one of strength, the four railroad unions voted for a nationwide rail strike.

In mid-August, President Woodrow Wilson called both the brotherhood chiefs and the railroad managers to a White House conference, and when he found no concessions would be made by either side, proposed a compromise which generally was agreeable to labor. A few days later, Wilson met with forty railroad presidents in the White House. It was a hot August day and many of the railroad executives felt they had been called to Washington to be given a public reprimand by a tough-minded schoolmaster. Wilson did not succeed in selling them his compromise, and the conference broke up in bitterness. The four railroad union leaders at once called a nationwide strike for Labor Day, September 4, 1916. Wilson addressed a joint session of Congress on August 29, asking for legislation that would provide for an eight-hour day. William C. Adamson, Georgia Democrat, long-time friend of labor, and chairman of the House Interstate Commerce Committee, sponsored the Adamson Act, which was passed on September 2, 1916, and was signed by President Wilson the following day. The new law, which generally followed the lines of Wilson's compromise, gave the operating brotherhood the eight-hour day effective January 1, 1917, but without extra pay for overtime. The effect of the law was to give the operators a major boost in pay.

The Labor Day strike was called off, but the Adamson Act hardly solved the problem since the railways held the legislation to be unconstitutional and carried the dispute into the federal courts. The eight-hour day became a political issue in the hotly contested 1916 presidential campaign. Charles Evans Hughes challenged Wilson's labor record and picked up business support when he called the president's action a shameful proceeding. The railroads across the country refused to abide by the Adamson Act on January 1, 1917, and the operating workers felt cheated out of a victory. Early in March, the nation seemed quite close to involvement in the world war, and the operating brotherhoods, noting the delay by the Supreme Court, grew afraid that the emergency of war might delay or prevent the eight-hour law from going into effect. On March 15, the brotherhood leaders called for another general strike for Saturday, March 17, 1917.

As the nation faced a new transportation crisis, Daniel Willard soon assumed a major role in avoiding a nationwide rail strike. Willard was a member of the advisory commission of the Council of National Defense, and it was known that he had always been able to see the railroad workers' point of view. When his efforts to arbitrate between labor and management failed in New York City, Willard made a quick trip down to Washington on Friday night, March 16, to see Franklin K. Lane, secretary of interior, and a fellow member of the advisory commission. On Saturday morning, with the strike deadline only a few hours away, Willard and Lane made one last effort. Lane risked the displeasure of the Supreme Court, but did receive the private assurance from a justice of the Court that the high court on the following Monday, March 19, would deliver a final and irrevocable decision on the eight-hour case. Willard took a fast train back to New York City, and the labor leaders, now assured that a final decision was near at hand, voted to delay the strike forty-eight hours. At noon on Monday, the Supreme Court, in a five to four decision, upheld the constitutionality of the Adamson Act. The operating brotherhoods had gained their eight-hour day. With this decision in the case of *Wilson v. New*, the Supreme Court had fully affirmed the nearly absolute control which Congress held over the interstate operations of American railroads. Only two weeks later, Congress met in an extraordinary session to hear a special message from Woodrow Wilson. The nation was about to declare war on Germany.[10]

Chapter XIII

• • • • • • • • • • • • • • •

The Baltimore
and Ohio
Goes to War

THE SAME WEEKS THAT SAW THE CONCLUSION OF THE
eight-hour day issue also saw war coming closer and closer to
America. The Germans resumed unrestricted submarine activity
in January 1917, and Woodrow Wilson severed diplomatic relations on February 3, 1917. German submarines sank three American vessels during the weekend of Willard's hectic traveling
between New York and Washington in mid-March. On April 2,
President Wilson delivered his war message to Congress, and four
days later that body declared war on Germany. The role of individual railroads in the total war effort was to be greatly determined by
action taken by the national government in Washington. Daniel
Willard had a major part in many of those events.

As the nation turned from neutrality to an all out war effort,
the expanding economy quickly put a strain on the American railroads. There were few precedents to help the railroads of the country put together a coordinated system of wartime transportation. In
the fall of 1915, when troubles faced the nation on the Mexican
border, Wilson had asked the American Railway Association to set
up a special committee to deal with military transportation between the War Department and the railroads. When the National
Guard was mobilized in the summer of 1916, thousands of troops

were moved efficiently to Texas and the Mexican border. As the mass movement of troops was about to start, President Willard was spending a weekend with top B&O officials at the company resort hotel at Deer Park, Maryland. Of the western troop movement, Willard told his fellow officials: "When we have troop trains to move, they are to have the right of way over everything except a train carrying the President of the United States. We will stop everything—freight trains, passenger trains—everything will give way to the steady and comfortable movement of the troops."[1]

American railroads, in general, were not too well prepared for the war tasks which lay ahead. The increased regulation of the Progressive Era had created a situation in which the railroads received little sympathy from either the general public or the ICC when rate increases were requested. Even though the general price level had increased 30 percent between 1900 and 1915, most requests for rate and fare increases were denied by the ICC. Average freight rates in 1916 were actually a shade lower then those of 1900. In the early teens, many railroads had delayed maintenance and improvement programs because of increasing operating ratios. Many lines were having to rely on borrowed money since risk capital was hard to obtain. The financial condition of several systems, such as the Wabash, the Rock Island, the New Haven, and the Frisco, was quite desperate by the middle teens. More than 37,000 miles of line, nearly one-sixth of the national total, were being operated by receivers or trustees in 1916.

The Army Appropriation Act of August 29, 1916, which had provided for the creation of the Council of National Defense, had also included the Federal Possession and Control Act, permitting the president, in a wartime emergency, to take over and control any system of transportation. In a sense this was an insurance policy against a future crisis. During the early spring of 1917, Daniel Willard heard from his friend Secretary of Interior Franklin K. Lane and later read in a Washington paper that President Wilson was considering having the federal government take over all the railroads with Willard as the director-general. Willard did not feel that such a drastic step was necessary. With the active support of Lane and the Council of National Defense, Willard, as chairman of the advisory commission, on April 8, 1917, sent telegrams to more than fifty railroad presidents inviting them to Washington to discuss the role of American railways in the war emergency.

On April 11, 1917, Daniel Willard met with his fellow railroad presidents and their top subordinates in the Willard Hotel in Washington. Their railroads represented perhaps 90 percent of the national rail mileage. After some discussion, the presidents approved and signed a resolution, prepared by the scholarly Fairfax Harrison, president of the Southern, stating that they would endeavor to operate the rail systems of America as if they were "a continental railway system." To coordinate these efforts, they created an executive committee, thereafter known as the Railroads' War Board. The five-man board was chaired by Fairfax Harrison and included Howard Elliott, president of the New Haven; Julius Kriettschnitt, chairman of the board of the Southern Pacific; Hale Holden, president of the Burlington; and Samuel Rea, president of the Pennsylvania. Ex-officio members of the board were Daniel Willard and Edgar E. Clark of the Interstate Commerce Commission. Working with an extensive staff in Washington, plus branch offices across the country, the Railroads' War Board suggested a reduction of duplicate passenger service, urged the heavier loading of freight cars, and set up car pools of freight equipment to relieve car shortages. The government endorsed these efforts, but late in May 1917, Congress passed the Esch Car Service Act which gave the ICC authority to set up rules governing the movement of all railroad cars.

In the last months of 1916 and throughout 1917, there was a growing shortage of freight cars. Earlier, in 1914 and 1915, when all lines had been seeking more traffic, there was often a surplus of cars. Earlier in 1915, the surplus was 300,000 cars or nearly one-seventh of the national total, but these surplus cars quickly disappeared with the increase in defense traffic. In March 1916, there was a shortage of 19,000 cars, which increased to 115,000 cars by November. By April 1, 1917, the shortage had grown to 145,000 cars and by November 1 of that year, it was up to 158,000 cars. The problem was compounded by the fact that the railroads of the nation owned 20,000 fewer freight cars in January 1917, than they had in 1914. They also owned fewer locomotives in 1917 than in 1914. The planned purchase of the 3,400 engines in 1917 was delayed because the government gave a higher priority to the building and shipping of engines needed by the Allies in Europe. The under maintenance of track and terminal facilities in the middle teens also made the problem worse.

Shortly after America declared war, officials of the army, navy, and United States Shipping Board all started to issue priority orders for many of their rail shipments. Many eastern lines soon found that most war shipments carried such "preference tags." Bad planning made the traffic problem worse. When the Hog Island shipyard was started on a salt swamp near Philadelphia, thousands of freight cars carrying "priority" building materials arrived weeks before there were any unloading facilities. Too many traffic officials sending out war shipments in 1917 had forgotten a lesson taught the nation half a century earlier by that tough old Union commander, William Tecumseh Sherman. As Sherman approached Atlanta in 1864, he had insisted that boxcars should never be used for storage, but had to be unloaded upon arrival in Georgia. Belatedly, the government attempted to bring some order out of the confused abundance of priority orders in August 1917, when Wilson appointed Judge Robert S. Lovett of the Union Pacific to be director of priority. Lovett seemingly believed he had no authority to cancel existing priority orders, but, at least, he gave out few new ones.

The rail traffic jam of 1917 was partially caused by the fact that so much war freight was headed to eastern Atlantic ports for shipment to Europe. The crisis grew worse in the weeks before Christmas 1917, because of an early and very severe winter. In December the average freight car moved only twenty-one miles per day, as compared to twenty-six in November, and twenty-eight in the preceding summer. Daniel Willard later wrote: "The amount paid by the Company for cleaning snow and ice from its tracks during the last winter [1917–18] was greater than the aggregate amount paid out for the same purpose during the entire six preceding winters."[2]

The Baltimore and Ohio, as an eastern trunk line, shared in the heavy wartime passenger and freight traffic, but never experienced any traffic jams or crammed freight yards as serious as those found to the north on the Pennsylvania Railroad. The B&O was also fortunate in being able to obtain much new equipment during 1917. In that year, the road acquired 32 new locomotives, 100 passenger cars, and 4,511 freight cars. An additional 28 locomotives and 1,125 freight cars, expected during 1917, were deferred because of the "superior needs of the Government and its Allies."[3] During the year the B&O retired from service 47 locomotives, 31 passenger cars, and 1,607 freight cars. All of the retired equipment was old and inferior to the new acquisitions. The book value of the total equipment roster of the road increased more than $8 million during 1917. Total operating revenues increased nearly 10 percent during the year, but operating expenses rose even faster because of higher wages and the greater cost of fuel and other supplies. Thus the operating ratio, which had been 72 percent in 1916, rose to 77 percent in 1917.

The fifteen divisions of the Baltimore and Ohio reported moving 644 troop trains during the year July 1, 1916, to June 30, 1917, with the Baltimore division and the Ohio division moving the greatest number. Early in the twelve months, the troops were moving toward the Mexican border, but the ninety-one troop trains of June 1917, were carrying soldiers destined eventually for European service. Many of the troop trains were carrying recruits to the fresh, new training camps being built to feed, house, and train as many as 35,000 volunteers and draftees in a single cantonment. Three of these huge new camps—Meade in Maryland, halfway between Washington and Baltimore; Taylor, located at Louisville, Kentucky; and Sherman, at Chillicothe, Ohio—were directly served by the lines of the B&O. Others, such as Camp Dix in New Jersey and Camp Benjamin Harrison near Indianapolis, were very close to the Baltimore and Ohio system.

An increasing number of the recruits in the training camps were former railroad employees. In the seven months, April 1, to October 31, 1917, the number of B&O workers who joined the armed services amounted to 1,760—1,029 volunteers and 731 draftees. Of this group, 823 came from the transportation department, 506 from maintenance of equipment, and 204 from maintenance of way. By the early winter of 1917–18, the number 1,760 was shown on a huge red, white and blue service flag proudly flying at the top of the B&O headquarters on Charles Street in Baltimore. The first gold star earned by a B&O employee was for John E. White, a former fireman on the Staten Island lines of the B&O. White, as a member of the reserves, was one of the first American soldiers in France. A motorcycle dispatch bearer, White "died of a gunshot wound on December 23 [1917] . . . somewhere in France."[4]

As more and more men put on uniforms, many women were employed to replace them. By May 5, 1917, 100 women had been employed to ease the labor shortage on the Baltimore and Ohio. Most of the new employees were clerical workers, but other women were car-cleaners at the Camden Station in Baltimore, ran drill presses, or were busy as blacksmith helpers. On the Cleveland division, Grace Vaughn was a station agent.

As total war came to America, operating expenses rose very rapidly on every railroad in the nation. Daniel Willard reported that in 1917, wages were 40 percent higher than in 1910. Locomotive fuel costs nearly doubled between 1916 and 1917, increasing from 10.3 cents per locomotive mile in 1916 to 19.9 cents in 1917. The total operating expense for a B&O locomotive climbed from thirty cents per mile in 1910 to fifty-nine cents per mile in 1917. Between 1914 and 1917, various types of iron and steel used by the railroad had increased in price from 125 to 483 percent. A dollar's worth of track spikes in 1914 had climbed to $2.89 by early 1918. Early in 1917, B&O officials estimated that the most important purchases for the year were going to be up 39 percent over 1916. In an issue of the *Baltimore and Ohio Employees Magazine*, they appealed to the workers to economize: "'If the cost of your living were 39 percent higher this year than last, you'd economise wouldn't you? And you'd do the same thing for your family!'"[5]

Fairfax Harrison and Daniel Willard, in the fall and early winter of 1917, were finding it increasingly difficult to run the railways of the nation as a "continental" rail system. Every single railroad in the nation was prone to keep and use any geographic or strategic traffic advantage it possessed. This was especially a problem since there was no way to compensate a disadvantaged line when the "continental" method of operation required redirection or diversion of traffic. As the severe winter of 1917–18 set in, the railroad crisis and the shortage of freight cars grew worse. President Frederick D. Underwood of the Erie Railroad was ready to admit that operations on his line were at the breaking point. The extreme cold weather before Christmas found New England nearly out of coal. As the crisis grew, the Interstate Commerce Commission recommended that the government take over the railroads under the authority of the Federal Possession and Control Act of August 29, 1916. On the day after Christmas, President Wilson issued a proclamation providing for federal operation of the nation's railroads as of noon, December 28, 1917. Early in January 1918, when he described the problem to Congress, Wilson said his action was not because of a failure on the part of the railroads, but rather because there were some things that government could do which private management could not. Given the existing conditions in December 1917, the federal take over was necessary and inevitable. The United States was the last of the warring nations to take such action.

In his proclamation of December 26, 1917, President Wilson appointed William G. McAdoo to be the director-general of American railroads. As a young Georgia lawyer, McAdoo had moved to New York City in the early 1890s to practice law and sell railway securities. Early in the new century, he became interested in the financial and engineering problems necessary for the completion in 1909 of several railroad tunnels under the Hudson River connecting New Jersey and lower Manhattan. In this project, he worked closely with such men as J. P. Morgan and Alexander J. Cassatt of the Pennsylvania. As a Democrat, McAdoo had helped manage President Wilson's 1912 campaign and was rewarded with his appointment as secretary of the treasury. As the war emergency grew, Wilson found many additional jobs to give his able cabinet member. His numerous positions inspired the pun, "McAdoo's work is never McAdone."

In general, the nation applauded the selection of McAdoo to head up the Railroad Administration, but some eastern rail executives, such as Fairfax Harrison and Dan Willard, were not too pleased with the appointment. Willard was unhappy with the government take over and McAdoo seemingly had never been impressed with the B&O president. Willard retained his position as chairman of the advisory commission, but played no role in the work of the Railroad Administration. During the twenty-six months of federal control, Willard remained president with corporate control of the Baltimore and Ohio, but the actual operations of the line were in the hands of men responsible to McAdoo. The Railroad Administration officials even denied Willard the use of his business car "No. 99" unless a special request was made for its use.

The new director-general of railroads at once sought the advice of his longtime friend Alfred Holland Smith, president of the New York Central. Smith, who became a temporary assistant to McAdoo, argued that an early concern must be the raising of railroad wages and McAdoo was soon to agree. McAdoo made Walker D. Hines, chairman of the board of the Sante Fe, his assistant director. Other top men in McAdoo's staff included Carl R. Gray, president of the Union Pacific after the war; John Skelton Williams, the first president of the Seaboard Air Line and later assistant secretary of the treasury under McAdoo; and William S. Carter, president of the Brotherhood of Locomotive Firemen and Enginemen.

The details of federal operation and control of the nation's rail lines were provided in the Railroad Control Act passed by Congress on March 21, 1918. This act provided that the individual railroads of the nation would receive an annual rental from the federal government equal to the average net railway operating income of each line for the three years June 30, 1914 to June 30, 1917. This base period included the heavy traffic year of 1916–17 but also the lean year of below average traffic in 1914–15. The legislation also provided for maintenance and repairs during the federal period of control, and promised that when control ended, the property would be "returned to it in substantially as good repair and in substantially as complete equipment as it was at the beginning of Federal Control."[6] This clause was to result in many disputes and claims of under maintenance when the roads eventually were returned to private control and operation. The return of the lines to private management was promised within twenty-one months following the ratification of the treaty ending the war. Congress also provided a fund of $500 million to help finance the expense of federal operation.

McAdoo and his staff insisted that all rail freight should, if at all possible, move over the shortest route. At the same time, terminal managers were to dispatch freight only where it seemed probable that prompt delivery at the destination was likely. Such procedures resulted in the greater use of lightly used lines and also a reduction of traffic over greatly congested routes. Greater emphasis was also placed on the return of empty freight cars from the Atlantic seaboard. The Railroad Administration also achieved certain economies by using standardized methods in repair and maintenance work and by having standard specifications for new cars and motive power. During the twenty-six months of federal control, the McAdoo staff spent $380 million when they ordered 100,000 new freight cars and 1,930 locomotives. Most of the locomotives were either switchers or Mikado freight engines (2-8-2). One hundred of the USRA light Mikado locomotives, having 64-inch drivers and weighing 146 tons, were delivered to the B&O during 1918.

The nation's rail passenger service also was changed during the McAdoo years. The highest priority during 1918, of course, was efficient troop movement. In the period from January 1, 1918, to the Armistice, the railroads carried 6,496,000 men, or an average of more than 20,000 per day. Much duplicate passenger service was eliminated, especially where several different railroads offered comparable service between two cities. Walker D. Hines figured that $95 million had been saved by eliminating trains and consolidating terminals and ticket offices. Many Pullman and dining cars were taken off the trains, and "a la carte" service was generally abolished. One gain for Willard's passenger service came with federal operation—Baltimore and Ohio passenger trains going to New York City were given trackage rights on the Pennsylvania line under the Hudson to enter New York in the Pennsylvania Station. When the war was over, the Pennsylvania naturally insisted that B&O travelers must return to the inconvenience of crossing the Hudson River by ferryboats to enter or depart from New York City.

McAdoo soon gave high priority to railroad labor. The director-general created a Railroad Wage Commission in January 1918, and this body soon reported that the cost of living had climbed 40 percent between December 1915 and December 1917. Average yearly wages on American railroads, which had been $828 in 1915, had only climbed to $1,004 by the end of 1917. The wage commission discovered that more than half of all rail employees were making no more than $75 per month and that 80 percent were paid no more than $100 per month in December

1917. As of December 1915, average pay for American railroad workers was: section men—$38 per month; section foremen—$64 per month; passenger brakemen—$85 per month; and passenger locomotive engineers—$178 per month. The wage commission recommended pay increases on a sliding scale, basing them on the wages as of December 1915. Workers receiving under $46 per month were given a $20 raise, the $85 per month worker got a 40 percent boost, the $100 per month man went up 31 percent, and the $150 per month employee received an increase of 16 percent. Workers making as much as $250 per month received no increase at all. The wage increases went into effect on May 25, 1918, with the new payroll rates retroactive to January 1, 1918. Years later, McAdoo wrote: "I have never done anything in my life that gave me so much satisfaction as raising the pay of the railroad employees."[7]

Later in 1918, McAdoo extended the eight-hour work day to all rail workers and also made changes in work rules for those running the trains which later would become a basis for featherbedding. The new work rules were a contributing factor in the growth of the railroad work force, climbing from 1,732,000 in 1917 to 1,841,000 in 1918, and more than 2,000,000 in 1920. McAdoo left the Railroad Administration late in 1918 and in January 1919 was succeeded by Walker D. Hines. Hines also granted additional pay increases after the war. The yearly average wages for the industry increased from $1,004 in 1917 to $1,419 in 1918; $1,485 in 1919; and $1,820 in 1920. As a result, the portion of the railroad revenue dollar going to railroad labor increased from forty cents in 1917 to fifty-five cents by 1920.

In addition to high labor costs, railroad supplies and fuel greatly increased in price during the war years. McAdoo and Hines were forced in June 1918 to raise both freight rates and passenger fares. Average freight rates were boosted 28 percent and passenger fares were pushed up 18 percent. These increases could not be made retroactive, and thus operational costs climbed faster than revenues. This trend continued after the Armistice. The national operating ratio for the entire industry climbed from 70 percent in 1917 to 81 percent in 1918, 85 percent in 1919, and 94 percent in 1920. The total operating expenses, including the rentals paid individual lines, for the twenty-six months of federal operation (January 1, 1918, to March 1, 1920) exceeded total revenues by just over $900 million.

Daniel Willard was not happy to see the railroads of the nation taken over by the federal government late in December 1917. He certainly believed that his own road, because of the millions of dollars spent on additions, betterments, and new equipment between 1910 and 1917, was ready and able to meet almost any increased war traffic. Nor did he like to see the operating ratio of the Baltimore and Ohio climb from 72 percent in 1916 to 77 percent in 1917, 92 percent in 1918, and even higher in 1919 and 1920. He and his board of directors in the early months of 1918 contended that the annual compensation of just over $29 million offered by the Railroad Administration to the Baltimore and Ohio was nearly $4 million below the annual rental due the railroad. Eventually the Railroad Administration and Willard's railroad compromised on a figure of $30,031,009.14 for the year 1918.

But Willard was a loyal American, and he at once made every effort to have every Baltimore and Ohio employee give full support to the total war effort. Even though he did not travel in "No. 99," he went all over the system talking to company employees in terminals, yards, and shops. He laid particular emphasis on the prompt repair of locomotives. Early in 1918 he said: "For instance, if a locomotive is in need of repairs, it should be repaired immediately, even though some of you have to remain longer at work. Every twenty-four hours' delay in moving to the seaboard the coal and other freight which should go abroad to our troops may mean twenty-four hours' delay in the trenches of Europe."[8] Director-general McAdoo made the same point on an inspection trip over the B&O lines in September 1918, when he said: "Every bad-order locomotive is a Prussian soldier."[9]

During the year 1918, the number of Baltimore and Ohio employees in the armed services naturally increased. By June 1918, 3,138 had been drafted and 1,770 had enlisted for a total of 4,908. By the end of the war later in the year nearly 7,000 Baltimore and Ohio workers had put on the uniform to serve their country. Of this number, 97 had died in the defense of their flag while 103 more had been wounded. Those who remained back home were loyal supporters of the several bond drives in the war years. Nearly 85 percent of the 65,000 employees supported the Third Liberty Loan Drive and purchased bonds worth more than $4 million. In the fall of 1918, in the Fourth Liberty Bond Drive, 61,316 subscribers out of a total employee roster of 69,996, or 87.7 percent, subscribed $5,667,750 with an average subscription of $92.43 per person. The general offices plus the Wheeling division and the Ohio River division all had 100 percent participation. B&O employees also subscribed more than $4 million to the Victory Loan Drive which was held after the Armistice.

During both 1917 and 1918, more than 400 workers, in addition to their own home "victory gardens," had gardens on

B&O property. Several hundred acres of unoccupied land owned by the B&O were made available to interested employees in Willard's "right-of-way gardens" campaign. Baltimore and Ohio workers also helped during the epidemic of "Spanish influenza" which was crippling eastern states in the early fall of 1918. When the hospitals of Cumberland and Keyser reached their capacities with flu victims in the first days of October, a special nine-car "hospital" train filled with doctors and volunteer nurses was dispatched west to the Cumberland area.

It was during the days of the influenza epidemic of late 1918 that Daniel Willard experienced both a personal triumph and a personal tragedy. In October 1918, General Pershing in France cabled the War Department that he needed a top railroad executive to help him straighten out the French railways in the American sector of the western front. Secretary of War Newton D. Baker cabled Pershing he would send the best railroad man in America to help solve the problem. Baker invited Willard to go to France, and the B&O president quickly accepted. A colonel's commission in the United States Army, signed by President Wilson, was sent to Baltimore, and tailors were called in to prepare Willard's uniforms. Colonel Willard never got to France. At the very end of October, his oldest son Harold and Harold's wife died of influenza within twenty-four hours of one another. The double tragedy gave Willard no opportunity to enjoy the final war honor offered him.

Many changes had occurred in traffic, revenue, and income patterns during the first decade of Willard's presidency of the Baltimore and Ohio.

TABLE 14. Baltimore and Ohio System Traffic and Financial Growth
1909–20 (Including affiliated lines)

Year	Miles of Road	Total Revenue	Net Revenue	Expenses to Earnings (%)	Average Passenger Fare (cents per mile)	Average Freight Rate (cents per ton-mile)	Dividend on Common Stock (%)
1909–10	4,434	$ 90,163,401	$26,967,817	70	1.90	.58	6
1910–11	4,434	89,968,130	25,230,624	72	1.91	.58	6
1911–12	4,455	94,040,594	27,218,145	71	1.93	.58	6
1912–13	4,456	103,329,992	26,902,182	74	1.93	.56	6
1913–14	4,515	99,164,009	24,760,621	75	1.92	.57	6
1914–15	4,535	91,815,797	27,890,289	70	1.97	.57	5
1916	4,545	116,968,881	32,508,586	72	2.01	.57	5
1917	4,989	139,851,909	31,758,243	77	2.09	.59	5
1918	5,151	175,259,574	13,325,983	92	2.62	.76	4.5
1919	5,153	182,620,016	12,271,984	93	2.59	.79	2
1920	5,155	231,949,443	5,545,135	98	2.94	.87	—

The change in the fiscal year came as a result of the decision of the Interstate Commerce Commission in the middle of the decade to have all railroads use the calendar year as the fiscal year. Thus in 1916, the B&O shifted from a year beginning July 1 and ending June 30 year to a year starting on January 1 and ending December 31. The increase of about 400 miles of line between 1908–9 and 1909–10 was a result of Willard's insisting that all affiliated lines be fully included in the accounts and reports of the railroad.

The decade of the teens saw American railroads possess a dominant position in the commercial traffic of the nation—both freight and passenger. In 1916, more than 77 percent of the intercity freight traffic went by rail. In the same year—well before the appearance of the "family car"—98 percent of all intercity commercial passenger traffic was by rail.

During the decade, the cost of living had more than doubled, and railroad freight rates and passenger fares had increased about 50 percent. Thus the railroad revenue had grown much faster than the real increase in traffic. The total dollar revenue on the B&O had climbed about 150 percent in the decade while the total freight ton-mileage had climbed only about 65 to 70 percent in the same ten years. Total passenger mileage in those years had grown less than 30 percent. In 1910 passenger revenue had been about one-fourth as large as the freight revenue—by 1920 it was no more than one-fifth of the revenue generated by freight traffic. Some of the new freight traffic was clearly the result of the establishment by Daniel Willard in 1916 of a new commercial development department. By the end of 1917, Willard was able to report that this new agency was "instrumental in bringing about the location on the System of 815 industries requiring side track facilities, including 223 coal developments."[10]

The traffic mix of the war years on the Baltimore and Ohio was not greatly different from that of the prewar period.

TABLE 15. Commodities Carried on the Baltimore and Ohio

	1911–12		1918	
	Tons	*Percent*	*Tons*	*Percent*
Products of Agriculture	3,203,250	4.95	4,577,492	4.80
Products of Animals	934,902	1.45	1,104,578	1.16
Products of Mines	43,115,160	66.63	61,656,682	64.67
Products of Forests	2,626,988	4.06	3,555,600	3.73
Manufactures	10,165,098	15.71	15,681,855	16.45
Misc. & Merchandise	4,658,772	7.20	8,760,022	9.19
Total	64,704,170	100.00	95,336,229	100.00

A major change that came with federal operation in 1918 and after was the tremendous increase in the expenses of operation. During 1917 the extra labor costs of the eight-hour day plus great increases in locomotive fuel costs had pushed the operating ratio from 72 percent in 1916 to 77 percent in 1917. In 1918 this ratio rose to 92 percent. Total revenue climbed about 25 percent in 1918, but operating expenses went up 48 percent over 1917. Maintenance of way and structure expense climbed from $15 million to $25 million, maintenance of equipment from $27 million to nearly $49 million, and transportation costs climbed from $59 million to $78 million. The only major operating expense to decline during 1918 was that of the traffic department—the railroad had plenty of business. The advertising budget for 1918 thus dropped nearly 80 percent from that of the previous year. McAdoo's major boost in railroad wages during the year was, of course, the main reason for the great increase in operating expenses. This trend continued in 1919 and 1920, and the operating ratio continued to climb in those years.

The railroad plant and capital structure of the B&O had also grown in the decade. The bottom line figures on the balance sheet of assets and liabilities had nearly doubled in the decade, climbing from $602 million in 1909–10 to $1,013 million in 1920. During the period, the investment in the road had climbed from $214 million to $246 million, while the value of equipment had increased from $73 million to $151 million. In 1920 the equipment roster included 2,638 locomotives, 95,780 freight cars, 1,317 passenger cars, and 2,661 pieces of work equipment. In the decade, the holdings of securities in subsidiary or affiliated companies had increased from $185 million to $287 million. The B&O continued to have a substantial holding of the securities of the Philadelphia and Reading. The capital stock of the Baltimore and Ohio had basically remained unchanged in the ten years—$60 million of preferred stock and $152 million of common stock. However, the long term debt of the railroad, which was $321 million in 1910, had increased to $561 million by 1920. Annual interest paid on this funded debt had increased from $11 million paid in 1910 to $22 million paid in 1920. This substantial increase in long term debt and annual interest payments did not augur well for the long term financial health of the company.

The twenty-six months of federal operation had caused a great increase in the operating ratio, and also a decline and then a temporary cessation of dividends on the common stock. Reduced dividends of 4.5 percent in 1918, and 2 percent in 1919, were paid on the common stock, being charged against the accumulated surplus of the company. No dividends were paid on the common stock in 1920. Dividends on B&O common stock would not be resumed until 1923. The war years, with their higher costs of operation, increasing operating ratio, and declining dividend record, brought a drop in the common stock on Wall Street. During 1913, after a half dozen years of $6 annual dividends, B&O common stock was quoted from a low of $90 to a high of $106. In 1917 the range in price was from $38 to $85 a share and in 1920 it ranged from $27 to $49. The world war and the twenty-six months of federal operation (January 1, 1918 to March 1, 1920) had been hard on the Baltimore and Ohio. Daniel Willard would face some difficult problems in the early 1920s.

Chapter XIV

. . . .

Prosperity and a Birthday Party

IN THE EARLY YEARS AFTER WORLD WAR I, THERE WAS A rather general belief in America that, in some way, the prewar climate of government-railroad relations should be improved. Three weeks after the Armistice, Woodrow Wilson in a message to Congress urged that body to give high priority to the entire railroad problem. Across the nation, a great variety of opinion could be found concerning the future of railroads. The retiring director-general, William G. McAdoo, held that federal control could well be extended for another five years. The most extreme suggestion was that of Glen E. Plumb, a specialist in railroad law and the legal counsel of the four operating unions. Under Plumb's proposal, the federal government would purchase all the lines, with the management and operation in the hands of a fifteen-member board composed of government officials, labor, and rail executives. The Plumb plan was widely endorsed by organized labor and railroad workers who had fared quite well during the months of federal control.

Even though government ownership of railroads was gaining acceptance in the rest of the world, the American public generally did not approve of the proposal made by Plumb. Railroad owners and executives, such as Daniel Willard and Howard Elliot of the New Haven, were very hostile to the Plumb plan and proposed instead a full return to private ownership with an improved program of regulation by the government. President Wilson tended to favor this approach, and in 1919–20, Congress gave much time to a new mode of rail regulation. The combined efforts of Congressmen John Esch of Wisconsin and Albert Cummins of Iowa were merged in the Esch-Cummins Act, or the Transportation Act of 1920, which was signed by President Wilson just a day before the railroads were handed back to private control on March 1, 1920.

The Transportation Act of 1920 provided for the return of the railroads to private management and also greatly increased the scope and power of the Interstate Commerce Commission. The ICC, increased from nine to eleven members, could now fix both maximum and minimum rates, and was to set rates so that they would assure the nation's railways a "fair rate of return" (originally set at 5.5 percent) on the railroad investment. One-half of any excess beyond a 6 percent return was subject to recapture by the government. To help the railroads operate in the black, the act guaranteed the individual lines a net operating income for the first six months of private operation (March 1, 1920 to September 1, 1920) equal to half the annual rental paid during the years of federal control. This six-month assistance program cost the federal government $530 million. The new legislation also gave the commission supervision of all new rail security issues and also made future mergers and consolidations subject to commission approval. At the same time, the commission was directed to work toward an orderly consolidation of the nation's railways into a limited number of larger systems. The legislation of 1920 also created a nine-member labor board with extensive jurisdiction over railroad wages, rules, working conditions, and labor disputes.

Daniel Willard felt that the Transportation Act of 1920 was a constructive piece of railroad legislation. He knew Senator Cummins, chairman of the Senate Committee on Interstate Commerce, quite well, and no doubt had indirectly influenced the final language found in the completed legislation. Willard and many other railroad presidents were especially in favor of the "fair rate of return" clause in the 1920 act. Certainly Willard's Baltimore and Ohio, along with most other lines, availed itself of the guaranteed "rental" income from the government for the first six months of individual control and operation.

The first two years (1920–22) of private direction of the B&O were a very difficult period for Daniel Willard and his top subordinates. Both the increased expenses of operation and the record high operating ratio of 1920 had to be reduced in some way. To settle a labor dispute with rail workers in the summer of 1920, the new railroad labor board ordered another wage boost of about 22 percent, effective May 1, 1920. Locomotive fuel, which cost the B&O only $1.14 per ton in 1916, had risen in 1920 to an average cost of $3.75 per ton. Fortunately for all railroads, the ICC, in the late summer of 1920, substantially increased all passenger fares and also pushed up freight rates ranging from a 40 percent increase in the East to 25 percent in the West and the South. Average freight rates on the Baltimore and Ohio rose about 34 percent as a result this ICC action.

The modest postwar depression of 1920–21 soon started to reverse this trend to higher and higher costs. Between 1920 and 1922, the overall cost of living declined about 20 percent. In 1921 the labor board cut railroad wages about 12 percent, effective July 21, 1921. At the same time, the railroad work force on the Baltimore and Ohio was cut from 72,000 workers on March 1, 1920 to under 59,000 in the early spring of 1921. During 1921 the Baltimore and Ohio traffic department cut freight rates by $7.5 million per year. The effect of these several changes let the B&O put a cap on operating expenses. Gross revenues of $231 million in 1920 dropped to $199 million in 1921 and rose slightly to $201 million in 1922. Total operating expenses of $226 million in 1920 declined sharply to $167 million in 1921 and to $165 million in 1922. The operating ratio which had stood at a record 97 percent in 1920, declined to 84 percent in 1921 and 82 percent in 1922.

The revival of business in 1922 was disturbed by two strikes, one by coal miners in the spring and later by one of the railroad shop workers in the summer. A strike of both anthracite and bituminous coal miners began in April 1922 and continued until late August. As a result, the B&O suffered a decline in coal traffic for the year. The second labor trouble started when a nationwide strike of railway machinists, blacksmiths, sheet metal workers, boilermakers, electrical workers, and carmen and their helpers started on July 1, 1922. These shop craft workers refused to accept a 10 percent wage reduction ordered by the railway labor board effective July 1. The strike by at least one-quarter of the total B&O work force naturally required a wholesale hiring of thousands of nonunion men. The shop craft strike finally ended September 15, 1922.

The Baltimore and Ohio made a favorable settlement with its shop men more easily than some of the other railroads. President Willard went to his workers and said, in effect: "Now we have made a settlement with you, let's pull off our coats and all go to work together—for the road. No bad feelings. Bygones are bygones."[1] To a newspaper reporter, Willard gave a positive opinion: "I am not so much interested as to what my men do when they are striking, as to what they are doing when they are working."[2] Willard had good reason to wish for a positive mood of cooperation with his workers. The strike had interrupted his efforts to work out a plan of worker cooperation suggested by W. H. Johnston, president of the machinists' union, and O. S. Beyer, Jr., a well-known efficiency engineer. The Johnston-Beyer proposal was for a cooperative plan between the workers and management with rewards given to workers who proposed practical changes in work methods and practices which would increase productivity and efficiency. The plan was introduced successfully in the B&O shops in 1922–23 and later extended to other departments of the railroad. Of the expanded plan, Willard wrote in 1926: "The policy of cooperation between management and the employees inaugurated in 1923 has been expanded with mutual benefits to all."[3]

Even though Baltimore and Ohio passenger traffic declined slightly during the decade, President Willard believed that first-class passenger service was essential to the prosperity of the road. Early in 1923, Willard told a group of longtime B&O employees that the three main essentials in the handling of passenger trains were: "1. To go safely—2. To go comfortably—3. To go on time."[4] The B&O president said that he had resisted suggestions to speed up passenger schedules because passenger comfort was more important. For several years, Daniel Willard had been trying to have his railroad noted for the smooth starting and stopping of its passenger trains. B&O passenger trains in the 1920s had a good "on time" record. In August 1929, the more than 17,500 passenger trips of the B&O system had an "on time" record of 95.4 percent for the month. Of the sixteen divisions in the system, the lowest average was 87.8 percent, while five divisions had averages from 97 to 100 percent on time.

Daniel Willard inaugurated two all-Pullman trains in the midtwenties, the *Capitol Limited,* put in daily service to Chicago in May 1923, and the *National Limited,* running west to Cincinnati and St. Louis, put in service in April 1925. Both trains were first-class, boasting such luxury items as a lounge car, train secretary, valet, maid, manicure, and shower bath. The luxury features of the two new trains made Willard feel a little guilty for he well realized that the Baltimore and Ohio was, in reality, a "day coach road." In one instance, he stopped a discussion concerning Pullman service by saying: "We are spending too much time on the problem of the Pullman passenger. Eighty per cent of our patrons ride in the day coaches; yet we barely give them twenty per cent of our attention."[5]

On one occasion, Daniel Willard became involved in railroad travel even fancier than first-class Pullman—the rail travel of European royalty. Early in 1926, Sam Hill, a resident of the state of Washington and the son-in-law of late James J. Hill, asked Willard to help him with the travel arrangements for the forthcoming visit to America by Queen Marie of Romania. Hill was hoping that something might be done to lower the cost of the extensive royal American tour. The rules of the Interstate Commerce Commission were quite strict about issuing railroad passes, even for visiting royalty. Willard said he would see if something could be done about the problem and promised to approach the ICC. Willard's fellow railroad presidents, who often spoke of Daniel as the fair-haired boy of the commission, were not too surprised when, in due course, the ICC issued a special "visiting royalty" rate. The new tariff permitted any line, if it so desired, to allow a royal entourage to pass over its line for a total cost of one dollar for the entire trip. The B&O and many other lines, including the New York Central, the Pennsylvania, and the three Hill roads, all offered the special rate to Queen Marie and her party. As a result, the coast to coast tour in the autumn of 1926 became a remarkable travel bargain for the visiting queen.

Many Baltimore and Ohio passenger trains, Pullman or coach, carried dining cars in the 1920s. The operation of several dozen diners was fairly expensive. New first-class diners cost as much as $60,000 in the 1920s, and the B&O accounting office figured it cost about half a dollar for every person served in a diner even before a single penny was spent on food. E. V. Baugh, the manager of the dining car and commissary department during the twenties, justified the service this way: "The one big reason that we have a Dining Car Department is because we want to be hospitable to our patrons in all respects—to make them feel the comfort, convenience and homelike atmosphere of our accommodations as soon as they step on our trains."[6]

Baugh was proud of his road's reputation for high quality cuisine. Being situated near the Maryland tidewater made it easy for the Baltimore and Ohio menus to include Chesapeake Bay oysters and a great variety of other seafood. E. V. Baugh and his diner stewards tried to provide substantial portions at moderate prices. The menus of the decade included both a special dollar and a quarter dinner, as well as a commercial traveler's meal for seventy-five cents. When Willard's "No. 99" was at the rear of a B&O passenger train, the Baltimore and Ohio president would often send his steward, Jim Ennis, through the train to the regular dining car for one of the specialties of the railroad. If Willard and his

Cheerful B&O chef keeps busy in his well-planned and efficient galley. *(Courtesy, Smithsonian Institution)*

business car guests gave a unanimously favorable verdict on the Chesapeake Bay fish or the crisp corn meal muffins, a personal thank you note from the president, and perhaps his signed photograph, were often sent forward to the cook in the busy and compact galley. It was the ambition of every B&O dining car chef to have an autographed picture of Daniel Willard to attest to his culinary skill.

On September 1, 1926, the Pennsylvania Railroad terminated the right of the Baltimore and Ohio passenger trains to use the Pennsylvania Station in New York City. This right had been given the B&O in the spring of 1918 as a wartime measure during the federal operation of American railroads. At the same time that the B&O resumed the use of the tracks of the Reading and Central of New Jersey railroads for passenger service between Philadelphia and Jersey City, it also started a new service for getting passengers in and out of New York City. Late in August 1926, the B&O inaugurated a fleet of motor coaches to carry passengers between several new stations in New York City and Brooklyn and train side in the B&O terminal in Jersey City. The *Baltimore and Ohio Magazines* described the favorable reaction of the first patrons of the new service: "Perhaps they wanted to get that stimulating whiff of salt air which is but one of the joys of crossing over, rather than traveling under, the always interesting and majestic Hudson."[7]

Not many years after Willard's road had turned to a competitive mode of transport to help get its passengers in and out of New York City, another change took place in downtown Baltimore. For many decades, the city fathers of Baltimore had insisted that a man on horseback, blowing a warning horn at each intersection, had to ride ahead of any switch engine moving cars along Pratt Street in the area just east of the Mount Clare shops. The horseman, who was supposed to protect horse-drawn traffic from the trains, was often dubbed "Paul Revere" by the small boys of the neighborhood. As automobiles and trucks replaced horses and wagons on Pratt Street in the postwar years, the city of Baltimore finally repealed the ancient ordinance and allowed brakemen to warn Pratt Street traffic of the approaching cars. By the 1920s, most of the freight cars were being moved along Pratt Street by stubby, saddle-tank dockside switchers known as "Little Joes." In an effort to fool the horses on Pratt Street, a few of the "Little Joes" were covered with an overall cab to make them resemble street cars.

Even though total passenger traffic on the Baltimore and Ohio declined by more than one-fourth between 1920 and 1929, Daniel Willard acquired dozens of new passenger locomotives during the decade. All of the new passenger motive power was much larger than the "Little Joes" that frequented Pratt Street. By the turn of the century, the older American type (4-4-0) passenger engines had largely been replaced by Ten-Wheelers (4-6-0) or by the new Atlantics (4-4-2). The development of a firebox too wide to be placed between or over the drivers made a trailing truck necessary. Thus the Atlantic locomotive, with its trailing truck, became a logical successor to the 4-4-0. In the first decade of the twentieth century in the Loree and Murray years, the Baltimore and Ohio purchased about fifty Atlantics, engines having seventy-eight- or eighty-inch drivers and weighing from 75 to 100 tons.

When Daniel Willard started to replace wooden passenger cars with ones built of steel, passenger engines larger than the Atlantics were going to be required. A few Pacific type (4-6-2) engines had been built by Schenectady for President Oscar Murray in 1906. Between 1911 and 1917, Daniel Willard ordered about 80 Pacifics in four different orders, each time purchasing Baldwin built engines from his good friend Sam Vauclain. Thirty more Pacifics were provided by the United States Railroad Administration in 1919. President Willard ordered more Pacifics built by Baldwin in 1922, engines with seventy-four-inch drivers and weighing 144 tons.

The best known B&O Pacific locomotives were the twenty ordered from Baldwin in 1927 and named for American presidents.

The engines were named in sequence from Washington through Arthur. There was only one *President Adams*, which honored both John and John Quincy Adams. Painted an olive green with lettering and striping in gold, the engines had eighty-inch drivers, weighed 163 tons, had 50,000 pounds traction power, and came equipped with a stoker, power reverse, and a tender water scoop. The man who supervised the introduction of the presidential Pacifics was Col. George H. Emerson, chief of motive power and equipment since 1920. Colonel Emerson was in Russia with American military forces when Samuel Vauclain recommended him strongly to Daniel Willard. In 1928 Colonel Emerson was responsible for building and adding the experimental *President Cleveland* to the presidential fleet of Pacifics. This locomotive was similar to the other twenty but was built with an experimental water-tube firebox at the back end of the boiler. The Baltimore and Ohio never seriously considered using the 4-6-4 or the 4-8-4 engines for passenger traffic. Until the appearance of the diesel locomotive twenty years later, Willard's road used the Pacific to haul the "varnish."

Naturally during the twenties, most of the new motive power acquired was for the larger and more important freight service. Dozens of the older Consolidations (2-8-0) were retired by the B&O during the 1920s. The great bulk of the freight engines purchased during that decade were Mikados (2-8-2), Santa Fes (2-10-2) or Mallets. Willard had purchased many Mikados in his first years as president, and more were acquired during the twenty-six months of federal control. Between 1920 and 1923, Baldwin built 135 heavy Mikados for the Baltimore and Ohio. By 1927 about 600 of these sturdy engines were included in the B&O roster of freight motive power.

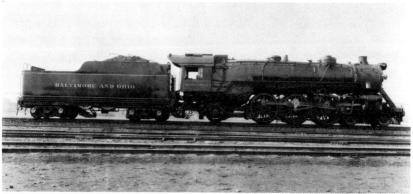

The *President Washington*, one of the fast Pacific-type locomotives built for service between Washington and New York. *(Courtesy, Baltimore and Ohio Railroad)*

The Capitol Limited passes the C&O Canal on its way to Chicago in the early 1920s.
(*Courtesy, Baltimore and Ohio Railroad*)

The first Santa Fe (2-10-2) type locomotives, with its extra pair of drivers as compared to the Mikado, was purchased by the Baltimore and Ohio from the Baldwin Locomotive Company in 1914. Between 1923 and 1926, the Baltimore and Ohio purchased 125 still larger Santa Fe locomotives, 75 from Baldwin, and 50 from the Lima Locomotive Company. These engines had sixty-four-inch drivers, weighed 218 tons, and provided 84,300 pounds of tractive power. Santa Fe locomotive crews called these engines "Big Sixes" because they were big, and their four-digit number all started with the number six. The 150 Santa Fe engines which the B&O had acquired by 1926 were chiefly used on the Cumberland, Pittsburgh, Akron, and Toledo divisions.

The B&O had purchased its first Mallet or articulated locomotive in 1904. Willard purchased sixty Mallets between 1911 and 1916, and more were acquired during the years of World War I. Early Mallets were 0-8-8-0 in wheel style, but later a forward truck was added (2-8-8-0). Most of the Mallets had fifty-eight-inch drivers, and the largest weighed nearly 250 tons with 118,000 pounds of tractive power. In 1922 Willard purchased sixteen Mallets from the Seaboard Air Line, with engine crew gossip saying that SAL executives had purchased engines too large for clearance on their line. By 1927 Willard's road was operating 135 of the huge Mallets. All of the Mallets were stoker-fired since it was considered impossible to hand-fire a locomotive with more than 55,000 pounds of tractive power.

Locomotive crews, as well as B&O labor generally, had something to celebrate in the mid-1920s. The month of October 1926 marked the fifteenth anniversary of the inauguration of the safety first movement on the Baltimore and Ohio Railroad. When the new president, Daniel Willard, pushed for a company-wide safety first movement in the fall of 1911, the Baltimore and Ohio was the first railroad in the East to do so and the second in the nation. In October 1911, General Manager Arthur W. Thompson had named a general safety committee and instructed each division to organize safety committees. At the Baltimore meeting, President Willard announced the first principle of the safety first movement would be "Safety Above Everything Else."[8] The general safety committee believed the best way to sell "Safety First" to all employees was through a company magazine, and in October 1912, the first issue of the *Baltimore & Ohio Employees Magazine* appeared.

Yearly accident and death figures for B&O employees clearly indicate the success of the safety first campaign in the first fifteen years of the program. During the four years from 1911 through 1914, when the average number of B&O employees was just over 61,000, the average yearly figures for deaths and injuries from accidents while working were 171 and 12,658 respectively. Comparable figures for the years 1922 through 1925, when the average work force was 67,000, were 67 deaths and 5,909 injuries. The 60 percent reduction in deaths and 53 percent decline in injuries clearly indicate the success of the safety first movement on the Baltimore and Ohio. This improved record in the number of accidents naturally resulted in savings in the relief department. Disablement benefits paid workers because of accidents declined from $337,000 paid in 1916, to $231,000 paid in 1928. Relief department funds paid out for accidental deaths to employees declined from $185,000 in 1916 to $90,000 for the year 1928.

On the other hand, the number and size of pensions paid to retired Baltimore and Ohio employees increased during the decade of the 1920s. Back in 1904, an average yearly pension of $190 had been paid to 354 Baltimore and Ohio pensioners. By 1920 the number of former workers receiving average annual pensions of $319 had increased to 1,102. A more liberal pension policy was adopted by the railroad in 1926, effective October 1, 1926. As a result, in 1927 there were 1,664 former workers receiving average yearly pensions of $511. In the *Annual Report* for 1929, Daniel Willard wrote: "Pensions are paid by the Company to superannuated and infirm employees and charged to operating expenses.

Superintendents inspect the road in a Tin Lizzie in the 1920s.
(Courtesy, Baltimore and Ohio Railroad)

No part of such pension payments is contributed by employees."[9] The number of pensioners in 1929 was 2,301 and the average pension for the year was $544. In 1929 the average annual earnings for railroad workers was $1,749 while factory workers received $1,543 and school teachers only $1,312.

Daniel Willard believed that his railroad had suffered from undermaintenance during the twenty-six months of federal control and operation. He was certain that his line in 1920 was not in the top-grade condition it had enjoyed on the eve of the conflict. After the final settlement with the federal government was completed, Willard grew a bit philosophical when he wrote in mid-1924: "The Company did not receive in settlement the full compensation and guaranty to which it believed itself rightfully entitled. . . .That portion of its rightful claims which it did not receive may be considered as the Company's contribution to the winning of the war and the readjustment that followed."[10]

Many Baltimore and Ohio officials believed that it took six years after the termination of federal control before the physical condition of the road was returned to its prewar status. During the decade of the twenties, the Baltimore and Ohio spent more than $90 million in additions and betterments to the road. Very small amounts were spent in both 1921 and 1922, but more than $10 million was spent in each of the four years 1923, 1924, 1926, and 1927, and $18 million was spent in 1929. The great bulk of the total

Locust Point from the air in the 1920s. Fort McHenry is in the foreground. (*Courtesy, Baltimore and Ohio Railroad*)

money came from new capital investment. Very little new road was constructed in the decade, but a great number of modest improvements were made through the entire system. In 1920 an eight-story office building was purchased in Baltimore to relieve crowded conditions in the company's general headquarters. As heavier and heavier locomotives were put on the line, many bridges needed to be rebuilt and reinforced. Dozens and dozens of bridges were upgraded, and some new ones built, including a $2 million bridge across the Miami River in 1921. Automatic signal protection was installed on forty miles of heavy traffic line early in the decade.

Throughout the decade, much money was invested in new yard facilities at Locust Point and the construction of new grain elevators in that area. In the midtwenties, a track elevation program near Philadelphia was completed, and, in the same years, the B&O, along with the Reading, constructed a $4 million vegetable and produce terminal in the same city. The entire Metropolitan branch northwest of Washington was upgraded during the decade. As the American public purchased millions of automobiles in the decade, the protection of railroad grade crossings became a growing problem. During the twenties, the Baltimore and Ohio spent many millions of dollars to eliminate dozens of grade crossings and to safeguard hundreds of grade crossings with warning lights. During 1928 the B&O installed 191 such signals at grade crossings.

The decade of the 1920s was a period of quite modest growth in Baltimore and Ohio mileage. The average yearly mileage of the operated B&O system grew only a little more than 400 miles in the decade, increasing from 5,155 miles as shown in the *Annual Report* for 1920 to 5,568 miles in 1930. During the ten years, several very small additions in mileage were made, but the major increase came in 1926–27 when the system-wide mileage increased more than 300 miles. In 1926 the Interstate Commerce Commission approved the purchase by the Baltimore and Ohio of 96 percent of the capital stock of the Cincinnati, Indianapolis and Western Railroad. The stock was acquired and the 321-mile line became a part of the Baltimore and Ohio system in 1927.

The Cincinnati, Indianapolis and Western consisted of a 296-mile main line from Hamilton, Ohio (twenty-four miles north of Cincinnati) via Indianapolis to Springfield, Illinois, plus a twenty-five mile branch line in Indiana running south from Melcher to Brazil. The main line of the Cincinnati, Indianapolis, and Western was the result of the merger of two earlier roads—the Cincinnati, Hamilton and Indianapolis and the Indianapolis, Decatur and Springfield. The Cincinnati, Hamilton and Indianapolis was a ninety-nine-mile road from Hamilton to Indianapolis opened in 1869, while the road west of Indianapolis had been built during the 1870s. Early in the twentieth century, the Cincinnati, Indianapolis and Western had been the western portion of the Cincinnati, Hamilton and Dayton. In 1916 the Baltimore and Ohio had acquired the Toledo and Cincinnati, the portion of the CH&D located in western Ohio. The new acquisition in 1927 gave the B&O a third line across Indiana, an entrance to the capital of the Hoosier State and a second route to the capital of Illinois.

In the late 1920s, the Baltimore and Ohio also purchased large blocks of stock in several railroads in Ohio, Maryland, and Pennsylvania. During 1927 the B&O acquired about 18 percent of the capital stock of the Wheeling and Lake Erie Railway, a line in northern and eastern Ohio whose two principal routes ran from Wheeling to Toledo and from Zanesville to Cleveland. Also in 1927, Willard's road purchased about 40 percent of the capital stock of the Western Maryland Railway, an 800-mile road consisting of a line from Baltimore to central West Virginia, plus several branches in southern Pennsylvania. Early in 1929, the Baltimore and Ohio sold its entire holdings of stock in the Wheeling and Lake Erie and purchased a substantial majority of the stock of the Buffalo, Rochester and Pittsburgh Railway. For some years, the B&O had owned trackage rights for portions of the Buffalo, Rochester and Pittsburgh, a 520-mile road whose principal line ran from Pittsburgh to Buffalo and Rochester in New York. In the summer of 1929, the B&O also entered into an agreement to acquire a majority of the capital stock of the Buffalo and Susquehanna, a 228-mile road running from Sagamore, Pennsylvania, up to Addison and Wellsville in south central New York. None of these roads were included officially in the operated mileage of the B&O during the 1920s.

The long tenure and generally successful presidency of Daniel Willard was certainly aided by the quality and relative lack of turnover in the twelve-man board of directors of his railroad. Only thirty different men served on the board during the twenty-one-year period, 1920 through 1940. Four men—John R. Morron, Paul M. Warburg, Robert Garrett, and John J. Cornwell—were on the board throughout the twenties. John Morron, a New York banker and one-time president of the Peter Cooper Glue Company, served on the B&O board from 1914 throughout the remainder of the Willard presidency. The German born Paul Warburg was a partner in Kuhn, Loeb and Company in New York and, after serving ably on the first Federal Reserve Board from 1914 to 1918, was a Baltimore and Ohio director from 1919 through 1931. Robert

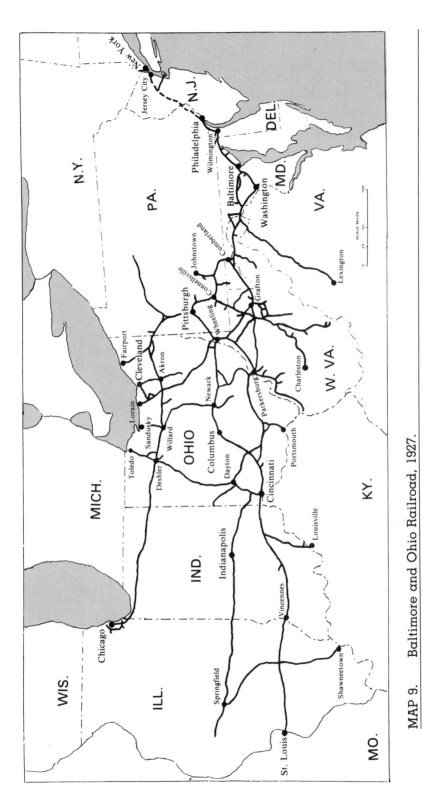

MAP 9.   Baltimore and Ohio Railroad, 1927.

New mileage acquired since 1910 included lines in West Virginia, Ohio, Indiana, and Illinois.

SCALE MILES

0   25   50   100

Garrett, grandson of John Work Garrett, Baltimore banker and discus thrower in the 1896 Olympic Games, was elected a director at the age of thirty-eight in 1913 and was still on the board when Willard retired in 1941. John T. Cornwell, Democratic governor of West Virginia 1917–21, was elected a director in 1920 and retained a seat on the board throughout Willard's presidency. Cornwell, a lawyer as well as an editor, became the general counsel of the Baltimore and Ohio in 1922.

Four more men—George M. Shriver of Baltimore, Joseph E. Widener of Philadelphia, Frederick H. Rawson of Chicago, and Henry Ruhlender of New York—were all elected to the board in 1922. Shriver and Widener remained on the board throughout the Willard years, while the other two left the board in the mid-thirties. In addition to his longtime interest in railroads, Widener was the owner of racetracks and had a notable art collection. George Shriver had joined the Baltimore and Ohio at the age of eighteen in 1886 as an accounting clerk. Two years later, he became a secretary to the president, Charles Mayer, and later was a presidential assistant to Leonor Loree and Oscar Murray. He was elected second vice president in 1911 and in March 1920, became the senior vice president in charge of the accounting, treasury, claims, and relief departments. Vice President Shriver was of real assistance to Daniel Willard in the frequent refunding operations of the 1920s and 1930s.

In 1923 Newton D. Baker and John F. Stevens joined the board of directors. Baker, a Cleveland lawyer and mayor of that city from 1912 to 1916, and secretary of war from 1916 to 1921, was a longtime friend of Daniel Willard and remained on the board until his death in 1937. John F. Stevens, a well-known consulting engineer, friend of James J. Hill, and chief engineer of the Panama Canal, remained on the board until his retirement at the age of eighty-seven in 1940. Shorter terms on the board were served by W. Averell Harriman, who joined the board at the age of twenty-three in 1914 and remained until 1922, and Bernard Baruch, who was a director from 1927 to 1933.

Willard's business relationship with the new directors during the twenties was excellent. The presence of Shriver and Cornwell on the board gave him two staunch allies on any issue that might arise. Willard was a man who disliked having an issue voted on before he knew fairly well the attitude of the men who were going to decide the issue. During the middle and late twenties, the board of directors seemed well satisfied with the record of the B&O. Dividends were up and gross corporate income was rising. The officials of the National City Bank of New York in 1929

Willard and his board of directors, in boardroom of Baltimore headquarters, November 6, 1929.
(*Courtesy, Baltimore and Ohio Railroad*)

saw the B&O traffic trend as a rising one and wrote: "It has also been demonstrated that its [B&O] present heavy traffic is being handled with great efficiency and with a lower trend of costs of operation."[11] Naturally such reports were pleasing to the Baltimore and Ohio directors. In 1929 it was easy for the board to reelect Daniel Willard as president at an annual salary of $150,000.

Although the Baltimore and Ohio Railroad received his first attention, during the twenties Daniel Willard found time for other areas of service. In 1921 he served as the chairman of the board of directors of the American Railroad Association. In 1926 he was made a member of the board of directors of American Telephone and Telegraph, and the next year President Herbert Hoover appointed him a member of the board of visitors to the United States Naval Academy. He had been a member of the board of trustees of Johns Hopkins University since 1914 and in 1926 was elected president of that body. The deans and professors at Johns Hopkins quickly discovered that Willard liked to have specific details and facts about the university he was advising. Soon Willard was carrying in an inner coat pocket small cards containing vital university statistics just as he did for his railroad. During the twenties, Willard received three of his thirteen honorary degrees, the three granted by Ohio University (1927), Syracuse University (1927), and Pennsylvania Military College (1928). Willard might easily have been taken for a professor himself with his black suits, dark derby or homburg, and somber haberdashery. Willard would send Ennis, his personal servant, to a men's store for an assortment of neckties, select *one* from the group, and send Ennis back to purchase a dozen of that single style and color.

Clearly the most important single event in the decade was the celebration of the railroad's centennial during 1927. President Willard noted the event in his annual New Year's greeting to the officers and employees of the Baltimore and Ohio which appeared in the January 1927 issue of the *Baltimore and Ohio Magazine*:

> The year of 1926 just ended has been one of the most satisfactory in the history of the Baltimore and Ohio Company. Business has been good, employment upon the whole has been steady and we all have much to feel thankful for.
>
> The New Year of 1927 will mark the one hundredth anniversary of the Baltimore and Ohio Railroad. It is a notable event, not alone in the history of the Baltimore and Ohio Company, but also in the history of our country, for in our country's development the railroad has played a most important part.[12]

The year-long birthday party and centennial of the railroad was celebrated in a variety of ways. Earlier, Albert C. Ritchie, governor of Maryland from 1919 to 1934, had been authorized by the Maryland legislature to appoint a centennial celebration commission. Other centennial committees had been formed by the mayor of Baltimore, the Maryland Bankers Association, and the Baltimore Association of Commerce. The top planning group on the railroad itself was led by Edward Hungerford, an author and journalist with years of experience in public relations and advertising. In 1925 Daniel Willard had hired Hungerford to be the centenary director for the year-long birthday party. Hungerford and his committee soon had developed plans which included a centennial dinner on February 28, 1927, the writing of a two-volume history of the railroad, plus a transportation exhibit and a railroad pageant planned for the fall of 1927.

The first major event in 1927 was the centenary dinner on the evening of February 28, 1927, exactly one hundred years after the granting of the Baltimore and Ohio charter by the Maryland legislature. The 725 guests, all male, who crowded into the main floor and twenty boxes of the Lyric Theater that evening included political leaders of Baltimore, all 150 members of the Maryland legislature, many big names from Washington, top Baltimore and Ohio officials, representatives of rail labor unions, and several presidents of nearby railroads. Two special trains, composed of business cars, Pullmans, and B&O diners, brought dozens of bankers and rail officials down from New York and Philadelphia to the Mount Royal Station, located not far from the Lyric. Far more wished to attend the affair than could possibly be accommodated. In fact, 239 additional guests were served in the ballroom of the nearby Belvedere Hotel. Daniel Willard presided at the Lyric while Vice President George Shriver did the honors at the Belvedere. After their meal, the Belvedere guests moved over to the balcony of the Lyric for the evening's program.

Daniel Willard, who always ran things on time, promptly called the gathering to order at 7:30 by ringing a silver-plated locomotive bell erected at the speakers' table. The dinner, which had been planned by E. V. Baugh, the B&O dining car manager, was excellent, but spartan by Victorian Era standards. During the meal, music was provided by the Baltimore and Ohio Symphony Orchestra and the Women's Chorus. Following the dinner, Daniel Willard noted the absence of Governor Ritchie, who was ill in Annapolis, introduced several railroad presidents at the speakers' table, and briefly spoke of further centennial programs planned for the year. The keynote speaker of the evening was Newton D. Baker, longtime friend of Willard and a director of the Baltimore and Ohio since 1923. Baker paid full tribute to the early business leaders of Baltimore who, a century earlier, had seen a vision of building a railway over the mountains to the Ohio River. The program was concluded with a short three-act pageant which portrayed early events in the founding of the railroad. The festive affair was over before eleven, and the Washington and New York guests were soon departing on their special trains from the Mount Royal Station.

Each of the departing guests of the B&O that evening had been presented one of the Baltimore and Ohio Centenary Medals, cast in bronze and 2-3/4 inches in diameter. The obverse of the medal displayed either the New York to Chicago *Capitol Limited* or the New York to St. Louis *National Limited*, encircled by the words, "One hundred Years—Safety—Strength—Speed." On the reverse side was Peter Cooper's *Tom Thumb*, surrounded by the legend—"The Baltimore and Ohio Railroad Company, 1827–1927." One of these medals was given to each of the B&O pensioners and all employees with forty or more years of service. Other employees and the general public could purchase the medal for $1.50.

Daniel Willard and Edward Hungerford were soon discussing the kind of outdoor celebration they should provide for the general public. Should it be a huge parade in Baltimore or perhaps an outdoor pageant? Hungerford told Willard there were two ways one could take a steamship out of New York harbor—a short two or three day coastal trip or a big liner all the way to Europe meaning a trip of a week or more. Willard asked Hungerford how much the longer trip—or really "big celebration" might cost. Hungerford made a guess and Willard replied: "We will take the steamer for Europe."[13] The reply really meant they would give an outdoor railroad pageant several times, rather than have a single day parade with all its possible problems of rain or bad weather. The Centenary Exhibition and Pageant of the Baltimore and Ohio Railroad— soon to be known across the country as "The Fair of the Iron Horse"—would cost over $1 million and bring over 1,250,000 visitors to the fair.

It took some time to decide upon a site for the Fair of the Iron Horse. The mayor of Baltimore, Howard W. Jackson, generously offered a city park, but the problems of track building, tree removal, and restoration costs made the proposal impractical. Next, they looked at a racetrack near Laurel, halfway between Baltimore and Washington. Willard, Hungerford, and several vice presidents visited the site. As they were walking down the track toward the racetrack, Willard found not one, but two, loose spikes in the cross ties. Picking them up, he turned to Charles W. Gallo-

way, his vice president in charge of operations and maintenance
and said "My compliments, Mr. Galloway."[14] The Laurel location
also proved impossible, and eventually a site near Halethrope,
eight miles out of Baltimore on the main line to Washington, was
selected. The site was a thousand-acre tract purchased for the B&O
by John W. Garrett half a century earlier for a possible future car
shop.

With the site selected, workers quickly moved in to construct buildings and prepare the grounds for the exhibit and the
pageant. The largest building, 62 feet wide and 502 feet in length,
was built to house the major exhibits and called the Hall of Transportation. In a small tower on top of the building was hung the
railroad's oldest bell, taken from the belfry of the Ellicott City
depot. For displaying equipment, several exhibition tracks were
located back of the exhibit hall. In front of the exhibit hall were the
court of honor and the stage for the pageant, including a railroad
parade track and road for the passage of rail equipment and other
vehicles used in the show. The parade track was continued on
around the entire area in an oval which facilitated both the movement and storage of the rail equipment used in the pageant. Facing
the stage was an 800-foot-long grandstand with a seating capacity of
12,000. The large canopy over the grandstand was blue and white,
the same color as the roofs of all buildings on the fairgrounds. Just
back of the grandstand were the main line B&O tracks with a

Visitors inspect locomotives at Fair of the Iron Horse, 1927.
(Courtesy, Baltimore and Ohio Railroad)

temporary station giving service directly to downtown Baltimore and Washington. Across the tracks, ample parking space for automobiles was provided.

The Baltimore and Ohio had been unique among American railroads in the way it had held on to its earliest cars and engines. Many of these old pieces had been shown both at the 1893 Chicago Fair and again at St. Louis in 1904. Early in the spring of 1927, this collection of ancient equipment was moved from storage in Martinsburg to a Baltimore roundhouse where the slow work of reconditioning was started. Colonel Emerson made certain that such famous old B&O engines as the *Atlantic*, the *Thomas Jefferson*, the *William Mason* and the *Thatcher Perkins* would be ready for the show. This old equipment, plus Major Pangborn's famous collection of full-sized wooden models of early American and European locomotives, was invaluable for the exhibit area and the pageant. Other railroads also loaned historic equipment for the Fair of the Iron Horse. President P. E. Crowley of the New York Central had the replica of the *DeWitt Clinton* and train (which first operated in 1831 on the Mohawk and Hudson), taken out of its location in the Grand Central Terminal and sent to Baltimore. The Pennsylvania Railroad loaned the Camden and Amboy (1831) *John Bull* and one of the finest modern British engines, the *George V* of the Great Western Railway was brought over from England. Additional equipment came from other American and Canadian railroads. Henry Ford loaned the *Satilla* (1860), an old Atlantic and Gulf engine.

The Hall of Transportation contained a variety of railway exhibits. The thirty-two Pangborn models were placed along the entire length of the hall. A distinctive feature was two large miniature railroad layouts showing the long development of the Baltimore and Ohio. A variety of other exhibits revealed the century-long progress made in brakes, signals, track, stokers, bridges, and other railway equipment. At either end of the Hall of Transportation were two other buildings. To the west, the traffic building contained exhibits and models of waybills, baggage, depots, coal wharves, grain elevators plus a huge bas-relief map of the entire area served by the Baltimore and Ohio. To the east, the allied service building contained exhibits prepared by the United States Post Office Department, the American Railway Express, the Western Union Telegraph Company, and the Pullman Company.

During the Fair of the Iron Horse, the centenary pageant was shown every afternoon except for Sundays. The pageant was presented in the form of a drama, set to music, with hundreds of

Indians, settlers, townspeople, highway vehicles, nineteen floats, and much railroad equipment showing transportation developments over more than two centuries. The moving pageant, placed in a straight line would have reached more than four miles and required well over an hour to pass a given point. Again, Daniel Willard was adamant that every performance must start exactly on time.

Admission to the Fair of the Iron Horse, both the exhibits, and the pageant was free. Grandstand seats for the pageant were not reserved, but blocks of seats were set aside for groups coming from a distance. Willard and Hungerford had guessed that daily attendance at the fair might average 20,000 to 25,000 persons. On the opening day, Saturday, September 24, 1927, 46,000 visitors passed through the gates and attendance figures continued to increase. The closing date was extended to Sunday, October 16. On Saturday, October 15, well over 100,000 came to the fair even though there was a Notre Dame-Navy football game at nearby Annapolis. Total attendance for the twenty-three-day fair was more than 1,300,000, or an average of over 50,000 per day. During the long three weeks, 270,000 railroad tickets to Halethrope had been sold at the Camden station in Baltimore, 136,000 cars had been parked at the fair grounds; and 174,000 "hot dogs" had been consumed by hungry visitors as they viewed their favorite "Iron Horse." Needless to say, both Willard and Hungerford were well pleased with their birthday party.

The year of 1927 had been not only a centennial year, but also another good traffic revenue year for the Baltimore and Ohio. The 1920s had generally been years of prosperity.

TABLE 16. Baltimore and Ohio System Traffic and Financial Growth 1921–29

Year	Miles of Road	Total Revenue	Net Revenue	Expenses to Earnings (%)	Average Passenger Fare (Per Mile) (¢)	Average Freight Rate (Per Ton-Mile) (¢)	Dividend on Common Stock (%)
1921	5,235	$199,077,853	$32,005,760	84	3.29	1.10	—
1922	5,212	200,843,170	35,821,795	82	3.30	1.06	—
1923	5,207	255,594,435	56,270,474	78	3.26	1.01	2.5
1924	5,196	224,318,795	51,566,162	77	3.22	1.03	5
1925	5,197	237,546,940	58,447,343	75	3.18	.99	5
1926	5,552	257,573,385	66,101,085	74	3.13	.99	6
1927	5,553	246,082,068	59,911,006	76	3.11	.98	6
1928	5,548	236,818,681	64,267,813	73	3.08	.97	6
1929	5,577	245,418,776	64,848,742	74	3.04	.99	6.5

During the 1920s, there had been a major change in the ratio between freight and passenger traffic and revenue on most American railways, including the Baltimore and Ohio.

TABLE 17. Baltimore and Ohio Revenues 1921–29
(in millions of dollars)

	Freight	Passenger	Mail and Express	Other
1921	$157	$29	$ 5	$8
1922	160	27	7	7
1923	209	31	7	9
1924	180	29	7	8
1925	194	28	8	8
1926	212	28	9	9
1927	204	26	8	8
1928	197	24	8	8
1929	205	22	10	8

Freight revenue on the B&O increased about 30 percent between 1921 and 1929 while passenger revenue dropped by about 25 percent. In 1921 freight revenue on the B&O was about five times that of passenger. Eight years later, in 1929, freight revenue was nine times as large as passenger revenue. However mail and express revenue, also carried on passenger trains, doubled during the eight years. Other B&O revenue, both transportation and non-transportation, remained very stable during the period.

The drop in rail passenger traffic during the decade is not surprising. During the twenties, the number of automobiles had increased from 8 million to 23 million, and many small intercity buses had started to provide service over the growing highway system. By 1929 intercity travel (in passenger-miles) provided by private cars was about five times that provided by railroad. In 1929 the railroads of the nation were providing 77 percent of all intercity commercial travel, compared to 98 percent in 1916. The small intercity bus lines were providing about 15 percent of all commercial intercity travel in 1929. Even though rail travel was declining there was no reduction in passenger schedules. The 1930 *Official Guide of Railways* was of record size—1,760 pages.

The loss of rail freight traffic to the intercity truck was only minor during the 1920s. In 1929 American railroads were moving 455 billion ton-miles of freight, or about 75 percent of the total, compared to 77 percent in 1916. In that same year, highway trucks were moving only 3 percent of all intercity commercial freight. The remaining 22 percent moved over the Great Lakes, rivers, canals, and pipelines.

During the twenties, there were no major changes in the types of freight carried on the Baltimore and Ohio. Throughout the decade, the products of mines continued to account for about three-fifths of the total tonnage. There were some changes as compared to the turn of the century. In 1929 products of agriculture made up 4 percent of the total (9 percent in 1901); animals and products—1 percent (1.5 percent in 1901); products of mines—61 percent (61 percent in 1901); products of forests—4 percent (6 percent in 1901); manufactures—22 percent (14 percent in 1901); and miscellaneous—8 percent (8.5 percent in 1901). Basically, in the long quarter of a century, the tonnage losses in agriculture, animal, and forest products were made up with gains in manufactures.

Once the American economy had recovered from the postwar depression of 1921, the cost of living and the general price was quite stable. This was also true of railroad freight rates and passenger fares. Neither freight rates per ton-mile nor passenger fares per mile on the Baltimore and Ohio changed much during the decade. President Willard and his fellow executives did manage to materially reduce expenditures on the railroad during the decade. As a result, there was a significant increase in annual net revenue during the twenties, permitting a marked reduction in the operating ratio, from 84 percent in 1921 to 74 percent in 1929.

The Baltimore and Ohio, as it celebrated its centennial in the late twenties, was the oldest of the major trunk line railroads in the Northeast, but it was certainly not the largest of the rival systems. In 1927 both the Pennsylvania and the New York Central were operating systems much larger both in mileage and total operating revenue. In the late 1920s, the number of employees on the B&O ranged from 70,000 to 75,000. This was less than half the number working on the New York Central and only about 40 percent of the Pennsylvania work force. The same general comparison held for the amount of passenger service offered by the three systems. In 1930 the total passenger train schedules of the Baltimore and Ohio were only about one-third of those operated by the Pennsylvania and much less than half that of the New York Central.

There had been some changes in the financial structure of the total B&O system during the decade, but the totals shown on the annual balance sheet had only modestly increased—$1,013,000,000 in 1920 and $1,117,000,000 nine years later in 1929. The investment in the road itself had increased from $246 million to $285 million in 1929. A greater growth was shown in the value of equipment, increasing from $151 million in 1920 to $259 million in 1929. The locomotive roster had declined in the decade dropping from 2,638 engines in 1920 to 2,364 in 1929. However, in the nine years, the average tractive power per engine had climbed by nearly one-quarter, increasing from 41,000 pounds in 1920 to 51,000 in 1929. The freight car fleet had modestly grown—95,780 in 1920 and 102,072 in 1929. The average freight car capacity in the nine years had gone from forty-seven tons up to fifty tons. Even though the passenger traffic had declined, there was a real increase in passenger equipment—1,317 cars in 1920 and 1,732 cars in 1929. The Baltimore and Ohio had $286 million invested in subsidiary companies in 1920. By 1929 this figure had grown to $332 million.

Modest changes had also occurred on the liabilities side of the balance sheet. During the nine years, there had been significant increases in B&O common stock, climbing from $152 million in 1920 to $256 million in 1929. The increase had come in the late twenties, $63 million being sold in 1927 and an additional $41 million being taken by B&O stockholders during 1929. During the decade, the amount of preferred stock remained constant at $60 million. The long term debt of the railroad had slightly declined during the twenties, being $561 million in 1920 and $550 million in 1929. Of this debt in 1929, nearly $72 million was in equipment trusts or obligations. The annual interest charges on the funded debt had grown modestly, from just over $24 million in 1920 to over $25 million in 1929, or an average interest rate of under 5 percent.

The best news revealed in the annual reports during the decade was the resumption of dividends for the common stock holders. No dividends on the common stock had been paid during the three years 1920–22, and in those years the stock market quotations from B&O common shares had ranged from a low of 27 to a high of 60. By 1923 the net revenue had climbed to more than $56 million with a decline in the operating ratio to 78 percent. President Willard noted the good news in his *Annual Report* for 1923: "The year 1923 was notable for the general revival of business and industrial activity in which your company shared to a gratifying extent. . . . Consequently declarations were made of two quarterly dividends of 5 percent per annum, effective for the second six months of the year."[15] Dividends of 5 percent were paid in 1924 and 1925, and the rate was raised to 6 percent in 1926, and to 6.5 percent for 1929.

The good earnings and the increased dividend rate rather quickly affected the market quotations for B&O stock. Baltimore and Ohio common stock hit a high of 84-7/8 in 1924, and 94-1/2 in 1925. In 1926 it ranged from a low of 83-1/2 to a high of 109-3/4. It continued to climb, reaching a high in the middle of 1929 of 145-1/8 a share. But the pleasant days of a centennial birthday party, high dividends, and a bull stock market were not to last. Hard times were ahead for Daniel Willard in the 1930s.

Chapter XV

• • • • • • • • • • • • • • • •

The Depression Years

THE 1930S WERE YEARS OF TRIAL AND DISAPPOINTMENT FOR Daniel Willard and his railroad. For several years after 1930, each year saw a sharp decline in total B&O revenue and traffic. By 1933 the roster of Baltimore and Ohio workers was less than half the total in 1927. Road improvements were few, and even some rather basic maintenance was delayed whenever possible. Money on the railroad was so hard to find that the *Baltimore and Ohio Magazine* was suspended from June 1932 to March 1934. In 1932 dividends on both common and preferred stock were dropped. Baltimore and Ohio common stock declined along with the rest of the market. Between 1929 and 1932, the average of industrial stocks declined from a high of 452 down to 58. In the same years, United States Steel dropped from 262 to 22 and General Motors from 73 to 8. The decline for B&O stock was even sharper, dropping from a high of 145 in 1929 to a low of under 4 per share in 1932. As major bond issues became due, the B&O obtained its first Reconstruction Finance Corporation loan in 1932, and six years later requested, and received, government approval for a plan for the modification of interest charges and security maturity dates.

Even though the decade was to prove a bleak one, the year of 1930 started out on a happy note for Daniel Willard. On January

275

13, 1930, over 1,600 men and women honored Willard at a banquet held in the crowded ballroom of the Lord Baltimore Hotel in Baltimore. The Daniel Willard Testimonial Dinner, sponsored by the labor organizations of the Baltimore and Ohio, was in recognition of Willard's twenty years as the president of the Baltimore and Ohio. Hundreds of labor leaders were present plus officers and directors of the railroad, bankers and merchants from Baltimore and New York, railroad presidents, and political leaders from Washington who all praised Daniel Willard. Labor officials conferred a newly created degree, "Doctor of Humanities," upon the longtime president. William Green, president of the American Federation of Labor, was unable to be present, but his telegram of congratulations, which was read to the banquet, concluded with the words: "No man is more deserving than Mr. Willard of the honor and tribute which you and the representatives of labor will pay him. May he long be privileged to serve as president of the Baltimore and Ohio Railroad to carry on the great humanitarian and constructive work in which he is engaged."[1]

A few weeks later, *Time* magazine made the same point when it wrote of Willard: "He has a conscience in dealing with labor. Any man can go directly to him with his troubles."[2] *Time* also

President Herbert Hoover rides the B&O in 1930.
(Courtesy, Baltimore and Ohio Railroad)

noted that Willard was popular in Washington. The B&O president was in sympathy with the ICC plans for major rail mergers, had won favor with Harding at the time of the 1922 shopmen's strike, and had provided the B&O trains which carried Herbert Hoover on much of his campaign travels in 1928.

The euphoria of the mid-January banquet did not last long. The B&O monthly traffic reports in the late winter and spring of 1930 were far from encouraging. By the end of the year, it was seen that the year's total revenue was only $206 million, nearly $40 million below that of 1929. The next year saw the decline in car loadings and traffic fall even faster, with 1931 revenue more than $48 million below that of 1930. Even though expenses were cut and many employees laid off, the operating ratio started to climb, from 73.6 percent in 1929 up to 75.7 percent in 1931. In the same years, the interest charges on the funded debt actually increased from $29 to $31 million per year. In the midst of the decline in traffic, Daniel Willard celebrated his seventieth birthday on January 28, 1931. He offered his resignation to the board of directors, but they would not hear of his leaving. Though he repeatedly offered his resignation during the thirties, he was to remain at his post for another decade.

Early in 1931, Daniel Willard discussed the financial dilemma facing the railroads of the nation with several other top rail executives. There was a general agreement that only a substantial boost in freight rates and a pay cut for railroad labor would solve the financial woes of the rail industry. The railroads of the country requested a 15 percent hike in freight rates, but the Interstate Commerce Commission eventually approved only a qualified 3 percent boost in freight rates.

Most railroad presidents in 1931 believed that railroad labor would never accept any reduction in wages. They were aware that in a July 1931, conference railroad labor leaders had resolved to ask Congress for legislation adopting a six hour work day without any reduction in pay. The labor leaders pointed out that the number of rail employees on Class I railroads had dropped from 1,858,000 in 1923 to 1,661,000 in 1929, a decline of more than 10 percent. The decline in employment had, of course, grown worse since 1929. The B&O work force, for example, had dropped from 66,000 at the end of 1929 to 47,000 at the end of 1931. The average national rail employment for 1931 was down to 1,259,000. Average annual wages for railroad workers had declined from $1,744 in 1929 to $1,664 in 1931, a decrease of about 5 percent. This decline was not a drop in wage scale, but rather in hours of work, since the average hours of labor had gone from 2,617 hours in 1929 to 2,414 hours in

1931. In the same two years, the cost of living in the United States had been reduced more than 10 percent.

In spite of these facts, Willard believed there remained a chance that the railroad brotherhoods might possibly consider a voluntary wage reduction. He decided to try to get management and labor together. Daniel Willard invited three nearby railroad presidents, W. W. Atterbury (Pennsylvania), Patrick Crowley (New York Central), and John J. Bernet (C&O), along with the leaders of the operating brotherhoods, Alvanley Johnston (engineers), David B. Robertson (firemen), S. N. Berry (conductors), and Alexander J. Whitney (trainmen), to dine with him at the Biltmore Hotel in Manhattan on October 12, 1931. Willard discovered that the labor leaders were at least willing to discuss the subject of a possible cut in wages. Willard believed a 10 percent reduction in wages was needed.

In November 1931, Willard succeeded in persuading the Association of Railway Executives to select a committee of nine railway presidents to speak for the carriers in any possible negotiation of reduced wages. The nine men selected represented lines across the nation, three each from eastern, southern, and western roads, but none of the giant lines such as the New York Central, Pennsylvania, Santa Fe, or Union Pacific were represented. Preliminary conferences between the nine presidents and labor representatives were held late in November and again in December. Willard was selected as chairman of the carriers' committee and David B. Robertson was made chairman of the labor group. During these early discussions, President Willard was asked by a labor representative if railroad officials would also take a cut in pay. Willard replied that his salary had recently been reduced by 20 percent. In fact, as of November 1, 1931, all B&O officials had taken pay reductions of at least 10 percent.

As the wage negotiations were approached, railroad labor knew that Willard had great sympathy for the problem facing the railroad worker. Daniel Willard hated to see the growing ranks of unemployed railroaders. He spoke of this in a speech he made in 1931 before the Wharton School of Finance and Commerce in Philadelphia when he said: ". . . I can think of nothing more deplorable than the condition of a man, able and anxious to work, with no resources but his labor and, perhaps with others even more helpless, dependent upon him . . . while I do not like to say so, I would be less than candid if I did not say that in such circumstances I would steal before I would starve."[3] These were shocking words, and many Americans were critical of his language, but they proved that Willard knew the problems of the laboring man.

A mammoth negotiating conference was held in the Palmer House in Chicago in mid-January 1932. About 1,500 labor chairmen and leaders representing twenty-one different railroad unions, plus the nine railroad presidents with all their aides and assistants, met in large and small sessions in the Palmer House during the last three weeks of January. Daniel Willard talked in small conferences both at the Palmer House and in his two rooms several blocks away in the Congress Hotel. David Robertson, general chairman of the Brotherhood of Locomotive Firemen and Enginemen, told his fellow labor officials that Willard could be trusted to treat labor fairly. More and more, labor leaders were ready to admit, at least to themselves, that some wage reduction seemed reasonable. Willard's position of leadership in the wage negotiations that winter was illustrated when his picture was placed on the cover of *Time* magazine for January 11, 1932.

Willard seemed to be talking and persuading endlessly day after day. Robertson asked Willard if he would speak again to all 1,500 labor leaders in the large ballroom of the Palmer House. Willard agreed and told his audience he was quite confident that a wage reduction of 10 percent would mean that few additional workers across the nation would have to be laid off. The labor men seemed convinced and cheered Willard as he left the ballroom. Late on Sunday evening, January 31, 1932, labor leaders and railroad presidents signed a document providing for a 10 percent wage reduction for the next ten months. When Willard finally left his room in the Congress Hotel to return home to Baltimore, he discovered that labor leaders had placed a huge basket of flowers in "No. 99," his B&O business car.

The wage reduction was to save Willard's railroad considerable money. During the year February 1, 1932, to February 1, 1933, the Baltimore and Ohio saved from $5 million to $6 million in wages. In the late 1920s, railroad wages on the B&O amounted to about 46 percent to 47 percent of all operating revenue. By 1931 this had increased to above 50 percent. The cut in wages helped reduce this figure to 44 percent by 1933–34. The January 1932 wage reduction agreement resulted in savings of more than $200 million for American railroads in the first year of the agreement. By 1932 the cost of living was about 20 percent below that of 1929. In September 1932, the carriers attempted to negotiate another 10 percent cut in wages. Railroad labor declined to consider any further reduction, but did agree to continue the original 10 percent cut another nine months or until October 31, 1933.

The Emergency Railroad Transportation Act, earlier recommended by the Interstate Commerce Commission, was passed by

Congress in June 1933. The act established the federal coordinator of transportation, a position to which Joseph B. Eastman was appointed by President Franklin D. Roosevelt. Eastman was empowered to promote an economy of rail operation by eliminating duplicate services and seeking to reduce general expenses. When the carriers in 1933 requested a further reduction in pay, Roosevelt asked Eastman to intervene. The result was a further extension of the 10 percent wage reduction for an additional eight months until June 30, 1934. A modest recovery during 1934 had resulted in a slight increase in prices and the cost of living. Eastman directed that the 10 percent reduction be changed to 7.5 percent for the last six months of 1934, to 5 percent for the first three months of 1935, with a full restoration of 1931 wage rates to take effect on April 1, 1935. With the economic recovery continuing, railroad wages were adjusted upward in the late 1930s. Average annual railroad wages, which had been only $1,445 a year in 1933, had climbed to $1,913 by 1940. In the same seven years, the average B&O work force had grown from 36,500 to 41,000.

The decline in traffic in the decade naturally resulted in a major reduction in additions, betterments, and new equipment in the 1930s. During the prosperous, expanding 1920s, Willard's road had spent nearly $100 million for such improvements. Since Willard and his top officials believed the traffic drop in the winter of 1929–30 to be only temporary, no reduction in the improvement program occurred in 1930. More than $14 million was invested in various improvements including pier improvements at Locust Point, the building of several new bridges, new passenger and freight terminal facilities at Cincinnati, new signal facilities on eighty-eight miles of road, and the elimination of numerous grade crossings throughout the entire system. During 1930 the B&O also purchased sixty-two new steel passenger cars and more than 3,200 new freight cars.

Things were different in 1931 when Willard wrote in his *Annual Report* that year: "Because of the general conditions prevailing, expenditures for additions and betterments were confined chiefly to improvements that had been under way and were nearing completion."[4] In 1931 no money was spent for additional equipment. During the rest of the decade, most years were little different from 1931. Few years saw more than $1 or $2 million spent for improvements, and the total for the decade was probably little more than 30 percent of that spent during the 1920s. Ordinary track maintenance declined greatly between 1930 and 1932. During 1930 the average mile of Baltimore and Ohio track had 138 cross ties replaced—in 1932 the number of new ties per mile was down to 54, the lowest figure for the decade. In 1930 more than

Stone bridge at Relay, Maryland, with hotel and station in the distance.
(Courtesy, Baltimore and Ohio Railroad)

2,100 man-hours of labor by section men were expended on each mile of B&O track—by 1932 the figure was down to 855 man-hours per mile of track. Money was so tight in 1933 that, with the approval of the ICC the Baltimore and Ohio arranged to borrow $4,500,000 from the Public Works Administration, at 4 percent interest, the money to be repaid in semi-annual installments from 1935 to 1944. These funds were to be used for the purchase and installation of 35,000 tons of rail and for the reconditioning of 240 locomotives and 5,000 freight cars, the repairs to be made in B&O company shops.

During the decade, far more equipment was retired than purchased. Between 1930 and 1940, the roster of locomotives declined from 2,364 to 2,065; passenger cars from 1,732 to 1,274; and freight cars from 102,072 to 83,515. In 1933 the B&O retired 333 locomotives, 270 passenger cars, 9,865 freight cars, and 1,233 units of service equipment. Naturally, the 299 engines and the more than 450 passenger cars and 18,000 freight cars lost in the decade were the oldest and poorest owned by the railroad. By getting rid of the older and smaller engines, the average pounds of traction power per locomotive increased from 51,288 pounds in 1930 to 56,446 pounds in 1940. In the same way, the average capacity of B&O freight equipment increased from 50 tons in 1930 to 53 tons in 1940.

The new equipment purchased by the Baltimore and Ohio in the eleven years from 1930 through 1940 consisted of 44 new locomotives, 95 passenger cars, and nearly 13,000 freight cars. No new equipment was acquired during 1931, 1933, or 1934, and the years with the major acquisitions were 1930, 1932, 1935, 1937, and 1940. The 44 locomotives acquired in these years, consisting of 7 steam engines and 37 diesels, was the smallest number of new engines acquired for a number of decades. The steamers included two Mallets, a Hudson type (4-6-4) engine named the *Lord Baltimore*, and the *George H. Emerson*, named for the chief of motive power and equipment in the 1920s and 1930s. The *George H. Emerson*, built in 1937 for passenger service, was an experimental (4-4-4-4) engine, with eight seventy-six-inch drivers, a tractive power of 65,000 pounds, and a weight, including tender, of 368 tons.

The diesels acquired during the eleven years included several new passenger engines plus twenty-five switch engines purchased in 1940. The first diesel acquired by the B&O was a small sixty-ton 300 horsepower switcher, purchased in 1925 for use in the B&O Twenty-sixth Street yards in Manhattan. The city of New York had recently prohibited all steam locomotives on Manhattan Island, and the Baltimore and Ohio decided to try the new type of motive power rather than electrify its yards. The little switcher was one of the first diesel locomotives in the nation.

The Baltimore and Ohio purchased its first road diesel in 1935 when it inaugurated two air-conditioned, streamlined passenger trains, one to operate from Washington to Jersey City and New York, and the second to operate on the Alton Railroad between Chicago and St. Louis. The Alton train consisted of eight steel alloy streamlined cars, while the eight car *Royal Blue* streamliner from Washington to New York had cars built of aluminum alloy. Starting in August 1935, the *Royal Blue* was pulled by the new two-unit road diesel, replacing the steamer *Lord Baltimore*. The Baltimore and Ohio financed the purchase of the twin road diesel, the two streamliner trains, plus 820 steel gondola cars, largely with $1,900,000 of equipment trust certificates sold to the Public Works Administration. In 1937 the Baltimore and Ohio acquired two more diesel powered streamliners to operate as the *Capitol Limited* between Washington, D.C., and Chicago.

Even though the equipment on the Baltimore and Ohio declined during the 1930s, there was a modest increase in mileage of the B&O during the decade. Between 1929 and 1940, the average mileage operated by Willard's line increased from 5,577 miles to 6,292 miles. The major increase in mileage occurred in the fall of 1931 when the Interstate Commerce Commission approved the application of the Baltimore and Ohio to operate both the 520-mile Buffalo, Rochester and Pittsburgh and the 228-mile Buffalo and Susquehanna as integral parts of the B&O system effective January 1, 1932. The Baltimore and Ohio had acquired a majority of the capital stock of both lines two years earlier in 1929.

During the thirties, the Baltimore and Ohio continued to have major financial interests in several roads which it did not operate. Since the early years of the century, the Baltimore and Ohio had a substantial stock interest in the Reading Railroad, which in turn controlled the Central Railroad of New Jersey, over whose tracks B&O trains reached Jersey City and New York. The Reading was one of the railroads allocated to the Baltimore and Ohio in the ICC plans (under the 1920 Transportation Act) for the consolidation of the nation's railways into a limited number of systems. As of 1933, the B&O owned 600,800 shares of Reading common stock plus 235,065 shares of first preferred, and 345,600 shares of second preferred stock. These holdings amounted to 42.21 percent of voting stock of the Reading Railroad.

The Western Maryland was a second line in which the Baltimore and Ohio held a major financial stake. The Western Maryland, chartered in 1853, had slowly built a line west and north of Baltimore quite near the main line of the Baltimore and Ohio and so closely parallel to the Maryland-Pennsylvania border that it once called itself the "Mason-Dixon Line." Eventually it controlled an 850-mile system, extending north to York, Pennsylvania, and west to Cumberland, Maryland, Connellsville, Pennsylvania, and Elkins, West Virginia. Control of the line, for a time, was held by the city of Baltimore and in 1902 it was sold to the Gould interests. In 1927 the Baltimore and Ohio acquired 159,000 shares of Western Maryland common stock plus enough preferred stock to give the B&O 40 percent of the outstanding capital stock of the company having a par value of more than $31 million.

In 1929 the Interstate Commerce Commission charged that this acquisition by the B&O violated the Clayton Anti-Trust Act and ordered the B&O to divest itself of the Western Maryland stock. The falling stock market in the early 1930s made such a large sale difficult. Eventually the ICC ordered the Baltimore and Ohio to place all its Western Maryland stock with the Chase National Bank of New York City as trustee. This arrangement continued during the decade, with the B&O still owning a substantial share of the Western Maryland stock. As of 1939, the Western Maryland operated 859 miles of road with 3,800 employees and had total operating revenues of more than $16 million.

Early in the decade, the Baltimore and Ohio became financially interested in the Chicago and Alton Railroad, a 1,000-mile line which extended from Chicago to St. Louis and Kansas City and connected with the B&O at Chicago, Springfield, and St. Louis. The line had been originally chartered in 1847 and during the 1850s constructed a 220-mile road from Joliet, Illinois, to Alton on the Mississippi River. The line was in default by 1930. When the property was sold at public auction in December 1930, it was purchased by interests identified with the Baltimore and Ohio. A new company, the Alton Railroad, which was fully controlled by the Baltimore and Ohio, took over the Chicago and Alton system, with the Interstate Commerce Commission giving full approval to the reorganization process on July 31, 1931. The Baltimore and Ohio issued $25 million of capital stock for the new Alton Railroad. The acquisition of the Alton by the Baltimore and Ohio was also in accord with the plan of the ICC for the consolidation of the rail properties in the United States into a limited number of large rail systems, as provided by the Transportation Act of 1920.

Both the Alton and the Western Maryland were scheduled to become part of the Baltimore and Ohio system in the Big Four railroad merger plan supported by President Hoover and approved

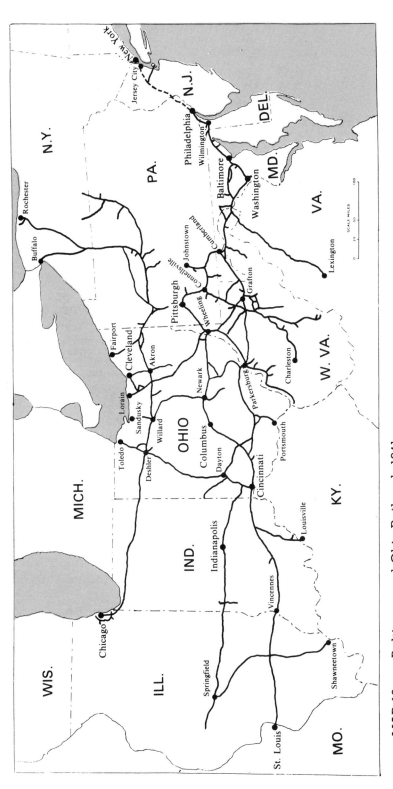

MAP 10.   Baltimore and Ohio Railroad, 1941.

Most of the additional mileage gained in the late 1920s and the depression 1930s was located in northwestern Pennsylvania and western New York.

by the Interstate Commerce Commission in July 1932. Under this plan, four major eastern railroads—the New York Central, Pennsylvania, Baltimore and Ohio, and Chesapeake and Ohio—would each be permitted to acquire several smaller lines to become the dominant system in the area between the Hudson and the Mississippi and north of the Potomac and Ohio rivers. The Baltimore and Ohio, under the plan, was also to be allowed to acquire the Lehigh and Hudson, giving Willard's road a possible entrance into New York City. At once Daniel Willard began to dream of financing and building a railroad bridge across the Hudson from New Jersey to midtown Manhattan near Fifty-seventh Street. The projected bridge over the Hudson river never reached the planning stage—finances were difficult and the War Department insistence that any such structure would have to be 200 feet above the Hudson created serious engineering problems. By the mid-1930s, both the bridge and the entire major merger project had been forgotten.

While Willard's road fully controlled the Alton, the new line was operated as a separate company, and its accounts were in no way connected with those of the Baltimore and Ohio. As of 1939, the Alton was operating 958 miles of road in Illinois and Missouri, had 4,490 employees, and had an equipment roster of 167 locomotives, 87 passenger, and 2,941 freight cars. Its operating revenue in 1939 amounted to $16,622,000, including $11,738,000 of freight revenue and $3,634,000 of passenger revenue.

A second separate railroad company, fully controlled and owned by the Baltimore and Ohio, but not included in the regular operations of the parent system, was the Baltimore and Ohio Chicago Terminal Railroad. In 1897 the Chicago Terminal Transfer Railroad had been organized from several earlier transfer and switching lines which basically served the railroads using the Grand Central Station completed in the early 1890s. By 1910 the Chicago Terminal Transfer Railroad had fallen into financial difficulties and receivership. Early in 1910, the Baltimore and Ohio purchased the property, and reorganized it as the Baltimore and Ohio Chicago Terminal Railroad.

In the early teens, this terminal railroad not only owned the Grand Central Station, but also had extensive tracks and yards serving the roads using that station: the B&O; the Soo lines; the Chicago Great Western; and the Pere Marquette. Its 75 miles of main line plus 200 miles of side tracks extended in a great arc south and west of Chicago and served plants, warehouses, and elevators extending from Hammond, Indiana, and Chicago Heights in the south to La Grange, Bellwood, and Franklin Park to the west and north of Chicago. By 1939 the Baltimore and Ohio Chicago Terminal Railroad had 83 miles of first main track, 290 miles of sidings, more than 2,000 employees, and a yearly revenue of over $4 million.

The decade of the 1930s saw declining traffic and often deficits instead of profits, but through the depression years, the Baltimore and Ohio managed to introduce many improvements both in passenger and freight service. Even though 1930 was a year of dropping revenue, that was the year that air-conditioning was introduced on the Baltimore and Ohio. The air-conditioned dining car, the *Martha Washington*, was put into service on April 23, 1930. Between 1927 and 1929, the Pullman Company had been testing mechanical air-conditioning for some of its sleeping cars. On May 24, 1931, Willard's railroad began operating the first completely air-conditioned passenger train, the *Columbian*, between Washington and New York. A short year later, on April 20, 1932, the Baltimore and Ohio inaugurated the first air-conditioned, long-distance sleeping car train, the *National Limited*, between New York and St. Louis. The *Capitol Limited*, a New York to Chicago B&O train, was likewise equipped on May 22, 1932. By 1936 the railroad had put air-conditioning in 275 of its passenger cars. Willard insisted that all his principal through trains be air-conditioned before he had air-conditioning added to his traveling office, busi-

The *National Limited* introduced air-conditioning on its New York to St. Louis run in April 1932. This was the first long-distance air-conditioned train in the nation. *(Courtesy, Baltimore and Ohio Railroad)*

ness car "No. 99." The new service caused favorable comment in much of the nation's press. An editorial in the *Los Angeles Times* enviously noted the cool *Columbian* back East but remarked that in the West "we refrigerate our fruit but roast our passengers."[5]

The Baltimore and Ohio not only made summer travel more enjoyable, but it also had something for those who liked winter sports. During the winter of 1935–36, the B&O line out of Buffalo, New York, operated a special "snow train" excursion to Allegheny State Park. Sports fans could enjoy both tobogganing and skiing on the snow-covered slopes of the park. "Snow trains" were also operated out of Baltimore and Pittsburgh. Later in the decade, fishing "specials" were scheduled for midwestern fishermen so they could enjoy saltwater angling in Chesapeake Bay.

Even with the Depression, the Baltimore and Ohio was able to establish new safety records for both its employees and its passengers. During the first four months of 1930, the employee accident rate per million man-hours worked dropped to under eight. Of the eighteen divisions in the B&O systems, the St. Louis division had the best record, only 3.16 accidents per million hours of work during the first four months of 1930. The Baltimore and Ohio was also proud of its safety record for passenger travel. In the December 1935 issue of the *Baltimore & Ohio Magazine*, it was pointed out that no passenger had lost his life on B&O passenger trains since May 1919.

Other improvements in B&O passenger service were made during the decade. Starting the 1930, reclining seats were placed in many of the B&O day coaches. Early in 1937, twenty new air-cooled motor coaches were put in service to transfer B&O passengers from Manhattan Island to train side in Jersey City. A little later, a stewardess-nurse service was inaugurated on the *Shenandoah*, a through train between New York and Chicago. The chief duties of the new attendants were to look after the comforts of women and children travelers and to serve hot meals at reasonable prices from the diner to day coach passengers. Passenger travel had also been made less expensive, since the Interstate Commerce Commission, early in 1936, had issued an order reducing most passenger fares to about two cents per mile for coach travel and three cents per mile in Pullman cars.

During 1936 a number of businessmen were asked to rate American rail travel, and the results were given in the *Baltimore & Ohio Magazine:* "One hundred and one American business men who travel extensively were recently asked what they thought of the service they got on the different railroads they had used, and an analysis of their opinions showed that the B. & O. had the highest rating among eastern lines."[6] The survey was sponsored by the magazine *Sales Management*. The 101 men had traveled an average of 16,138 miles and spent from fifteen to eighteen nights apiece on sleeping cars during the past twelve months. They were asked which railroads were good and poor in seven factors: running time, cleanliness, temperature control, roadbed, service, food, and equipment. Ten railroads were selected for having the greatest percentage of "good" reports in relation to the number of men using them. Among these ten railroads, the Union Pacific was first, the Santa Fe second, and the Baltimore and Ohio ranked fourth. Only two other heavy passenger carriers in the East were in the group of ten lines and their ranking was fifth and tenth. The B & O ranked much higher than either of these two eastern competitors with respect to cleanliness, temperature control, service, food, and equipment. With respect to running time and roadbed, the two eastern rivals ranked higher than the Baltimore and Ohio.

There were also improvements in freight service during the 1930s. A free pick-up and delivery service for less-than-carload freight shipments paying not less than forty-five cents per 100 pounds was approved by the ICC and put into effect by the B&O and other eastern railroads in mid-November 1936. There had been great increases in the operating efficiency in freight service by all railroads in America since World War I. Across the nation

Rear brakeman and club car porter check the weather as the *Capitol Limited* pauses at Relay Station. *(Courtesy, Smithsonian Institution)*

between 1921 and 1940, the length of the average freight train had increased from 37.4 to 49.7 cars, and the average speed of freight trains rose from 11.5 to 16.7 miles per hour.

TABLE 18. Increases in Operating Efficiency of Railroad Freight Service 1921–40

	National Average		Baltimore and Ohio	
	1921	1940	1921	1940
Average freight car capacity (in tons)	42.5	50.0	46.0	53.0
Net tonnage carried by average freight trains (in tons)	651	849	713	942
Annual ton-mileage of freight service per employee (in ton-miles)	181,000	358,000	241,000	428,000

No doubt in 1921, the Baltimore and Ohio was ahead of the average American railroad in the efficiency of its freight service, basically because Daniel Willard had worked so diligently to upgrade his line in the years just before America entered World War I. Of course, it could not be expected that the Baltimore and Ohio, with its mountainous route, could match either the train length or the tonnage of a road like the New York Central. Patrick E. Crowley, president of the New York Central from 1921 to 1931, had been so proud of the long freight trains which ran over his easy "water level" route that some newsman liked to call him "Pull Eighty Cars" Crowley.

The Baltimore and Ohio, like all railroads of the nation, suffered from increased highway competition during the 1930s. Total passenger revenue declined during the decade from $18.5 million in 1930 to $10.6 million in 1940. In 1930 passenger revenue amounted to about 11 percent of the freight revenue, but a decade later, it had dropped to only 6 percent. In 1930 across the nation, intercity travel by private automobiles (in passenger miles) was already five times as large as that by rail. Ten years later, private auto travel was easily ten times that moving by rail. Early in the decade, Daniel Willard had said: "The railroads never will get back the travel constantly turning to private automobiles. The public likes to ride in its own car."[7] Buses and, later in the decade, even air carriers were causing rail travel to decline. In 1930 rail passenger travel was nearly four times that of bus and air—by 1940 it was little more than twice the combined bus and airliner travel.

Freight traffic was also being lost to the highway in the decade. Between 1930 and 1940, total rail ton-mileage in the nation slightly declined. However, highway truck freight, even though the cost of three to four cents per ton-mile was higher than railroad freight, more than tripled in the decade. Across the nation, the rail shipment of automobiles and automotive parts declined from 59 percent of the total movement in 1929 to only 37 percent in 1939. Rail shipment of citrus fruit dropped from 76 percent by rail in 1929 to 56 percent in 1939. Livestock movement by rail also dropped in the decade from 89 percent in 1929 to only 43 percent in 1939. On the Baltimore and Ohio, livestock shipments dropped from 623,000 tons in 1929 to 304,000 tons in 1939. In the same decade, less-than-carload-lot freight moving on the Baltimore and Ohio declined from two million tons in 1929 to one million tons in 1939.

Daniel Willard's road in the 1930s was losing traffic to farmers' trucks carrying hogs and cattle to market, but the Baltimore and Ohio continued to be interested in the farmers and their problems. The B&O had been sponsoring farm programs since the early years of the century. The Second Annual B&O State Poultry Show was held at the high school in Taylorsville, Illinois, in mid-December 1923, with 140 boys and girls from fourteen counties participating. At the December show, the Baltimore and Ohio offered cash prizes for the winners in two projects, egg setting and flock management. In 1926 a Baltimore and Ohio "Dairy Products Special" train made many stops in eastern Pennsylvania, Delaware, Maryland, and West Virginia to help the cattle raisers of those states "realize the necessity for purebred stock."[8] The railroad was also an early sponsor of 4-H activity in the states served by the B&O. Throughout the twenties and thirties, the B&O 4-H Potato Clubs in Indiana were active with the best potato producers showing their exhibits at the Indiana State Fair each summer. By the late 1930s, 4-H Club members were producing up to 200 bushels of potatoes per acre, well above the 90 bushel per acre yield typical in the Hoosier State.

As in the decade of the twenties, there was relatively little turnover in Willard's board of directors during the depression thirties. Only twenty-one different men served as Baltimore and Ohio directors during the decade. Six men, John J. Cornwell, Robert Garrett, John R. Morron, George M. Shriver, John F. Stevens, and Joseph Widener, all of whom had been on the board all or most of the previous decade, continued on the board throughout the 1930s. As Paul Warburg, Henry Ruhlender, Bernard Baruch, and

Newton D. Baker left the board in the early or mid thirties, they were replaced by Howard Bruce, Carl A. de Gersdorff, Harry Bronner, and A. H. Sprague. Lawyers and bankers continued to make up the bulk of board membership. Even though Baltimore and Ohio presidents had traditionally not been on the board, Daniel Willard was a director in the early Depression years of 1930, 1931, and 1932. Willard later returned to the group in 1941, when at the age of eighty, he gave up the presidency for the less active chairmanship of the board of directors.

By far the most important problem facing the B&O board during the 1930s was the deteriorating financial condition of the railroad. During the prosperous mid and late 1920s, the gross corporate income had ranged from $43 million in 1924 to a high of $57 million in both 1926 and 1929. These sums had generally been nearly twice the annual fixed charges, which ranged from $25 million to $30 million during the same years. All of this had changed with the collapse of traffic in the early depression thirties. By 1931 the B&O gross corporate income was down to $35 million, while the fixed charges were more than $31 million. After paying preferred 4 percent and common 3.5 percent dividends in 1931, the road had a deficit of $7.5 million. The real crisis came the next year when gross corporate income dropped to $28.5 million, some $6 million less than the fixed charges due that year. In 1932 dividends were not paid on either the preferred or the common stock.

The deficit of $6.3 million in net corporate income for 1932 was compounded by the fact that the Baltimore and Ohio had $63,250,000 of twenty-year, 4.5 percent convertible bonds which matured on March 1, 1933, just three days before President Roosevelt would enter the White House. It was clear, both to Daniel Willard and his Senior Vice President George M. Shriver, that the poor stock market conditions of 1932–33 would make it impossible to refund or refinance the maturing securities. Fortunately, after lengthy negotiations in the summer and fall of 1932 with the ICC and the Reconstruction Finance Corporation, a refunding plan was approved on November 15, 1932. Under the plan, the RFC loaned the Baltimore and Ohio sufficient funds to repay half of the maturing bonds, with the bondholders accepting new refunding and general mortgage 5 percent bonds for the remaining 50 percent. Well before the March 1, 1933, due date, more than 99 percent of the bondholders had accepted the proposal.

A slight economic recovery came in 1933, and the Baltimore and Ohio managed to pay its fixed charges, leaving a net corporate income of $204,000 for the year. However, modest deficits of more than $3 million in net corporate income appeared both in 1934 and

1935. Additional financial help from the Reconstruction Finance Corporation was obtained, and by the end of 1935, the RFC debt owed by the railroad had climbed to more than $51 million. Railroad revenues climbed in 1936 and 1937, and the B&O managed a net corporate income in 1936 of more than $4 million and suffered a deficit of less than $1 million for the year 1937.

The greatest financial crisis for Willard and his railroad came in 1938. A serious economic recession appeared in that year and the gross revenue of the Baltimore and Ohio declined by nearly $35 million. Operating expenses declined only $24 million, as compared to 1937, and the operating ratio climbed to nearly 78 percent, the highest figure in the decade. The income available to pay the fixed charges in 1938 was only $19 million, well under the year's fixed charges and interest due which amounted to $32 million. The deficit for the year, the highest during the decade, amounted to more than $13 million. In his *Annual Report* for 1938, Daniel Willard admitted that the financial problem facing his railroad was indeed serious:

> Since 1931 the Company has been required to meet maturities of its funded debt aggregating $172,585,700. Most of these maturities have occurred at times when the securities markets were so depressed as to make payments or refunding by ordinary means impossible. . . . The present indebtedness of the Company to the Reconstruction Finance Corporation aggregates the principal sum of $87,566,578.44. . . . Obligations of the Company aggregating approximately $185,000,000 (including the debt to the Reconstruction Finance Corporation referred to above) will come due during the next four years. It is evidently essential, therefore, that by some means fixed interest charges be reduced.[9]

Fortunately, Daniel Willard had some good friends in his time of need. Even though he had voted for Herbert Hoover in 1932, the B&O president had a good friend in the White House in 1938. Whenever Franklin Roosevelt journeyed to Hyde Park, he normally took the B&O line, which he considered his favorite railroad. The genial B&O president also had a good friend in Jesse Jones, chairman of the Reconstruction Finance Corporation. In Congress, Willard also had many friends who viewed him as a liberal with an excellent railroad labor record. In January 1938, Willard obtained still another loan, in the amount of $8,233,000, from Jesse Jones and the RFC. To obtain the money, some of which was needed to meet B&O payrolls, the B&O officials put up a varied collateral including the 184-mile Chesapeake and Ohio Canal, which had not been in operation since 1923. Later, in the summer of 1938, Daniel Willard, Jr., the president's son and assistant general counsel for the B&O, arranged with Jesse Jones for the Public Works Administration to purchase the aging canal outright for $2 million. Current plans, as of the summer of 1938, were to restore portions of the canal near Washington under the sponsorship of the National Park Service. In November 1938, the ICC permitted the Baltimore and Ohio president to initiate a plan with his bondholders for a possible moratorium on interest payments.

Late in July 1939, the United States Congress passed the Chandler Bill which was later signed by President Roosevelt. This legislation approved the Baltimore and Ohio Plan for Modification of Interest Charged and Maturities which provided that the maturity dates on some bonds would be extended for several years. The plan also provided that, for a period of eight years, the annual fixed charge of about $31 million would be modified so that $19 million would remained fixed, with the remaining amount to be paid depending upon company earnings. No dividends were to be paid on any stock until all back interest had been fully repaid. Burton K. Wheeler, chairman of the Senate Interstate Commerce Committee, had added so many technicalities to the legislation that in practice only the Baltimore and Ohio Railroad would be able to take advantage of it. A large majority of the bondholders approved the modification plan. Thus with the substantial help from a friendly federal government, Daniel Willard's railroad had been saved from a receivership and a reorganization like that which had faced John Cowan and Oscar Murray forty years earlier. As the seventy-eight-year-old railroad president argued for the legislation in the spring of 1939, he declared: "If I thought business conditions were to remain as bad as they are, I would say put us in receivership. . . . The railroads are going to come back again. . . . I haven't lost confidence in the United States!"[10]

Daniel Willard's confidence in the nation and her railroads was soon to be justified. The gross revenue on the Baltimore and Ohio in 1939 climbed to $161 million, $26 million over the figure for 1938, and increased to $179 million in 1940. In 1939 there was a small deficit, but in 1940 the income available for fixed charges left a modest net corporate income of $5.5 million.

New York City, and the nation, celebrated the modest economic recovery at the end of the decade by sponsoring and enjoying the New York World's Fair in 1939 and 1940. The Baltimore and Ohio, along with other eastern railroads, sponsored a major railroad exhibit at the fair. Edward Hungerford, who had managed the Baltimore and Ohio Centennial and the Fair of the Iron Horse in 1927, produced a pageant at the New York Fair entitled "Railroads on Parade." The Baltimore and Ohio officials sent to the

World's Fair such historic locomotives as the *William Mason*, the *Thatcher Perkins*, and the *J. C. Davis*, along with a streamlined Pacific locomotive, designed by Otto Kuhler, and normally in service with the *Royal Blue*.

TABLE 19. Baltimore and Ohio System Traffic and Financial Decline and Recovery 1930–40

Year	Miles of Road	Total Revenue	Net Revenue	Earnings to Expenses (%)	Average Passenger Fare (per mile) (¢)	Average Freight Rate (per ton-mile) (¢)	Dividend on common stock (%)
1930	5,569	$206,660,435	$53,518,060	74	2.97	1.01	7
1931	5,556	158,474,627	38,553,187	76	2.85	1.00	3.5
1932	6,308	125,882,823	34,227,888	73	2.42	.99	—
1933	6,312	131,792,253	41,422,552	69	2.25	.94	—
1934	6,310	135,539,395	36,201,611	73	2.18	.92	—
1935	6,351	141,873,643	36,409,503	74	2.15	.95	—
1936	6,396	168,992,681	45,392,347	73	2.02	.93	—
1937	6,371	169,436,436	40,576,920	76	1.95	.87	—
1938	6,345	134,722,330	29,738,309	78	2.09	.91	—
1939	6,306	161,030,252	41,129,176	74	2.00	.91	—
1940	6,293	179,175,465	46,574,666	74	1.85	.90	—

Between 1930 and 1940, freight revenue had declined about 10 percent while passenger traffic had dropped well over 40 percent. In the decade, passenger revenue had declined from $18,600,000 to $10,600,000. In 1930 freight revenue was about nine times that of passenger, while ten years later the ratio was 15 to 1. The railroad share of all freight movement in the nation had dropped from about 74 percent to 61 percent. In the same period, truck traffic across the country had climbed from 4 to 10 percent and that of pipelines from 5.5 to nearly 10 percent. The share moving via water had increased only slightly.

During the decade, the national railroad share of all intercity commercial travel declined from 68 percent to 64 percent. Interurban travel dropped by more than half, while the share carried by highway buses climbed from 18 to 26 percent. Air travel had also grown, especially as hundreds of new DC-3 airliners provided air service from coast to coast. By 1940 air travel amounted to nearly 3 percent of all passenger miles of travel. Across the country in 1940, private automobile travel in passenger-miles was nearly a dozen times that moving by rail.

During the 1930s, Baltimore and Ohio mail revenue had remained quite stable at about $3 million per year, while express revenue had declined more than 50 percent. In tonnage totals, the freight mix on the B&O in 1940 was: products of agriculture, 4 percent; animals and products, 1 percent; products of mines, 62 percent; products of forests, 3 percent; manufactures, 21 percent; and miscellaneous, 9 percent. These figures were little different than those a decade earlier. American railroads generally had about 55 to 56 percent of their tonnage listed as mine products.

TABLE 20. Soft Coal Production and Movement 1899–1940
(in millions of tons)

Year	Total United States Production	Price Per Ton at Mine	Carried by B&O	Carried by C&O	Carried by Norfolk & Western
1899	193	$1.04	9	4	4.5
1912	450	1.11	17	17	—
1918	579	2.58	45	27	—
1920	568	3.75	48	29	—
1926	573	2.06	52	55	43
1932	309	1.31	28	44	—
1940	461	1.91	36	60	—

Throughout the first four decades of the twentieth century, the products of mines, especially soft or bituminous coal, had led in tonnage figures among all types of traffic on the Baltimore and Ohio. Mine products in all four decades ranged from 60 to 62 percent of total tonnage. Its share of total freight revenue was not so high since freight rates for the haulage of coal were fairly low. In 1932 the 28 million tons of coal moving over the B&O paid a rate of .67 cents per ton-mile, while the system wide freight rate was .99 cents per ton-mile. The highest level of national soft coal production came in the last year of World War I, 1918. The 573 million tons (1926) was the highest production year for the 1920s, and the 309 million tons in 1932 the lowest for the depression 1930s. Total soft coal production rose to 620 million tons in 1944, but by the 1950s was normally under 500 million tons per year. Both fuel oil and natural gas were becoming competitors with coal for home heating by the 1920s and 1930s. Between 1926 and 1970, the national production of natural gas had increased some fifteenfold and its residential use increased more than a hundredfold. Even with increased industrial use, many were speaking of coal mining as a depressed industry.

The Baltimore and Ohio, by the decade of the 1920s, was facing increased competition for hauling West Virginia coal from both the Norfolk and Western and the Chesapeake and Ohio. After 1930 the C&O moved easily ahead of the B&O in hauling soft coal. During the depression thirties, all three lines were finding a substantial fraction of their coal cars were at mine sidings or some nearby railyard as "no bill" cars and being held for shipping orders. In periods of low demand for coal, often several thousand coal cars were thus used serving as a form of rolling storage for unsold coal.

In general, the range of the operating ratio (earnings to expenses) on the B&O was much like the decade of the 1920s. The lower figures for 1932 and 1933 were basically the result of the 10 percent wage reduction achieved early in 1932. Average freight rates during the decade were modestly declining, while average passenger fares showed a marked reduction. Daniel Willard liked low passenger fares and vigorously protested the efforts of other eastern railroads to raise passenger fares late in the decade: "I am definitely in favor of the railroads meeting the challenge of bus competition, which so far in the east we have not done."[11] The Interstate Commerce Commission agreed with Willard and confirmed lower fares early in 1940.

Dividends on both preferred and common stock were stopped in 1932 and neither would be resumed until well after World War II. A direct consequence of the loss of dividend payments was a major collapse in the price of B&O common stock. From highs of 145 in 1929 and 122 in 1930, it dropped to a low of 3-3/4 in 1932. It reached a high of 37-7/8 in 1933, and 34-1/4 in 1934, but soon began to fall. The range for B&O common in 1938 was from 4 to 11 and in 1940 it hit a low of 2-3/4 with a high of 6-3/8 per share.

During the decade of financial problems, some increases had appeared in the balance sheet of the Baltimore and Ohio. Between 1929 and 1940, the totals shown on the balance sheet had grown about 20 percent from $1,013,000,000 in 1929 to $1,231,000,000 in 1940. The investment in the road had climbed from $285 million in 1929 to $311 million in 1940, while the value of equipment in the eleven years had declined from $259 million to $253 million. The amount invested by the parent company in subsidiary roads had grown from $332 million in 1929 to $400 million by 1940. On the liabilities side of the balance sheet, there had been no change in the common stock, $256 million, or the preferred stock, $60 million, during the eleven-year period. The long-term debt had increased during the long decade, increasing from $550 million in 1929 to $673 by 1940. Equipment trusts or obligations, included in this funded debt, had dropped from $72 million in 1929 to only $25 million in 1940. Total annual interest charges in the eleven years had gone from $25 million in 1929 to more than $31 million in 1940.

With the start of World War II in Europe, the United States began to strengthen its own defense posture. As part of this effort,

President Roosevelt in 1939 asked Daniel Willard and Carl Gray, the retired president of the Union Pacific, to study the capacity of the nation's railways to handle the increased traffic that would accompany the defense buildup. This would be the last major governmental assignment assumed by Willard. A year later, the Willard family was deeply saddened by the death of their second son, the forty-six-year-old Daniel Willard, Jr., who died on May 17, 1940. The younger Willard, a lawyer, had entered the employ of the B&O in 1924 and at the time of his death was assistant general counsel on the railroad.

Daniel Willard had turned seventy early in the Depression, in January 1931. Each year after that, except during the deep financial crisis of 1939, Willard had placed his resignation before his board and each time it had been unanimously declined. Willard did not press the matter since his health was good and he loved his job. On January 28, 1941, Willard celebrated his eightieth birthday, and a few months later, in May, he once again offered his resignation with the strong suggestion that it should be accepted. With reluctance, the board accepted his request and on June 1, 1941, elected him chairman of the board. Daniel Willard was to receive the same salary for the chairmanship, $60,000 per year, that he had been getting as president in the late 1930s. The cut to $60,000 had been made when the B&O was on the brink of receivership in the years 1937–38. Willard also owned 1,005 shares of B&O stock in 1941, stock that had paid no dividends for a decade. After more than thirty-one years, "Uncle Dan" Willard had given up the direction of the Baltimore and Ohio. As he relinquished his long-held presidency, he said: "I wish I were only sixty and could keep on, I love it."[12]

Willard's successor as president was the fifty-seven-year-old Roy Barton White, who in 1902 had started his railroad career as a telegraph operator on a line later to be part of the B&O system. In the teens, he was a B&O division superintendent in Indiana and Illinois and from 1923 to 1926 the general manager at New York City for the B&O. In 1926 he moved on to the Central Railroad of New Jersey where he was president until 1933, when he was elected president of the Western Union Telegraph Company. White was a railroader at heart and was happy to return to the Baltimore and Ohio even though it meant taking a $25,000 cut in salary. The board gave White the same $60,000 a year salary they were paying Willard. In 1941 White owned 1,000 shares of B&O common stock.

Daniel Willard served only thirteen months as chairman of the Baltimore and Ohio board. After being ill for six weeks, Willard died of a heart condition on July 6, 1942, in the Union Memorial Hospital in Baltimore. He was buried in the Willard family plot at Hartland, Vermont, and was survived by his widow and four grandchildren. In his long career, Willard had spanned the years from the days of Jay Gould, Edward H. Harriman, and Jim Hill to an era of stiff federal regulation in the midtwentieth century. In noting his passing, his fellow board members wrote of Willard: "His leadership in employer-employee relations was an asset not only to the Baltimore and Ohio but redounded also to the benefit of industry generally and to the country as a whole."[13] In their note of condolence to Mrs. Willard, President and Mrs. Franklin Roosevelt wrote of Willard: ". . . who was my faithful friend and counselor through many, many years. Daniel Willard was one of the great figures in modern railroading."[14] Daniel Willard had left his successor a first-class railroad which provided excellent service. However, the new president, Roy White, would face many new challenges in the months and years ahead.

Chapter XVI

. . . .

The Baltimore and Ohio Again Aids a Nation at War

AS AMERICA MADE A MODEST RECOVERY FROM THE Depression in the late 1930s, more and more of the news in the press and on the radio was shifting from the home front to foreign affairs. Radio commentators like H. V. Kaltenborn and Lowell Thomas were covering such stories as the plans of the Japanese warlords for a new order in East Asia or the threat that Adolf Hitler might occupy Austria. Such newscasts, plus the background for war articles in weekly news magazines, made many Americans think about another world war. When Hitler's armies marched into Poland in the early days of September 1939, most Americans were still resolved that they should avoid the conflict. Even so, they were soon willing to have the United States sell airplanes and war munitions to Britain and France.

In 1939 when the American defense and war production reached $1 billion, the nation was still in a depression with 9.5 million Americans, 17 percent of the civilian labor force, unemployed. But the war in Europe brought an upswing in the American economy and also in railroad traffic. Operating revenues for the entire rail industry in 1939 were up more than 10 percent over the previous year. They climbed again in 1940 to $4,296,000,000, a higher figure than for any year since 1930, with an operating ratio of only 72 percent, lower than any year in the 1930s. In 1941 the revenue of the nation's railroads climbed another 25 percent to well over $5 billion.

As Hitler's troops moved into Poland in the late summer of 1939, the top railroad executives of the nation decided to make every effort to escape the federal control they had endured a score of years earlier between 1917 and 1920. At the same time, they were aware that some form of overall coordination of the complex transportation of the nation would be required. The man in the White House, Franklin Roosevelt, was a friend of the railroads. During his presidency, FDR traveled almost 250,000 miles by rail, more than any other chief executive. He was also aware that rail operating efficiency had greatly increased in the two preceding decades. Not long after the invasion of Poland, Roosevelt called to Washington a railroad executive who had led in some of the recent railroad innovation. Ralph Budd, president of the Burlington Railroad and an early sponsor of diesel-powered streamlined passenger trains, urged the president to leave the nation's railways under private control. Budd convinced the president that a fully coordinated transport service could be obtained by the full support and cooperation of the ICC, the Shippers' Advisory Boards, and the Association of American Railroads.

When the German onslaught through the low countries in May 1940, ended the "Phony War" on the Western front, President Roosevelt quickly asked Congress for a greater defense program. On May 28, 1940, he set up the Council of National Defense, composed of six members of his cabinet. He also established the advisory commission to the council, composed of seven industrial leaders. Ralph Budd was, at once, appointed to the group as the commissioner of transportation. In his new position, Ralph Budd was charged with the coordination of truck, bus, air, and pipeline transportation, as well as that of railroads. Through his efforts, he motivated fellow rail executives to reduce the bad-order freight car ratio (the portion of freight cars not in service because of needed repairs). The percentage of bad-order freight cars declined from 13 percent in 1939 to only 5.4 percent in 1941. Budd managed to avoid many of the problems that had bothered America's transport facilities during World War I. Budd continued to advise Roosevelt until the end of 1941.

Shortly after Pearl Harbor, President Roosevelt established the Office of Defense Transportation (ODT) to continue the direc-

Roy B. White, president, 1941 – 53.
(Courtesy, Baltimore and Ohio Railroad)

tion of wartime transport. The director of the new agency was Joseph B. Eastman, veteran member of the ICC and federal coordinator of transportation from 1933 to 1936. Eastman relied heavily upon the earlier work of Ralph Budd. This early transportation planning, plus the all-out efforts at cooperation in the rail industry, was so successful that during World War II the federal government took over the nation's railroads only during brief labor difficulties in December 1943 and January 1944.

Daniel Willard's successor, Roy B. White, had to face the prospect of operating his railroad in wartime during the first year of his presidency. In the opening paragraph of his *Annual Report* for 1941, he wrote concerning the effect of Pearl Harbor: ". . . The railroads, already so satisfactorily functioning in providing adequate transportation in the National Emergency, then became a strong and essential arm of our National Defense. . . . This Company proposes to do everything it is possible for it to do in accomplishing an early victory."[1] As the new president faced the problems of a railroad serving a nation at war, he was soon to have a number of new officials among his top subordinates. Several major officers, some of them nearly as old as Dan Willard, either died or retired in the early war years. George M. Shriver, longtime director and senior vice president, finance and accounting, died in May 1942 and was succeeded by Russell L. Snodgrass, a Canadian-born lawyer who had worked with the Reconstruction Finance Corporation before coming to the Baltimore and Ohio. Harry A. Lane, chief engineer on the B&O since 1917, died in 1941 and was succeeded by Alfred C. Clark. Col. George H. Emerson, chief of motive power and equipment retired in 1942, after twenty-one years in that position. The increased wartime activity on the Baltimore and Ohio did not bring any salary increase for Roy White, whose salary of $60,000 in 1943 was the same as at the time of his election in 1941. John J. Cornwell, director and general counsel, had a salary of $40,000 in 1943 while the several vice presidents were paid from $25,000 to $36,000 that year.

President White and his top staff did not have to worry about inadequate traffic in the early war years. The gross revenue in 1941 of more than $227 million was 27 percent larger than that of 1940, with freight revenue up more than 25 percent and passenger traffic climbing more than 30 percent. In 1942 the gross revenue increased to $306 million, one-third larger than that of the previous year. The passenger revenue in 1942, the first full year of war for the nation, was nearly twice that of 1941, while the freight traffic had increased more than 30 percent in the year. As the war traffic expanded, so too did the work force on the Baltimore and Ohio. The number of employees on White's railroad grew from 47,000 in 1941 to nearly 55,000 in 1942, 60,000 in 1943, and over 64,000 in 1944 and 1945.

The increase in Baltimore and Ohio equipment during the four years of the war in no way matched the growth in the work force. This problem was one also faced by nearly every railroad in the nation. As compared to the first year of World War I, 1917, the railroads of the United States in 1942 had 31 percent fewer locomotives, 24 percent fewer freight cars, and 35 percent fewer passenger cars. The number of railroad workers in the United States had dropped about 27 percent in the same twenty-five years. However, the smaller work force in 1942 was operating heavier engines with a greater average tractive effort which pulled longer, faster, and heavier trains. The average freight car in 1942 had a capacity of fifty tons, compared to only 41 tons in 1917, and thus the 1,745,000 freight cars in 1942 had a total carrying capacity nearly as great as that of 1917. The 42,000 locomotives moving troops and war munitions toward the front in 1942 had a total tractive effort roughly equal to the more numerous engines operating in the first year of World War I.

Even so, some additional equipment was urgently needed during the four years of World War II. Joseph Eastman was hardly any more successful in his requests for additional equipment than Ralph Budd had been. The ever watchful War Production Board seemed to trim and cut every request for additional rail equipment made by Eastman. During the war years, the railroads were permitted to have only about 60 percent of the 4,000 new locomotives requested by Eastman. Only 40 percent of the 300,000 additional freight cars were approved, and less than 40 percent of the extra passenger equipment that was requested.

Between 1941 and 1945, the equipment roster of the Baltimore and Ohio increased only modestly. The motive power roster only climbed from 2,062 to 2,099 locomotives. In the same period, freight cars increased from 87,996 in 1941 to 88,961 in 1945, while passenger equipment went from 1,199 to 1,229 cars. During the five years 1941 through 1945, Roy White's railroad spent more than $60 million on new equipment, with largest annual expenditures in the three years of 1941, 1944, and 1945. Relatively little money was spent during the war years on new passenger equipment. As the new, more powerful engines and larger freight cars were acquired during the war years, dozens of old engines and hundreds of older worn out freight cars were retired.

More than 150 new locomotives were added to the motive power roster from 1941 through 1945, with about 40 percent of the new engines being diesels. Included in the diesel fleet were several freight units, nine passenger diesels acquired in 1945, and about forty diesel switchers. During the summer of 1942, the Baltimore and Ohio purchased three, four-unit diesel freight locomotives, with each of the three multi-unit engines rated at 5400 horsepower and costing about $500,000 per locomotive. When the new diesel motive power left Chicago on August 31, 1942, with a train of seventy-six loaded tank cars, it was one of the first eastern lines to use the new type of power for freight service.

The largest of the new steam locomotives acquired during World War II by the B&O were the thirty articulated locomotives of the EM-1 Class (2-8-8-4) purchased from Baldwin between 1943 and 1945. The sixteen sixty-four inch drivers produced 115,000 pounds of tractive power, and the engines, including the tenders with a capacity of twenty-five tons of coal and 22,000 gallons of water, weighed just over one million pounds each. Everybody agreed the new, fully-equipped motive power was the finest on the Baltimore and Ohio. After looking over the first one delivered, President White turned to A. K. Galloway, Colonel Emerson's successor as general superintendent of motive power and equipment, and said: "Well, I must say, they have everything!"[2]

Of course, the bulk of the B&O motive power remained the several hundred Mikados (2-8-2) or "Mikes" which Daniel Willard had purchased during his long presidency. The first engines of this wheel type built in America had been produced by Baldwin in 1897 for the Japanese railways and were named for the ruler of that nation. During the anti-Japanese hysteria of World War II, the Baltimore and Ohio, along with a handful of other railways, tried to rename Mikado locomotives as the "MacArthur" type. However, most railroads and all the older workers never accepted the attempted change in name. In 1943 at the Mount Clare shops, B&O

workers started to convert twenty of the older Mikes into mountain type (4-8-2) engines. The rebuilt locomotives had longer boilers, more steam pressure, seventy inch drivers instead of sixty-four inch drivers, and tenders with greater water and coal capacity.

During the war, the Baltimore and Ohio also purchased or built more than 10,000 new freight cars, with most of the new equipment being acquired in 1941, 1944, and 1945. All of the new freight cars were built of steel. The new freight cars included more than 4,500 hoppers, over 2,000 gondolas, about 2,700 box cars, and 100 caboose cars built in the company shops.

Much more money was spent for new equipment during the war years than for betterments along the line of the Baltimore and Ohio. The operated mileage of the Baltimore and Ohio, other than affiliated lines, declined during the war years, dropping from 6,283 miles in 1941 to 6,132 miles in 1945. During 1942 the line of the Valley Railroad of Virginia, long an unprofitable branch, was abandoned, and some mileage was also abandoned in New York. These two abandonments caused a decrease of more than 120 miles of operated line. Also in 1942, the Alton Railroad, which had been operated as an affiliated line by the Baltimore and Ohio since the early 1930s, was forced into bankruptcy. With the eventual reorganization of the line in the mid-1940s, the Baltimore and Ohio gave up control of the property.

The betterments along the Baltimore and Ohio lines during the war years consisted of a variety of modest improvement programs. Early in the war, more than 300 new industries were located along the Baltimore and Ohio system. About ninety of these new projects were of some size, and half of these major developments were devoted to new war production. The B&O was glad to provide minor line relocations, along with the needed sidings, to meet the needs of the newly located plants. To accommodate the heavier engines and tonnage of the war years, more than 200 B&O bridges were upgraded and strengthened during the war. New block signals were also installed on more than 200 miles of main line during the years 1942 through 1945. Flasher lights were erected at a number of grade crossings early in the decade. In 1942 yard facilities were improved at Locust Point near Baltimore, and in 1943 new diesel repair and fueling facilities were built at Willard, Ohio. New yard tracks and sidings were added at a number of points along the lines of the war busy Baltimore and Ohio.

In the early days of the war, President Roy B. White urged all Baltimore and Ohio employees to meet the challenges of the war: "Our first duty is to carry on unflinchingly our job as a transportation agency. We must deliver the goods. . . . The better we

do our job as B&O-Alton men and women, the quicker our arma-
ments will grow to a strength this foe cannot withstand, and the
fewer the casualties to the men in the armed services."[3] But quite
soon, large numbers of Baltimore and Ohio personnel were themselves in the armed services. During the summer of 1941, several
months before Pearl Harbor, the War Department had approached
the B&O relative to the formation of a Military Railway Unit. In
the winter of 1941–42, the 708th Headquarters, Railway Grand
Division was formed, being lead by officers largely drawn from
Baltimore and Ohio officials and men.

    Early in 1942, increasing numbers of Baltimore and Ohio
workers were enlisting or being drafted into the several branches
of the armed forces. Soon, about 25 per day or 700 per month were
giving up the work clothes or uniforms of the railroad to serve
Uncle Sam. By the end of 1942, the number had grown to 6,959
and by the end of March 1943, it was up to 8,293. The number in
the armed services had increased to more than 13,000 by the end of
1943 and to more than 16,000 by the end of 1944. By the time of VJ
Day in August 1945, the Baltimore and Ohio Service Flag showed
that 17,178 men and women had left the railroad to serve their
country. Gold stars marked the deaths of 201 B&O workers who
would not be coming back from the conflict. Two former B&O
workers, Johnny Squires, messenger from Louisville, Kentucky,
and Emile Deleau, Jr., a trackman from Cambridge, Ohio, were
both listed among the war dead and also had earned the nation's
highest military award, the Congressional Medal of Honor. When
President Roy White wrote his "victory message" to the 64,000
B&O workers in mid-August 1945, nearly 500 war veterans had
already returned to work on the railroad. That same summer, in
occupied Germany, a former B&O worker, Col. John S. Major of
the 708th Railway Grand Division, celebrated the American victory by placing a B&O emblem over the swastika on the cab of a
captured German locomotive.

    The thousands of Baltimore and Ohio employees supported
the war effort in ways beyond the moving of war freight and troop
trains. Most employees subscribed generously to the several war
bond drives during the four war years. In 1944 nearly 44,000 different B&O workers were participating in a payroll deduction plan for
the purchase of War Bonds. Many departments and offices had 100
percent participation in the bond drives, and numerous workers
were having 10 percent, or more, of their pay withheld for bond
purchases. By the end of the war, B&O workers had purchased
nearly 1,300,000 bonds with a total maturity value of over $36
million. As in World War I, the Baltimore and Ohio urged its

workers to contribute to the war effort by planting Victory Gardens on land made available along the railroad right-of-way. Division superintendents assigned such plots to weekend gardeners, and their efforts were aided by a free booklet, *Victory Gardens*, supplied by the Agricultural Development Department of the railroad.

From 1941 through 1945, more than 17,000 B&O employees left for the armed services at the same time that the total work roster on the system climbed by about 17,000 workers. As a result, hundreds of older workers delayed their retirement, many retired workers returned to the railroad, and thousands of new employees joined the railroad for the first time. Many of the new employees were women. As in World War I, they filled a great variety of jobs in shops, offices, stations, and trains. In midwar President White pointed out that one woman employee worked on a track maintenance crew for twenty-three months without missing a single day. Early in the war, several women were added to the Baltimore and Ohio Police Department and assigned to day and night duty in guarding railroad waterfront property in Baltimore. In the first eight months of 1943, B&O officials recruited 450 high school

Women workers on the B&O in World War II at Camden Station of Baltimore. *(Courtesy, Baltimore and Ohio Railroad)*

women graduates to work in Baltimore, with more than half the new workers assigned to waybill, ticket, and payroll duties in the accounting department. In the spring of 1944, Eleanor Roosevelt, wife of the United States president, paid a tribute to the women of the B&O family: ". . . During this war period women as employees have become very much more important in many occupations which were formerly entirely in the hands of men. . . . You and I are on the home front, and our part of the war is to remember that the more we do to speed the day of victory the better."[4]

The need for labor, especially lower paid unskilled labor, became so great that by 1944 the Baltimore and Ohio was availing itself of special agreements made between the war manpower commission and the Mexican government for the temporary employment of Mexican nationals on American railroads. By the late summer of 1944, about 1,350 Mexicans had been imported to work on track crews up and down the B&O lines. More were brought in during the spring of 1945. By the end of the war, a total of 2,816 Mexican workers had been brought in to work on the railroad. The end of the war brought an end to the labor shortage, and most of the Mexican workers had returned home by the end of 1945.

The B&O workers who remained on the job at home during the war, like all railroaders across the nation, were faced with a steady climb in the cost of living. Prices went up about 5 percent by 1941 and another 10 percent in 1942. Railroad workers across the nation became restive and by the summer of 1941, operating and nonoperating unions were agitating both for a wage boost and paid vacations. When negotiations failed early in the fall of 1941, President Roosevelt appointed a special mediating board headed by Wayne L. Morse, dean of the University of Oregon Law School. Railroad labor was unhappy with the Morse board recommendations and called a strike for Sunday, December 7, 1941. The Morse board was reconvened by Roosevelt and on December 2, 1941, granted a program of short paid vacations plus a new wage scale. Average annual rail wages across the nation rose from $2,045 in 1941 to $2,307 for 1942. The average wages on the Baltimore and Ohio climbed from $2,141 in 1941 to $2,368 in 1942.

The high wages in war plants, the continued inflation, and the growing prosperity of the entire rail industry soon made railroad labor desire another boost in pay. Late in 1942 and early in 1943, a new series of wage demands were presented to management. A series of recommendations made by government-created emergency boards during 1943 failed to satisfy the railroad unions. As the railroad labor leaders considered a strike vote, one of them said: "If we strike, we aren't striking against the carriers, we are striking against the government."[5] Finally, a nationwide rail strike was called for December 30, 1943. President Roosevelt called a series of White House conferences between the contending parties and then took over the nation's railroads on December 27, 1943.

The strike was called off, and the War Department formally took possession of the railroads, retaining control until January 18, 1944. The real management of the roads remained with the top rail executives, several of whom put on army colonel's uniforms and received $360 in army pay during the twenty-two days of federal operation. One of the colonels directing rail operations was Roy White who directed rail operations in the Allegheny region, an area including some eighty different carriers. The unions finally accepted Roosevelt's offer of additional wage increases, effective retroactively to February 1, 1943. Again the rail workers of the nation had shown that political pressure on the White House could produce wage boosts greater than those available by the normal channels of the Railway Labor Act. Baltimore and Ohio average wages were $2,587 in 1943, $2,702 in 1944, and $2,624 in 1945, figures quite close to the national averages.

Both wages and prices had climbed substantially during the four war years, but this was not true of either freight rates or passenger fares. Across the nation, average freight rates between 1941 and 1945 had only climbed from .93 cents to .96 cents per ton mile and passenger fares had increased from 1.75 cents to 1.87 cents per passenger-mile. On the Baltimore and Ohio, average freight rates had gone from .894 cents to .896 cents per ton-mile and passenger fares only from 1.85 cents to 1.94 cents per passenger-mile.

During the Second World War, rail passenger traffic seemed to nearly explode in volume. For the nation, the total passenger traffic in 1944 was twice that of 1918 and nearly sixfold greater than that of 1932. During the forty-five months of war (1941 to 1945), 113,891 special troop trains in the nation moved 43,700,000 members of the armed forces, or an average of nearly 1 million men per month. The growth of passenger traffic was equally great on the Baltimore and Ohio. B&O passenger revenue of more than $51 million in 1944 was almost one-sixth as large as the freight revenue, was more than four times the passenger traffic of 1940, and nearly six times that of 1933. The distance traveled by the typical passenger greatly increased, climbing from 116 miles in 1941 to 193 miles in 1944. The heavy passenger traffic continued well into 1945, the last year of the conflict. In 1945 the B&O carried nearly 14 million passengers, including 14,862 groups of military personnel with a total of 1,563,000 men.

The greatly increased passenger traffic in the early 1940s unfortunately led to an increased number of railroad accidents across the country. Between 1942 and 1945, several major railroad wrecks resulted in more than 300 deaths, an accident rate much higher than for the two preceding decades. The Baltimore and Ohio suffered one of the first accidents, when on the early morning of September 24, 1942, the *Ambassador*, from Detroit to Washington hit the rear of the *Cleveland Express* near Dickerson, Maryland, some thirty-five miles northwest of Washington, D.C. The *Cleveland Express* had stopped for minor repairs on the foggy morning. The following *Ambassador* had seemingly ignored the warning torpedoes placed on the track by the flagman. A dozen passengers and two train crewmen died in the accident, the worst rail collision on the Baltimore and Ohio since a 1907 crash in West Virginia.

No doubt one of the most frequent and best known travelers on the Baltimore and Ohio in the war years was Franklin Roosevelt. The president loved to travel by rail, although he disliked to travel much faster than fifty miles an hour. The president's heavily armored private car, the "Ferdinand Magellan," often rode on B&O rails when he traveled in the northeastern United States. FDR had long admired Daniel Willard, and there were rumors that the president did not favor the Republicanism he associated with the top management of the rival Pennsylvania. In any event, during World War II, he often used the Baltimore and Ohio for his numerous trips north to visit Hyde Park. Frequently, he boarded his private car on a siding near the Bureau of Engraving not far from Fourteenth Street S.W., took the B&O line north to Jersey City, and then rode the New York Central West Shore division up the Hudson to Highland, New York, where a private car met the train and drove on to Hyde Park.

Very little new passenger equipment was added during the war years, but a number of the diners were modernized. In the late 1920s, twenty Baltimore and Ohio diners had been built and designed to reveal the elegance and charm of colonial days, with Hepplewhite chairs, a Sheraton sideboard, and side-wall brackets reminiscent of colonial pewter. Most of these diners were modernized during the war starting in 1943. The cars were repainted in brighter colors with new carpeting and new drapes at the windows. The older, heavier chairs were replaced with modern, lighter chairs, permitting the seating capacity to be increased from thirty-six to forty-eight, a real blessing in the crowded trains of the war. As each car was modernized, the car names—"Priscilla Alden," "Nelly Custis," or "Abigail Adams"—were changed to numbers.

The renovation program also resulted in savings in cleaning and maintenance. The top passenger traffic officials, however, did not permit any lowering in the quality of the food served in the Baltimore and Ohio dining cars.

Even with the great increase in wartime passenger traffic, the economic bread and butter of the Baltimore and Ohio remained its basic freight traffic. Between 1940 and 1944, B&O freight revenue nearly doubled, climbing from $158 million in 1940 to $202 million in 1941, $264 million in 1942, $300 million in 1943, $315 million in 1944, and $293 million in 1945. The 1944 freight revenue was nearly triple the low figure of $106 million in 1932. The expanded freight traffic of the war years included not only the normal civilian peacetime shipments, but also the varied mix of wartime munitions. During 1942 Baltimore-bound freight trains carried loads of ship parts to the Bethlehem-Fairfield shipyard in Baltimore for the completion there of the seventy-fifth Liberty ship, the *Daniel Willard*. The sponsor of the 10,500-ton cargo vessel, completed in the late fall of 1942, was fourteen-year-old Mary Beale Willard, granddaughter of the late Baltimore and Ohio president.

War needs naturally increased the shipment of coal. In 1944 Baltimore and Ohio freight trains carried more than 62 million tons of coal, more than twice the tonnage carried in the early depression 1930s. Roy White's railroad also experienced a major increase in the shipment of oil. In the summer of 1941, total railroad deliveries of oil to the East by rail tank car were only 11,250 barrels per day. But as German submarines pinched off coastal tankers, rail deliveries to eastern states rose to more than 1 million barrels per day. The Baltimore and Ohio actively shared in this new traffic, but soon was running short of available tank cars. H. L. Holland and F. H. Einwachter, both of the Mount Clare shops, worked out a simple answer to the problem when they fitted four wooden tanks, each lined with thin sheet steel, into ordinary boxcars. The converted boxcar "tankers" each held 12,200 gallons of oil, compared to the normal tank car capacity of 8,000 to 10,000 gallons. During 1943 an average of 850 tank cars per day moved over the lines of the B&O. In 1944 the Baltimore and Ohio was carrying more than 4.6 million tons of petroleum and other oil products, amounting to more than 3 percent of its total freight tonnage.

As the Baltimore and Ohio prospered in the early 1940s, its tax bill naturally increased. The total taxes paid by the railroad increased from $11.6 million in 1940 to $16.2 million in 1941, $46.8 million in 1943, and $49 million in 1944. The taxes per dollar of operating revenue climbed from seven cents per dollar of operating revenue in 1941 to nearly thirteen cents per dollar in 1944. In the same period, the tax per share of capital stock climbed from $5.14 in 1941 to $15.54 in 1944.

As the Baltimore and Ohio and other American rail lines noted the high taxes they had paid during the Second World War, they soon noted the contrasting tax picture of the nation's railways in 1917–18, and the period twenty-five years later in 1941–45. During the federal operation under William G. McAdoo in World War I, the government management of the railroads cost American taxpayers roughly $2 million every day. In contrast, American railroads during World War II paid federal income taxes of nearly $3 million each day of the war. Since critics of the rail industry could not refute these figures, American railroads in postwar years enjoyed a new prestige. In the postwar 1940s, there was little talk of governmental ownership of American railroads.

The taxes paid during World War II by the Baltimore and Ohio and other railroads were large because the yearly gross revenues in the war years were of a record size. The Baltimore and Ohio gross revenue of $306 million in 1942 climbed to $358 million in 1943, and $387 million in 1944, before declining a bit to $364 million in 1945, the last year of the war. The average annual gross revenue from 1941 through 1945, was $328 million, nearly twice the $165 million average yearly revenue for the eleven years 1930–40, and well above the $245 million yearly average for the five years 1925–29. In each of these years, 1941–45, the B&O income available for fixed charges was well above the amount due for interest on the funded debt. As early as the end of 1941, the improving revenues indicated that the B&O would easily meet the financial needs of the 1938 Plan for Modification of Interest Charges and Maturities. At a testimonial dinner given to Daniel Willard in Baltimore early in December 1941, the eighty-one-year-old chairman of the board reported: "I am glad to be able to say this evening that in 1941 we expect to have sufficient net income at the end of the year, five years before the termination of the plan, to provide for the payment in full of all deferred interest and obligations."[6]

The prosperity of the early 1940s was sufficient for the Baltimore and Ohio to pay off a substantial share of its funded debt during the war years. By 1943 there had been a net reduction in interest bearing obligations of more than $58 million. More bonds were paid off in the last two years of the war, and in the *Annual Report* for 1945 Roy White was able to report that the debt reduction during the war amounted to $105 million, which reduced annual interest payments by more than $5 million.

Even with these debt reductions, the Baltimore and Ohio faced a financial problem in 1944 because in that year, more than $112 million of interest–bearing debts were due, including $71 million of 4 percent Reconstruction Finance Corporation Notes. The B&O officials in the fall of 1944 proposed an adjustment plan for the refunding of these debts under the provisions of Chapter XV of the Bankruptcy Act. The adjustment plan called for the refunding of these debts, including the RFC loan, with new maturity dates being evenly spaced between 1965 and 2010. Under the plan, the RFC notes were to be exchanged for 4 percent collateral trust bonds to mature in 1965. Critics of the B&O and their adjustment plan often spoke of the entire proposal as the B&O "bankruptcy of 1944," but the B&O never came close to receivership in the process of proposing the debt adjustment. However, full approval of the proposed adjustment plan was required both by the Interstate Commerce Commission and the appropriate federal courts. The ICC and the courts were slow in making up their minds on the proposal.

In the summer of 1945, Burton K. Wheeler, Democratic United States senator from Montana and chairman of the Senate Committee on Interstate Commerce, attempted to hasten the proceedings by asking for a thorough investigation of the RFC debt owed by the Baltimore and Ohio. Eventually, the Baltimore and Ohio adjustment plan was fully approved by the Interstate Commerce Commission and the United States Supreme Court in 1946. At the same time that President White was proposing the adjustment plan, top legal officials of the railroad were working to complete the simplification of the corporate structure of the railroad by terminating the corporate existence of certain subsidiary lines. Between 1941 and 1944, the number of separate subsidiary lines in the B&O system was reduced from 107 to 70 carrier corporations.

As in an earlier world conflict a quarter of a century before, the Baltimore and Ohio had served the nation well. The editors of the *Baltimore & Ohio Magazine* wrote of the final victory in 1945: "And in this story, no small portion of glory will be assigned to the railroads—particularly those of this country. It would be difficult indeed to find a single agency that contributed more to the success of allied arms."[7] The year 1945 had been a year of war, of victory, and of transition to peace. President White and his fellow workers on the Baltimore and Ohio would soon face new challenges in the postwar years.

Chapter XVII

. . . .

Postwar Problems

IN THE MONTHS AFTER THE VJ DAY CELEBRATION, ROY White saw the high traffic and revenue figures of World War II quickly collapse. In the early postwar months, serious strikes in the steel, automotive, coal, and electrical industries resulted in a sharp drop in freight traffic on the B&O and all across the country. Freight revenue on the B&O in 1946 declined more than 14 percent below that of 1945, while passenger revenue dropped more than 25 percent in the year. In June 1946, little more than a year after the war had ended in Europe, the monthly earnings on White's railroad, something over $25 million, were *exceeded* by total expenses (wages, materials, fuel, taxes, rent, and interest) by more than $597,000. For the entire year, total B&O operating revenue was just under $305 million, a drop of more than $56 million below the 1945 figure. In spite of White's best efforts, the operating expenses for 1946 were reduced by only $21 million and, as a result, the operating ratio, which was 82 percent in 1945, climbed to 90 percent in 1946.

A major problem facing Roy White throughout his presidency was that of inflation. Between 1939 and 1951, the consumer price index had climbed 87 percent, with most of the increase coming after the close of World War II. Costs and expenses faced by the B&O in these years were well above the general increase in the cost of living. The average annual payroll cost per employee on the B&O in 1951 was $4,254, more than twice the $2,119 figure for 1939. Between 1939 and 1951, the average rate of pay per straight time hour increased 126 percent. In the same twelve years, the cost of fuel for B&O locomotives climbed 138 percent while the cost of material and other supplies rose 134 percent. The freight rate per ton-mile on the B&O increased only 43 percent while average passenger fare went up 63 percent. Roy White summarized the problem in his 1951 report to the railroad's stockholders: "Since 1939 the disparity between cost and rate levels has widened. . . . Energetic efforts have been exerted to narrow the gap through the only avenues available—increased efficiency, economy, and adequate rates. Much has been accomplished in improving efficiency and economy, but so far we have not succeeded in obtaining adequate rates."[1]

Even though the early postwar years saw a decline in revenue, a modest increase in total dollar revenue soon appeared. The $305 million operating revenue of 1946 climbed to $360 million in 1947 and to $400 million the following year. Traffic dropped off in 1949, but soon recovered, increasing to $451 million in 1951 and a record $460 million in 1953, the year that Roy White gave up the presidency to Howard E. Simpson. Such yearly operating revenues were well above those of World War II, which had peaked in 1944 at $387 million. But most of this increase was caused by inflated prices and higher freight rates and passenger fares, which had increased by roughly 50 percent in the postwar years. The actual ton-mileage and passenger-mileage figures for White's last year as president were well below the record traffic figures of World War II. The highest ton-mileage figure in the postwar years of White's presidency was in 1951 when the B&O recorded more than 30 billion ton-miles of freight. This was more than 10 percent below the record war years of 1943 and 1944, both of which saw B&O freight trains produce over 34 billion ton-miles of freight service.

The drop-off in passenger service on the Baltimore and Ohio was even greater in the late forties and early fifties. The year 1951 was a fairly good year on the B&O for postwar passenger traffic with a more than $26 million of passenger revenue. But the passenger mile figure in 1951 of 799 million passenger-miles was less than one-third of the record 2,483 million passenger-miles of 1945 and the still higher 2,758 million passenger-miles of 1944.

Nor did the B&O show any growth in mileage in the years after World War II. During the eight years of White's postwar leadership, 1946 through 1953, the average mileage of line providing freight service held quite steady at just under 6,100 miles. In the same years, the mileage of passenger service declined from 4,800 miles in 1946 to 3,500 miles in 1953. Certainly no B&O president in the midtwentieth century could be expected to match the expansion record of the earlier Thomas Swann who had doubled the B&O mileage between 1848 and 1853, or to quadruple the system as John W. Garrett had done in the quarter of a century after 1858. "Uncle" Daniel Willard in his thirty-one-year tenure had been bucking the trend of rail mileage growth in his more than 1,500-mile expansion of the B&O. The American rail network had been declining in miles of operated line since early in the Willard presidency—in 1916 the American rail mileage stood at a record figure of more than 254,000 miles. By the B&O centennial year of 1927, the figure had dropped to 249,000 and continued to decline to 232,000 miles in 1941 and 222,000 in 1953.

Early in World War II, the Alton Railroad, which had been a line affiliated with the B&O for several years, had been forced into bankruptcy. Even though it still owned several million dollars of Alton notes at the end of the war, the B&O had little interest in regaining control of the Alton in the postwar period. Thus Roy White and the B&O did not object when the Alton Railroad was consolidated on June 1,1947, with the Gulf, Mobile and Ohio, a relatively new railroad formed in 1940 out of the Mobile and Ohio and the Gulf, Mobile and Northern. Isaac B. Tigrett, a Tennessee banker and president of the Gulf, Mobile and Ohio, had his good Texan friend, Jesse Jones, help obtain approval by federal officials in Washington, D.C., for the acquisition of the Alton.

Roy White spent many millions of dollars on improvements and betterments on his 6,000-mile system in the postwar years. The bulk of the new money was spent on new equipment, but between 1946 and 1953, an average of well over $10 million a year was spent for improvements on road, track, and terminal facilities. The amounts spent yearly on road improvements during the eight years ranged from a low of about $9 million in 1949 to a high of between $14 and $16 million in each of the years of 1947, 1948, and 1951.

Between 1946 and 1949, a variety of road improvements were planned and completed from Baltimore west to Chicago and St. Louis. Several new spurs and added trackage were built to serve the coal fields in Ohio and other midwestern states. During the four years, more than 250 bridges were replaced or rebuilt to accommodate the heavier freight trains that were being operated. New freight terminal yards, Barr Yard in Chicago, Cone Yard in East St. Louis, and Mill Creek Yard in Cincinnati, were all planned and completed during the late 1940s. Teletype installations were being installed during the same years. During 1947 and 1948, automatic track signals were put in place along 130 miles of heavily used line and new interlocking facilities were also added. A new Union Station at Akron was opened in 1949. During the early 1950s, more than 150 additional bridges were rebuilt or replaced, dozens of additional highway crossings were given additional protection, and several new interlocking plants were installed. In 1950 and 1951, a second track was added to a tunnel near Grafton, West Virginia, and later centralized traffic control was installed on the line between Grafton and Parkersburg and the line from North Dayton to Lima, Ohio. A new import ore pier was completed in Baltimore by 1952 and the Cumberland yard was modernized. Also in the 1950s, numerous steam locomotive repair shops were being converted to handle the repair and maintenance of diesel engines.

Between 1946 and 1953, far more money was spent on new equipment than on road improvements. In 1946 the $25 million spent on all improvements was about equally divided between road and equipment items. In the following seven years, equipment expenses exceeded road improvement costs by margins ranging from 40 to more than 200 percent. In both 1947 and 1948, more than $40 million was spent each year on new equipment, a figure roughly three times that spent on road improvements. A great majority of the new equipment expenditures went for hundreds of new diesel locomotives.

In the early postwar years, Alexander K. Galloway, superintendent of motive power since 1942, was still acquiring a few steam locomotives. In 1946 three steam passenger locomotives were built in the B&O shops and the following year, thirty steam freight locomotives were added to the motive power roster. Seven of these were built in company shops, while ten articulated Mallets (2-6-6-4) were purchased from the Seaboard Air Line that same year. B&O engine crews liked the big engines that came from the southern road, since they were trouble free and easy to handle. In 1948 three additional steam locomotives were constructed in the B&O shops. In 1949 two steam engines were modernized there.

With passenger traffic in decline in the postwar years, far more money was spent on freight cars than on new passenger equipment. Between 1946 and 1948, the B&O placed in service 2,400 new box cars and more than 15,300 additional hopper cars. In addition new AB brakes were installed on 5,800 freight cars. The AB brake permitted both faster application and quicker recovery of air pressure. The new freight equipment was badly needed since 1947 saw a marked increase in postwar freight traffic. The 1947 wheat crop was of record size, and the year also saw a marked

B&O Mallet hauls coal train over the summit of the Alleghenies near Altamont, Maryland.
(Courtesy, Baltimore and Ohio Railroad)

President Truman escorts Winston Churchill on B&O train enroute to Fulton, Missouri, in 1946. *(Courtesy, Baltimore and Ohio Railroad)*

increase in the production of bituminous coal. As a result, the 94,700 cars the B&O had on its freight equipment roster in 1947 were all in heavy use. Freight crews endeavored to cut the average turn-around time for all freight equipment. The average turn-around time was reduced from 14.8 days in December 1946, to 13 days in December 1947. More freight equipment was procured in the early 1950s. Between 1951 and 1953, the B&O placed in service 2,200 box cars, 5,000 hoppers, 500 covered hoppers, 1,000 gondolas, and nearly 400 flat cars. As the new equipment was put in operation, hundreds of older cars were, retired. In 1952 and 1953, much new marine equipment for the B&O was also purchased. Included in the new fleet were four new tugboats for New York Harbor. Two of the tugboats were named the *Roy B. White* and the *Howard E. Simpson*.

Across the nation, more than thirty-five different railroads were buying new passenger trains in the late 1940s. Hundreds of millions of dollars were being spent on the sleek, new streamlined passenger equipment. The Chicago Railroad Fair of 1948 and 1949 was placing much emphasis on the dozens of new streamlined passenger trains being put in service by the Burlington, Great Northern, Pennsylvania, Southern Pacific, and other major lines. As of midcentury, probably 30 percent of all rail passengers were riding the new equipment.

The investment made by the B&O in new passenger equipment in these years was really quite modest. In 1946 ten passenger cars were rebuilt for new daylight service between Washington and Cincinnati. The two sections of the new, fast *Cincinnatian* were christened the same day, January 7, 1947, in Cincinnati and Washington. In Washington, D.C., Mrs. Robert A. Taft, wife of the senior senator from Ohio, who was also a former B&O director, christened the new train by breaking a bottle of Potomac River water on the coupler of the train's observation car. In 1949 sixteen new passenger cars, ordered three years earlier, were delivered for a new streamliner the *Columbian* running between Washington and Chicago. Included in the design of the new train was a vista-dome car with its upper deck high level observation compartment. Featured in the front of the car was an instrument panel including a clock, altimeter, barometer, and speedometer.

There was no great rush of passengers for the new equipment. The *Cincinnatian* had so few passengers that in 1950 it was shifted to a Cincinnati to Detroit run. Earlier, at the end of 1949, the B&O had been permitted to discontinue its last passenger service on its old main line between Baltimore and Mount Airy, forty miles to the west. In order to reduce passenger service losses, the B&O, in 1953, purchased eight Budd Company rail motor cars called the RDC. These self-propelled cars, powered by a pair of 275-horsepower diesel engines, were economical to operate and had a top speed of eighty miles per hour. The B&O placed five of the cars on the Baltimore to Washington route and to increase traffic, offered a special two dollar round trip fare. The RDC could reasonably be operated with a two-man crew, but railroad brotherhoods soon were insisting on a full four-man crew, including a fireman and brakeman. Thus, railroad labor was largely responsible for the fact that few RDC units were in operation by the mid-sixties.

Shortly after the war ended, the B&O, along with other rail carriers, acquired the ownership of the sleeping cars of the Pullman Company. Early in the decade of the 1940s, the Justice Department had charged the Pullman Company with being a monopoly. In a final decision in May 1944, the courts ordered Pullman to separate its manufacturing and operating divisions and required that one of the two divisions be sold. The Pullman Company decided to sell its equipment and in March 1947, the United States Supreme Court approved the sale of the Pullman sleeping cars to more than fifty operating railroads. In the B&O *Annual Report* for 1948, President White reported the acquisition of 155 standard sleeping cars from the Pullman Company. These cars were obtained through the purchase of 3.41 percent of the capital stock of the Pullman Company.

During the postwar years of the White presidency, 1945 to 1953, the B&O, along with all the other railroads of the nation, lost considerable freight and passenger traffic to other modes of transportation. Between 1945 and 1953, the total intercity freight carried by American railroads declined from 691 billion ton-miles to 613 billion ton-miles, while the rail share of the total freight movement dropped from 67.3 percent to 52.5 percent. In the same eight years, the truck share of the freight traffic climbed from 6.5 percent to 17.7 percent, while that moving on rivers and canals went from 2.9 percent up to 5.9 percent. The loss in passenger traffic to the bus, airplane, and private automobile was even more drastic. The 31 billion passenger-miles of rail travel on American railroads in 1953 was only one-third of the 1945 figure, and the rail share of all share of all commercial intercity traffic dropped from 72.9 percent in 1945 to 46.4 percent. The portion moving by bus climbed from 21.4 percent to 28.9 percent, while the share of air carriers increased from 2.7 percent to 21.6 percent. Of course, the great bulk of passenger travel in the postwar years was in private automobiles. In 1944 total private auto travel was only 17 percent larger than commercial intercity travel. Already by 1950, intercity private auto travel was nearly six times as great as all commercial travel.

The B&O officials felt that the United States government was giving an unfair advantage to the competitors of the railroads by giving them large governmental subsidies. In his 1949 *Annual Report*, President Roy White wrote:

> Railroads do not seek to stifle competition, they only ask that it be fair. . . . In 1948 $1,704,000,000 was expended by railroads to build and maintain roadways and structures required for safe efficient railroad operation. Every cent of this was private capital. . . . In the same year, American taxpayers—including the railroad industry—put up $2,701,000,000 to build, maintain and operate public highways.[2]

Roy White clearly felt that the highway trucks and buses that were taking away freight and passenger traffic were receiving an unfair advantage from the government.

About the same time, railroads were complaining that the United States Post Office had set parcel post rates so low that it was hurting both freight traffic and the Railway Express Agency. Post Office figures indicated that parcel post operations ran a deficit of $50 million in fiscal 1947 and more than $85 million in 1948. In 1949 Postmaster General Jesse L. Donaldson told a congressional committee: "Personally, I feel that the Post Office has gone into the freight business."[3] In his budget message to Congress for the fiscal year 1950, President Harry S. Truman said: "The low rates for parcel post have led to substantial diversion of express traffic from common carriers. . . .I, therefore, strongly urge . . . revision of the postal rate structure."[4] The *Baltimore & Ohio Magazine* in 1949 ran a series of articles pointing out how the government was using taxes to help competitors of the railroads. In their September 1949 issue, they reported that: "in 1948, for carrying their 6 percent of the first class mail the airlines were paid $41,000,000. The same year for carrying 94 percent of the first class mail, the railroads was paid $26,000,000."[5]

During the twelve year presidency of Roy White, many improvements had been achieved in operating efficiency on the B&O. The average net tons carried on a B&O freight train had increased from 1,042 tons in 1941 to 1,501 tons by 1952. The gross tons of freight per hour of crew time had increased from 24,474 tons to 35,438 tons. Much of the increased efficiency had been achieved in the war years, but the push for new economy and better service continued after VE and VJ Days. In March 1947, the B&O introduced "sentinel service" in which shippers of carload freight were assured of a definite delivery date when the shipment was moving between thirty of the principal cities located on the B&O system. The improved service was made possible by the use of a new teletype communications system which gave better control of freight car movement and location data. Roy White said the letters "SX" were used to designate the new service since the letters were the Morse Telegraph code letters for dollars. It was hoped that sentinel service would make money both for the shipper and the railroad. Many shippers were soon applauding the new service and a traffic manager in Philadelphia called sentinel service the "best piece of transportation news since pre-war."[6]

Other improvements appeared in the postwar years. In the spring of 1950, White's railroad introduced a "time saver service" for LCL (less than carload lot) freight—a service which promised second day delivery for small shipments between New York City and midwestern cities such as Chicago, St. Louis, and Indianapolis. Safety and accident records also were improved in the late forties and early fifties. Roy White liked to remind his workers that when accidents happened, everybody was a loser. G.W. Elste, superintendent of the B&O safety department, sponsored an active safety campaign in the postwar years and the program soon paid dividends. In 1941 the B&O employee casualty ratio was 8.81 per million hours of work. By 1952 it had declined to 4.74 per million hours. Between 1942 and 1953, the B&O safety record was below the national average for all Class I railroads. For its outstanding safety performance, the B&O won an E.H. Harriman Safety Award in September 1953. Roy White also managed to achieve a decrease in loss and damage costs in the postwar years. Freight loss and damage payments of $5.7 million in 1947 had dropped to $3.5 million per year by 1950. The B&O had established an apprentice training program for 700 young employees studying to become machinists, blacksmiths, moulders, or patternmakers. Other B&O training programs had also been set up for freight and passenger sales and diesel maintenance.

Even though passenger traffic was declining on his line, President White continued to upgrade and improve passenger service in the postwar years. In the spring of 1947, "serva-seat service," providing inexpensive meals at the seats of coach passengers, was begun on several long-distance trains. Also that year, the B&O introduced a plan for securing passenger tickets by charging them to credit cards. About the same time, a new service permitted *Royal Blue* passengers to talk by phone from the moving train to almost any other phone in the nation. In the early summer of 1948, general passenger agent Dan Moorman opened a new ticket office in downtown Washington to facilitate passenger travel to and from the capital. A few months later, the new travel center was very busy as about 10,000 people moved via the B&O to the nation's capital for the inauguration of President Harry S. Truman in January 1949. Included in the crowd were 1,600 West Point cadets who were housed in seventy Pullman cars and fed by B&O dining car stewards in dining rooms set up in a large freight shed. A year later, ten deluxe sleepers were added to the B&O passenger car roster, the cars assigned to the *Capitol Limited* and the *Ambassador*.

Probably the greatest problems facing Roy White and top company officials in the late 1940s and early 1950s were the rather continuous wage demands and strike threats made by railroad labor. Serious strike problems faced the B&O and all American railways in 1946, in 1948, and again in 1950. New demands for higher wages and work rule changes, first made by labor in June 1945, had finally been solved by arbitration, but the engineers and trainmen were not satisfied and threatened nationwide strikes in the spring of 1946. Finally, an angry Harry Truman ordered seizure of the railroads by the government and, in a nationwide radio address, accused Alvanley Johnston, grand chief of the 78,000 engineers, and Alexander Fell Whitney, president of the 211,000 trainmen, of "obstinate arrogance." The aroused American president said: "This is no contest between labor and management. This is a contest between a small group of men and their government."[7] The 2,000 telegrams received at the White House the next morning supported the tough talk by a ratio of 30 to 1.

The same sort of rail labor crisis occurred in mid-1948 and again in 1950. Strikes, or the threat of one, won pay boosts, cost of living allowances, and the forty-hour work week. The demand of firemen for an extra fireman in each diesel unit was refused and that decision was confirmed. Late in the summer of 1950, the editors of *Time* outlined the successful strategy of railroad labor: "It was about ten years since the respectable bosses of the railroad brotherhoods made the big discovery: if they acted like John L. Lewis and those fellows, if they just sat stubbornly through wage negotiations and thumbed their noses at mediators and fact-finding boards, a New Deal Government would give them everything they wanted."[8]

Whenever President Truman had the army take over the railroads to end a strike threat in the early postwar years, Roy White put on his United States Army uniform and again became Colonel White. Placed in charge of the railroads of the Allegheny region, he was in nominal control not only of his own B&O, but also of twenty-two other major roads in the East. White was one of seven railroad presidents, all given the rank of colonel, who were in charge of rail operations across the country under the legal direction of the War Department.

Much of the increase in railroad pay at midcentury was a natural consequence of the inflation and increased cost of living in

TABLE 21. Average Yearly Compensation for B&O and United States Rail Workers 1945–53

Year	B&O	United States
1945	$2,781	$2,721
1946	3,200	3,068
1947	3,428	3,219
1948	3,718	3,595
1949	3,882	3,707
1950	3,983	3,765
1951	4,254	4,133
1952	4,480	4,343
1953	4,578	4,415

the postwar years. Between 1945 and 1953, the cost of living in America increased by 48.6 percent. The wage increase for American railroad workers in the years 1945 to 1953 amounted to 62.3 percent, somewhat higher than the inflation figure.

In 1953, the 54,067 employees of the road, like all the railroad workers in the nation, were grouped under five major classifications: (1) executives; (2) professional and clerical; (3) maintenance of way and structures; (4) maintenance of equipment and stores; and (5) transportation. Lowest paid of the five groups were the maintenance of way workers (roadmasters, bridge builders, section men, and signal men) who numbered 9,948 workers (18.4 percent of the total B&O work force) and averaged an annual pay of $3,503. In this group, section workers often made no more than $3,000 per year. Also below the company average were the 16,149 shopmen, blacksmiths, machinists, and electrical workers in the maintenance of equipment group (29.9 percent) whose average annual pay was $4,002. The 8,666 professional and clerical workers (16 percent) had an average pay of $4,344 in 1953. The 18,681 dispatchers, station agents, telegraphers, yardmen, engineers, conductors, firemen, and trainmen who made up the transportation group (34.5 percent) had an average yearly pay of $4,898, but conductors or engineers with good runs might make as much as $8,000 per year. The 623 B&O executives, many of whom worked in the headquarters building in downtown Baltimore, made up just over 1 percent of the total work force and in 1953 had average pay of $9,798. The median family income in the United States in 1953 was $4,233.

TABLE 22. Baltimore and Ohio System Traffic
and Financial Status 1941–53

Year	Miles of Road	Total Revenue	Net Revenue	Expenses to Earnings (%)	Average Passenger Fare (per mile) (¢)	Average Freight Rate (per ton-mile) (¢)	Dividend on Common Stock (%)
1941	6,284	$227,503,022	$ 66,584,604	72	1.85	.89	—
1942	6,247	306,254,193	102,012,995	67	2.10	.88	—
1943	6,149	358,142,152	107,557,799	70	2.11	.88	—
1944	6,144	387,193,036	100,124,282	74	1.86	.91	—
1945	6,132	361,373,218	64,711,672	82	1.94	.90	—
1946	6,153	304,984,718	29,772,426	90	2.13	.93	—
1947	6,194	360,294,194	59,917,683	83	2.13	1.04	—
1948	6,192	400,190,447	75,969,221	81	2.60	1.21	—
1949	6,202	356,708,017	63,350,441	82	2.88	1.29	—
1950	6,201	402,541,895	77,966,026	81	3.17	1.28	—
1951	6,188	451,277,841	84,949,720	81	3.27	1.30	—
1952	6,186	442,676,674	91,158,868	79	3.26	1.41	.75
1953	6,185	460,848,985	94,782,837	79	3.19	1.45	1

As just listed, the higher revenue figures in postwar years were due far more to inflation and higher freight rates and passenger fares than to any increase in tonnage figures or passenger travel.

TABLE 23. Decline in Baltimore and Ohio Passenger Travel and Revenue 1941–53

	Passenger Revenue (in millions of dollars)	Passenger-Miles (in millions of miles)
1941	$14	748
1942	27	1,273
1943	40	1,887
1944	51	2,758
1945	48	2,483
1946	36	1,694
1947	24	1,142
1948	25	947
1949	22	762
1950	22	704
1951	26	800
1952	24	744
1953	22	679

The total B&O passenger travel in 1953 was only about one-quarter of that in the late war years of 1944 and 1945. During the war years, B&O freight revenue was about five times as large as passenger revenue. By the early fifties, passenger revenue made up only about 5 percent of the total B&O operating revenue. Except for the war years, B&O passenger service, like that of all American lines, had been a deficit operation ever since 1930. In 1950 the combined passenger deficit of all Class I railroads was about 33 percent of the total net freight income. In this respect, the B&O was in worse shape than many other eastern lines. The passenger deficit of the Chesapeake and Ohio in 1950 was only 21 percent of its net freight income, while that of the Norfolk and Western was 22 percent, that of the Pennsylvania was 38 percent, and that of the New York Central was 45 percent. The comparable figure for the Baltimore and Ohio was 47.5 percent.

The mix of revenue commodities moving on B&O freight trains at midcentury had changed very little from earlier years—the products of mines still constituted about 60 percent of the total tonnage with a variety of manufactured products accounting for about 30 percent. Higher freight rates granted after World War II, plus a modest increase in freight volume during the Korean War

(1950–53), did push up the B&O net revenue and permitted a modest drop in the operating ratio.

By 1948 the annual net revenue had passed the $75 million mark, and the operating ratio had declined several points to 81 percent. In the *Annual Report* that year, President Roy White was able to report: "On November 15, 1948, a dividend of One Dollar ($1.00) per share was declared on the Company's Preferred stock. That dividend was the first one declared on either class of the Company's stock since 1931. . . . In announcing the dividend it was stated that future dividends will be dependent entirely upon the Company's earnings."[9] Company earnings did hold up, and in 1949 another dollar was paid to the holder of preferred stock. In the following year, 1950, this was raised to the full dividend of four dollars per year. Another full dividend was paid on preferred stock in 1951, and in 1952 not only was the four dollars preferred stock dividend paid, but common stock shareholders received a seventy-five cent per share dividend, their first dividend in more than twenty years. In 1953 the common stock dividend was raised to one dollar. The resumption of dividends had a modest effect on the price of B&O common stock. During World War II, B&O common ranged in price from 2-1/8 to a high of 28-7/8. In 1946 and 1947, the range was from 7-5/8 to 30-1/4. In 1949 the high quotation for the year was only 11-3/8, but this climbed to 29-3/8 in 1952 and 30-3/8 in 1953.

During the very years that the B&O was starting to resume the paying of dividends on its stock, officials in Washington started to investigate allegations of possible fraud in the relations between the Reconstruction Finance Corporation and the B&O during the consideration of the B&O debt readjustment plan in 1944. In the spring of 1951, W. Stuart Symington, the newly appointed administrator of RFC ordered a special investigation of the relationship between the B&O and the RFC during the readjustment of the B&O large debt to that corporation in 1944. Earlier, New Hampshire's Republican senator, Charles W. Tobey, had claimed that the B&O "bankruptcy" in 1944 had been "collusive and irregular."[10] Senator Tobey had also pointed out that Cassius M. Clay, who had been in charge of the railroad section of the RFC from 1932 to 1941, later moved on to the B&O where he was solicitor general from 1941 to 1945. By early 1952, RFC officials were convinced that, while there may have been errors in judgment in the affair, no fraud, collusion, or illegality was involved. In any event, the B&O in 1954, during Howard Simpson's second year as president, paid off $40 million of the collateral trust bonds held by the RFC.

Only minor changes occurred in the B&O general balance sheet during the twelve year presidency of Roy White. The grand total of $1,265,000,000 of assets or liabilities in 1941 had increased to only $1,309,000,000 by 1953. The investment in road and equipment of $581 million in 1941 had increased to $949 million by 1953 because nearly all of the subsidiary companies of 1941 were fully brought into the B&O in the dozen years of White's presidency. During the twelve years, the common stock remained at a total of $256 million and the preferred stock at $60 million, while the total long-term debt declined from $677 million in 1941 to $587 million in 1953.

Roy White had excellent relations with his board of directors during the twelve years he was B&O president. Only nineteen different men served on the twelve-man board during 1941–53. When White succeeded Dan Willard in 1941, the directors came from only five cities: Baltimore (5), New York (3), Philadelphia (2), and one each from Chicago and Cincinnati. By 1953 the geographic spread in the board was greater: Baltimore (3), New York (2), and one each from Philadelphia, Chicago, Cincinnati, St. Louis, Toledo, Parkersburg, and Cleveland. Seven directors served all twelve years with White: Howard Bruce, a Baltimore banker; J. Hamilton Cheston, a Philadelphia lawyer-banker; Richard R. Deupree, president of the Procter and Gamble Company in Cincinnati; Robert Garrett, a Baltimore banker and grandson of John Work Garrett; Stewart McDonald, chairman of the board of Maryland Casualty in Baltimore; John C. Traphagen, New York banker and insurance executive; and Harold I. Young of New York and St. Louis, president of the American Zinc, Lead and Smelting Company. Robert Garrett had been a board member since 1913, Bruce since 1932, and Cheston and Traphagen since 1939.

Other long-time board members who joined the board in the mid-1940s included John D. Biggers, glass manufacturer from Toledo; James D. Cunningham, a Chicago manufacturer; Richard Harte, a hardware manufacturer from Parkersburg; and Arthur W. Steudel, president of the Sherwin-Williams Company in Cleveland. During most of the White presidency, the executive committee of the board consisted of five men: McDonald, chairman; Bruce; Cheston; Traphagen; and White. After the departure of general counsel John J. Cornwell from the board in 1945, President White had no fellow B&O officials serving on the board of directors.

Several events of importance occurred toward the end of White's presidency. The surprise attack on South Korea by communist North Korea late in June 1950 was answered by the air, sea, and land forces of the United States and the United Nations. The war, which was bitterly fought until an armistice line was established late in 1951, meant that American railroads again were needed to aid and support the defense mobilization of the nation. Increased traffic, some car shortages, and extra rail workers were the order of the day in the months of 1950–51. Early in 1951, Roy White summarized his view of the latest war effort by the B&O: "We have good equipment. We have good leadership. We have one of the finest groups of loyal, well trained employees in the country. With everybody cooperating we will get the big job done."[11]

Two happier events came in 1952 and 1953. On February 28, 1952, the post office issued a three-cent commemorative stamp marking the one hundred and twenty-fifth anniversary of the granting of the charter to the B&O Railroad by the Maryland legislature. The bright blue, three-cent stamp showed three stages of rail transportation: a horse-drawn rail car, the *Tom Thumb*, and a modern diesel locomotive. A year and a half later, the long history of the railroad was again recognized with the opening of the B&O Transportation Museum on July 2, 1953. The location of the new museum was the large (237-foot diameter) roundhouse and the adjoining Mount Clare Station located at Pratt and Poppleton Streets about one mile west of downtown Baltimore. Dozens of historic locomotives and cars, most of them original equipment, were placed in the roundhouse, while the Mount Clare Station was filled with models, rail artifacts and memorabilia with the first stone of the B&O given a position of prominence. The dedication of the museum was marked by the reenactment of the July 4, 1828, ceremony and was attended by President Roy White, Executive Vice President Howard Simpson, Gov. Theodore R. McKeldin of Maryland, Baltimore city officials, and other railroad dignitaries.

While the tenure of Roy White in the B&O president's chair was much shorter than that of Daniel Willard, his twelve years of leadership meant that his presidency was the third longest among the fifteen B&O top executives. White's twelve years and three months in that office were about six months longer than that of Louis McLane, president from 1836 to 1848. Roy White had his seventieth birthday early in August 1953, and unlike Willard, gave up his office at the normal age of retirement. At the board of directors meeting on August 19, 1953, Executive Vice President Howard E. Simpson was elected president to succeed the retiring Roy White, effective September 1, 1953. Roy White was elected to the board of directors and was also appointed chairman of the board, an office that had not existed since the death of Daniel Willard.

White's years of leadership had been years of considerable progress for the B&O. During the years 1941–53, the company's
funded debt had been greatly reduced, dividend payments had
been resumed, many improvements in service had been achieved,
and the transition to dieselization had been pushed vigorously. A
testimonial dinner for the retiring president and the new president
was held at the Lord Baltimore Hotel on October 26, 1953, and
attended by 900 associates and friends of Roy White and Howard
Simpson.

The fifty-seven-year-old Howard Simpson was born in
Jersey City, New Jersey, and at the age of fifteen, obtained his first
job as a clerk in the Central Railroad of New Jersey. After a variety
of positions, he joined the B&O in 1931, where most of his work
continued to be in the passenger and traffic departments. The jo-
vial and hard working Simpson was one of the nation's few top rail
executives to rise through the passenger department. Simpson's
ability as a salesman would be tested in the decade of the 1950s.

Chapter XVIII

• • • • • • • • • • • • • • •

The Baltimore
and Ohio Accepts
the Diesel

IN THE POSTWAR YEARS OF PRESIDENT ROY WHITE AND Howard Simpson, many rapid and important technical improvements were made on the Baltimore and Ohio. But by far, the greatest change was the virtual disappearance of the steam locomotive and the full acceptance of the diesel. During the sixteen years between VJ Day and Simpson's departure from the B&O presidency in 1961, the raw bleat of the diesel horn slowly replaced the sound of the steam locomotive whistle known to generations of Americans.

In the B&O locomotive roster of 1945, steam engines outnumbered diesel units by a ratio of nearly fifteen to one. By 1953 there were two dozen more diesels than steamers on the Baltimore and Ohio motive power roster. In the spring of 1958, Howard Simpson announced that his railroad was using diesel power for all operations. During 1959 and 1960, the last B&O steam locomotives were retired. The motive power roster as of December 31, 1960, consisted of 1129 diesel units and no steam locomotives.

Rudolph Diesel, a French-born German mechanical engineer, had invented the diesel locomotive in the 1890s. Diesel sold the American manufacturing rights in 1898 to Adolphus Busch, a rich St. Louis brewer. Busch was a pioneer in mechanical refrigeration, but he never applied the new engine to rail transportation. The first American efforts to use the diesel in self-propelled rail cars ended in failure. Finally, the General Electric Company solved the problem by linking the diesel engine with an electric generator which, in turn, ran a traction motor. The Central Railroad of New Jersey in 1925 purchased a sixty-ton, 300 horsepower diesel-electronic locomotive to be used in switching service at Manhattan Island. This first diesel, with its ability to develop maximum power at slow starting speeds, was very useful in yard service. A few weeks later the Baltimore and Ohio purchased the second diesel locomotive for use in the Twenty-sixth Street yards in New York City.

During the postwar years, the dieselization program of the Baltimore and Ohio did lag a bit behind the national average, but it was not a bad record for a system where as much as 44 percent of all freight tonnage was coal. The B&O did not acquire diesels as fast as the Chesapeake and Ohio, another big coal carrier, but its diesel program was well ahead of the Illinois Central, a third major coal road.

Diesel motive power available after World War II had numerous advantages and few liabilities compared to the steam locomotive. The new diesel electrics were not cheap, since the average unit carried a price tag of between $125,000 and $200,000. In the first postwar decade, the Amercian railroad industry spent about $3.3 billion for 21,000 diesels, or an average of about $157,000 per unit. Both in the original cost and in dollars per horse power, diesels cost much more than the steamers they were replacing. However, in low maintenance costs, long hours of service per day, and modest fuel consumption, diesels showed real economic advantages over the steam engine.

In the first postwar decade, when more than 20,000 new diesel units were being acquired, fewer than 400 new steam locomotives were built for domestic use. In 1952 the diesel roster of motive power across the nation exceeded steamers by a ratio of five to four. After 1953 not a single American railroad ordered a new steam locomotive, and by 1955 more than fifty railroads owned no steamers at all. Most of the remaining steam motive power was placed in storage, including the immense 7,000 horsepower "Big Boys" of Sherman Hill fame out on the Union Pacific. By 1962 the steam engine roster across the country was below one hundred, and it was soon easier to find a steam locomotive in a city park or in a museum than operating on an American railroad.

Diesel power had numerous advantages over the steam engine; the two greatest were the savings in fuel and water. When Ralph Budd's *Zephyr* made its nonstop, dawn-to-dusk trip from

Denver to the Chicago World's Fair late in May 1934, it traveled nearly three miles per gallon of fuel oil, and the total fuel cost of the 1015-mile trip was less than than fifteen dollars! The new postwar diesels were not quite capable of moving a ton of freight per mile on a spoonful of oil as some of the ardent diesel proponents had claimed. But a gallon of diesel fuel oil could produce about 200 ton-miles of freight service. At the same time, coal for locomotive tenders was going up in price—more than 60 percent between 1945 and 1950. Such increases made more and more rail executives look with interest at diesel power. Total fuel costs for motive power across the nation declined from 8 percent of the revenue dollar in 1948 when only one locomotive in five was a diesel, to less than 4 percent in 1967 when active steam engines in the industry dropped to less than two dozen. Compared to the thirsty steam engine, the diesel used hardly any water. By the late 1950s, when dieselization was nearly complete, the railways of the nation had been able to retire nearly $50 million of water-supply tanks and equipment used earlier for their steamers.

Diesels also offered additional advantages. Maintenance and shop repair costs were low. It was soon discovered that diesels normally required only one-quarter as many man hours of maintenance as steam engines since the extensive daily firebox and boiler servicing was not required. Diesels could be operated for thousands of miles without major servicing, and needed repairs could be quickly made since diesel replacement parts were standardized. While the typical steamer required an hour or more of "firing up," the diesel could achieve full power rather quickly from a cold engine. The high horsepower at low speeds permitted faster starts and improved schedules. The lower center of gravity of the diesel allowed faster speeds on curves, while the lack of reciprocating parts in the diesel unit cut down on track stresses created by a steamer. All of these assets permitted larger freight loads at faster speeds. Some railroad men claimed that diesel motive power could result in three freight cars doing the work of four cars behind a steam engine.

The leaders of the Baltimore and Ohio were soon equally enthusiastic about the worth of the diesel. When President Roy White told B&O workers in the early winter of 1950–51 that their railroad was ready to meet the emergency of the Korean crisis he wrote: "The backbone of our present strength is our greatly increased Diesel power. By April 1951 our expanded Diesel program is expected to be in full effect. . . . Diesel engines save money. They not only reduce maintenance of equipment expenses but have a marked effect in lowering fuel costs. . . . They are easier on our roadbed. . . . and reduce the cost of track maintenance."[1]

The reductions in fuel, water, and enginehouse expenses which accompanied the B&O dieselization program in the postwar years clearly supported the views of Roy White on the importance of diesel motive power. A comparison of 1945 when only one engine in fifteen was a diesel, with 1957 when the B&O was operating more than 1,100 diesels, reveals the savings that came with diesel power. Both years were years of good revenue for the road—1945 with a gross revenue of $361 million and on operating ratio of 82 percent, and 1957 with a gross revenue of $461 million and an operating ratio of 81 percent. In the twelve-year period, B&O total locomotive fuel costs dropped from $23.6 million to $21.2 million, and declined from 18 percent of all transportation costs in 1945 to 11 percent in 1957. The decline continued to only 8.5 percent in 1960. Total fuel costs per revenue dollar were 6.5 cents in 1945, 4.6 cents in 1957, and 3.6 cents in 1960.

Substantial savings were also made in water and enginehouse expense in the same years. The cost of water for B&O train locomotives declined from $954,000 in 1945 to $529,000 in 1957, and $147,000 in 1960, and represented .75 percent, .30 percent, and .10 percent of all transportation costs in the respective years. Enginehouse expenses for yard and train locomotives dropped from 5 percent of all transportation expense in 1945 to 3.7 percent in 1957.

During the same dozen years, the portion of total operating expenses going for maintenance of way and structures declined from 18 percent in 1945 to 14.2 percent in 1957. Some of these savings came from the dieselization program, but a large portion were clearly a result of the introduction of dozens of new mechanical spike pullers, power tampers, rail layers, and spike drivers purchased by the Baltimore and Ohio in the early 1950s. Of this new mechanized maintenance of way equipment, C. R. Riley, chief engineer of maintenance said: "These machines do everything but talk."[2]

The diesel locomotive, like the earlier electric locomotives, had the added advantage of being able to reverse its electric motors, using them as brakes. This braking effort was normally sufficient to reduce a train's speed within proper limits on a 2 percent descending grade. This dynamic braking effort was soon found to be very effective on the steep mountain grades in the West. When diesels began to be used on Baltimore and Ohio freight trains, B&O crewmen soon found dynamic braking quite helpful on the long Allegheny grades of Maryland, West Virginia, and Pennsylvania. Shop repair crews soon saw dramatic savings in the number of iron brake shoes which needed to be replaced each year.

The *Capitol Limited*, headed by diesel-electric locomotives, passes through the Potomac River valley enroute to Chicago. (*Courtesy, Baltimore and Ohio Railroad*)

The operating economy of the diesel was so great that soon diesels were replacing electric motive power as well as steam. In the early twentieth century, more that 6,000 miles of line had been electrified, and by the days of World War II, over 850 electric locomotives were in use across the nation. Being able to offer most of the advantages of electric motive power without the worry of maintaining electrified track, the new diesels began to replace many electric units. Electric locomotives numbered only 585 units in 1957, and were down to 321 in 1967. Quite early the Baltimore and Ohio shifted from electric to diesel power for its tunnel operations under downtown Baltimore. For a number of years, B&O officials had included nine electric locomotives in their motive power roster to the ICC. By 1952 the electric units had all been retired.

In 1945, the last year of World War II, the Baltimore and Ohio motive power roster consisted of 9 electric, 1968 steam, and 137 diesel locomotives. Some of the diesel units dated back to the depression thirties, but the great majority had been acquired during the years of World War II. About half of the 137 units were yard switchers, but more than 40 units were being used on long run passenger service and several units were being used on through freight service to Chicago and St. Louis. In his *Annual Report* of 1945, Roy White mentioned as one of the highlights of 1945 the high quality of the diesel freight service: "Three freight diesel locomotives operated daily, 1944 and 1945, between Cumberland, Md., and Washington, Ind., without missing a trip—averaging 138,000 miles per locomotive per annum."[3] In the same year and over the same territory, more than two dozen modernized MacArthur (2-8-2) steam engines averaged only 80,000 miles a year, a figure perhaps 50 percent higher than the annual mileage for most B&O steam freight engines.

With such a good performance record, it is a bit surprising that no additional diesels were purchased during 1946. Instead, President Roy White on the last page of his 1946 *Annual Report* wrote: "Satisfactory progress is being made in construction of coal-fired gas turbine locomotives being developed by the Locomotive Development Committee sponsored by the Baltimore and Ohio and several other railroads, coal companies, and Bituminous Coal Research, Inc."[4] Several important coal carrying lines, including the Norfolk and Western and the Illinois Central, along with the Baltimore and Ohio, had high hopes for their experimental coal-fired gas turbine engine. Their expectations for this new power were never realized, and, within a few years, all of the large coal carriers were increasingly shifting to diesel power.

When White succeeded Daniel Willard in 1941, there were only fifty-three diesel units on the railroad. By 1953, the year of White's retirement and the election of Howard Simpson, the B&O had 810 diesel units in its roster of motive power.

TABLE 24. Motive Power Roster of the Baltimore and Ohio 1945–60

	Diesel	Steam	Electric	Total
1945	137	1,968	9	2,114
1947	150	1,891	9	2,050
1949	338	1,644	9	1,991
1951	423	1,275	9	1,707
1953	810	787	—	1,597
1955	911	508	—	1,419
1957	1,106	233	—	1,339
1959	1,130	44	—	1,174
1960	1,129	—	—	1,129

Very early in the B&O diesel program, it became apparent that the new motive power was doing far more than its share of work. In 1949 the 338 diesel units were moving 19 percent of the freight, carrying 38 percent of the passengers, and doing 45 percent of the switching, while the steam engines, nearly five times as numerous, were taking care of 81 percent of the freight service, 62 percent of the passenger service, and 55 percent of the switching. In 1953, for the first time, the diesel fleet of 810 units outnumbered the 787 remaining steamers. The B&O diesel roster in 1953 consisted of 470 freight units, 81 passenger units, and 259 switchers. In that year, B&O diesel power was providing 74 percent of the freight service, 68 percent of the passenger service, and 64 percent of the switching. The Baltimore and Ohio was still lagging behind the nation at large where in the entire industry the diesel figures were 75 percent of the freight, 80 percent of the passenger, and 83 percent of the switching or yard service. National motive power figures for 1953 were 22,500 diesels and 11,800 steam locomotives.

The new president, Howard Simpson, continued the dieselization program which Roy White had pushed vigorously. During 1953, the year he was elected to the presidency, Howard Simpson and his general superintendent of motive power, Alexander K. Galloway, spent $25 million for new equipment, including the acquisition of 112 diesels. During the year 1955, the Baltimore and Ohio purchased 91 additional diesels and at the same time retired 146 aging steamers. In 1956 company officials added another 99 diesels while retiring 70 steam locomotives. In his *Annual Report* for that year, Simpson could point to record high revenues of more than $473 million as well as advances in the diesel program. Of the latter he wrote: "There are now in service 1,010 Diesel locomotive units—583 freight, 103 passenger, and 324 yard switchers. . . . At the end of 1956 Diesel power was handling 86% of the freight traffic, 99% of the passenger traffic, and 83% of yard switching."[5]

During 1957 more than $35 million was spent on new equipment, including ninety-seven new diesel units—sixty-nine freight and twenty-eight yard switching units. In the same twelve months, 204 aging steam engines were retired. With the retirement of more and more steamers, many Baltimore and Ohio towns were seeing their last steam operation. Lima, Ohio saw its last P-7 Pacific when engineer C. V. Veldy took #5319 out of town on October 10, 1956. The aging Pacific had originally been christened the *President Arthur*, as one of the twenty president-type engines built by Baldwin for Daniel Willard in 1927.

In 1957 Simpson's railroad had 233 steam locomotives and was one of the few railroads with that many steamers still in operation. *Railway Age* reported that twenty-six major American lines still had a total of 1,377 steam locomotives in service at the end of 1957. Nearly half of the remaining steamers still in service were of three types: 286 Mikados, 225 switchers (0-8-0) and 155 Mallets (2-8-8-2). The editors of *Railway Age* noted that the "Norfolk & Western, Illinois Central, Baltimore & Ohio, Nickel Plate, Union Pacific, and Duluth, Missabe & Iron Range . . . still move a considerable portion of tonnage with steam power."[6] The same issue of *Railway Age* noted the permanent retirement of the Norfolk and Western experimental locomotive, *Jawn Henry*. Maintenance costs of the huge 4,500-horsepower, coal-fired steam turbine electric had become prohibitive.

The economic recession of 1957–58 caused a major decline in rail traffic, and the Baltimore and Ohio revenue in 1958 of $392 million was 16 percent below that of the previous year. This fact hastened the complete dieselization of the Baltimore and Ohio as Howard Simpson noted in his 1958 *Annual Report*: "Since March 1, 1958, because of lower traffic volume, the Baltimore & Ohio has been completely dieselized, which substantially reduced locomotive repair cost."[7] In 1957 the B&O spent $5,096,000 on repairs of the steam locomotives, a figure which declined to only $304,000 in 1958. The B&O roster of steam engines dropped to ninety-seven in 1958 and only forty-four in 1959.

The increased usage of diesels on the railroad made both the management and the engine crews happy. Operating officials in West Virginia were pleased with the savings in equipment and time that resulted when they discovered the five four-unit diesels could replace twenty-eight Mallets as "helper" engines for heavy freights on the rugged Cranberry grade east of Rowlesburg and the Cheat River grade west of town. Steam helpers averaged two hours and seven minutes up the 2.2 percent Cranberry grade to Terra Alta, and about three hours and twenty minutes for the round trip. The new diesel "helpers" could climb the same grade in about one hour and make the round trip in one hour and fifty minutes. During the years of transition, B&O engineers had to be ready to operate a diesel one day and a steamer the next. As they shifted from steam to diesel power, many of the engineers said: "It's just like moving from a Ford to a Cadillac."[8]

In the early use of the diesels, two or more units were often used together as a single locomotive with all the controls in the leading unit. Baltimore and Ohio top officials, like rail managers across the nation, were concerned about the reaction of the brotherhoods toward a multi-unit engine—was it one locomotive or two or three? B&O officials gave such multiple-unit locomotives a single number, regardless of the number of units linked together. The locomotive engineers accepted the arrangement, but insisted on a higher daily pay scale for each added diesel unit.

The rate of pay might increase for engineers, but the number employed declined greatly as steamers gave way to diesels. Across the nation in 1951, steamers still outnumbered diesels by a ratio of five to four, and the number of locomotives in service stood at 40,036. That year the number of employed locomotive engineers was 58,898. By 1962 the number of locomotives had dropped to 28,098, including only 54 steam engines, and the roster of engineers had declined to 38,225. The same general decrease in the number of locomotive engineers also occurred on the Baltimore and Ohio.

As Simpson's line purchased more and more diesels during the 1950s, some steam repair shops had to be modernized to take care of the new motive power. During 1951 the large steam locomotive repair shop at Glenwood, Pennsylvania, not far from Pittsburgh, was converted into a modern repair facility for diesels. By using the older building, William C. Baker, vice president for operation and maintenance, estimated a savings of perhaps $3 million. The Glenwood shops employed up to 300 men and had the capacity to make heavy annual repairs to at least 200 diesels. Diesel repair facilities were also installed at a dozen other locations from Philadelphia to East St. Louis. By the end of the decade, the bulk of heavy diesel repair was being concentrated at the Glenwood shops and at a new modernized repair facility at Cumberland,

Maryland. By the summer of 1961, the Cumberland shop was operating as assembly line method and employing more than 400 men on a twenty-four hour, seven-day-a-week operation. Diesels requiring only light repairs could be returned to service within sixteen hours.

In its annual report to the Interstate Commerce Commission for 1960, the Baltimore and Ohio railroad included a motive power roster consisting of 1,129 diesel units and *no* steam locomotives. For the first time in nearly 130 years, not a single steam engine was operating on the tracks of the B&O. About two-thirds of the diesel units in 1960 had been obtained from the Electro-Motive Division of General Motors, while the Baldwin-Lima-Hamilton Corporation and Alco Products had each supplied about 15 percent of the total fleet. The 1,129 diesel units were of four types: 453 freight units (1,350 to 1,600 horsepower); 63 passenger units (2,000 to 2,250 horsepower); 349 switchers (600 to 1,200 horsepower); and 264 GP multi-purpose road switchers (1,500 to 1,750 horsepower).

In the decade and a half since World War II, the motive power roster of the Baltimore and Ohio declined from 2,114 engines in 1945 to only 1,129 in 1960. However, the smaller number of diesel units in 1960 produced a somewhat greater total tractive effort than that of the larger locomotive roster of 1945. The shift to all diesel motive power had brought tremendous increases in operating efficiency and corresponding reductions in fuel, repair and maintenance costs. The savings that had accompanied the dieselization program on the Baltimore and Ohio had helped the road face many of the economic problems of the postwar years.

Chapter XIX

. . . .

The Simpson Era: Years of a Declining Traffic

WHEN HOWARD E. SIMPSON COMPLETED HIS *ANNUAL Report* for 1953, the year in which he had succeeded Roy White as president, he was quite optimistic concerning the future of the Baltimore and Ohio. The more than $460 million of operating revenues for the year were so large that he started out his annual report with the words: "The year 1953 was one of the best in the history of your company."[1] In the fall of 1953, he had been elected a member of the board of directors and also the executive committee of the Association of American Railroads. Late in October of the same year, some 900 friends and associates had honored both Col. Roy White and the new B&O president at a testimonial dinner at the Lord Baltimore Hotel in Baltimore.

However the record of the eight years of his presidency, 1953–61, did not really live up to Simpson's early optimism. Only the two years 1956 and 1957 saw operating revenues exceed the year 1953, and by 1961, B&O revenues had declined to $351 million, almost 25 percent below the figures for 1953. There was no comparable decline in operating expenses, and the road's operating ratio stayed above 80 percent after 1953, hitting 86 percent by 1961. The net income, after fixed charges, which had been $28 million in 1953, exceeded that figure only in 1956, declined to $15

Howard E. Simpson, president, 1953–61. *(Courtesy, Baltimore and Ohio Railroad)*

million by 1959, and showed a large deficit in 1961. Payroll costs during the Simpson years continued to climb, increasing about 45 percent (per employee) between 1953 and 1960. In the decade of the fifties, most American railroads were facing the same problems that were troubling Howard Simpson. Between 1950 and 1960, the share of all intercity freight moving by rail dropped from 56.2 percent to 43.7 percent. It was not surprising that by 1960, Howard Simpson was seriously considering a railroad merger as a solution to his road's growing economic problems.

During the eight years of the Simpson presidency, the Baltimore and Ohio also experienced a decline both in mileage and in number of employees. In the postwar years from 1945 to 1953, the average mileage operated by the B&O was quite stable, remaining very close to 6,180 miles throughout the period. However, during the Simpson years, the operated mileage of the B&O declined from 6,185 miles in 1953 to only 5,902 miles in 1961. One of the major losses of mileage came in 1955 when the B&O sold to the Wellsville, Addison and Galeton Railroad, about ninety-eight miles of "detached" mileage south of Wellsville and Addison, New York and extending southward to Burrows, Pennsylvania. This mileage had become isolated from the remainder of the system in a disastrous flood of 1942. The reconstruction of the washed-out line could not be economically justified, and abandonment of the destroyed mileage had been authorized by the Interstate Commerce Commission.

In these same years, there was an even more marked decline in the number of workers employed on the B&O. The total roster of employees had decreased from 54,067 in 1953 to 45,481 in 1957 and only 29,892 in 1961, the year that Simpson gave up the

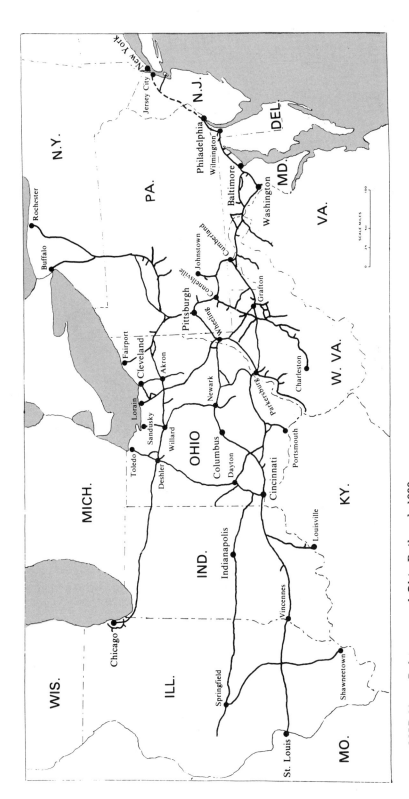

MAP 11   Baltimore and Ohio Railroad, 1962.

In the years since 1941, the B&O system had declined more   Pennsylvania, and Virginia.
than 400 miles. Major losses in mileage were in New York,

presidency. This decline of 81 percent in eight years was even greater for the B&O than the national decrease in rail employment, which dropped 68 percent in the same period (1,206,000 workers in 1953, and 717,000 in 1961). The decline in employment was due to a modest decline in traffic, but even more to a major increase in operating efficiency. Back in 1940, the annual freight service per B&O employee was 428,000 ton miles. By 1953 the amount of annual freight service per employee had climbed to 519,000 ton-miles, and by 1961 the figure had risen to 773,000 ton-miles. The increased operating efficiency gained in the 1950s was helped significantly by the dieselization program and also by the greatly increased use of new machines in the maintenance of way department.

Even though Howard Simpson was facing problems in the fifties, he continued to obtain excellent media and public relations coverage for his railroad. In April 1954, Dave Garroway gave the television audience across the nation a view of the varied passenger and freight activity of the B&O Locust Terminal on the NBC TV show "Today." The Baltimore harbor was unusually busy that spring because a waterfront strike had nearly closed the port of New York City. In early September 1959, Dave Garroway and his "Today" show again featured the B&O when the story was told of how modern track machines had nearly replaced the legendary railroad "gandy dancer." Late in February 1955, Steve Allen in his NBC "Tonight" show gave an estimated TV audience of five million viewers a detailed tour of the B&O Museum in Baltimore. On Abraham Lincoln's birthday in 1956, still another TV program, "Wide, Wide World," gave a dramatic portrayal of Lincoln's funeral train as it arrived at the B&O Camden Station in Baltimore back in 1865.

During 1956 several pieces of historic equipment from the B&O Museum appeared in two Hollywood movies. MGM's movie *The Swan*, which starred Grace Kelly, used a late-nineteenth-century locomotive, the *A.J. Cromwell*, and a *Royal Blue* coach in a railroad sequence. About the same time, two older B&O engines, the *Lafayette* and the *William Mason*, were used extensively in a Walt Disney movie, *The Great Locomotive Chase*, a Civil War film starring Fess Parker and Jeff Hunter. The following year, the B&O received much attention from the media when a B&O special twelve-car train carried Queen Elizabeth II and her royal party from Washington, D.C. to Staten Island in New York City. Howard Simpson's business car was used by the queen and Prince Philip for their journey over the B&O line. Throughout the 1950s, the B&O had wished all its friends and patrons a Merry Christmas by decorating and lighting the "Tree-by-the-Tracks." This famous Christmas tree was a fifty-foot, century-old, red-berried holly tree which stood beside the road's right-of-way at Jackson, Maryland, just two miles north of the Susquehanna River bridge.

In the 1950s, Howard Simpson experienced the same kind of nagging labor problems that had faced Roy White in the early postwar years. During 1953 there was considerable activity among the several railroad unions, each striving to gain a "better" wage agreement in order to gain new members. The fifteen non-operating unions were strongly pushing for additional "fringe" benefits such as increased vacations, health and accident insurance, and double pay for working on holidays. The railroad labor front was fairly quiet during 1954. In the following year, the several unions representing conductors, trainmen, and firemen all were making fresh wage demands, while the non-operating unions finally achieved a substantial health and welfare insurance plan. During 1956 all the operating and non-operating unions asked for additional pay increases. In that year, the average annual pay for railroad workers in the nation for the first time exceeded $5,000. In 1956 a three-year wage agreement was made, extending from November 1, 1956 until November 1, 1959, and providing for annual wage increases as well as extensive fringe benefits. By 1957 these fringe benefits (vacations, holidays, insurance, etc.) were amounting to about $500 a year per employee beyond the straight time hourly wage rate.

TABLE 25. B&O Employee Payroll Costs 1953–60	
1953	$4,578
1954	4,726
1955	4,998
1956	5,422
1957	5,686
1958	6,199
1959	6,574
1960	6,642

The wage increase of about 45 percent in the seven years was in marked contrast to the cost of living which had climbed only about 12 percent in the same period. Quite clearly, the railroad unions were still successfully following a tough-minded wage strategy which permitted their wage scales to keep well ahead of the modest inflation typical of the fifties.

Howard Simpson and his fellow railroad presidents were to be more successful in their efforts to eliminate firemen from freight diesel locomotives. By 1959 there were 28,000 diesel units and only 750 steam engines in the nation. Railroad presidents across the nation were calling the fireman's shovel an "expensive antique" since the diesel fireman had no coal to shovel and no boiler to tend.

On the diesel, the fuel oil was fed automatically to the engine, but thousands of firemen were still working on diesels. Top rail officials across the nation pointed out that recently in Canada, a royal commission had decided that diesel firemen were no longer needed for freight service. Many countries in Europe had made the change, even taking firemen out of some passenger trains. When officials of the firemen's union brought up the safety issue, railroad managers quickly pointed out the "extra pair of eyes" in the engine, since the head-end brakeman shared the locomotive cab with the engineer.

Early in 1959, the Association of American Railroads, led by its top executive Daniel P. Loomis, started a campaign for the reduction of featherbedding by railroad labor, a redefinition of the "work day" for train crews, and the orderly removal of all firemen in freight and yard diesels. Early in November 1959, railroad management spelled out the details of their attitude concerning the diesel fireman issue: "Management would determine when a fireman should be used on a diesel and other nonsteam locomotives in freight and yard service. Firemen on passenger trains would not be affected."[2] The reaction of the operating brotherhoods was naturally immediate and far from mild. H. E. Gilbert, president of the Brotherhood of Locomotive Firemen and Enginemen, called the proposal "inhuman and unrealistic."[3]

Several different commissions to arbitrate the diesel fireman issue were appointed between 1959 and 1963 by Dwight D. Eisenhower and John F. Kennedy. The presidential commissions included such well-known figures as Samuel I. Roseman, New York jurist and former advisor to Presidents Franklin Roosevelt and Harry Truman; Clark Kerr, president of the University of California; and James P. Mitchell, former secretary of labor. Each time the arbitration boards agreed with the railroad managers and decided for the eventual elimination of yard and freight engine firemen. And each time Gilbert's union refused to accept the finding of the commission. The threat of a railroad strike brought congressional action in August 1963, and one more arbitration board was set up by President Kennedy. This board in Arbitration Award No. 282 again agreed with the railroad managers, and on April 27, 1964, the United States Supreme Court confirmed the right of the railroads to eventually eliminate most firemen from freight and yard diesels.

Even with the high cost of labor and the loss of much passenger revenue and some freight traffic, the B&O spent well over $200 million for property improvements during the eight years between 1953 and 1960. The yearly expenditures varied from a low of $8 million in 1959 and $12 million in 1960, when operating revenues were declining, to the higher amounts of $37 million in 1956 and $53 million in 1957, when operating revenues were much higher. During the mid and late fifties, about two-thirds of the money available each year was spent on new equipment with the remainder going for road improvement and betterment. Hundreds of new expensive diesel units were being acquired in these years, and thus the lion's share of the equipment money went for new motive power. With passenger traffic in decline, relatively little money was spent on passenger cars in the Simpson years. However, much new freight equipment was purchased: 1,400 cars in 1953; 2,700 in 1956; 4,000 in 1957; and 2,600 in 1958. Many additional older freight cars were rebuilt and modernized.

During the Simpson era, a great variety of improvements in road, track, terminal, and repair facilities were made. A number of new and improved interlocking plants were installed during the middle and late 1950s. In the same years, a system of centralized traffic control was put in operation on several segments of track with very heavy freight and passenger traffic. Nearly every year, dozens of additional automatic protective devices at grade crossings were installed, many of which resulted in payroll savings since manual protection could be eliminated. As more and more diesels were acquired, additional maintenance facilities for the new motive power were added throughout the system. In 1955 new diesel fuel oil storage facilities were completed at Cumberland, Maryland; Keyser, West Virginia; East Dayton, Ohio; and Indianapolis, Indiana. By 1956 work was underway on a new freight terminal at Twenty-third Street, New York City.

In 1957 the new passenger station at Pittsburgh, made necessary by the new Penn-Lincoln Parkway, was completed. Much of the financing of the new station was provided from funds received from the state of Pennsylvania for B&O property purchased for the highway improvement. Many old bridges were improved and other new ones built during Simpson's eight years. One of the largest of the bridges built in the period was the Staten Island Arthur Kill Bridge, the world's longest railroad vertical lift bridge which was opened on August 25, 1959. The new structure, which took three years to construct, had a 558-foot central span which could be raised to a maximum height of 135 feet. Since the new bridge aided navigation on the Arthur Kill, the United States government had assumed more than 90 percent of the $11 million cost of the project.

Portions of the improvement budgets were spent on entirely new technology. Early in 1955, two TV cameras were installed in the Potomac yard in Washington, D.C., for the instant identification and checking of freight car numbers, making the B&O one of the first railroads to employ this technique. One rail official pointed out that TV needed no coffee breaks, asked for no overtime pay, and never complained about the weather. Far more expensive was the huge Datamatic Electronic Computer which was installed on the tenth floor of the B&O general office building in Baltimore late in 1958. The new computer was expensive, but officials were certain it would soon be saving both time and money. Howard Simpson said of the new computer:

> Installation of the large electronic computer in the General offices . . . required several years of exhaustive research and preparation. Payroll, freight revenue accounting and car accounting are being performed on this new equipment in less time than by conventional methods formerly employed. In addition, the computer had been integrated with the tape-to-card data processing system in sixty-five freight yards.[4]

One of the most important innovations introduced in the 1950s was the new massive and modern machines available for track maintenance. These new rail layers, ballast regulators, spike pullers, power tampers, and spike drivers made it easier for section men to use brain instead of brawn in maintaining the track and roadway. The B&O purchased hundreds of the new track and road-bed machines during the 1950s. C. R. Riley, the chief engineer of maintenance, was enthusiastic about the new equipment and claimed they kept the B&O right-of-way in top-flight condition. As a result of the combination of skilled hands and responsive equipment, the B&O section crews in 1955 were able to top all previous records in the amount of new and repaired rail laid and ties installed. During 1957 the new machines were used in 93 percent of the surfacing work of 2,145 miles of tracks surfaced during the year. The machinery helped reduce labor costs on the B&O. The maintenance of way labor force on the B&O declined from 14,290 workers in 1945 to only 4,154 in 1961. In the sixteen years, such employees had dropped from 22 percent of the total B&O labor force to only 14 percent.

The hundreds of new diesels and all the new technology could not seem to slow the continued decline in passenger traffic and revenue. In the first postwar years during the presidency of Roy White, the passenger traffic had declined from $48 million and 2,483,000,000 passenger miles in 1945 to $21 million and 679,000,000 passenger miles in 1953. The decline in revenue had been less steep than that of total travel since average passenger fares had climbed from 1.9 cents per mile to 3.2 cents per mile during the eight years. The drop in revenue and travel continued under Howard Simpson, declining to $14 million and 483,000,000 passenger miles in 1961.

In the first year of his presidency, Howard Simpson had told his stockholders about the status of passenger travel on the B&O: "The continuing improvement in public roads and increase in number of automobiles and buses make highway motor transport our greatest competitor for passenger traffic. An increasing number of passengers traveling long distances move by airplane."[5] The official national figures for commercial intercity travel in the postwar years clearly supported the statement by President Simpson.

TABLE 26. Commercial Travel and Percentage of Total Passenger Miles 1945–61

Year	Railroads (in millions)	Percent	Buses (in millions)	Percent	Air Carriers (in millions)	Percent
1945	91,826	72.9	27,027	21.4	3,362	2.7
1950	31,790	45.3	26,436	37.7	10,072	14.3
1955	28,548	36.3	25,519	32.4	22,741	28.9
1957	25,900	31.4	25,300	30.7	28,900	35.1
1961	20,308	26.3	19,703	25.6	34,642	44.9

Bus travel had continued to be slightly less popular than travel by railroad during the 1950s, but by 1957 air travel had moved out in front as far as commercial travel was concerned. In 1960 it was estimated that private automobile travel was roughly nine times that of the combined total of rail, bus, and air travel.

Even though he was well aware of the downward trend of rail travel in the early postwar years, Howard Simpson seemed reluctant to give up on passenger service. Simpson had been a specialist in passenger traffic for many years, and he was eager to make an extra effort to keep and maintain as many passenger trains as possible. In the summer of 1954, eleven new duplex roomette-bedroom sleepers, built by Budd, were added to three B&O trains: the *Capital Limited*, the *National Limited* and the *Diplomat*. Between 1956 and 1958, several new slumbercoaches, providing sleeping accommodations at coach fare plus a small space change, were added to B&O trains between Chicago and Baltimore. Simpson was also happy when three special B&O rail diesel cars (RDC) made the 768-mile Washington to Chicago run in a record time of 12-1/2 hours during the Memorial Day weekend in 1955. But Simpson admitted that some passenger trains must be discontinued where a train's revenue was well below the out-of-pocket cost. During 1953 nine B&O passenger trains were discontinued. Each year saw additional passenger service cut, and between 1949 and

1957, more than one hundred B&O passenger trains were taken out of service.

Baltimore and Ohio passenger traffic officials in 1954 protested when they learned that the Post Office Department was thinking of diverting first class mail from the railways of the nation to air carriers. In fact, mail revenue on B&O passenger trains actually increased a bit during the eight Simpson years, climbing from $9,168,000 in 1953 to $9,330,000 in 1958 and $10,288,000 in 1961. During the 1960s, all American railroads suffered a marked decline in mail revenue. Baltimore and Ohio express revenue also declined rather sharply, dropping from $4,123,000 in 1953 to $1,752,000 in 1958 and $1,650,000 in 1961.

The continuing decline in rail travel plus the increased operating costs, especially the higher wages paid train crews, meant that all American railroads were facing higher and higher passenger service deficits in the decade of the 1950s. By 1957 the B&O was estimating that its annual losses or deficits caused by its passenger service had risen to more than $33 million. In mid-November 1957, the B&O filed petitions with regulatory bodies in Maryland, Delaware, and Pennsylvania seeking to discontinue the six remaining round trip passenger trains each day between Baltimore and New York City. Such permission was granted the following spring, and all the New York to Baltimore service ended on April 29, 1958. The B&O accountants worked under Walter L. Price, vice president of finance and accounting, figured the savings from the discontinuance amounted to about $5 million a year. The figures indicated that the B&O had been losing $2.40 for every dollar taken in fares for the passenger service between Baltimore and New York.

The drop in passenger service on the B&O during the Simpson presidency is most graphically seen in comparing a 1955 B&O passenger timetable with one for 1961. In the six years, the size of the timetable had dropped from forty-four to sixteen pages, and the number of individual schedule tables had declined from thirty-one to ten. In 1945 B&O passenger trains had been operating on 4,788 miles of the entire 6,097 mile system. By 1953 passenger trains were running on only 3,521 miles of the B&O system, and in 1961 passenger trains were running on only 2,270 miles of B&O track.

Of course, the money lost on passenger traffic had to be made up on the larger more profitable freight operations. But even here, the overall picture was not too bright. American business was generally profitable during the Eisenhower 1950s, and the nation's industrial output rose by about 40 percent during the decade. But the railroads did not share in the expansion. Between 1950 and 1960, the intercity freight moving by rail declined from 597 billion ton-miles to 579 billion ton-miles. The railroad's share of all intercity freight traffic dropped in the decade from 56 percent in 1950 to 44 percent in 1960 with trucks, river barges, and pipelines all making substantial gains. Annual freight revenue ton-mileage on the B&O in each of the three years—1958, 1959, and 1960—was about 10 percent below the figure for 1950.

The problem was further compounded by the fact that rail expenses were climbing faster than income. The B&O average freight rates per ton-mile changed very little in the decade while the consumer price index climbed about 23 percent. In the winter of 1960–61, Simpson's cost accountants pointed out that between 1950 and 1960 the cost of a ton of steel rail had climbed from $72 to $115 per ton, typewriters from $137.50 to $225, freight car couplers from $67.50 to $87.50, crossties from $1.93 to $2.75, and a seventy-ton hopper car from $6,100 to $10,200. The cost of wages on the B&O had climed 66 percent in the decade. Clearly, the B&O was saved from financial disaster through the reduction of her work force in the decade and by the increasing operating efficiency of dieselization, longer trains, and new track maintenance machinery.

But there were some bright spots in the freight picture during the decade. Industrial development was pushed throughout the 1950s. New industries along the B&O lines were started every year. A $50 million petro-chemical plant was started in 1953 and 180 new plants were established in 1954, 179 in 1956, and 166 in 1960. A number of new coal mines were opened along the B&O routes, and by 1958 the B&O was carrying 11 percent of the national production of bituminous coal. However, this good news was dampened by the fact that soft coal production across the country was declining by about 20 percent during the decade. In 1957 the B&O celebrated ten years of its sentinel service. The supervision of the carload freight service, with its twin features of siding-to-siding dependability plus automatic records, was supervised in the office of A. W. Conley, general superintendent of transportation. In December 1958, Howard Simpson and Gov. Theodore R. McKeldin of Maryland opened the new $5.5 million Locust Point Fruit Terminal in Baltimore harbor. A joint venture with the United Fruit Company, the new facility was called "the world's largest and most modern banana discharging terminal."[6]

A new door-to-door trailer on flat car (TOFC) service was started on the Baltimore and Ohio in July 1954. To place the new service in operation, the B&O leased 150 new twenty-four-foot trailers and assigned thirty-five flat cars to the new venture. By the spring of 1955, TOFC was expanded to forty-two cities on the B&O system. In 1957 George E. Dove was named the manager of the new department of railroad trailer service. By 1960 the service, now generally referred to as "piggyback" service, was expanded to include containers, or demountable trailer bodies. Specially built cranes were used to transfer either the highway trailers or the containers to and from the flat cars. By 1959 the B&O had assigned 297 trailers and 225 flat cars to piggyback service. Piggyback freight tonnage had grown from 36,000 tons in 1955 to 107,000 tons in 1958 and 536,000 tons in 1961. The annual revenue from the new service had increased from $.5 million in 1955 to $3 million in 1958 and $6.6 million in 1961. The growth had been very rapid, but piggyback revenue in 1961 still amounted to only 2 percent of the total freight revenue for the year.

Even with dieselization and innovations in freight service, the B&O by the end of the decade, was in serious financial trouble. In a message to all B&O men and women, President Simpson early in 1959 wrote: "During my five-year tenure as president, one of my guiding principles has been to keep you as well informed of our program as possible. . .in good times and bad. . . .We have passed through lean periods in the past, but in my opinion the situation in which we now find ourselves is one of the most serious we have ever faced."[7] Not quite two years later *Forbes*, in reviewing the conditions of American railroads in 1960 wrote: "Diesel savings and wartime profits pulled the railroads through the Fifties. . . . But the chronic disease—loss of traffic—remained largely untreated."[8] Later in the article, the *Forbes* editors had high praise for the aggressive management of such lines as the Norfolk and Western and the Chesapeake and Ohio, but rated the B&O in the bottom quarter of eighteen major lines for overall operating efficiency. *Forbes* also gave low ratings to the two nearby, longtime rivals of the B&O, the Pennsylvania and the New York Central.

Full support for the *Forbes* view of the B&O financial status is found in the traffic and revenue figures for the decade.

The mix of commodities moving on B&O freight trains in the Simpson years was much like that of earlier years, with the products of mines making up about 60 percent of the total tonnage. However, the share of the revenue coming from such traffic was less than for the tonnage. For example, in 1953 the coal and coke traffic on the B&O made up 44 percent of the total freight tonnage but only 27 percent of the total freight revenue. Obviously the freight rates for coal and other mine products were much less than the company wide average of 1.45 cents per ton-mile.

TABLE 27. Baltimore and Ohio System Traffic and Financial Status 1953–61

Year	Miles of Roads	Total Revenue	Net Revenue	Expenses to Earnings (%)	Average Passenger fare (per mile) (¢)	Average Freight Rate (per ton-mile) (¢)	Dividend on Common Stock (%)
1953	6,185	$460,848,986	$94,782,837	79.4	3.19	1.45	1
1954	6,182	378,088,687	66,586,097	82.4	3.09	1.39	1
1955	6,167	432,061,417	81,645,451	81.1	3.07	1.34	2
1956	6,019	465,484,696	90,343,770	80.6	3.13	1.34	2.5
1957	6,000	461,303,581	88,042,180	80.9	3.23	1.42	2.5
1958	5,937	382,540,431	73,692,970	80.7	3.15	1.44	1.5
1959	5,917	395,179,011	74,167,223	81.2	3.07	1.43	1.5
1960	5,909	389,402,595	69,178,360	82.2	2.98	1.37	1.5
1961	5,902	351,369,044	46,891,655	86.6	3.03	1.32	.6

During the Simpson years, the share of B&O revenue resulting from passenger service had further declined, dropping from $22 million in 1953 to $14 million in 1961. During the same eight years, the number of passengers on B&O trains dropped from 3,717,000 per year to 2,377,000 per year, and the annual total passenger-miles declined from 679,000,000 to 483,000,000.

With the modest increase in traffic in the middle 1950s, the annual dividend on the common stock was raised to 2 percent ($2.00) in 1955 and 2.5 percent ($2.50) in 1956 and 1957. As revenue declined in the following years, the dividend rate was cut to 1.5 percent ($1.50) in 1958, and to only 0.6 percent (60 cents) in 1961. Dividend rates of 1.5 percent to 2.5 percent were actually not much below the average rate of return for all Eastern railroads during the decade. The rate of return for Eastern railways for the ten years 1951 through 1960 saw four years average below 3 percent and in only three years barely exceeded 4 percent. With such low dividends for B&O common stock, the shares were not much sought after in the stock market. In only four years of the Simpson presidency did the B&O common sell for more than $50 per share: 1955, 1956, 1957, and 1959.

The decline in revenue in 1960 was not too great, but after taxes, rents, fixed charges, and dividends had all been deducted from the net revenue, there remained only $2,611,000 of net income for the year. The decrease of more than $38 million in revenue in 1961 created a real financial crisis. After taxes, rents and fixed charges were paid for the year the net income showed red ink to the extent of $31 million, a deficit much larger than any faced by the railroad in the Depression.

The B&O board of directors which faced the financial crisis during the Simpson presidency was a remarkably stable group.

Jervis Langdon, Jr., president, 1961–64.
(Courtesy, Baltimore and Ohio Railroad)

Between 1953 and 1961, only sixteen different men served on the twelve-man board, many of whom had also served under Roy White. During most of the eight years, the executive committee of the board consisted of Howard Bruce (chairman), J. Hamilton Cheston, Howard Simpson, John C. Traphagen, and Roy B. White. During the eight years of the Simpson era, there was a modest decline in the company's general balance sheet, since the assets/liabilities total declined from $1,309 million in 1953 to $1,153 million in 1961. A portion of this decrease resulted from the major debt refunding operation accomplished in 1955 by Howard Simpson and his board. Of the refunding project, President Simpson wrote: "The greatest achievement of the year [1955] was the refinancing of roundly $350,000,000 of Company debt. It was the largest refunding operation ever undertaken by an American railroad."[9] As a result of the refunding operation, the funded debt of the B&O declined from $532 million in 1954 to $491 million in 1956 and annual interest paid dropped from $23 million to $19 million in the same years. In 1956 Howard Simpson and the board appointed Jervis Langdon, Jr., as general counsel for the B&O. The fifty-one year old Langdon, who had earlier served on the legal staffs of the New York Central and the Chesapeake and Ohio, still believed that railroads had a bright future. In 1958 Langdon was elevated to vice president and general counsel.

By the late 1950s, Howard Simpson and his board became well aware of a new rail merger movement starting to appear. In 1955 the Louisville and Nashville asked the ICC to approve the merger of the 1,043-mile Nashville, Chattanooga and St. Louis into the L&N. In 1957, the year the ICC approved the L&N merger request, there were 116 Class I railroads (above $3 million in annual operating revenues) in the nation. Many rail executives thought this was far too many. In the dozen years after 1957, more than fifty merger applications were to be sent foward to the Interstate Commerce Commission. In 1959 the Norfolk and Western, one of the larger coal carriers, obtained approval for its control of the 600-mile Virginian Railway. There was no great enthusiasm for mergers in the B&O board room. Perhaps the directors recalled "Willard's Law," attributed to Uncle Daniel— "No Management will willingly merge itself out of a job"; or put another way—"If you have to merge, make sure the other fellow loses out, not you."[10]

But as the traffic and revenue picture grew worse in the late 1950s, it became apparent that some type of merger might be the best solution to the financial problem facing the B&O. Shortly after Alfred E. Perlman, president of the New York Central, had turned down the first merger proposals made by the Pennsylvania, he looked further south. Early in 1959, Perlman approached Cyrus S. Eaton and Walter J. Tuohy, the two leaders of the Chesapeake and Ohio, along with Howard Simpson and proposed a merger of the three roads. Eaton and Tuohy noted the weak financial position of Perlman's road and insisted that the B&O/C&O merger must precede any merger with the New York Central. By June 1960, they were asking the permission of the ICC to purchase control of the B&O common stock. Howard Simpson clearly preferred a three-way merger with the leadership of the newly merged line to be equally shared. In September 1960, he wrote to the B&O family: "It is clear that neither the three railroads nor the public interest will be advanced by the current struggle of the C&O and the Central for control of the B&O."[11]

But the merger did not work out as Howard Simpson had hoped. Early in February 1961, Walter J. Tuohy, the president of the Chesapeake and Ohio announced that his road had bested the New York Central since the C&O controlled 61 percent of the stock of the B&O. Changes in control soon brought some changes in management. At their regular monthly meeting held in New York City on May 17, 1961, the board of directors elected Howard Simpson chairman of the board and chief executive officer. Chairman Roy White, whose health had been failing for sometime, was named honorary chairman. At the same meeting, Jervis Langdon, Jr., was named president effective June 1, 1961.

Things did not improve on the B&O during the summer of 1961 as the growing deficit became more apparent. A spokesman for the brokerage house of Merrill Lynch, Pierce, Fenner & Smith spoke of the B&O position as "a weak financial position, poor credit, and large requirements for deferred maintenance."[12] Coal company patrons of the B&O were complaining of poor service and numerous bad order cars. The sixty-five-year old Simpson decided to quit. At their meeting on December 20, 1961, the board accepted Simpson's request to retire as the chief executive officer of the company with these duties to be assumed by President Langdon on January 1, 1962. Howard Simpson did retain his position on the board of directors. Within a little more than a year, the B&O would come under the complete control of the Chesapeake and Ohio.

Chapter XX

· · · · · · · · · · · · · · · ·

The Baltimore and Ohio Is Taken Over by the Chesapeake and Ohio

THE CHESAPEAKE AND OHIO, WHICH GAINED CONTROL OF the Baltimore and Ohio in the early sixties, began as a short line built to serve the local needs of the farmers and merchants of central Virginia. Chartered as the Louisa Railroad in 1836, the twenty-one-mile line was built within a year by the use of slave labor. By 1850 the little road had reached Richmond and changed its name to the Virginia Central. During the 1850s, the standard-gauge Virginia Central was extended westward, and in 1861 was a 189-mile line running from Richmond via Gordonsville, Charlottesville, and Staunton to the end of the track at Jackson's River. War torn and weary in 1865, the company faced the rigors of Reconstruction with only $100 in gold in its treasury. The undaunted owners of the road reorganized their line as the Chesapeake and Ohio and sought fresh capital for an extension to the Ohio River. Eventually they found Collis P. Huntington willing both to finance and build the line to Huntington, West Virginia. The road suffered two receiverships, but by the turn of the century was a prosperous 1,445-mile line extending from Newport News, Virginia, west to Cincinnati and Louisville. In the 1880s and after, the Chesapeake and Ohio had been a serious competitor of the B&O in the haulage of the soft coal mined in West Virginia.

In the first half of the twentieth century, the financial control of the prosperous C&O shifted several times. Between 1900 and 1909, the Pennsylvania and the New York Central owned large blocks of C&O stock. During the 1920s, the Van Sweringen brothers, Mantis James and Oris P., acquired stock control of a large system of railways including the Nickel Plate, the Chesapeake and Ohio, the Erie, and the Pere Marquette. From the mid-1930s until 1954, the Wall Street rebel financier, Robert R. Young, and his Allegheny Corporation controlled the Chesapeake and Ohio. During the Young years of control, the C&O in 1947 acquired the Pere Marquette with its 1,941 miles of line in Michigan, Ohio, Indiana, Illinois, Canada, and New York. By 1950 the headquarters of the enlarged C&O were located in Cleveland. A diversification of C&O traffic followed the Pere Marquette merger and merchandise traffic produced 45 percent of C&O freight revenues by 1955. The C&O continued to originate more coal traffic than any other United States railroad, serving the extensive coal fields of eastern Kentucky and southern West Virginia. In 1954 Robert Young sold his C&O securities to Cyrus S. Eaton, a Cleveland investment banker. Eaton acquired a prosperous 5,000-mile railroad with annual revenues averaging $350 million per year and a good dividend record that stretched back for decades. He also acquired Walter Joseph Tuohy, who had been president of the C&O under Robert Young.

Walter J. Tuohy, born on Chicago's south side in 1901, was the son of the Chicago police sergeant. He held a series of odd jobs while attending De Paul University night school where he was granted a B.C.S. degree in 1925 and a L.L.B. degree in 1929. During the Depression, he went into the coal business and became president of Chicago's Globe Coal Company in 1939. Robert Young brought Tuohy to the Chesapeake and Ohio as a vice president in 1943, and he became president five years later. Eaton was so impressed with Tuohy that he soon gave him a free hand concerning the future of the C&O.

Tuohy, like Robert Young, was a small man (five feet six inches and only 125 pounds), but he was big on drive, imagination, and innovation. Shortly after becoming the C&O president, Tuohy became aware of the basic economy of the diesel locomotive. Within the C&O, the older officials assumed that the patrons of the

Walter J. Tuohy, president, 1964–65.
(Courtesy, Chessie System Railroad)

largest soft coal carrier in the nation would not stand for dieselization. This did not deter Tuohy. The C&O president talked to all the major coal operators and plainly told them the C&O would have to use diesel power if the coal freight rates were to be maintained at the present low levels. By 1955 diesel power was in use for 93 percent of all C&O operations. It was one of the first of the major coal carriers to shift completely from steam to diesel power.

Walter Tuohy brought the same kind of drive and business acumen to the railroad merger opportunities that were appearing at the end of the 1950s. Referring to the vast number of competing rail lines in the nation he said: "One hundred ten class one railroads are just too many."[1] When Alfred Perlman, president of the New York Central, early in 1959 suggested a three-way merger of his line plus the C&O and the B&O, Walter Tuohy was quick to note that his road was financially strong while Perlman's line was quite weak. In the late fifties, the Chesapeake and Ohio was paying regular four dollar dividends on less than half the gross revenues of the large New York Central, which was hard pressed even to pay annual dividends of fifty cents.

Soon Perlman and Tuohy were both in the market for the common stock of the Baltimore and Ohio. *Fortune* magazine in its article, "Mating Time for the Railroads," pointed out that for many railroads the real alternative was merger or insolvency. A *Fortune* cartoon of the rail merger fever carried the following caption: "In the center foreground an angry Al Perlman of the New York Central is arguing his claim to Howard Simpson of the Baltimore & Ohio, who's being clutched by Walter Tuohy of the Chesapeake & Ohio. That's Tuohy's boss, Board Chairman Cyrus Eaton, rubbing his hands."[2]

A hectic competition for B&O stockholder support ensued between Perlman and Tuohy. B&O shareholders were offered bargain priced weekends in the Chesapeake and Ohio fancy Greenbrier Hotel in White Sulphur Springs. Both New York Central and C&O agents rushed to Europe to argue with the officers of several large Swiss banks which held more than 500,000 shares in trust for hundreds of foreign owners. Of the Swiss bankers who committed themselves, most seemed to favor Tuohy's railroad.

By the last weeks of 1960, the Chesapeake and Ohio was reported to have acquired 30 percent of the B&O stock. The New York Central had barely 10 percent of the outstanding shares. Early in February 1961, Tuohy announced that his road controlled 61 percent of the B&O stock. By the spring of 1961, the amount thus controlled had risen to nearly 70 percent. Walter Tuohy and the C&O held a clear majority of the B&O stock, but to legitimatize their control of the road, they needed full approval by the Interstate Commerce Commission.

Hearings before the ICC on the C&O's application for authority to acquire stock control of the B&O started in June 1961 and continued intermittently for thirty-seven days into the early fall of that year. Top B&O officials plus many C&O officers testified in favor of the C&O/B&O unification. Included among the top C&O brass were Walter Tuohy; John E. Kusik, senior vice president of finance and accounting; and Gregory S. DeVine, vice president of coal traffic. The C&O officials contended that unification could stop the B&O slide toward bankruptcy and that the C&O was willing to spend up to $250 million over five years to overhaul the ailing road. They pointed out that the two roads, which were complementary rather than competitive lines, could coordinate their operations so that the stronger line could save the weaker. New York Central officials at the hearings tried to refute the case made by Tuohy and claimed that since a C&O/B&O merger was an end-to-end proposition, few savings would result. Perlman aides also contended that their own line would lose millions of tons of traffic to a unified C&O/B&O system. The hearings were held in seven cities, heard testimony from 486 witnesses, and resulted in 5,600 pages of testimony. Final briefs to the ICC were filed by the B&O and the C&O in January 1962. By this time, Al Perlman had decided his case was lost and withdrew his opposition to the application of the C&O. Late in 1961, Al Perlman and James M. Symes, Pennsylvania chairman, along with their respective boards, had decided to ask the ICC to approve a New York Central-Pennsylvania merger.

The C&O and B&O officials had to wait nearly a year while the eleven member commission made up its mind concerning the proposed merger. During 1961 and 1962, Jervis Langdon managed to cut expenses while modestly increasing revenue. B&O operating revenues in 1962 were up $14 million and expenses down $20 million, leaving a modest net income of $1.6 million in place of the huge deficit of 1961. Facing a passenger service deficit of $9 million a year, Langdon in March 1962, announced his road was considering a petition to suspend all passenger service. Such a petition was not made, but he did slow the schedules of both the *Capitol Limited* and the *National Limited* in mid-1962. Of an earlier trip to Chicago in the *Capitol Limited*, Langdon said: "The train traveled so fast through the Alleghenies that I found it difficult to shave, much less keep my coffee in its cup."[3]

On New Year's Eve 1962, the ICC announced that by a split vote of eight to three, they had approved the C&O bid to control the B&O. In doing so, the commission had gone against the wishes of the national administration, the brotherhoods, and several eastern railroads. But top B&O and C&O officials were happy. Jervis Langdon of the B&O said: "Through measures of coordination both roads can tackle the problem of cost reduction and improved utilization of their plant and equipment."[4] The *Baltimore Evening Sun* said the ICC action should result in one of the strongest rail systems in the East. In Cleveland, Cyrus Eaton and Walter Tuohy wrote their shareholders: "The Interstate Commerce Commission . . . approved as consistent with the public interest C&O's control of the Baltimore & Ohio, the nation's first railroad and one of its most important."[5]

The ICC order became effective on February 4, 1963, and at 12:01 A.M. on Monday, February 4, the Chesapeake and Ohio formally took control of the Baltimore and Ohio in a midnight ceremony in Baltimore in the portrait filled, paneled boardroom of the nation's oldest railroad. The affiliation of the 6,000-mile B&O and the 5,000-mile C&O produced an 11,000-mile rail system reaching from the Atlantic to the Mississippi and from the Great Lakes to the southern borders of Virginia, West Virginia, and Kentucky. The bulk of the C&O mileage lay either south of the B&O (in Virginia, West Virginia, and Kentucky) or to the north in Michigan. Several major cities—Washington, Huntington, Louisville, Cincinnati, Columbus, Chicago, Toledo, and Buffalo—were served by both roads. As the two lines came under a single management, the B&O obtained more than $200 million in loans from the C&O and its bankers, money which was to be used over a five-year period to repair 9,000 old freight cars, buy 18,000 new ones, enlarge tunnels to accommodate piggyback traffic, and improve its yards. In 1964 C&O officials started steps to also include the 800-mile Western Maryland in the C&O/B&O systems. The two larger roads, as of 1964, owned about two-thirds of the stock of the smaller line. Finally in March 1968, the ICC approved control of the Western Maryland by the C&O/B&O system.

Early in 1963, Baltimore and Ohio shareholders started to exchange their stock for C&O shares of stock, stock that was paying a yearly dividend of four dollars per share. Also in February 1963, three C&O officials, Cyrus Eaton, Walter Tuohy, and John E. Kusik, joined the B&O board of directors. Several other new members were elected to the board, and only four men who had been on the board in 1961 remained on the new board elected in February 1963. Starting in 1964, the annual reports of the two roads came out in a combined report under the title *C&O/B&O Railroads Annual Report*. The *Annual Report* for 1964 listed nineteen department heads and corporate officers of the two lines. Of the nineteen men, only four had held comparable positions on the B&O. Six vice presidents in the group provided a unified direction for the two roads in the areas of personnel, operations, taxes, planning, public relations, and finance. None of the six came from the Baltimore and Ohio. Some of the top B&O officials of 1960–62 may have felt in 1964 that "Willard's Law" relative to mergers was coming back to haunt them. The vice president for C&O/B&O finance, Hays T. Watkins, Jr., had been with the C&O since 1949 and later would become the top executive of both the C&O and CSX.

Further unification of the two lines came late in 1964 when Jervis Langdon gave up the B&O presidency to become chairman and chief executive officer of the Rock Island Lines. Walter Tuohy was elected president of the B&O, but a year later he was succeeded by Gregory S. DeVine, who had spent thirty years in the coal business before joining the C&O in 1957. When Tuohy died in 1966, DeVine was elected president and chief executive officer of both the C&O and the B&O, positions he held until his retirement in 1971. The growing C&O dominance over the Baltimore and Ohio could be seen in the B&O board of directors, which by 1970 included six men also on the C&O board. The six were Cyrus Eaton, Gregory DeVine, C. Vernon Cowan, Hays T. Watkins, John E. Kusik, and Milton S. Eisenhower, president of Johns Hopkins University and younger brother of a former United States president. In 1970 the C&O held about 94 percent of all the B&O common stock.

In at least one instance, the efforts of C&O officials to fully combine the two companies did not succeed. Back in 1934, one of the best efforts of the C&O public relations department had been the introduction of "Chessie" (short for Chesapeake), a cat drawn by the Viennese artist Guido Gruenewald. Chessie's picture and the slogan "Sleep like a Kitten" became known the nation over. In the 1964 *C&O/B&O Annual Report*, it was suggested that a second cat known as "Bessie" (for the B&O) should be introduced as a mate for Chessie. Shareholders were invited to respond to the suggestion. Evidently the response was minimal for no future mention ever appeared about "Bessie." A few years later a new corporate symbol—the silhouette of the Chessie kitten inside the letter C—began to appear on Chessie System cars and locomotives.

As the decade of the 1970s began, the C&O/B&O system employed 49,000 men and women whose combined efforts moved 900 freight and 61 passenger trains each day. The two roads in 1970 had nearly equal total operating revenues—$453 million for the C&O and $479 million for the B&O. In 1971 Gregory DeVine reached the age of sixty-five and retired as president and chief executive officer of the C&O/B&O. His successor was the forty-five-year-old Hays T. Watkins, who, after receiving an M.B.A. from Northwestern University in 1948, joined the C&O the following year. Watkins was treasurer by 1960, vice president of finance in 1964, and vice president of administrative group in 1967. In 1972–73, his second year as president and chief executive officer, Watkins had the name "Chessie System" adopted as a marketing appellation for the Chessie railroads—the C&O, B&O, and Western Maryland. By 1974 Cyrus Eaton had given up his board chairmanship, and Hays Watkins became president and chairman of the Chessie System. During most of the 1970s, Watkins was also president of the B&O. In 1979 John T. Collinson succeeded Watkins as Baltimore and Ohio president.

The new Chessie System symbol—Chessie in the letter C—was soon to appear on both C&O and B&O equipment. However, the two roads continued to be operated as separate lines, even though top management and policy decisions were made at the Chessie headquarters in Cleveland. This C&O/B&O combination thus was saved from many errors made in a later merger, that of the Pennsylvania and New York Central into Penn Central in 1968. From 1964 until the appearance of the Chessie System, the combined C&O/B&O annual reports contained separate sections for the operating statistics of the two railroads. The Baltimore and Ohio prepared separate brief annual reports starting in 1972. Full

Hays T. Watkins, president, 1970–72 and 1975–78. *(Courtesy, Baltimore and Ohio Railroad)*

annual statistics for the B&O continued to appear in such places as *Railway Age* and *Moody's Transportation Manual.* Throughout the 1960s and the 1970s, the Baltimore and Ohio continued to be the weaker and less prosperous of the two railroads.

During the 1970s, the total operating revenues of the Chessie System increased from $1,045 million in 1970 to $1,859 million in 1979, with the net earnings in the same period climbing from $35 million to $120 million. Much of the increase in the decade was due more to inflation than to greater actual traffic. Late in 1974, there was a two-for-one stock split, doubling the number of shares of common stock. The dividend of four dollars of 1970 on the smaller number of shares had climbed to $2.32 ($4.64) per share in 1979 on the doubled number of shares. The number of employees on the Chessie System had declined about 10,000 during the decade to just over 39,000 in 1979.

In the late 1960s, the Chesapeake and Ohio had entered into an extended consideration of a possible merger with the Norfolk and Western Railway, but the proposed consolidation was never completed. A decade later, Hays T. Watkins and the Chessie System were interested in a still larger merger with several lines located in the South. In mid-1967 the 9,000-mile Seaboard Coast Line was the result of a merger of two major southeastern lines, the Atlantic Coast Line and the Seaboard Air Line. Later, the Louisville and Nashville was added and the Seaboard Coast Line became the Seaboard Coast Line Industries, with their three lines known as the Family Lines.

Late in September 1980, the Interstate Commerce Commission approved the merger of the Chessie System with the Seaboard Coast Line Industries. On November 1, 1980, the CSX Corporation was created as the new holding company for the two rail systems. Prime F. Osborn, III, of the Seaboard/Family Lines became chairman and Hays T. Watkins of Chessie was elected president. Press reporters were told by both of the top executives that the *C* stood for Chessie, the *S* for Seaboard, and that the *X* indicated that the new system was much larger than one plus one. The new board of directors of twenty-four basically was half from Chessie and half from Seaboard. The Chessie System kept its headquarters in Cleveland, Seaboard was based in Jacksonville, Florida, and CSX set up its headquarters in Richmond, Virginia. CSX had 70,000 employees, 27,000 miles of road in twenty-two different states, assets in excess of $7.5 billion, and total revenues of nearly $5 billion, including earnings from large real estate holdings of coal, oil, and gas. CSX had extensive mileage in all parts of the nation east of the Mississippi except for Wisconsin and New England. In May 1982, Prime Osborn retired as chairman and was succeeded by Hays Watkins. The new president was A. Paul Funkhouser of Seaboard.

TABLE 28. Baltimore and Ohio System Traffic and Financial Status 1962–84

Year	Miles of Road	Total Revenue	Net Revenue	Expenses to Earnings (%)
1962	5,870	$ 365,783,000	$ 81,704,000	77.6
1963	5,849	371,661,000	81,729,000	78.0
1964	5,823	381,889,000	90,002,000	76.4
1965	5,743	399,722,000	100,257,000	74.9
1966	5,759	416,107,000	107,447,000	74.1
1967	5,748	411,809,000	99,293,000	75.9
1968	5,731	441,021,000	107,876,000	75.5
1969	5,596	461,127,000	117,600,000	74.5
1970	5,552	479,190,000	110,626,000	76.9
1971	5,550	495,812,000	120,600,000	75.7
1972	5,501	502,383,000	134,686,000	73.1
1973	5,473	555,426,000	153,289,000	72.4
1974	5,425	648,383,000	203,722,000	68.6
1975	5,412	614,406,000	150,846,000	74.4
1976	5,408	684,737,000	176,314,000	74.2
1977	5,406	762,860,000	214,562,000	71.8
1978	5,265	830,746,000	59,891,000	92.8*
1979	5,163	922,248,000	65,076,000	92.9
1980	5,208	945,950,000	56,597,000	94.0
1981	5,198	1,059,277,000	58,429,000	94.5
1982	5,023	899,937,000	2,952,000	99.7
1983	5,518	918,591,000	4,212,000	99.5
1984	5,317	1,050,905,000	56,452,000	94.6

The marked increase in operating ratio in 1978 and later years is due to a major change in accounting policies.

At the time of the appearance of the CSX Corporation, the Baltimore and Ohio represented roughly one-fifth of the mileage, the revenue, and the work force of the parent company.

The decline in Baltimore and Ohio mileage in the two decades was happening to railroads all across the country. The B&O decline of 563 miles was a drop of almost 10 percent, but, in the entire nation, the decline of rail mileage was 26 percent for the two decades. The threefold increase in total revenue in the two decades, $365 million up to $1,050 million, was chiefly the effect of inflation, since consumer prices had tripled between 1962 and 1984. In the twenty-two years, the average revenue per ton-mile had climbed from 1.4 cents to 3.1 cents per ton-mile in the nation. The total B&O ton-mileage had changed little in this period, increasing from 24 billion ton-miles in 1962 to a high of about 29 billion ton-miles in the midsixties, but declining to about 26 billion ton-miles by 1984. Coal traffic had become more important in the sixties and seventies increasing from 28 percent of all revenue in 1962 and 33 percent by 1984.

Thanks to the financial assistance of the parent company and the good top management out of Cleveland, the B&O operating ratio declined in the mid-1960s and early 1970s. This was in marked contrast to operating ratios of 81 percent to 86 percent for the last years of the Howard Simpson presidency. The sudden increase in the operating ratio up to 93 percent and higher after 1978 was caused by major changes made in accounting practices on all Chessie roads. For the first time, such items as taxes and depreciation were figured as operating expenses. Earlier such items had been deducted from operating revenue only after the operating ratio had been determined.

Passenger traffic on the Baltimore and Ohio, as on all roads, continued to drop during the 1960s. Between 1962 and 1970, B&O passenger revenue declined from $27 million (about 7 percent of total revenue) to less than $7 million (1.4 percent of total revenue). By 1970 the combined C&O/B&O passenger timetable was a single sheet of paper folded into eight double pages. The only remaining B&O passenger service consisted of travel from Baltimore to Chicago, Baltimore to St. Louis, and Cincinnati to Toledo. A coach ticket from Baltimore to Chicago in 1970 cost $38.25 or about 4.7 cents per mile for the 807-mile, eighteen-hour trip.

By 1970, there was a growing public concern over the long list of train discontinuances in the nation—from 20,000 intercity trains in 1929 to only 500 in 1970. In October 1970, Congress passed legislation which created the National Railroad Passenger Corporation. Under this act, Amtrak passenger service on a limited national rail network was put in operation on May 1, 1971. All passenger service operated by the Baltimore and Ohio ended on that date. This ended the long period of deficit-ridden B&O passenger service, where the red ink had amounted to as much as $9 million per year in the early 1960s. However, the Baltimore and Ohio was required to make a one-time payment in 1971 of $29.6 million to the National Railroad Passenger Corporation to obtain relief from the responsibility of providing intercity passenger service. Since 1971 only a limited amount of Amtrak passenger service has been routed over Baltimore and Ohio lines.

The number of workers employed on the Baltimore and Ohio, along with all the railways of the nation, declined markedly during the 1960s and 1970s.

TABLE 29. Decline of Rail Employment and Increases in Wages 1962–84

Year	B&O Workers	Railroad Workers in the United States	Average Annual Wages in the United States
1962	27,787	700,146	$ 6,659
1965	24,901	639,961	7,490
1968	22,768	590,534	8,654
1971	20,608	544,333	11,023
1974	17,192	525,177	14,235
1977	16,212	482,731	18,518
1979	16,647	482,789	22,585
1981	15,417	436,397	26,698
1983	12,763	322,030	32,125
1984	12,117	323,030	34,064

The decline in B&O employment in the twenty-two years (1962–84) had been about 54 percent, while across the nation the decrease was not very different. Certainly both in the nation at large and on the B&O, the productivity in ton-mileage per worker had greatly increased in the two decades.

The workers themselves were being rewarded for their greater productivity, since average wages had climbed about five-fold in the two decades, while the cost of living had gone up only threefold. The average wage for a B&O employee in 1977 was $17,886, quite close to the average that year for all railroad workers. In 1977 the 580 B&O officials and executives as a group had average yearly pay of $30,108. In the same year, the 2,109 clerical and professional workers averaged $16,162 per year, while the lower paid 3,030 maintenance of way employees made an average of $14,822. Higher still were the 3,350 maintenance of equipment and stores workers with $16,673, and the 7,143 transportation and train crews with $19,269 per year. Such annual pay would have seemed a dream world indeed to the 5,000 workers who received less than $500 per year as they built the B&O across the mountains of western Virginia to the Ohio River in the early 1850s during the presidency of Thomas Swann.

The year 1977 marked the 150th anniversary of the founding of the Baltimore and Ohio. On the back page of the *Chessie System Annual Report* for 1976, Hays T. Watkins, Chessie chairman and president, wrote: "1977 marks the sesquicentennial of the Baltimore and Ohio Railroad, as well as the 150th anniversary of America's Railroads."[6] Watkins and the other top system officials in Cleveland had no intention of having a Dan Willard type of celebration comparable to the 1927 Fair of the Iron Horse. However, the sesquicentennial year was marked in a variety of ways.

Daniel Willard on February 28, 1927, had held a giant banquet and party at the Lyric Theater in Baltimore for 950 guests, all of them male. Fifty years later, on Monday, February 28, 1977 (the sesquicentennial of the B&O charter), Hays Watkins had a smaller party for 350 guests, men and women, at the Baltimore and Ohio Railroad Museum in Baltimore. The guests included representatives of government, business, labor, and the press. An Amtrak special from Washington, with seven shiny Amfleet cars eased up to the museum doors after a short staged race with the *Tom Thumb* and the *Best Friend of Charleston*. After a reception in Mount Clare Station and Museum, the guests moved to the adjoining roundhouse where tables were placed on the covered turntable surrounded by ancient engines and wooden passenger coaches. After the dinner, brief remarks were made by Hays T. Watkins; Stephen Ailes, president of the Association of American Railroads; Charles J. Chamberlain, chairman of the Railway Labor Executives Association; Mayor William D. Schaefer of Baltimore; and Blair Lee, lieutenant governor of Maryland. The speaker's platform was on the open vestibule of a post-Civil War passenger coach. Robert C. Byrd of West Virginia, Senate majority leader, entertained the guests with some country-style fiddling. The B&O giant, white 150th birthday cake had been baked by the chefs of Chessie's Greenbrier resort hotel.

Other special events also marked the railroad's birthday. On April 19, 1977, Chessie shareholders mixed business with a salute to the B&O when they held their annual meeting in the B&O Museum roundhouse. After the meeting, the shareholders enjoyed B&O birthday cakes with refreshments and later toured the museum. During the year, shareholders were invited to purchase for sixteen dollars a sesquicentennial plate of B&O blue china showing a painting of Charles Carroll laying the B&O's first stone on July 4, 1828. The general public was invited to ride on more than forty round-trip and one-way tours of a Chessie steam special train scheduled out of a number of cities in eight midwestern and eastern states. Thousands of rail fans and steam locomotive buffs crowded the train from April until early October 1977. The Chessie public relations department also published a thirty-two-page booklet, *The Story So Far*, which reviewed the 150-year growth of the B&O, with a heavy emphasis on the nineteenth century.

The Baltimore and Ohio board of directors in the sesquicentennial year of 1977 naturally had few connections with an older independent B&O. Robert Garrett, grandson of John Work Garrett, had left the board in the early 1950s after serving nearly forty years as a director. But there were still a few directors from Baltimore. The eighty-year old Howard E. Simpson, B&O president from 1953–61, was on the board, as was Milton S. Eisenhower, president emeritus of Johns Hopkins University, the school which bore the name of a major friend of the railroad in the mid-nineteenth century. Another Baltimore director was W. James Price, a partner in the investment banking firm of Alexander Brown and Sons, the banking family in whose house the early dreams of a railroad to the Ohio River had been discussed in the early weeks of 1827.

During the century and a half, the Baltimore and Ohio had grown up with the country as it faced both the rigors of war and depression. President John Work Garrett had seen much of his railroad literally torn apart since his lines were so often between the contending forces of the Blue and the Gray in the Civil War. Half a century later, Daniel Willard helped the nation prepare for World War I, and in the decade after Pearl Harbor, Roy White directed rail wartime activity in both World War II and the Korean Conflict. During the nineteenth century, the presidents of the railroad frequently had to face the problems of economic panic and depression—Louis McLane in 1837, Chauncy Brooks in 1857, and John Garrett in 1873. The panic and depression of the mid-1890s was so severe during the administration of Charles Mayer that the B&O was forced into a receivership successfully solved by John Cowen and Oscar Murray. A generation later, the B&O barely escaped a second receivership during the severe depression in the presidency of Daniel Willard. In the long corporate history, the railroad's labor policy became more liberal. John Garrett (1858–84) was a vigorous foe of organized railroad labor, while half a century later, Daniel Willard (1910–41) was a staunch friend of the workers.

The Baltimore and Ohio never received any federal or state land grants because of its early conception in an area far removed from the frontier. But it did receive substantial financial aid from the city of Baltimore and the state of Maryland, both in the first construction directed by President Philip Thomas and in its eventual completion to the Ohio River years later in the presidency of Thomas Swann. As the new railroad eventually reached the Ohio River and beyond, the prosperity and economy of both Baltimore and Maryland greatly benefited from the new link to the West. The federal government aided the projected railroad by allowing such United States Army engineers as Col. Stephen H. Long and Lt. George Whistler to aid in the early surveying and planning of the route west of Baltimore. The preeminence of the Baltimore and Ohio in the early rail development in the nation was so great that the editor of the *American Railroad Journal* spoke of the new line as the railroad university of the United States.

In its long history, the pioneer Baltimore and Ohio was proud of its many "firsts"—the first road to place an electric locomotive in regular service, the first completely air conditioned train, and one of the first to use a diesel-electric locomotive. In the spring of 1844, the first telegraph line in the nation was constructed along the B&O track between Baltimore and Washington, D.C. History seemed to be repeating itself when, in the summer of 1983, the parent CSX Corporation reached an agreement with Southern New England Telephone to place a fiber optics communication system along the CSX rights-of-way. In the last century and a half, the Baltimore and Ohio has grown with the nation, and its long development reveals much of the history of America's rail industry.

Appendices

Appendix I

Presidents of the Baltimore and Ohio Railroad, 1827–1984

Philip E. Thomas	1827–36	Oscar G. Murray	1904–10
Joseph W. Patterson	1836	Daniel Willard	1910–41
Louis McLane	1836–48	Roy B. White	1941–53
Thomas Swann	1848–53	Howard E. Simpson	1953–61
William G. Harrison	1853–55	Jervis Langdon, Jr.	1961–64
Chauncy Brooks	1855–58	Walter J. Tuohy	1964–65 (C&O control)
John W. Garrett	1858–84	Gregory S. DeVine	1965–69 (C&O control)
Robert Garrett	1884–87	Hays T. Watkins	1970–72 (C&O control)
Samuel Spencer	1887–88	J. W. Hanifin	1973–74 (C&O control)
Charles F. Mayer	1888–96	Hays T. Watkins	1975–78 (C&O control)
John F. Cowen	1896–1901	John T. Collinson	1979–83 (C&O control)
Leonor F. Loree	1901–4	J. W. Snow	1984– (C&O control)

Appendix II

Mileage of the Baltimore and Ohio, 1830–1980

Year	B&O	United States	Year	B&O	United States
1830	13	23	1910	4,434	240,293
1835	116	1,098	1915	4,535	253,789
1840	116	2,808	1920	5,155	252,845
1845	213	4,633	1925	5,197	249,398
1850	213	9,021	1930	5,569	249,052
1855	411	18,374	1935	6,351	241,104
1860	515	30,626	1940	6,293	233,670
1865	521	35,085	1945	6,132	226,696
1870	588	52,922	1950	6,201	223,779
1875	1,314	74,096	1955	6,167	220,670
1880	1,449	93,267	1960	5,909	217,552
1885	1,695	128,320	1965	5,743	211,925
1890	1,845	163,597	1970	5,552	206,265
1895	2,094	180,675	1975	5,412	199,126
1900	3,200	193,346	1980	5,208	179,000
1905	4,025	218,101			

Sources: B&O Annual Reports; Association of American Railroads.

Appendix III

Baltimore and Ohio Passenger and Freight Revenue, 1831–1980 (in thousands of dollars)

Year	Passenger	Freight	Average Passenger Fare (cents per mile)	Average Freight Rate (cents per ton-mile)
1831	$ 27*	$ 4*	—	—
1835	93*	170*	—	—
1840	177*	256*	—	—
1845	370*	369*	3.14 est.	4.10 est.
1850	438*	905*	—	—
1855	608*	3,103*	—	—
1860	698*	3,224*	—	—
1865	3,997*	6,099*	2.40 est.	2.00 est.
1870	10,840**	—	—	—
1875	14,444**	—	—	—
1880	18,317**	—	—	—
1885	3,791	12,825	—	—
1890	5,614	16,991	1.82	.69
1895–96	5,316	16,818	1.76	.63
1900–1	9,054	35,553	1.97	.50
1905–6	13,701	60,002	2.00	.56
1910–11	15,208	67,629	1.91	.58
1914–15	14,059	70,780	1.97	.57
1920	31,183	182,710	2.94	.87
1925	27,904	193,558	3.18	.99
1930	18,567	173,706	2.97	1.01
1935	9,887	122,787	2.15	.95
1940	10,619	158,106	1.85	.90
1945	48,215	293,496	1.94	.90
1950	22,285	353,483	3.17	1.28
1955	18,651	383,955	3.07	1.34
1960	15,884	340,021	2.98	1.37
1965	10,111	364,203	3.15	1.23
1970	2,661	451,890	4.15	1.58
1975	—	593,718	—	2.40
1980	—	913,355	—	3.93

*Main Stem Revenue only

**Total Revenue

Sources: B&O Annual Reports; Poor, *Manual of the Railroads of the United States; Moody's Transportation Manual.*

Appendix IV

Baltimore and Ohio Operating Ratio and Dividends, 1831–1962

Year	Operating Ratio or Expenses to Earnings (%)	Dividends (in $)	Year	Operating Ratio or Expenses to Earnings (%)	Dividends (in $)
1831	35	.37 1/2	1866	60	8.00
1832	55	1.35	1867	60	8.00
1833	70	.75	1868	73	8.00
1834	67	—	1869	68	8.00
1835	61	1.12 1/2	1870	69	8.00
1836	76	—	1871	63	8.00
1837	95	—	1872	61	9.00
1838	74	—	1873	65	10.00
1839	77	—	1874	64	10.00
1840	63	2.00	1875	69	10.00
1841	61	2.00	1876	64	10.00
1842	51	—	1877	62	8.00
1843	51	2.00	1878	56	7.00*
1844	47	2.50	1879	54	8.00*
1845	49	—	1880	56	8.00
1846	51	3.00	1881	62	10.00
1847	53	3.00	1882	59	10.00
1848	54	—*	1883	56	10.00
1849	52	—*	1884	60	10.00
1850	45	—*	1885	66	10.00
1851	51	—*	1886	65	10.00
1852	53	—*	1887	68	8.00
1853	61	—*	1888	69	—
1854	55	—	1889	69	—
1855	57	—	1890	69	—
1856	54	6.00	1891	69	—
1857	60	3.00	1892 (9 mo.)	73	1.25*
1858	65	—	1892–93	72	2.50
1859	46	6.00	1893–94	69	2.50
1860	41	6.00	1894–95	69	—
1861	43	6.00	1895–96	73	—
1862	32	6.00*	1896–97	78	—
1863	30	6.00	1897–98	73	—
1864	38	7.00	1898–99	65	—
1865	56	8.00	1899–1900	66	2.00

Year	Operating Ratio or Expenses to Earnings (%)	Dividends (in $)	Year	Operating Ratio or Expenses to Earnings (%)	Dividends (in $)
1900–1	65	4.00	1932	73	—
1901–2	64	4.00	1933	69	—
1902–3	62	4.00	1934	73	—
1903–4	67	4.00	1935	74	—
1904–5	66	4.50	1936	73	—
1905–6	64	5.50	1937	76	—
1906–7	67	6.00	1938	78	—
1907–8	74	6.00	1939	74	—
1908–9	67	6.00	1940	74	—
1909–10	70	6.00	1941	72	—
1910–11	72	6.00	1942	67	—
1911–12	71	6.00	1943	70	—
1912–13	74	6.00	1944	74	—
1913–14	75	6.00	1945	82	—
1914–15	70	5.00	1946	90	—
1916	72	5.00	1947	83	—
1917	77	5.00	1948	81	—
1918	92	4.50	1949	82	—
1919	93	2.00	1950	81	—
1920	98	—	1951	81	—
1921	84	—	1952	79	.75
1922	82	—	1953	79	1.00
1923	78	2.50	1954	82	1.00
1924	77	5.00	1955	81	2.00
1925	75	5.00	1956	81	2.50
1926	74	6.00	1957	81	2.50
1927	76	6.00	1958	81	1.50
1928	73	6.00	1959	81	1.50
1929	74	6.50	1960	82	1.50
1930	74	7.00	1961	86	.60
1931	76	3.50	1962	78	—

For the years 1831–65 Operating Ratio is only for Main Stem.

*Paid a stock dividend.

Sources: B&O Annual Reports and *Moody's Transportation Manual.*

Appendix V

Baltimore and Ohio Equipment

Year	Locomotives	Freight Cars	Passenger Cars
1836	12	1,062	46
1848	57	1,201	65
1857	236	3,668	124
1866	290	3,846	164
1873	473	10,292	261
1877	590	11,521	307
1880	547	13,944	358
1885	666	21,408	504
1890	826	25,985	654
1895	890	26,635	660
1900	1,266	64,127	899
1905	1,798	80,338	1,206
1910	2,055	84,776	1,177
1915	2,399	86,097	1,261
1920	2,638	95,780	1,317
1925	2,459	99,668	1,432
1930	2,364	102,072	1,732
1935	2,225	96,595	1,234
1940	2,065	83,515	1,274
1945	2,099	88,961	1,229
1950	1,982	93,798	1,050
1955	1,419	91,489	1,019
1960	1,129	90,111	711
1962	1,148	75,182	547

Sources: B&O Annual Reports; Poor, *Manual of the Railroads of the United States; Moody's Transportation Manual.*

Appendix VI

Selected Material on Baltimore and Ohio Employees and Compensation, 1857–1962

Year	Number of Employees	Average Yearly Compensation ($)
1857	4,500 est.	—
1881	18,000 est.	—
1887	25,000 est.	—
1899	35,000 est.	563*
1905	52,000 est.	608*
1916	60,000	891*
1918	69,996	1,419*
1920	72,000	1,820*
1925	66,061	1,649*
1930	66,034	1,714*
1935	35,036	1,792
1940	41,007	1,986
1945	64,285	2,781
1950	53,592	3,983
1955	46,177	4,998
1960	33,401	6,642
1962	27,787	6,659*

*National average.
Sources: B&O Annual Reports; Association of American Railroads; *Moody's Transportation Manual.*

Notes

Chapter I

1. *Annals of Congress*, Fourteenth Congress, Second Session, p. 853.

2. When the northwestern counties of Virginia were admitted as the state of West Virginia in 1863 it became Wheeling, West Virginia.

3. Frederick J. Turner, *The Rise of the New West* (New York, 1906), p. 67.

4. Robert G. Albion, *The Rise of New York Port: 1815–60* (New York, 1939), p. 373.

5. *Ibid.*, p. 377.

6. David Hosack, *Memoir of DeWitt Clinton* (New York, 1829), pp. 346–48.

7. Francis Baily, *Journal of a Tour in the Unsettled Parts of North America, 1796–97* (London, 1856), p. 107.

8. Samuel Hazard, *The Register of Pennsylvania* I (1828), p. 407.

9. John Melish, *Information and Advice to Emigrants to the United States* (Philadelphia, 1819), p. 112.

Chapter II

1. William Prescott Smith, *The Book of the Great Railway Celebrations of 1857* (New York, 1858), p. 12.

2. *Niles' Register*, March 17, 1827.

3. *Ibid.*, June 23, 1827.

4. *Ibid.*, July 7, 1827.

5. *Ibid.*, October 27, 1827.

6. Alexander Brown and Sons to Thomas Kennedy, 20 February, 1828, in *The Early Correspondence of Alexander Brown and Sons with regard to the Building of the Baltimore and Ohio Railroad* (Baltimore, 1927).

7. *Second Annual Report of the Baltimore and Ohio Railroad* (Baltimore, 1828), p. 11.

8. *Niles' Register*, June 7, 1828.

9. Smith, *The Book of the Great Railway Celebrations of 1857* (New York, 1858), p. 13.

10. John Q. Adams, *Memoirs of John Quincy Adams* (Philadelphia, 1876), Vol. VIII, pp. 49–50.

Chapter III

1. John H. B. Latrobe, *The Baltimore and Ohio Railroad: Personal Recollections* (Baltimore, 1868), p. 7.

2. N. H. Ellicott to Philip E. Thomas, November 3, 1828, in Alfred R. James, "Sidelights on the Founding of the Baltimore and Ohio Railroad," *Maryland Historical Magazine* XLVII, December, 1953, p. 296.

3. Alexander Brown and Sons to W. and J. Brown and Co., Liverpool, December 28, 1829, in *The Early Correspondence of Alexander Brown and Sons.*

4. *Niles' Register,* May 22, 1830.

5. John H. B. Latrobe, *The Baltimore and Ohio Railroad: Personal Recollections* (Baltimore, 1868), p. 19.

6. *Niles' Register,* October 22, 1831.

7. William Prescott Smith, *The Book of the Great Railway Celebrations of 1857* (New York, 1858), p. 32.

Chapter IV

1. *Eleventh Annual Report of the Baltimore and Ohio Railroad* (Baltimore, 1837), p. 7.

2. *Fourteenth Annual Report of the Baltimore and Ohio Railroad* (Baltimore, 1840), p. 4.

3. *American Railroad Journal,* September 1, 1842, p. 157.

4. *Seventeenth Annual Report of the Baltimore and Ohio Railroad* (Baltimore, 1843), pp. 4–5.

5. "Report of the Baltimore and Ohio R. R. Company, Showing the Amount of Salaries paid the Officers of said R. R. Company" Document Q of the House of Delegates (Maryland), 7 February 1845.

6. John E. Semmes, *John H. B. Latrobe and His Times* (Baltimore, 1917), p. 362.

Chapter V

1. *American Railroad Journal,* April 24, 1845, p. 267.

2. W. Prescott Smith, *A History and Description of the Baltimore and Ohio Railroad,* (Baltimore, 1853), p. 76.

3. *Twenty-third Annual Report of the Baltimore and Ohio Railroad* (Baltimore, 1849), p. 12.

4. *Twenty-fifth Annual Report of the Baltimore and Ohio Railroad* (Baltimore, 1851), p. 9.

5. *American Railroad Journal,* April 27, 1850, p. 262.

6. *Twenty-third Annual Report of the Baltimore and Ohio Railroad* (Baltimore, 1849), p. 9.

7. *Twenty-sixth Annual Report of the Baltimore and Ohio Railroad* (Baltimore, 1852), p. 35–36.

Chapter VI

1. Helen Hopkins Thom, *Johns Hopkins: A Silhouette* (Baltimore, 1929), p. 31.

2. *Twenty-fifth Annual Report of the Baltimore and Ohio Railroad* (Baltimore, 1851), p. 13.

3. *Twenty-sixth Annual Report of the Baltimore & Ohio Railroad* (Baltimore, 1852), p. 33.

4. *Thirty-first Annual Report of the Baltimore and Ohio Railroad* (Baltimore, 1857), p. 10.

5. J. H. Sullivan, *Central Ohio Railroad Co.* (Baltimore, 1854), p. 14.

6. *Thirty-first Annual Report of the Baltimore and Ohio Railroad* (Baltimore, 1857), p. 11.

7. William Prescott Smith, *The Book of the Great Railway Celebrations of 1857* (New York, 1858), p. 176.

8. *Ibid.*, p. 195.

9. *Ibid.*, p. 203.

10. August Mencken, *The Railroad Passenger Car* (Baltimore, 1957), p. 121.

11. Edward Hungerford, *The Story of the Baltimore and Ohio Railroad, 1827–1927* (New York, 1928), Vol. I, pp. 271–73.

Chapter VII

1. Edward Hungerford, *The Story of the Baltimore and Ohio Railroad, 1827–1927* (New York, 1928), Vol. I, p. 336.

2. Festus P. Summers, *The Baltimore and Ohio in the Civil War* (New York, 1939), p. 44.

3. William Bruce Catton, *John W. Garrett of the Baltimore and Ohio: A Study in Seaport and Railroad Competition, 1820–74* (Ph.D. Dissertation, Northwestern University, 1959), p. 278.

4. Edward Hungerford, *The Story of the Baltimore and Ohio Railroad, 1827–1927* (New York, 1928), Vol. I, p. 350.

5. *Ibid.*, Vol. II, p. 9.

6. *Thirty-fifth Annual Report of the Baltimore and Ohio Railroad* (Baltimore, 1863), p. 46.

7. *Ibid.*, pp. 6–7.

8. *Thirty-sixth Annual Report of the Baltimore and Ohio Railroad* (Baltimore, 1864), p. 55–56.

9. *Thirty-seventh Annual Report of the Baltimore and Ohio Railroad* (Baltimore, 1865), p. 42.

10. William Bruce Catton, *John W. Garrett of the Baltimore and Ohio* (Ph.D. Dissertation, 1959), p. 310.

11. H. J. Jewett to John W. Garrett, November 13, 1862. In MS 1925, Baltimore and Ohio Collection, Maryland Historical Society.

12. *Thirty-seventh Annual Report of the Baltimore and Ohio Railroad* (Baltimore, 1865), p. 52.

13. Festus P. Summers, *The Baltimore and Ohio in the Civil War* (New York, 1939), p. 167.

14. H. J. Jewett to John Garrett, February 25, 1865. In MS 1925, Baltimore and Ohio Collection, Maryland Historical Society.

15. George H. Burgess and Miles C. Kennedy, *Centennial History of the Pennsylvania Railroad* (Philadelphia, 1949), p. 344.

16. A. Lincoln to J. W. Garrett, January 10, 1865 in Roy P. Basler, ed., *The Collected Work of Abraham Lincoln* (New Brunswick, New Jersey, 1953), Vol. VIII, p. 208.

17. *Thirty-ninth Annual Report of the Baltimore and Ohio Railroad* (Baltimore, 1867), p. 10. The war caused the Annual Reports to be published late: 1861 in 1863; 1862 in 1864; 1863 in 1865; 1864 in 1866; and 1865 in 1867.

Chapter VIII

1. *Commercial and Financial Chronicle*, April 7, 1877, p. 308.

2. *Forty-ninth Annual Report of the Baltimore and Ohio Railroad* (Baltimore, 1875), pp. 13–14.

3. *American Railroad Journal*, September 23, 1876, p. 1208.

4. H. V. and H. W. Poor, *Manual of the Railroads of the United States for 1885* (New York, 1885), p. v.

5. Allan Nevins, *The Emergence of Modern America, 1865–78* (New York, 1927), p. 297.

6. *American Railroad Journal*, April 1, 1871, p. 346; October 19, 1872, p. 1322; William H. Osborn to William Ackerman, May 16, 1883, in Thomas C. Cochran, *Railroad Leaders, 1845–90: The Business Mind in Action* (Cambridge, Mass., 1953), p. 427.

7. Cable from John W. Garrett to John King, September 29, 1873. Robert Garrett Family Papers, Manuscript Division, Library of Congress.

8. G. R. Blanchard to E. I. du Pont de Nemours & Co., May 18, 1869. Series B Letters, E. I. du Pont Papers in Eleutherian Mills Historical Library.

9. Clifton K. Yearley, Jr. "The Baltimore and Ohio Railroad Strike of 1877" in *Maryland Historical Magazine*, Vol. 51, No. 3, September, 1956, p. 188.

10. Robert V. Bruce, *1877: Year of Violence* (Indianapolis, 1959), p. 64.

11. *American Railroad Journal*, July 28, 1877, p. 959.

12. Robert V. Bruce, *1877: Year of Violence* (Indianapolis, 1959), pp. 312–13.

Chapter IX

1. *Forty-seventh Annual Report of the Baltimore and Ohio Railroad* (Baltimore, 1873), p. 13.

2. *Forty-fifth Annual Report of the Baltimore and Ohio Railroad* (Baltimore, 1871), pp. 11–12.

3. Edward Hungerford, *The Story of the Baltimore and Ohio Railroad: 1827–1927* (New York, 1928), Vol. II, pp. 118–19.

4. *Ibid.*, Vol. II, p. 222.

5. John King to John W. Garrett, January 5, 1874, Robert Garrett Family Papers, Manuscript Division, Library of Congress.

6. John King to Drexel Morgan & Co., December 27, 1877. In MS 1925, Baltimore and Ohio Collection, Maryland Historical Society.

7. *Forty-fifth Annual Report of the Baltimore and Ohio Railroad* (Baltimore, 1871), p. 12.

8. *Fiftieth Annual Report of the Baltimore and Ohio Railroad* (Baltimore, 1876), p. 19.

9. *Fifty-sixth Annual Report of the Baltimore and Ohio Railroad* (Baltimore, 1882), p. 24.

10. *Fifty-fourth Annual Report of the Baltimore and Ohio Railroad* (Baltimore, 1880), p. 14.

11. Robert Garrett to John W. Garrett, March 4, 1884, Robert Garrett Family Papers, Manuscript Division, Library of Congress.

12. *Fifty-eighth Annual Report of the Baltimore and Ohio Railroad* (Baltimore, 1884), p. 32.

13. *Railroad Gazette*, October 3, 1884, p. 711.

Chapter X

1. John K. Cowen, *Here and There: A Tale of Two Cities* pamphlet (no date or place of publication).

2. *Railroad Gazette*, October 14, 1887, p. 674.

3. *Ibid.*, December 16, 1887, p. 819.

4. *Ibid.*, November 30, 1888, p. 789.

5. John King to John W. Garrett, September 18, 1873. Robert Garrett Family Papers, Manuscript Division, Library of Congress.

6. *Sixty-second Annual Report of the Baltimore and Ohio Railroad* (Baltimore, 1888), p. 17.

7. *Railroad Gazette*, April 1, 1887, p. 216.

8. *Sixty-sixth Annual Report of the Baltimore and Ohio Railroad* (Baltimore, 1892), p. 12.

9. *Sixty-ninth Annual Report (1894–95) of the Baltimore and Ohio Railroad* (Baltimore, 1895), p. 10.

10. *Railroad Gazette*, March 6, 1896, p. 162.

Chapter XI

1. John Moody, *The Railroad Builders* (New Haven, 1920), p. 113.
2. Stuart Daggett, *Railroad Reorganization* (Boston, 1908), p. 31.
3. Albro Martin, *James J. Hill and the Opening of the Northwest* (New York, 1976), p. 433.
4. *Railroad Gazette*, p. 384, June 7, 1901.
5. *Seventy-eighth Annual Report of the Baltimore and Ohio Railroad* (Baltimore, 1904), p. 15.
6. Mark Sullivan, *Our Times: 1900–25* (New York City, 1940), Vol. III, pp. 201–02.
7. *Eighty-third Annual Report of the Baltimore and Ohio Railroad* (Baltimore, 1909), p. 13.
8. *Eighty-second Annual Report of the Baltimore and Ohio Railroad* (Baltimore, 1908), p. 16.

Chapter XII

1. *Railroad Gazette*, January 7, 1910, p. 49.
2. *Eighty-fourth Annual Report of the Baltimore and Ohio Railroad* (Baltimore, 1910), p. 8.
3. Edward Hungerford, *Daniel Willard Rides the Line: The Story of a Great Railroad Man* (New York, 1938), pp. 161–62.
4. *Ibid.*, p. 152.
5. *Eighty-seventh Annual Report of the Baltimore and Ohio Railroad* (Baltimore, 1913), p. 10.
6. *Baltimore and Ohio Employees Magazine*, May, 1913, p. 1.
7. *The Official Guide of the Railways June, 1916* (New York City, 1916), p. 520.
8. *Open Letter to Mr. Daniel Willard, President of the B&O Railroad re the History of the CH&DRR and the B&O RR.* (no place, 1919), p. 53.
9. *Ninety-second Annual Report of the Baltimore and Ohio Railroad* (Baltimore, 1918), p. 9.
10. Edward Hungerford, *Daniel Willard Rides the Line: The Story of a Great Railroad Man* (New York, 1938), pp. 190–97.

Chapter XIII

1. Edward Hungerford, *Daniel Willard Rides the Line: The Story of a Great Railroad Man* (New York, 1938), p. 203.
2. *Ninety-second Annual Report of the Baltimore and Ohio Railroad* (Baltimore, 1918), p. 15.

3. *Ibid.*, p. 8.

4. *Baltimore and Ohio Employees Magazine*, February, 1918, p. 6.

5. *Ibid.*, February, 1918, p. 20.

6. Walker D. Hines, *War History of American Railroads* (New Haven, 1928), p. 257.

7. William G. McAdoo, *Crowded Years: The Reminiscences of William G. McAdoo* (New York, 1931), p. 490.

8. *Baltimore and Ohio Employees Magazine* February, 1918, p. 9.

9. *Ibid.*, October, 1918, p. 5.

10. *Ninety-second Annual Report of the Baltimore and Ohio Railroad* (Baltimore, 1918), p. 11.

Chapter XIV

1. Edward Hungerford, *Daniel Willard Rides the Line* (New York, 1938), p. 235.

2. *Ibid.*

3. *Annual Report of the Baltimore and Ohio Railroad, 1925* (Baltimore, 1926), p. 10.

4. *Baltimore and Ohio Employees Magazine*, February, 1923, p. 27.

5. Edward Hungerford, *Daniel Willard Rides the Line* (New York, 1938), p. 240.

6. *Baltimore and Ohio Employees Magazine*, March, 1922, p. 18.

7. *Baltimore and Ohio Magazine*, October, 1926, p. 7.

8. *Ibid.*, February, 1927, p. 11.

9. *Annual Report of the Baltimore and Ohio Railroad, 1929* (Baltimore, 1930), p. 11.

10. *Annual Report of the Baltimore and Ohio Railroad, 1923* (Baltimore, 1924), p. 9.

11. *Over a Century of Railroading* (New York City, 1929), pamphlet in the Eleutherian Mills Historical Library.

12. *Baltimore and Ohio Magazine*, January, 1927, p. 5.

13. Edward Hungerford, *Daniel Willard Rides the Line* (New York, 1938), p. 255.

14. *Ibid.*, p. 260.

15. *Annual Report of the Baltimore and Ohio Railroad, 1923* (Baltimore, 1924), p. 6.

Chapter XV

1. *Baltimore and Ohio Magazine*, March, 1930, p. 6.
2. *Time* March 3, 1930, p. 45.
3. Edward Hungerford, *Daniel Willard Rides the Line* (New York, 1938), p. 198.
4. *Annual Report of the Baltimore and Ohio Railroad, 1931* (Baltimore, 1932), p. 8.
5. *Los Angeles Times* (editorial), May 25, 1931.
6. *Baltimore and Ohio Magazine*, October, 1936, p. 5.
7. *Time*, August 3, 1931, p. 12.
8. *Baltimore and Ohio Magazine*, January, 1927, p. 44.
9. *Annual Report of the Baltimore and Ohio Railroad, 1938* (Baltimore, 1939), p. 10.
10. *Time*, May 22, 1939, p. 72.
11. *Ibid.*, January 15, 1940, p. 51.
12. *Ibid.*, May 12, 1941, p. 86.
13. *Annual Report of the Baltimore and Ohio Railroad, 1942* (Baltimore, 1943), p. 18.
14. *Baltimore and Ohio Magazine*, August, 1942, p. 17.

Chapter XVI

1. *Annual Report of the Baltimore and Ohio Railroad, 1941* (Baltimore, 1942), p. 7.
2. Lawrence W. Sagle and Alvin F. Staufer, *B&O Power: Steam, Diesel, and Electric Power of the Baltimore and Ohio Railroad, 1829–1964* (Staufer Railroad Books, Medina, Ohio, 1964), p. 189.
3. *Railway Age*, January 10, 1942, p. 180.
4. *Baltimore & Ohio Magazine*, June, 1944, p. 3.
5. *Time*, November 1, 1943, p. 19.
6. *Railway Age*, December 13, 1941, p. 1010.
7. *Baltimore and Ohio Magazine*, January, 1946, p. 3.

Chapter XVII

1. *Annual Report of the Baltimore and Ohio Railroad, 1951* (Baltimore, 1952), p. 2.
2. *Annual Report of the Baltimore and Ohio Railroad, 1949* (Baltimore, 1950), pp. 18–19.
3. *Baltimore and Ohio Magazine*, March, 1950, p. 9.
4. *Ibid.*, March, 1950, p. 9.
5. *Ibid.*, September, 1949, p. 7.

6. *Ibid.*, July, 1947, p. 9.
7. *Time*, June 3, 1946, p. 20.
8. *Ibid.*, September 4, 1950, p. 14.
9. *Annual Report of the Baltimore and Ohio Railroad, 1948* (Baltimore, 1949), p. 6.
10. *Time*, June 11, 1951, p. 104.
11. *Baltimore and Ohio Magazine*, February, 1951, p. 5.

Chapter XVIII

1. *Baltimore and Ohio Magazine*, January, 1951, p. 1.
2. *Ibid.*, February, 1956, p. 8.
3. *Annual Report of the Baltimore and Ohio Railroad, 1945* (Baltimore, 1946), p. 1.
4. *Annual Report of the Baltimore and Ohio Railroad, 1946* (Baltimore, 1947), p. 18.
5. *Annual Report of the Baltimore and Ohio Railroad, 1956* (Baltimore, 1957), p. 12.
6. *Railway Age*, February 3, 1958, p. 22.
7. *Annual Report of the Baltimore and Ohio Railroad, 1958* (Baltimore, 1959), p. 7.
8. *Baltimore and Ohio Magazine*, July, 1957, p. 11.

Chapter XIX

1. *Annual Report of the Baltimore and Ohio Railroad, 1953* (Baltimore, 1954), p. 2.
2. *Trains*, January, 1960, p. 12.
3. *Ibid.*
4. *Annual Report of the Baltimore and Ohio Railroad, 1958* (Baltimore, 1959), p. 13.
5. *Annual Report of the Baltimore and Ohio Railroad, 1953.* (Baltimore, 1954), p. 5.
6. *Baltimore and Ohio Magazine*, January, 1959. p. 1.
7. *Ibid.*, March, 1959, p. 10.
8. *Forbes*, January 1, 1961, p. 25.
9. *Annual Report of the Baltimore and Ohio Railroad, 1955* (Baltimore, 1956), p. 3.
10. *Forbes*, January 1, 1961, pp. 25–26.
11. *Baltimore and Ohio Magazine*, September, 1960, p. 2.
12. *Trains*, September, 1961, p. 13.

Chapter XX

1. *Time*, February 17, 1961, p. 86.
2. *Fortune*, January, 1961, p. 115.
3. *Time*, August 10, 1962, p. 61.
4. *Annual Report of the Baltimore and Ohio Railroad, 1962* (Baltimore, 1963), p. 4.
5. *Chesapeake and Ohio Railway 1962 Annual Report* (Cleveland, 1963), p. 8.
6. *Chessie System 1976 Flash Annual Report* (Cleveland, 1977), p. 14.

Bibliography

Manuscript Collections

Robert Garrett Family Papers, Manuscripts Division, Library of Congress, Washington, D.C.
Baltimore and Ohio Collection, Maryland Historical Society, Baltimore, Maryland.
Baltimore and Ohio Archives, Baltimore and Ohio Museum, Baltimore, Maryland.
Baltimore and Ohio Papers, Eleutherian Mills Historical Library, Eleutherian Mills-Hagley Foundation, Wilmington, Delaware.

Books

Adams, John Q. *Memoirs of John Quincy Adams*. Philadelphia, 1876.
Adler, Dorothy R. *British Investment in American Railways, 1834–1898*. Charlottesville, Virginia, 1970.
Albion, Robert G. *Square-Riggers On Schedule*. Princeton, 1938.
_____. *The Rise of New York Port: 1815–1860*. New York, 1939.
Allen, Frederic Lewis. *The Great Pierpont Morgan*. New York, 1949.
Baily, Francis. *Journal of a Tour in the Unsettled Parts of North America, 1796–1797*. London, 1856.
Basler, Roy P., ed. *The Collected Works of Abraham Lincoln*. New Brunswick, New Jersey, 1953.
Bell, J. Snowden. *The Early Motive Power of The Baltimore and Ohio Railroad*. New York, 1912.
Black, Robert C. *The Railroads of the Confederacy*. Chapel Hill, 1952.
Blake, Nelson M. *William Mahone of Virginia, Soldier and Political Insurgent*. Richmond, 1935.
Browne, Gary Lawson. *Baltimore in the Nation*. Chapel Hill, 1980.
Bruce, Robert V. *1877: Year of Violence*. Indianapolis, 1959.
Burgess, George H., and Miles C. Kennedy. *Centennial History of the Pennsylvania Railroad Company*. Philadelphia, 1949.
Campbell, E. G. *The Reorganization of the American Railroad System, 1893–1900*. New York, 1938.
Catalogue of the Centenary Exhibition of the Baltimore and Ohio Railroad, 1827–1927. Baltimore, 1927.
Chandler, Alfred D., Jr. *Henry Varnum Poor: Business Editor, Analyst, and Reformer*. Cambridge, 1956.
_____. *The Railroads: The Nation's First Business*. New York, 1965.
Cleveland, Frederick A., and Fred Wilbur Powell. *Railroad Finance*. New York, 1923.
Cochran, Thomas C. *Railroad Leaders, 1845–1890*. Cambridge, 1953.
Cook, Roger, and Karl Zimmerman. *The Western Maryland Railroad: Fireballs and Black Diamonds*. San Diego, 1981.

Daggett, Stuart. *Railroad Reorganization*. Cambridge, 1908.

Davis, Burke. *The Southern Railway, Road of the Innovators*. Chapel Hill, 1985.

Davis, Patricia T. *End of The Line: Alexander J. Cassatt and the Pennsylvania Railroad*. New York, 1978.

Dictionary of American Biography. New York, 1928–1981.

Early Correspondence of Alexander Brown and Sons with Regard to the Building of the Baltimore and Ohio Railroad. Baltimore, 1927.

Faulkner, Harold U. *The Decline of Laissez Faire, 1897–1917*. New York, 1951.

Fishlow, Albert. *American Railroads and the Transformation of the Antebellum Economy*. Cambridge, 1965.

Gates, Paul W. *The Farmer's Age: Agriculture 1815–1860*. New York, 1960.

Greenberg, Dolores. *Financiers and Railroads, 1869–1889: A Study of Morton, Bliss and Company*. Newark, Delaware, 1980.

Grodinsky, Julius. *Jay Gould: His Business Career, 1867–1892*. Philadelphia, 1957.

Harlow, Alvin F. *The Road of the Century. The Story of the New York Central*. New York, 1947.

Harwood, Herbert H., Jr. *Impossible Challenge: The Baltimore and Ohio Railroad in Maryland*. Baltimore, 1979.

Henry, Robert S. *This Fascinating Railroad Business*. Indianapolis, 1942.

Hidy, Ralph W. *The House of Baring in American Trade and Finance*. Cambridge, 1949.

Hill, Forest G. *Roads, Rails and Waterways: The Army Engineers and Early Transportation*. Norman, Oklahoma, 1957.

Hilton, George W., and John F. Due. *The Electric Interurban Railways in America*. Stanford, California, 1960.

Hines, Walker D. *War History of American Railroads*. New Haven, 1928.

Holbrook, Stewart H. *The Story of American Railroads*. New York, 1947.

Hosack, David. *Memoir of DeWitt Clinton*. New York, 1829.

Hungerford, Edward. *Daniel Willard Rides the Line*. New York, 1938.

————. *Men of Erie*. New York, 1946.

————. *The Story of the Baltimore and Ohio Railroad, 1827–1927*. New York, 1928.

Kamm, Samuel R. *The Civil War Career of Thomas A. Scott*. Philadelphia, 1940.

Kennan, George. *E. H. Harriman, A Biography*. Boston, 1922.

Kirkland, Edward C. *Industry Comes of Age, Business Labor, and Public Policy, 1860–1897*. New York, 1961.

Lambie, Joseph T. *From Mine to Market: The History of Coal Transportation on the Norfolk and Western Railway*. New York, 1954.

Lane, Wheaton J. *Commodore Vanderbilt*. New York, 1942.

Latrobe, John H. B. *The Baltimore and Ohio Railroad*. Baltimore, 1868.

Lewis, Robert G. *Handbook of American Railroads*. New York, 1956.

McAdoo, William G. *Crowded Years: The Reminiscences of William G. McAdoo*. Boston, 1931.

McGrane, Reginald C. *Foreign Bondholders and American State Debts*. New York, 1935.

Martin, Albro. *Enterprise Denied: Origins of the Decline of American Railroads*. New York, 1971.

———. *James J. Hill and the Opening of the Northwest*. New York, 1976.

Melish, John. *Information and Advice to Emigrants to the United States*. Philadelphia, 1819.

Mencken, August. *The Railroad Passenger Car*. Baltimore, 1957.

Meyer, B. H. *History of Transportation in the United States before 1860*. Washington, D.C., 1917.

Moody, John. *The Railroad Builders: A Chronicle of the Welding of the States*. New Haven, 1920.

Munroe, John A. *Louis McLane: Federalist and Jacksonian*. New Brunswick, New Jersey, 1973.

Nelson, James P. *The Chesapeake and Ohio Railway*. Richmond, 1927.

Nevins, Allan. *The Emergence of Modern America, 1865–1878*. New York, 1927.

———. *Ordeal of the Union*. New York, 1947.

North, Douglass C. *The Economic Growth of the United States, 1790–1860*. New York, 1966.

Overton, Richard C. *Burlington Route: A History of the Burlington Lines*. New York, 1965.

———. *Burlington West: A Colonization History of the Burlington Railroad*. Cambridge, 1941.

Owens, Hamilton. *Baltimore on the Chesapeake*. Garden City, New York, 1941.

Pangborn, J. G. *The World's Railway* (reprint edition). New York, 1974.

Rae, John B. *The American Automobile*. Chicago, 1965.

Reizenstein, Milton. *The Economic History of the Baltimore and Ohio Railroad, 1827–1853*. Baltimore, 1897.

Ringwalt, J. L. *Development of Transportation Systems in the United States*. Philadelphia, 1888.

Ripley, William Z. *Railroads, Rates, and Regulation*. New York, 1912.

———. *Railway Problems*. New York, 1913.

Sagle, Lawrence W., and Alvin F. Staufer. *B&O Power: Steam, Diesel, and Electric Power of the Baltimore and Ohio Railroad, 1829–1964*. Medina, Ohio, 1964.

Salsbury, Stephen. *No Way to Run a Railroad: The Untold Story of the Penn Central Crisis*. New York, 1982.

Satterlee, Herbert L. *J. Pierpont Morgan, An Intimate Portrait*. New York, 1939.

Schotter, Howard W. *Growth and Development of the Pennsylvania Railroad Company*. Philadelphia, 1927.

Searcher, Victor. *Lincoln's Journey to Greatness*. Philadelphia, 1960.

Semmes, John E. *John H. B. Latrobe and His Times.* Baltimore, 1917.

Shaw, Ronald E. *Erie War West: A History of the Erie Canal.* Lexington, Kentucky, 1966.

Smith, William Prescott. *The Book of the Great Railway Celebrations of 1857.* New York, 1858.

Soule, George. *Prosperity Decade, From War to Depression: 1917–1929.* New York, 1947.

Starr, John W., Jr. *Lincoln and the Railroads.* New York, 1927.

Stover, John F. *American Railroads.* Chicago, 1961.

_____. *History of the Illinois Central Railroad.* New York, 1975.

_____. *Iron Road to the West: American Railroads in the 1850s.* New York, 1978.

_____. *The Life and Decline of the American Railroad.* New York, 1970.

_____. *The Railroads of the South, 1865–1900.* Chapel Hill, 1955.

Sullivan, Mark. *Our Times: 1900–1925.* New York, 1926–35.

Summers, Festus P. *The Baltimore and Ohio in the Civil War.* New York, 1939.

Taylor, George R. *The Transportation Revolution, 1815–1860.* New York, 1951.

_____ and Irene D. Neu. *The American Railroad Network, 1861–1890.* Cambridge, 1956.

Thom, Helen Hopkins. *Johns Hopkins: A Silhouette.* Baltimore, 1929.

Thompson, Robert L. *Wiring a Continent: The History of the Telegraph Industry in the United States, 1832–1866.* Princeton, 1947.

Trottman, Nelson. *History of the Union Pacific: A Financial and Economic Survey.* New York, 1923.

Turner, Charles W. *Chessie's Road.* Richmond, 1956.

Turner, Frederick J. *The Rise of the New West.* New York, 1906.

Turner, George Edgar. *Victory Rode the Rails: The Strategic Place of Railroads in the Civil War.* Indianapolis, 1953.

Ward, James A. *J. Edgar Thomson, Master of the Pennsylvania.* Westport, Connecticut, 1980.

Walsh, Richard, and William L. Fox (eds.) *Maryland, A History, 1632–1974.* Baltimore, 1974.

Weber, Thomas. *The Northern Railroads in the Civil War.* New York, 1952.

White, John H., Jr. *American Locomotives: An Engineering History, 1830–1880.* Baltimore, 1968.

_____. *The American Railroad Passenger Car.* Baltimore, 1978.

Winchester, Paul. *Graphic Sketches from the History of the Baltimore and Ohio Railroad.* Baltimore, 1927.

Articles and Pamphlets

Baer, Christopher T. *Canals and Railroads of the Midatlantic States, 1800–60.* Wilmington, Delaware, 1981.
Bateman, Carroll. *The Baltimore and Ohio: The Story of the Railroad that Grew Up with the United States.* Baltimore, 1951.
Brown, R. W. *Daniel Willard (1861–1942): From Woodburner to Diesels.* Newcomen Society, 1948.
Chronological and Alphabetical Lists of Presidents, Directors, and Officers of the Baltimore and Ohio Railroad. Baltimore, 1929.
Cowen, John K. *Here and There: A Tale of Two Cities* (No date or place of publication).
Cullen, Elizabeth O. "The Coming of the Railroads to Washington, D.C." Read before the Columbia Historical Society, May 20, 1958.
James, Alfred R. "Sidelights on the Founding of the Baltimore and Ohio Railroad." *Maryland Historical Magazine,* XLVII, December, 1953.
Open Letter to Mr. Daniel Willard, President of the B&O Railroad in the History of the CH&DRR and the B&ORR (no place), 1919.
Over a Century of Railroading. New York City, 1929.
"Report of the Baltimore and Ohio R. R. Company, Showing the Amount of Salaries Paid the Officers of said R. R. Company" Document Q of House of Delegates (Maryland), February 7, 1845.
Sagle, Lawrence W. "America's Oldest Railroad Shops—Mount Clare." *Railroad History.* No. 127, October, 1972.
Skidmore, Howard. (Ed.). *The Story So Far: Sesquicentennial of the Baltimore and Ohio Railroad, 1827–1977.* 1977.
Stover, John F. "America's Pioneer Railroad: 150 Years of The B&O." *Railway Age.* Vol. 178. April 25, 1977.
Sullivan, J. H. *Central Ohio Railroad Co.* Baltimore, 1854.
Ward, James A. "Image and Reality: The Railway Corporate-State Metaphor." *Business History Review.* LV, Winter, 1981.
Yearley, Clifton K., Jr. "The Baltimore and Ohio Railroad Strike of 1877" *Maryland Historical Magazine,* LI. September, 1956.

Dissertations and Theses

Burkhardt, Ronald John. "A History of the Ohio and Mississippi Railroad, 1848–65." Masters Thesis, Purdue University, 1971.
Catton, William Bruce. "John W. Garrett of the Baltimore and Ohio: A Study in Seaport and Railroad Competition, 1820–74." Doctoral Dissertation, Northwestern University, 1959.

Periodicals and Yearbooks

American Railroad Journal
Baltimore and Ohio Magazine
Book of the Royal Blue
Business Week
Commercial and Financial Chronicle
Forbes
Fortune
Los Angeles *Times*
Maryland Historical Magazine
Moody's Transportation Manual
Niles' Register
Official Guide of the Railways
Poor's Manual of the Railroads of the United States
Railroad Gazette
Railroad History
Railway Age
Register of Pennsylvania (Samuel Hazard, ed.)
Time
Trains
Yearbook of Railroad Facts

Railroad Annual Reports

Baltimore and Ohio, 1828–1981.
Chesapeake and Ohio (Chessie, CSX), 1953–82.

Index

Johnston, W. H., 250
Jones, Jesse, 293–94, 317
Jones, Talbot, 16, 20, 34
Jones, William E., 109
J. Q. Adams (locomotive), 41

Kaltenborn, H. V., 301
Kansas Pacific RR, 129
Kelly, Grace, 346
Kennedy, John F., 348
Kennedy, Thomas, 24
Kerr, Clark, 348
Kimball, Frederick J., 212
King, John Jr., 127–28, 130, 137, 138, 146, 148, 151, 169
Kingwood Tunnel, 70, 220
Knight, Jonathan, 12, 21, 22–23, 30, 31, 32, 33, 37, 40, 48, 50, 54
Knox, Philander C., 204
Koenig, Frederick, 170
Korean War, 329–30, 335
Kriettschnitt, Julius, 235
Kuhler, Otto, 295
Kuhn, Loeb and Company, 190, 221, 260
Kusik, John E., 362, 364

Labor unions, 135–36
Lackawanna RR, 136
Lafayette College, 161
Lafayette (locomotive), 346
LaFollette, Robert M., 204
Lake Erie, 121
Lake Erie Division, 150, 152
Lamon, Ward H., 101
Lancaster Turnpike, 8
Lane, Franklin K., 231, 234
Lane, Harry A., 303
Langdon, Jervis, Jr.: elected president of B&O, 357; leaves B&O for Rock Island RR, 364; mentioned, 356, 363
Latrobe, Benjamin H., 39, 40, 41, 48, 49, 50, 52–53, 54, 57, 59, 61, 62, 66, 69–71, 73, 113, 144, 145
Latrobe, Benjamin Henry, Sr., 13, 40
Latrobe, John H. B., 30, 35, 39, 40, 48, 59, 61, 62, 63, 73
Laying first stone of B&O, 25–27
Lee, Blair, 370

Lee, Robert E., 100, 106, 108–10, 146, 164
LeHigh RR, 136
Less-than-carload-lot freight declines, 291, 323–24
Lexington, Va., 141, 146
Lincoln, Abraham: and 1861 trip to Washington, D.C., 101–2; and massive troop movement of 1863, 110–11; requests coal from Garrett, 114–15; mentioned, 61, 107, 108, 110
"Little Joe" switch engines, 253
Little Miami RR, 84, 86
Little, Stephen, 186–87
Liverpool and Manchester RR, 31
Livestock shipments by rail decline, 291
Locomotives: early use on B&O, 29, 34–36; wind-powered car, 35; treadmill car, 35; first use on grades, 38; in 1840s, 54–57; cost of, 57; acquired in 1850s, 77; new engines purchased after Civil War, 134–35; during J. W. Garrett years, 159; in 1899, 188; during Loree years, 197; during Willard years, 218, 221, 253–56, 272; during WWII, 305–6; diesel, 333–42; mentioned, 44, 91, 168, 175, 213, 272, 318
Locust Point (Baltimore), 76, 90, 133, 156, 157, 172, 258–59, 280, 306, 346, 353
Loder, Benjamin, 74
Long Bridge across Potomac, 144
Long Island RR, 167
Long, Stephen H., 21, 22–23, 24, 30, 31, 33, 37, 372
Loomis, Daniel P., 348
Lord Baltimore (locomotive), 282, 283
Loree, Leonor, F.: elected B&O president by Pennsylvania RR, 195; early career, 195–96; plans for improving B&O, 196–98; resigns presidency of B&O, 198; later career, 198; mentioned, 185, 210, 217, 262
Lorman, William, 20
Los Angeles Times, 288
Loss and damage payments, 324
Louisa RR, 359